COVID-19 in Southeast Asia

Insights for a post-pandemic world

edited by
Hyun Bang Shin, Murray Mckenzie, and Do Young Oh

Published by
LSE Press
10 Portugal Street
London WC2A 2HD
press.lse.ac.uk

Cover design by Diana Jarvis https://www.roamland-studio.co.uk/
Cover image: © Veejay Villafranca 2021

Print and digital versions typeset by Siliconchips Ltd.

ISBN (Paperback): 978-1-909890-76-3
ISBN (PDF): 978-1-909890-77-0
ISBN (EPUB): 978-1-909890-78-7
ISBN (Mobi): 978-1-909890-79-4

DOI: https://doi.org/10.31389/lsepress.cov

The full text of this book has been peer-reviewed to ensure high academic standards.
For our full publishing ethics policies, see http://press.lse.ac.uk

Suggested citation:
Shin, Hyun Bang; Mckenzie, Murray; and Oh, Do Young (eds). 2022. *COVID-19 in
Southeast Asia: Insights for a post-pandemic world*. London: LSE Press.
DOI: https://doi.org/10.31389/lsepress.cov License: CC BY 4.0.

To read the free, open access version of this book online,
visit https://doi.org/10.31389/lsepress.cov or scan this QR code with
your mobile device.

Contents

PART II: MIGRANTS, (IM)MOBILITIES, AND BORDERS

List of figures

List of tables

Editors

Hyun Bang Shin is Professor of Geography and Urban Studies at the London School of Economics and Political Science and directs the LSE Saw Swee Hock Southeast Asia Centre. His research centres on the critical analysis of the political economy of urbanisation, gentrification, displacement, urban spectacles, and urbanism, with particular attention to Asian cities. He is a trustee of the Urban Studies Foundation and an editor of the *International Journal of Urban and Regional Research*.

Murray Mckenzie is a postdoctoral research assistant and research officer at the LSE Saw Swee Hock Southeast Asia Centre, and a strategic planning consultant. He holds a PhD in geography and urban studies from UCL and an MA in community and regional planning from the University of British Columbia. His research focuses on the roles of the arts, culture, and their contestation in processes of urban growth and change.

Do Young Oh is a research assistant professor at the School of Graduate Studies, Lingnan University, Hong Kong. He was previously a research officer, based jointly at the Saw Swee Hock Southeast Asia Centre and the Middle East Centre at the LSE, where he completed his PhD in regional and urban planning. His research interests focus on comparative urbanism and postcolonialism in East Asia.

Contributors

Laura Antona is an ESRC postdoctoral fellow at the University of Oxford and holds a PhD in human geography and urban studies from the LSE. Laura's research focuses on the experiences of migrant domestic workers in Singapore, focusing particularly on their experiences in refuges and during periods of detainment.

Katherine Brickell is Professor of Human Geography at Royal Holloway, University of London, and an associate of the Saw Swee Hock Southeast Asia Centre. She is the author of *Home SOS: Gender, Violence and Survival in Crisis Ordinary Cambodia* (Wiley, 2020) and is co-editor of *The Handbook of Contemporary Cambodia* (Routledge, 2017).

Joe Buckley is an independent researcher specialising in labour and social movements in Southeast Asia. He holds a PhD in international development from SOAS, University of London. He has published and consulted widely on labour relations and labour politics in Cambodia and Vietnam and is the author of *Vietnamese Labour Militancy: Capital-Labour Antagonisms and Self-Organised Struggles* (Routledge, forthcoming).

Thanapat Chatinakrob is a PhD candidate at the Manchester International Law Centre, University of Manchester. He has a strong interest in legal studies, especially regional and international laws across Southeast Asia. His interests lie in international dispute settlement mechanisms and policy implementation in the Thai context.

Theavy Chhom is a research associate at the Cambodia Development Resource Institute (CDRI), Phnom Penh. She is currently part of the USAID project on Gender and Inclusive Development Analysis (GIDA), with its focus on marginalised groups. The project aims to analyse existing gender gaps and key social, structural, and institutional barriers, with links to the COVID-19 crisis. She is leading qualitative methods including photovoice and focus groups through the lens of intersectionality.

Creighton Connolly (@Creighton88) is an assistant professor in the School of Graduate Studies and Institute of Policy Studies at Lingnan University, Hong Kong. He researches urban political ecology, urban–environmental governance, and processes of urbanisation and urban re-development in Southeast Asia, with a focus on Malaysia and Singapore. He is editor of *Post-Politics and Civil Society in Asian Cities* and has published in a range of leading urban studies and geography journals.

Maria Carmen (Ica) Fernandez works on the intersections of vulnerability, displacement, and spatial governance in the Philippines. She holds graduate degrees in urban and regional planning from the University of the Philippines and the University of Cambridge and co-convenes UrbanisMO.ph, an informal collective of development workers interested in difficult conversations about Philippine cities. Ica is currently a PhD researcher at the University of Cambridge.

Rachel Gong is a researcher at the Khazanah Research Institute, a policy think tank in Kuala Lumpur. Her current research covers digital policy issues such as digital inclusion, the digital economy, and digital governance. Her earlier research has been published in *Sociological Perspectives*, the *Journal of Consumer Culture*, and the *Journal of Technology in Human Services*. Rachel graduated *summa cum laude* from Princeton University and received her PhD in sociology from Stanford University.

Tessa Maria Guazon is a contemporary art curator and an associate professor in the Department of Art Studies, University of the Philippines Diliman. She is the principal investigator for the Manila case study of the SEANNET (Southeast Asia Neighbourhoods Network) research project. Her essays and reviews have been published in anthologies, academic journals, and exhibition catalogues.

Cornelius Hanung is a researcher and human rights defender from Indonesia. He has been involved in human rights and LGBTIQ movement in Southeast Asia and beyond for nearly a decade. Previously, he worked with the Asian Forum for Human Rights and Development

(FORUM-ASIA), ASEAN SOGIE Caucus, and Arus Pelangi Indonesia. He earned a Master's degree in Engineering and Management, and a diploma in International Human Rights Law from South Korea.

Francesca Humi works for the Kanlungan Filipino Consortium, a Filipino community charity in London. She previously worked in inclusive education at the LSE Eden Centre and in peacebuilding at International Alert Philippines. She has a BA in international development studies from McGill University and an MSc in empires, colonialism, and globalisation from the LSE.

William Jamieson is a PhD candidate in geography at Royal Holloway, University of London. His work is concerned with the integration of political geography and literary theory through critical creative writing methods to enhance our understanding of how space is 'read' and 'written' by capital. His project concerns the dynamics of land reclamation in Singapore and sand extraction across Southeast Asia. His fiction pamphlet, *Thirst for Sand*, was published by Goldsmiths Press in 2019.

Yi Jin is a postdoctoral fellow at the Asia Research Institute, National University of Singapore. He obtained his PhD in human geography and urban studies at the LSE. Trained with a background of sociology and human geography, Yi's research expertise includes urban redevelopment, urban governance, critical spatial theory, industrial heritage, the city and everyday life, and qualitative research methods.

Jarud Romadan Khalidi is a researcher at Khazanah Research Institute. His research interests include development economics, with a particular focus on exclusion, inequality, and poverty. He holds an MA in public policy from the National Graduate Institute for Policy Studies (GRIPS) Tokyo, and a Bachelor of Economics (Honours) from the International Islamic University Malaysia.

Sin Yee Koh is Senior Lecturer in Global Studies at Monash University Malaysia and an associate of the Saw Swee Hock Southeast Asia Centre. She is a human geographer working at the intersections of migration studies and urban studies. Her work uses the lens of migration and mobility to understand the circulations of people, capital, and aspirations in and through cities.

Sabina Lawreniuk is a Nottingham research fellow in the School of Geography at the University of Nottingham. She is the co-author of *Going Nowhere Fast: Mobile Inequality in the Age of Translocality* (Oxford University Press, 2020).

Al Lim is a PhD student in the combined programme in anthropology and environmental studies at Yale University. He holds an MSc in urbanisation and development from the LSE, as well as a BA (Honours) in urban studies from Yale-NUS College.

Justin Muyot lectures on public administration at the University of the Philippines and on economics at the University of Santo Tomas. He holds an undergraduate degree in business economics and an MPP/MPA dual degree from the Lee Kuan Yew School of Public Policy and the LSE. Prior to teaching, he worked in the executive and legislative branches of the Philippine government.

Maw Thoe Myar is a researcher in the Research and Policy Advocacy Department at the Center for Social Integrity (CSI), Myanmar. She holds an MA in social science from Chiang Mai University, Thailand. Her research interests include land access, human security, Karenni people, and migration.

Keng-Khoon Ng is a lecturer and programme head at the School of Architecture and Built Environment, UCSI University, Malaysia. He has an interdisciplinary PhD in architecture and urban studies from the National University of Singapore. Keng-Khoon's research interests focus on architecture, urban planning, and critical urban studies in Southeast Asian cities.

Rita Padawangi is Associate Professor of Sociology at the Centre for University Core, Singapore University of Social Sciences. She co-coordinates the Southeast Asia Neighbourhoods Network (SEANNET), an initiative for urban research and teaching. Her research covers the sociology of architecture, social movements, and participatory urban development.

Maria Karla Abigail (Abbey) Pangilinan is a development worker and urban planner who specialises in implementing social protection programmes in both urban and rural contexts. She has a master's degree in urban and regional planning from the University of the Philippines and an MSc in urbanisation and development from LSE.

Adrian Perkasa is a lecturer in the Department of History, Universitas Airlangga, Indonesia. Currently, he is a PhD candidate at the University of Leiden and a local principal investigator in Surabaya as part of the Southeast Asian Neighborhoods Network (SEANNET).

Tengku Nur Qistina is a senior researcher in the Social Policy and National Integration Department at the Institute of Strategic and International Studies (ISIS), Malaysia. Her focus is on gender and women's empowerment, where she provides gendered perspectives on Malaysian social policies. She has previously worked on and provided gendered perspectives on defence, security, healthcare, and the local Malaysian context. She obtained her LLB from the University of Manchester and her MA in national security studies from King's College, London.

Nastassja Quijano is a development professional specialising in monitoring and evaluation, with extensive experience in supporting, coordinating, and managing social and human development programmes. She holds an MSc in international development management from the University of Westminster, United Kingdom.

Farlina Said is an analyst in foreign policy and security studies at the Institute of Strategic and International Studies (ISIS), Malaysia. As a part of the think tank, she has been involved in crafting various dialogues and forums on cybersecurity, cyber diplomacy, and the implementation of UN cyber norms.

Ponpavi Sangsuradej is a Thai native and third-year PhD student at SOAS, University of London. Her research focuses on political discourse in Burma from 1945 to 1948.

Ashraf Shaharudin is a researcher at the Khazanah Research Institute, a policy think tank in Kuala Lumpur. His current research areas include open government data and agricultural policy. Ashraf holds a Bachelor of Engineering (Electrical and Electronic) from the University of Western Australia and a Master of Economics from the Universiti Putra Malaysia.

Thomas E.L. Smith is an associate of the Saw Swee Hock Southeast Asia Centre and Associate Professor of Environmental Geography in the Department of Geography and Environment at LSE. He is particularly interested in complex interactions between agricultural practices, land degradation, fire emissions characteristics, and their associated impacts. He is also a member of the multidisciplinary Tropical Catchments Research Initiative (TROCARI).

Hengvotey So has been a research assistant at the Cambodia Development Resource Institute (CDRI), Phnom Penh CDRI for four years. She is currently part of the USAID project on Gender and Inclusive Development Analysis (GIDA). In 2018, she was involved in the Zurich University-funded Skill for Industries project, which aimed to understand to impact of skills improvement in support of industrial growth in Cambodia.

Theng Theng Tan is an independent researcher. Prior to this, she was a researcher at Khazanah Research Institute, a policy think tank in Malaysia. Her research interest is in labour economics, especially issues related to gender inequality. She holds an MSc in economic policy from University College London and a Bachelor of Commerce (economics and finance) from the University of Melbourne.

Maddy Thompson is a Leverhulme Trust postdoctoral research fellow at Keele University. Her work examines the geographies of digital health, drawing on both local and international case studies. She also has interests in migration and mobility studies.

Siti Aiysyah Tumin is a researcher at the Khazanah Research Institute, a policy think tank in Kuala Lumpur. Her research interests are in labour economics and policies, the informal economy, social capital formation, and development economics. Siti is an economics graduate of the University of Warwick and the University of Cambridge.

Helena Varkkey is a senior lecturer at the Department of International and Strategic Studies, University of Malaya. Her research focuses on the governance of transboundary haze pollution and the political economy of palm oil in Southeast Asia. Her monograph on *The Haze Problem in Southeast Asia: Palm Oil and Patronage* was published in 2016. She is also a member of the multidisciplinary academic grouping Tropical Catchment Research Initiative (TROCARI).

Abellia Anggi Wardani completed her PhD training at Tilburg University, the Netherlands. She is interested in studying ethno-religious conflict, everyday peacebuilding, borderlands, cross-border trade, traditional markets, ethnography, and language. She is a research adviser at the Center for Social Integrity (CSI) Myanmar and is a lecturer in the Faculty of Humanities, Universitas Indonesia.

Moonyati Yatid is a policy analyst at the Global Foundation for Cyber Studies and Research (GFCyber). Her wide research experience and interest cover the areas of Technology, Innovation, Cyber Security as well as Oil, Gas and Energy (OGE).

Sokphea Young obtained his PhD from the University of Melbourne and is currently an honorary research fellow at University College London. He is the author of *Strategies of Authoritarian Survival and Dissensus in Southeast Asia: Weak Men Versus Strongmen* (Palgrave Macmillan, 2021).

Yimin Zhao is Assistant Professor in Urban Planning and Management at Renmin University of China. Trained as a human geographer, his research has been engaging with spatial politics in the urban change. After previous investigations on Beijing's green belts and *Jiehebu*, his current study develops along two lines of inquiry, one focusing on the infrastructural lives of authoritarianism in Beijing and the other looking into the urban mechanisms of 'Global China'.

Acknowledgements

This volume has grown out of the COVID-19 and Southeast Asia project, put together as a rapid response by the Saw Swee Hock Southeast Asia Centre (SEAC) at the London School of Economics and Political Science (LSE) to the prevailing COVID-19 pandemic, as SEAC aligned itself with the emergent scholarly endeavour to use the pandemic as a moment of reflection and learning for a better future. Initially, the project was part of SEAC's effort to quickly act on a sense of responsibility to the multidisciplinary network of Southeast Asia scholars, many of them early career researchers, who are ordinarily supported by the public events, research funds, and visiting appointments administered by SEAC. Reaching the advanced production stages of any scholarly work warrants a sense of accomplishment, but what we as editors feel in this instance is something other than the familiar satisfaction of overcoming the tedium of revision. It is, rather, a feeling that has more to do with the affective bonds of mutual support that have been created by supporting one another and our contributors through the various experiences of uncertainty, upheaval, sickness, and loss that the COVID-19 pandemic imposed. In this regard, we thank all the contributing authors to this volume, as well as the contributors to the LSE Southeast Asia Blog (https://blogs.lse.ac.uk/seac), whose enthusiastic and collegial responses to the editors' call for contributions in the summer of 2020 provided the early momentum for this book project.

We would also like to express sincere thanks to Gray Brakke and Malvin Kaur, both graduate interns at SEAC, whose invaluable assistance sustained the Centre's project on COVID-19 and Southeast Asia. We very much appreciate Gray's diligent and meticulous assistance in proofreading drafts and working with references, figures, and tables to make sure they conformed to the publisher's requirements, and Malvin's contribution to disseminating COVID-19 blogs contributed by most authors of this volume. The support of Katie Boulton, SEAC Centre Manager, also enabled the editors to push ahead with the completion as the project was reaching its final stage. We also owe our gratitude to

Professor Patrick Dunleavy as editor-in-chief of the LSE Press and Lucy Lambe at the LSE Library for their encouragement, guidance, and especially Professor Dunleavy's careful reading of some of our earlier drafts.

More than anything, the editors and SEAC appreciate the generous financial support from late Professor Saw Swee Hock and also from Mr Arvind Khattar, which allowed SEAC to embark on the COVID-19 and Southeast Asia project and to produce this volume. It is our great sorrow not to be able to personally present this volume to Professor Saw, who sadly passed away in February 2021, but we hope this volume constitutes part of his long-lasting legacy and imprint on SEAC and the London School of Economics and Political Science.

Last but not least, the editors thank our own family members, who had to endure long hours of working from home, which effectively turned our private home into work space that infiltrated personal lives.

1. Insights for a post-pandemic world

Murray Mckenzie, Do Young Oh, and Hyun Bang Shin

> a different ambition: to move the future which is just beginning to *take shape* into view against the *still* predominant past.
>
> Ulrich Beck

There may never be a 'post-COVID world', in the literal, posterior sense. However, if it is to serve as a novel scholarly appellation for the near future – the LSE's trans-institutional 'Shaping the Post-COVID World' initiative being one indication this is so – then our initial questioning of it might begin with Ulrich Beck's (1992, p.9) observations concerning the prefix 'post-', made nearly 30 years ago: as it gestures to a 'beyond' that cannot yet be known or named, the reality of that which is 'post-' can only be confronted through the familiar past and present that it purports to negate.

During the months in which this text was written, our world in many respects appeared to be in a moment of suspended transformation. Our intellectual lives, and the structures of daily life that sustain them, bore increasingly familiar features that mixed the improvisational with the decisive. The question of what will differentiate the arrangements that endure raises both a critical, scholarly imperative and an exigent impetus to act, or to shape the 'post-pandemic world' to the full extent that one can. Thus, the initial premise of this volume follows the widely read adjuration of Indian writer and activist Arundhati Roy (2020) to see the pandemic as 'a portal, [or] a gateway between one world and the next'. In her words, COVID-19 was an opportunity to rethink the world as it is and to ready ourselves to step into a new one, without, as she has put it, 'dragging the carcasses of our prejudice and hatred, our avarice, our data banks and dead ideas, our dead rivers and smoky skies behind us'. Roy's stirring rhetoric comes entwined with her critical rigour and perspicacity, and it is our wish for this volume to likewise evince both aspects – the hopeful and the incisive – in its treatment of

---

How to cite this book chapter:
Mckenzie, Murray; Oh, Do Young; and Shin, Hyun Bang. 2022. 'Insights for a post-pandemic world'. In: Shin, Hyun Bang; Mckenzie, Murray; and Oh, Do Young (eds) *COVID-19 in Southeast Asia: Insights for a post-pandemic world*. London: LSE Press, pp. 1–33. DOI: https://doi.org/10.31389/lsepress.cov.a License: CC BY 4.0.

the circumstances that COVID-19 brought differently or more clearly into view.

Nevertheless, so too do we yet harbour misgivings as to whether such questions of a 'portal' are the right ones to ask. Gautam Bhan, Teresa Caldeira, Kelly Gillespie, and AbdouMaliq Simone (2020) have opined that such monumental claims about COVID-19 – 'totality, catastrophe, portal' – evince an 'overreach, … romance, [and] rush to diagnose that inflames, encamps, and routes our imaginations'. They have argued that these tendencies reveal a northern paradigmatic imagination that slights the experiences of urban majorities in the global South, where emerging infectious diseases are but one risk among the many that constitute an enduring crisis to be contended with through the collaboratively improvisational practices of everyday life (see also Simone 2004). For many urban residents of the global South, there has been no lockdown, no social distancing, and no substantial change to provisions for sanitation or public health (Oldekop et al. 2020; Wasdani and Prasad 2020; Wilkinson 2020) – facts that often fall to critical social scientists to make known. Amid the circumstances of the pandemic, however, critical reflection and theorisation might compete with more urgent priorities to act, to contend with the exigencies of one's embeddedness, or to attend to solidarities rather than critique (Barbosa 2020).

This volume, then, collects the insights of an ensemble of social scientists – area studies, development studies, and legal scholars; anthropologists, architects, economists, geographers, planners, sociologists, and urbanists; representing academic institutions, activist and charitable organisations, policy and research institutes, and areas of professional practice – who recognise the necessity of critical commentary and engaged scholarship while at the same time making no claims that the pandemic's legacy or lessons can at this point be definitively known. Amid social sciences scholarship on COVID-19 at large, one readily finds evidence of disciplinary disjuncture and incoherence, as the deeper analysis and reflection through which concepts and theories will coalesce have remained in an incipient phase. What we do wish to convey, however, is our conviction that the sweeping consequences of COVID-19 will leave scarcely any focus of social research untouched, such that even social scientists who claim no expertise in infectious disease – most of us, of course – are likely to consider the relevance and possibilities of their research to have shifted in significant ways.

As we discuss in this introductory chapter, with reference to Beck's *Risk Society*, as cited above, there have been two fundamental perspectives that these social scientists' responses have been likely to take and with which we can argue for the value of these preliminary contributions. One is that which speaks from a situated position in relevant debates to challenge knowledge about the pandemic that has assigned selective and inequitable visibility to issues, people, or places, or which through its inferential or interpretive capacity has worked to set social expectations or assign validity to certain interventions with a bearing on the pandemic's course and the future it has foretold. The other perspective is that which has used the events and consequences of the pandemic to advance or renew understandings of social challenges, risks, or inequities that were already in place and which, without further or better action, are to be features of our 'post-pandemic world' as well.

By grounding this volume in Southeast Asia, we endeavour to help secure a place within these debates for a region that was among the first outside East Asia to be forced to contend with COVID-19 in a substantial way and which has evinced a marked and instructive diversity and dynamism in its fortunes. The relative success of Malaysia, Singapore, or Thailand in dealing with the pandemic can be counterposed with the greater difficulties of Indonesia or the Philippines; the worsening of authoritarian leanings, the manipulation of information, the exploitation of migrant workers, stirrings of unrest, and outbreaks of political instability and conflict can be counterposed with demonstrations of technological innovation and heartening instances of grass-roots mobilisation. As we explain in this chapter, our editorial commitments in this regard owe much to our disciplinary grounding in urban geography, where postcolonial critiques of knowledge and difference have become transformational reference points in the intellectual and theoretical landscape (see, e.g., Robinson 2011; Robinson 2016; Roy 2009; Sheppard, Leitner, and Maringanti 2013). These critiques, alongside human geography's foundational neo-Marxian analysis of relational capitalist urbanisation (see, e.g., Doucette and Park 2019; Song and Hae 2019), have together compromised the viability of an archetypal 'Southeast Asian city' as an object of research (see Rimmer and Dick 2009) and a 'metrocentric' approach that foregrounds only select metropolitan regions (Bunnell and Maringanti 2010; Goh and Bunnell 2013). As we describe below, and acknowledging the methodological nationalism evidenced in other domains of Southeast Asian area studies, our preference is to think in terms of a multitude of situated outcomes and experiences that in their relational connectivity are in fact constitutive of regional mappings bearing greater methodological utility than a priori framings can afford (Bunnell 2013; Ong 2011; Shin 2021).

The unfolding pandemic in Southeast Asia

Southeast Asia was among the first regions outside East Asia to be significantly affected by COVID-19. While Thailand was the first country to report a case of COVID-19 outside China, on 13 January 2020, the Philippines reported the first death from the disease outside China on 2 February. Singapore, the region's global business hub, was also seen as an early transmitter of the virus to other parts of the world. It is well known that an international sales conference held in mid-January 2020 in Singapore was a key early node from which the virus circulated to other parts of the world, including the UK, France, South Korea, and Spain (Mandhana, Solomon, and Jeong 2020). By April, the country's initially measured approach and preservation of relative normality had given way to an advisory against non-essential travel abroad, the closure of the border to non-residents, the suspension of religious services, and a 'circuit-breaker' lockdown that was especially impactful on migrant worker dormitories (*The Economist* 2020a; *The Economist* 2021b).

Despite the early emergence of cases, many parts of Southeast Asia were known to have been less severely affected by the COVID-19 pandemic in terms of the number of COVID-19 cases and the resulting death rates. There are two principal caveats to this observation, however. First, the tremendous economic impact of COVID-19 in the region – more severe than that of the Asian financial crisis in 1997–1998 – was expected to have a lasting detrimental impact on inclusive growth, which fostered a widespread but mostly frustrated desire for political change that likely will have consequences for regional stability as well (*The Economist* 2020b). The GDP of the Philippines was expected to shrink 9.0% in 2020 (OECD 2021); the economies of Malaysia and Thailand have been severely affected too. The global economic downturn and travel restrictions had pervasive impacts on everyday life, as reported in scholarship on garment workers (Lawreniuk 2020), microfinance borrowers (Brickell et al. 2020), and tourism operators (Do et al. 2021; Foo et al. 2020), for example. Second, as we conclude the writing of this chapter in June 2021, the identification of new clusters and the spread of more transmissible variants of the virus – partly attributable to recent festivals and the entry of infected foreigners – has been straining healthcare resources and causing worry in scantly vaccinated areas of continental Southeast Asia that had hitherto been able to avoid being host to major outbreaks (*The Economist* 2021a) (see Figures 1.1 and 1.2).

According to the COVID Performance Index maintained by the Lowy Institute (2021), an Australian think tank that assessed the performance

Figure 1.1. New COVID-19 cases, seven-day moving average

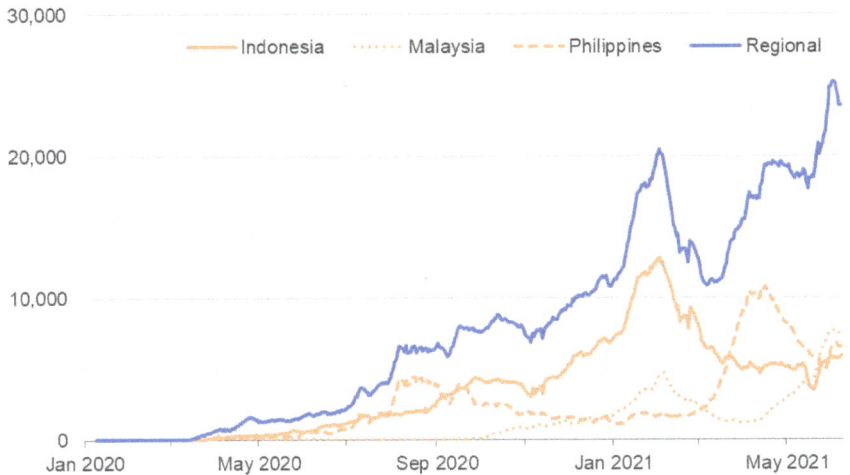

Source: World Health Organization.

Figure 1.2. New COVID-19 deaths, seven-day moving average

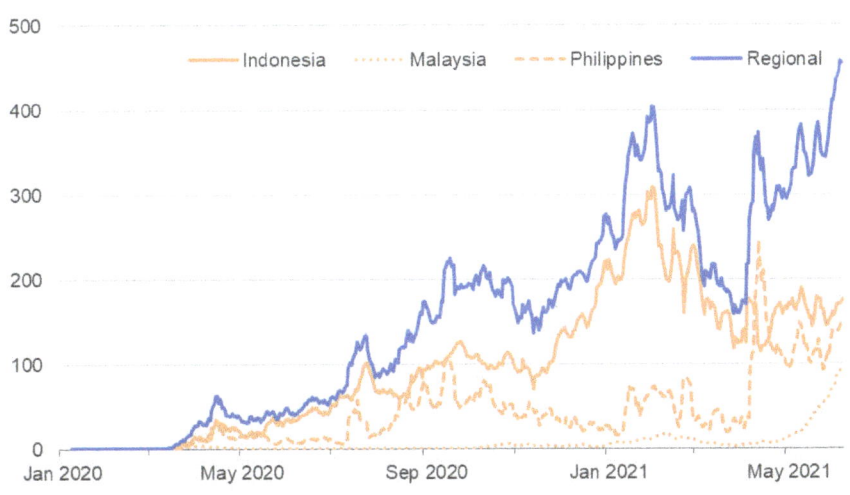

Source: World Health Organization.

of 116 countries in managing the pandemic, several Southeast Asian countries ranked highly as of 13 March 2021, including Thailand (4th), Singapore (14th), Malaysia (17th), and Myanmar (24th). While some observers have doubted the reliability of such data, it is notable that even the worst-hit parts of Southeast Asia performed relatively better than many advanced Western countries. For example, as of 8 June 2021, the UK had recorded 1,915 COVID-19 deaths per million people. While similar rates were reported in other European countries – such as France, Italy, and Spain – Indonesia and the Philippines, as the two countries in Southeast Asia with the highest number of cases, had respectively recorded only 194 and 205 COVID-19 deaths per million (see Table 1.1). Reasons for this success might include ASEAN-led regional health governance (Caballero-Anthony 2021; see also Davies 2019), a widespread mask-wearing culture (Ratcliffe 2020), early domestic and international travel restrictions (Elegant 2020), or a mixture of all of these factors (Meagher 2020).

Furthermore, although the region's share of global COVID-19-related deaths was low, differences between Southeast Asian countries

Table 1.1. Cumulative COVID-19 cases and deaths per million people across Southeast Asian countries, up to 8 June 2021

Country	Population in millions (2019)	Cumulative cases per million	Cumulative deaths per million
Philippines	107.29	11,893	204.8
Indonesia	266.91	6,980	194.1
SE Asia region	**651.88**	**6,449**	**125.99**
Malaysia	32.58	19,093	106.2
Myanmar	54.34	2,658	59.4
Thailand	66.37	2,750	19.5
Cambodia	15.29	2,278	17.4
Timor-Leste	1.28	6,138	14.1
Singapore	4.03	15,451	8.2
Brunei Darussalam	0.46	531	6.5
Vietnam	96.21	94	0.6
Laos	7.12	276.	0.4

Sources: World Health Organization (cumulative cases and deaths); United Nations Statistical Division (populations).

cannot be overlooked, as they reflect diverse socio-economic and political conditions within the region. As mentioned above, several Southeast Asian countries like Singapore and Thailand were able to control their COVID-19 outbreaks with sound public health systems, massive test-and-trace regimes, swift government responses, and society-wide engagement. In hard-hit nations such as the Philippines and Indonesia, the situations were more concerning. We saw the rise of authoritarian governance including clamping down on free speech and declaring martial law (Russell 2020). Philippine president Rodrigo Duterte infamously threatened lockdown violators that he would 'shoot them dead' and 'bury' them, while informal residents already living in vulnerable conditions were pushed into more difficult economic situations (Gutierrez 2020; *Reuters* 2020). In Indonesia, President Joko Widodo introduced a Sukarno-like martial law that included repressive measures towards the media to tighten domestic control and surveillance (Kuddus 2020). At the same time, in the country, drinking traditional *jamu* was promoted by the president to build immunity against COVID-19 (Kuddus 2020). In fact, these poor pandemic responses could be said to have resulted from the states being too weak to effectively mobilise society to tackle the spread of the virus, and not because they downplayed the risk (Pepinsky 2021). In this regard, as Greer et al. (2020) have argued, politics and policies are highly related to the effectiveness of COVID-19 responses.

A pandemic may also operate as an 'X-ray' image that reveals long-lasting societal fractures (McCann 2020). For example, the COVID-19 outbreak among migrant workers in large dormitories in Singapore exposed the inherent problems of its selective migration regime (Lin and Yeoh 2020). While more than one million low-skilled migrant workers served as the 'hidden' backbone of the Singaporean economy by providing cheap labour to four million Singaporeans (Li 2020), their well-being was largely overlooked by the Singaporean government. In Thailand, more than one million undocumented migrant workers from Cambodia and Myanmar were excluded from state legal protection while struggling to return to their home countries due to mobility restrictions (*Radio Free Asia* 2020). Refugees in the region were also excluded from social protection provided by the state, having been mistreated or stigmatised (Human Rights Watch 2021a; Thiri Shwesin Aung, Fischer, and Wang 2021).

It is also important to note that COVID-19 will be remembered as a moment of not only public health crisis but also political crisis.

As mentioned earlier, Myanmar was considered a country that had successfully tackled the outbreak, but a coup in February 2021 raised major political as well as health concerns in the region. In Myanmar, healthcare workers and civil servants led a civil disobedience campaign to fight against the return to military dictatorship. Frontline health workers' decision to risk their lives and boycott work reflected the political urgency amid a worsening pandemic situation (BMJ Opinion 2021). Thailand and Cambodia also experienced human rights crises in 2020: students, media, opposition parties, and human rights defenders were attacked and suppressed by states that aimed to silence critical voices (Human Rights Watch 2021a; Human Rights Watch 2021b). Global action to respond to emerging threats to democracy in the region remained largely insignificant. ASEAN's efforts to restore democracy in Myanmar were meagre despite convening several meetings (*Al Jazeera* 2021). Such circumstances raised concerns about the peaceful and equitable future of the region.

No one is safe until everyone is safe. This adage succinctly captures the challenges faced by Southeast Asia and the world. The extent of direct and indirect impacts of the pandemic on the region has varied, but the ever-changing pandemic situation suggested that globally coordinated responses to COVID-19 were necessary to overcome its multi-faceted challenges. In June 2021, Malaysia struggled to stop a sharp rise in COVID-19 cases and again imposed a two-week lockdown to stop the virus. There were also new surges of COVID-19 cases in Vietnam and Singapore. Vaccination was considered a key solution to tackle the virus, but the progress of vaccination campaigns varied across the region. As of 14 June 2021, Singapore was leading (80.19 doses per 100 people), followed by Cambodia (33.12), while in Vietnam less than two doses (1.60) had been administered per 100 people (Our World in Data 2021). Along with supply issues, distrust in military governments is one of the key reasons for low vaccination rates in the region (Thompson 2021).

While the mainstream media and government announcements focused on official programmes to address the pandemic, it would be erroneous to disregard bottom-up initiatives that built upon the strengths of local communities and civil societies. Community-based responses to the pandemic produced the possibility for more progressive changes in the region. For example, both Padawangi (Chapter 18) and Perkasa (Chapter 20) in this volume highlight community efforts to slow down the spread of the virus. On the other hand, in Vietnam, it was expected that the country's high public trust, building upon the transparency of COVID-19 information, could increase expectations and demands for further positive political changes (Truong 2020). In this regard, COVID-19 allowed us to imagine an alternative system driven by empowered people and communities. In the following section, we will look into what we can learn from the pandemic, laying out the key perspectives that guided our project.

Learning from the pandemic: our perspectives

As indicated above, this volume commences from Arundhati Roy's (2020) proposition that COVID-19 opened a 'portal' through which circumstances are brought more clearly into view and through which we might collectively venture in the imagination of future possibilities. Like the pandemic itself, this approach is not without precedent. In geography and urban studies, for instance, Ali and Keil (2006) surveyed the 2002–2004 SARS outbreak and concluded that, while the greater, faster, and more spatially complex connectivity of the global city network should be recognised as posing new risks for the transmission of emerging infectious diseases and new challenges for their containment, an inverse perspective was also worthy of better recognition, namely that the study of infectious disease might serve as a fruitful 'new entry point for the already lively debate on connectedness in the global city universe' (Ali and Keil 2006, p.493). There are two general and equally valid interpretations of what this 'entry point' – or 'portal' for Roy (2020) – represents. The first is in accordance with the principles of political ecology as a mode of geographical critique. As Ali and Keil have extended to COVID-19 in collaboration with one of this volume's contributors (Connolly, Keil, and Ali 2020), it is the literal sense in which infectious disease wedges open a view onto the ecological pressures that are attendant on socio-spatial change and its entanglement with natural and social processes and systems. The second is a broader interpretation, which commences from the position that *all* modes and domains of critique have had some, and often many, of their points of reference changed, with implications as well as possibilities for intellectual work that are impossible to ignore. Taking inspiration from Chen's *Asia as Method* (2010), it could be proposed that the coronavirus pandemic, as an imagined anchoring point for scholars in a host of contexts, locations, and disciplines, like the ambiguous 'Asia' Chen has in mind, can be strategically mobilised to generate 'alternative horizons and perspectives' (Chen 2010, p.212) that gain in political and integrative potential precisely by virtue of their emotional force.

Using this latter interpretation, which features implicitly in every contribution to this volume, we catalogued hundreds of English-language publications in the fields of development, human geography, planning, and urban studies for which to date (March 2021) COVID-19 had served as a 'portal', 'entry point', or 'method'. Nearly all of them had been written by scholars who claimed no expertise in infectious disease. Instead, many of them adopted the pandemic and its consequences, including the suspension of most primary research activities, as an appropriate juncture for the critical re-evaluation of each scholar's research area or sub-field. Such re-evaluation has been especially energetic in the geography of tourism, for example. In the three most highly cited papers, according to Google Scholar, of any of the publications we have catalogued thus far, Gössling, Scott, and Hall (2020), Hall, Scott, and Gössling (2020), and Higgins-Desbiolles (2020) have argued that COVID-19 exposed the critical flaws in global tourism's fundamental growth model, including its exposure to risk and its lack of resilience as well as its implication in the climate crisis. They have further highlighted associated problems such as deforestation, industrialised food production, and neo-liberal injustices such as labour exploitation and tax avoidance.

Ulrich Beck's *Risk Society* (1992, p.9), and his ambition to 'move the future which is just beginning to take shape into view against the still predominant past', affords a useful initial basis for summing up what it is that holds this outburst of scholarship together and what original critical undertaking it might collectively advance. Beck's compelling and well-known thesis, originally written in German in 1986, is that the late-capitalist logic of the production and distribution of *risks* has now become dominant over – and therefore in some sense a determinant of – the high-capitalist logic of the production and distribution of *wealth*. Those risks encompass the multitude of hazardous externalities that occur because of the expansion of techno-economic production, of which the accelerated transmission of emerging infectious diseases is a good example (Connolly, Keil, and Ali 2020), and that must consequently be identified and avoided, contained, or distributed.

Overall, the potential application of this lens to COVID-19 scholarship involves two essential perspectives. First, given their invisibility and uncertainty, risks acquire their social existence only through the knowledge that is available about them and thus are dependent on social construction: northern political and economic concerns related to emerging infectious diseases are a ready example (see King 2002). This is one of the essential premises of geographers' recent critical interventions into global health and 'the differentiated manner in which particular problems, populations, and spaces are rendered visible and amenable to intervention' therein (Brown, Craddock, and Ingram 2012, p.1183). Scholarship in this vein served a vital purpose in the year before this volume's publication by challenging the rationalities and causal interpretations, as well as their implicit social expectations and value judgements, through which the pandemic was understood and addressed in various contexts. In the responses of some governments to COVID-19, for example, an immoderate dependence on sophisticated analytics variously caused the neglect of other forms of public health knowledge, such as field experience; the neglect of the societal implications of containment measures, including worsening domestic violence and mental health (Dodds et al. 2020); and the neglect of the nuances of spatially uneven and unjust outcomes that are not easily conveyed in summary statistics or graphical forms (Everts 2020). In other instances, scholars have focused their criticism on the intensification of a medicalised surveillance capitalism, in which the modelling and monitoring of COVID-19 have been guided principally by profit motives rather than practical feasibility or a regard for data privacy and security. The trade-off between public health and civil liberties that was constructed in debates about digital pandemic containment technologies was an especially contentious aspect of this issue (Kitchin 2020) that is echoed in several of the contributions to this volume (see Chapters 4 and 5 in particular).

Second, risks are unevenly distributed in ways that might amplify existing inequalities or complicate them, as evident at all scales from the interpersonal to the global. In often-predictable ways, many of the risks and consequences of industrial *over*-production are displaced, by a combination of design and circumstance, onto the same disadvantaged groups for whom material scarcity remains a real predicament, such as the residents of Jakarta's informal settlements, who are among the people in the region most vulnerable to the risks of environmental pollution, flooding, and land subsidence (Firman et al. 2011). These groups, furthermore, are more likely to lack the information and resources needed to recognise and avoid the risks to which they are exposed. As Harvey (2020) argued early in the pandemic, the familiar refrain that 'we are all in this together' was no more than a rhetorical cloak over outcomes that were highly differentiated by class, gender, race, ethnicity, and other intersecting factors of oppression, largely originating in the dual burdens of exposure to the virus and to job losses that were disproportionately borne by the 'new working class' of the tertiary sector. This was as true of the millions of 'impoverished, hungry, thirsty' migrant workers that Roy (2020) observed trekking out of India's megacities in late March 2020 as it was for the most vulnerable communities of Chicago and New York (Maroko, Nash, and Pavilonis 2020).

Thus, there is also a two-part answer to the question of the pandemic's political meaning – the question of 'a portal to what?' There is, first, the part that seizes the opportunity to construct an objective community of global risk, potentially in the utopian terms of an imminent collectivity, facilitated by a 'great awakening' (Gills 2020) to new intersectional equivalences based on the degree and urgency of endangerment. Among the possibilities that social scientists have raised is that COVID-19 might serve as catalyst for a new global development paradigm (Oldekop et al. 2020), a sustainability transition (Cohen 2020; Goffman 2020; Wells et al. 2020), or more caring and inclusive approaches in urban planning and design (Forester 2020; Jon 2020; Pineda and Corburn 2020). The second part of the answer steps back from the commonality of positive social change – for, indeed, commonality might be precisely the grounds upon which responsibility is deferred – to ask whence risk's most charged political subjects are to come. This part of the answer, referring again to Beck, is that it might be the anxious solidarities of *negative* social change that prove more animating in the current era: negative in the sense that their foremost concern is not with need or want but with the demand to be *spared* from exposure to the manifold potential dangers we have collectively produced. In other words, it may be enough to say – as the ambiguous phrase 'post-pandemic' implicitly does – that what we are searching for in the present is a portal simply to 'something other than this'.

Learning from Southeast Asia

The way we have situated this study in Southeast Asia reveals the influence of our disciplinary grounding in urban geography, where, among the scholarly fields represented in this volume, there has been an especially sustained and impactful application of postcolonial critiques of knowledge and difference to theoretical debates. Among the most influential texts is Robinson's *Ordinary Cities* (2006), which makes a forceful argument against widely evinced practices in canonical urban studies through which only certain cities have become launching sites for novel theoretical propositions, and categorical divisions and hierarchies imposed on cities and world regions have amounted to incommensurability for the purposes of learning and understanding them. Robinson enjoined urban geographers to think in terms of 'a world of ordinary cities' (Robinson 2006, p.1) or a world in which conceptual innovations or insights can arise from any urban situation or process (see also Robinson 2016). Her intervention has helped to motivate geography and its adjacent disciplines to engage more systematically with the intellectual legacy of subaltern studies, with its methodological tools for resisting constrictive and hegemonic conceptions of political action, and especially with the injunction of Chakrabarty (2000) to 'provincialize' European thought by instating difference as an analytic through which academic knowledge is consciously produced. Accordingly, a recent bibliometric assessment of the cities that are now 'on and off the map' of urban globalisation research recommends cautious optimism about an evident but incomplete decentring of Euro-American cities, with select East Asian cities especially gaining representation, including Tokyo, Shanghai, and Beijing (Kanai, Grant, and Jianu 2018; see also Shin 2021 and Song and Hae 2019).

This volume, accordingly, is intended to make a modest effort to expand and enrich the representation of Southeast Asian experiences in English-language scholarship, a task we have set out to undertake by consciously mobilising regional contributors from the perspective of decolonisation and decentring knowledge production (see Chapter 26 in this volume). Our quick assessment of the first 834 English-language publications responding to COVID-19 in development, human geography, planning, and urban studies that we had collected as of March 2021 found that only 3.4% of them thoroughly described or analysed experiences of the pandemic in Southeast Asia – a figure that suggests the region has been afforded only two-fifths of the representation it is due based on its share of the world's population. What we cannot yet offer, however, is a rigorous analysis of the extent to which that 3.4% of publications resists the prevalent tendency to elide or assimilate southern social phenomena into dominant narratives originating in, or more attentive to, cities and regions of the global North. The urban theorist Ananya Roy (2009; 2011b) has been especially observant of the problem that it is insufficient to redouble efforts to compile empirical research on the subaltern urbanisms of the global South or to refashion them as desirably 'vibrant and entrepreneurial' (Roy 2011b, p.226). Rather, theoretical propositions about cities in the global South must be 'appropriated, borrowed, and remapped' (Roy 2009, p.820), or made to travel in all manner of ways to stimulate new insights and provocations beyond their places of origin if theory generated in the global North is to yield up its exclusive authoritative force. Consequently, urban geographers have developed an influential and highly innovative body of work focused on epistemologies and methodologies of comparative research, often encompassing cities occupying markedly different positions in relation to global economic and social flows (see Lees, Shin, and López-Morales 2016; McFarlane 2010; Robinson 2011).

Among Roy's enduring contributions to this literature is her argument for the strategic grounding of knowledge production in world regions and a reformulated 'area studies', albeit attentive to 'the spatiality of flow, juxtaposition, porosity, and relational connectivity' through which cities and regions are made (Amin 2004, p.34; see also Roy 2009). In taking 'Asia' as her consciously ambiguous focus, Roy's aim is not to adopt it as a territorial container for a multitude of urban meanings but rather to demonstrate how its circulating models, its inter-referenced plans and policies, and its aspirations to globality or futurity are in fact constitutive of the same geographical space for which they stand (see also Ong 2011); they affect a 'making and unmaking of the referent' that is 'Asia' (Roy 2011a, p.309). In so doing, these experiments and claims practise a form of self-recognition that is not a conferral of visibility onto a subaltern Other in and through which colonial difference is reinscribed, but instead achieve a centring, or 'worlding', of themselves that resists being subtended by implicitly Euro-American categories, concepts, or habits of thought (see Chakrabarty 2000). Chua (2011) and Pow (2014), for example, have interrogated Singapore's self-scripting of its own success and the attendant partial borrowings of its lessons, or a Singapore 'model', in a wide range of urban contexts – an essential precursor, perhaps, for the influence of Singapore's technology-focused pandemic response in places as distant as the Czech Republic (Kouřil and Ferenčuhová 2020). Park, Shin, and Kang (2020) have evinced a similar process of self-referencing in the case of South Korea's promulgation of its developmental model.

As Bunnell (2013) has observed, the beneficial implications of this perspective for Southeast Asian area studies and for a lessened reliance on methodological nationalism therein have been acknowledged far less among area studies scholars than have the corresponding implications for urban research. Rather, regional analyses of Southeast Asia depend predominantly on the a priori framings of either global economic macro-regions, in the view of which Southeast Asia typically occupies a supplementary position in relation to the Asia-Pacific, or of sub-regional economic areas, such as the Indonesia–Malaysia–Singapore growth triangle. While greater attention to Southeast Asia's intraregional, transnational urbanisms is broadly warranted by this situation, in Bunnell's view, the approach to intra-Asian urban aspirations developed in Roy and Ong's 2011 edited volume *Worlding Cities*, as well as in Bunnell's own editorial work (Bunnell et al. 2012), is distinctly capable of allowing mappings of regions-in-formation to cohere through existing linkages and relations as they are observed, whether movements of financial capital or the everyday dreams of disadvantaged urban residents. The point is not that a relational urban geography should necessarily displace differently scaled geographical analyses but that the methodological innovations of postcolonial urban studies – including sensitivities to forms in emergence, to the mutability of geographical constructions, and to the possibility of alternative topological mappings – have much to offer beyond the study of cities for which they were devised. Concurrently, we are also mindful of the danger of postcolonial perspectives 'falling into the epistemological pitfall of liberal pluralistic thinking' and of how such approaches may 'potentially neutralise or bypass historical violence and structural hierarchies' (Hae and Song 2019, p.11; see also Shin 2021, pp.65–67). To this extent, we are reminded of Roy's (2016, p.207) avowal that refers to how postcolonial approaches would help her 'undertake a political economy attentive to historical difference as a fundamental and constitutive force in the making of global urbanization'. Thus, while each of the chapters in this volume takes a starting point that falls within Southeast Asia as conventionally understood, more important in our view is that each conveys a regional formation-in-the-making that claims a positioning within this world in its own way.

That does not mean that this volume attempts to reach any conclusions as to what the enduring rearrangements instigated by COVID-19 in Southeast Asia are likely to be. Certainly, over the course of the pandemic, the imaginative force of a perpetually emergent and technologically sophisticated 'New Asia' (Chang 2005), comprising a selection of East and Southeast Asian megacities, has held force in commentaries on the successful management of outbreaks in China, Singapore, and

South Korea. Exemplary is the economist Yasheng Huang's analysis in the *Harvard Business Review* of the synergistic blend of collectivist mindsets, advanced digital infrastructures, and compliant adoption of contact-tracing technologies to which he ascribes those countries' shared success (Huang, Sun, and Sui 2020). As Ong (2008; 2016) has documented, Singapore's well-nurtured bioscientific capabilities have been among the principal beneficiaries of its competitive ambitions, as well as of its post-SARS sensitivity to epidemiological risk, and these capabilities have in turn been an overlooked impetus to Asia's incessant remaking, now 'as a genomic, epidemiological, and environmental continuity' (2016, p.xiv). Ong also observes, however, how less well-resourced states such as Indonesia have cautiously negotiated to preserve a measure of 'bio-sovereignty' amid capitalistic and cross-regional initiatives for global health.

Taken as a whole, it is through a lens that takes Southeast Asia's cities as 'milieus of intervention', or as launching points for 'a plethora of situated experiments', as posited by Ong (2011, p.2), that this volume best stands to bring a post-pandemic world into view. The workings of this analytic depend, in ethos and orientation if not in an explicitly conceptual sense (see Anderson and McFarlane 2011), on the foregrounding of various situated articulations of knowledges and practices, or 'global assemblages' (Collier and Ong 2005), through which the broader shifts instigated or illuminated by the pandemic can be productively grasped. Consequently, Ong (2011) has argued, canonical theories of the political economy of globalisation or of subaltern postcoloniality are liable to be made untenable in their hegemonic forms, for what is demonstrated is that neither singular causalities nor privileged social categories alone suffice to explain the multitude of situated outcomes and experiences that are engendered by such overarching phenomena as COVID-19. Our contributors' conclusions must perforce be open-ended; the concepts and methods they use and the challenges and initiatives they describe neither hold consistent from one chapter to the next nor collectively exhaust the most salient themes for social research arising from COVID-19 in this part of the world. Each chapter, however, initiates an intellectual engagement with a world amid crisis, and, while theoretical intervention is constrained by each chapter's brevity as well as the risk of being premature, the circumstances under which this book was produced have the benefit of bringing many of its contributors' personal and political entanglements to the fore, while giving voice to authors from the region, many of whom are early career researchers under-represented in mainstream English publications.

Learning from COVID-19 in the region

COVID-19 presented huge challenges to governments, businesses, civil societies, and people from all levels of society, but its impact was highly variegated, affecting society in multiple negative ways, with uneven geographical and socio-economic patterns. The collaborative scholarly initiative in which this volume originated began with our recognition that, despite the profound implications COVID-19 posed for Southeast Asia, critical perspectives on and from the region were under-represented in many academic forums, apart from a small number of regionally specific initiatives. With this in mind, we solicited contributions from a diverse selection of social scientists that contemplate the lessons COVID-19 might hold for a 'post-pandemic world' in and beyond Southeast Asia. Within these contributions, we have identified three major themes, which serve as the titles for the three parts of this book: (1) Urbanisation, digital infrastructures, economies, and the environment; (2) Migrants, (im)mobilities, and borders; and (3) Collective action, communities, and mutual action.

Urbanisation, infrastructure, economies, and the environment

Arundhati Roy's (2020) notion of the pandemic as a 'portal' is among the most arresting of a considerable number of arguments for viewing COVID-19 as a catalytic crisis that has modified or accelerated processes of social change that were already considered urgent matters in the social sciences. For instance, Cohen (2020) has observed that the pandemic's destabilisation of global financial markets, disruption of international supply chains and tourism, and prompt to reconsider patterns of work forced our thinking about prosperity and sustainability to advance abruptly in a direction broadly like the one in which governments, multilateral organisations, and research institutions had moving with respect to sustainable consumption for 30 years. Oldekop et al. (2020) have argued that the pandemic substantiates the case for a more global, rather than international, development paradigm that equally implicates countries of the global North and South in the shared challenges of the climate crisis and patterns of deprivation and inequality. Harvey (2020) has argued that the pandemic underscores the problems of the existing global model of capital accumulation, which was already troubled by protest movements and other challenges to its legitimacy as well as mounting signs of poor economic health, such as the excessive creation of debt.

It is now the task of the social sciences to ground these and other interlinked arguments for the pandemic's significance in the empirical specificities of an array of contexts, not least because in many cases one finds that the strained political systems of severely affected countries may have constrained both the durability and progressiveness of adaptive responses. In Part I of this volume, contributors do this with respect to several salient dimensions of social change, namely urbanisation, digital infrastructures, economies, and the environment. First, from a regional perspective, Connolly (Chapter 2) discusses how our urban economies became prone to infectious disease, as the rise of globalisation not only made cities interconnected but also facilitated the emergence of peri-urban and regional connections that created greater challenges in terms of containing epidemic outbreaks. Rapid urbanisation seen in regions such as Southeast Asia has not been accompanied by an adequate provision of infrastructure such as clean water supplies and housing appropriate for tackling the proliferation of infectious disease. To address these problems, Connolly calls for the incorporation of socio-ecological justice for our urban economies to achieve more socially inclusive and environmentally sustainable future development.

Chapters 3, 4, and 5 address digital technology and the economy. By taking Malaysia and Cambodia as their main case studies, the authors attend to the impacts of the pandemic on digital infrastructure. The use of digital technology for tackling the pandemic (e.g. app-based contact tracing) was a major area of innovation for pandemic-affected countries across the world. While the pandemic contributed to the deepening of digitalisation of social services including health and education, Gong, Shaharudin, and Tumin (Chapter 3) shed light on the ways in which such digitalisation may not create equitable opportunities for people, even though governments and businesses would encourage digital technologies to enhance the resilience of their labour force to the pandemic. For Yatid and Said (Chapter 4), the rapid adoption of digital technologies to control the spread of infectious disease raised concerns for data governance, especially with regard to ensuring data privacy and security. Young (Chapter 5) raises an important aspect of digital platforms as a double-edged sword based on his study of digital platforms and online communities in Cambodia. Digital platforms have been a key arena for communities to connect with each other; however, it is also important to be aware that digital platforms can be an invisible means of state surveillance.

Chapters 6, 7, and 8 examine the impact of the pandemic on select industries, namely real estate, business process outsourcing, and garment manufacturing. Here, we glimpse how the global pandemic affected the global production network and value production. Ng (Chapter 6) examines how cross-border investment practices in real estate markets responded to the COVID-19 pandemic. Focusing on Malaysia's 'My Second Home Programme', which encouraged offshore property investment, the chapter exposes the fragile conditions of domestic property markets that depended heavily on the mobility of international investors when such mobility was constrained by movement restrictions. He thus calls for state action to curb the industrial practices of building housing for profit, which exacerbates affordability problems for local populations.

In Chapter 7, on the business process outsourcing (BPO) industry in the Philippines, Thompson reveals the exploitative relationship between the global North and the global South, which drove BPO workers to face greater risks during the pandemic to support the lives of consumers in the global North. In Chapter 8, Brickell, Chhom, Lawreniuk, and So critically reflect upon the economic impact of the COVID-19 pandemic on garment workers who were trapped in what the authors conceptualise as 'global precarity chains'. In line with the arguments made by Thompson, Brickell et al. also shed light on the ways in which garment workers in Cambodia faced harsher life conditions, which were initially generated by the precarious position of the country's garment industry in global value chains but were further exacerbated by the pandemic pushing workers into greater indebtedness.

Chapter 9 turns to labour relations, taking the example of labour activism and campaigning in Vietnam. Here, Buckley examines the structure of labour relations in Vietnam's socialist market economy and discusses how the national campaign by the state-led labour organisation co-existed with self-organised labour activism at the grassroots level. For Buckley, this dual structure was effective in advancing demands for safer workplaces as well as broader reformist changes to promote fair wages and welfare benefits amid pandemic-generated economic hardship. While exposing limitations, this dual structure was deemed effective in terms of preventing acute impacts of pandemic on many Vietnamese workers.

Finally, Chapter 10 steps back to reflect on the relationship between Southeast Asian economies and socio-environmental conditions and how this relationship was reshaped by the pandemic. Here, taking the example of haze in Indonesia and Malaysia, Smith and Varkkey draw attention to the possibility of how haze-generated air pollution and the spread of infectious disease might have reinforced each other during the pandemic.

Migrants, (im)mobilities, and borders

The widespread imposition of restrictions on movement during COVID-19, including border closures, lockdowns, social distancing measures, and travel restrictions, signalled a profound resurgence of geographical closure, political disintegration, and territoriality that augured a very different post-pandemic world (Dodds et al. 2020; Radi, Pinos, and Ptak 2021; Ren 2020). Observers anxiously raised the prospect of various government responses and political debates reinforcing aspects of exclusionary nationalism and its linkages with authoritarianism, prejudice, and the politics of fear; however, it has also remained possible that the pandemic will prove to be an impetus for greater co-operation and cross-national solidarity (Bieber 2020). As a critical node in the control of transnational mobility, Singapore has already been centred within these debates and used to demonstrate that pandemic containment measures have tended to sustain existing regimes and the pathologisation of select mobilities, especially that of migrant workers (Lin and Yeoh 2020). These areas of inquiry are worked through and addressed from several places within Southeast Asia in the second part of this volume.

The salience of pre-existing structures of inequality impacting on migrant workers is well-demonstrated by Chapters 11 and 12, both of which take Singapore as their scene of analysis. In Chapter 11, Jamieson presents a critical and theoretically informed consideration of the preconditions for the uncontained outbreaks that afflicted migrant worker dormitories. His argument is that this exposure was enabled by the construction of the migrant worker as a pathological subject in the context of the 'logistical violence' of the global supply chains (Cowen 2014) within which the city-state had positioned itself as a global node. The model of 'logistical citizenship' that this entailed, for Singapore, in effect sequestered migrant labour from state or societal responsibility by way of formal and informal policy mechanisms, the nested hierarchies of agents and contracts, and the spatial logic of the dormitory – with enduring and exploitative consequences that must not be allowed to slip behind the premise of quarantine as a temporary measure. In Chapter 12, Antona reports on the experiences of live-in domestic workers, whose mobility was acutely circumscribed, especially during Singapore's 'circuit-breaker' containment measures. Describing domestic workers' confinement in the homes of their employers, where they were subjected to increased surveillance and control and tasked with greater responsibilities, and their reluctance to travel outside the city-state when their right to return became much less certain, Antona's most rousing finding is how few of her interlocutors regarded this as a meaningful change from ordinary circumstances, or as less of a 'new normal' and more of the 'same old'.

A similar critique of pre-existing inequalities is evident in Chapters 13 and 14, both of which address the plight of overseas Filipino work-ers (OFWs), ordinarily characterised as the Philippines' 'modern-day heroes' for the hardships they endure, and for the substantial benefits remittances provide to OFWs' households as well as the national econ-omy. In Chapter 13, Fernandez, Muyot, Pangilinan, and Quijano focus on the experiences of the over 600,000 OFWs whom the pandemic had forced to repatriate as of April 2021. The difficulties they faced upon return – including, *inter alia*, lengthy and inconvenient journeys from Metro Manila to their home provinces, limited access to financial assis-tance or protection against exposure to COVID-19, and the necessity of compensatory adjustments to household expenses, including the with-drawal of children from education – illuminated their underlying dis-advantages, precarity, and stigmatisation. So too did these difficulties illuminate shortcomings of governance, including underinvestment in community infrastructure and human capital, deferrals of responsibility to impoverished provincial and local governments, dilatory adaptation or policy responses, and insensitivity or misguidance in policy choices.

In Chapter 14, Humi presents a complementary analysis of the dif-ficulties faced by OFWs who remained employed in frontline health-care roles in the UK, where they constituted the nationality dying from COVID-19 in the greatest numbers among National Health Service (NHS) staff. She observes that the 'heroes' narrative is echoed in the af-finity that Britons hold for NHS workers, the insufficiency of which was demonstrated by gestures such as weekly performances of 'clapping for carers' while pay increases, adequate personal protective equipment, and secure immigration statuses were not forthcoming. Humi uses these circumstances to forcefully situate the control and exploitation of Filipino and other migrant labour with respect to colonial legacies, the disruptive interventions of international organisations, and the deleterious fragmentation of such imagined communities as the 'Filipino global nation'.

In Chapter 15, Tan and Romadan take a more policy-oriented approach to examining the societal consequences of the redoubled vulnerability of Malaysia's migrant workers during the pandemic. While poor living standards amplified migrants' viral exposure and rates of transmission, the inadequacy of governmental support for their employers worsened migrants' precarity of employment and attendant residential status. Tan and Romadan's point is that the argument for more effective government intervention in these circumstances is not only moral; there is also a compelling economic argument that encompasses (1) externalities such as the healthcare burden of the virus's poorly mitigated circulation; (2) the qualities of migrant workers that make them difficult to replace (i.e. their willingness to take lower-skilled and unappealing jobs); and (3) the dangerous assumptions (a) that the costly modernisation of production technologies can be achieved simply by impeding industries from utilising low-cost, labour-intensive strategies, and (b) that it is lower-skilled roles, typically filled by migrants, that technology is most likely to displace.

In Chapter 16, Koh discusses the significance of borders and bordering practices as technologies of selective inclusion and exclusion, which were strengthened by the pandemic as well as augmented by such tactics as travel bubbles and 'green' or 'fast' lanes. Her argument is that what we witnessed is not only the illumination of the enduring logics of injustice that inform existing borders and bordering tactics but also their greater entwinement with health security in ways that will reshape the unequal privileges of mobility and which therefore bear considerable and potentially lasting ethical and political significance. Of critical importance here, as in many contributions to this volume, are the underlying inequalities that impact individuals' health status and exposure to the virus, which are easily occluded by the legitimacy of public health considerations and the objectivity of testing for the virus or antibodies.

Koh's observations are complemented by Chapter 17, in which Wardani and Maw Thoe Myar share an anthropological perspective on the Myanmar–China border area from Muse, a small town in Myanmar's northern Shan State. Visiting the border crossing in July

2020, the authors detail the diverse mix of actors contending with un-expected macro-level changes in policy and trade and the uncertain-ty of the pandemic's course through various improvised means. Truck drivers camped within their stranded vehicles, found support in nearby communities, and haggled to offload perishable agricultural goods to local traders. Hawkers, smugglers, and peddlers worked flexibly be-tween formal and informal economic arrangements.

Collective action, communities, and mutual aid

Given the profound uncertainty brought by disrupted or accelerated processes of social change and the challenges of closure, disintegration, and enforced immobility, the third part of this volume sharpens our col-lective focus on the pandemic's diverse impacts on everyday life. There we find cause for hope. For, as Springer (2020, p.112) has suggested, one can find evidence of a 'resurgence of reciprocity' in every part of the world, as everyday acts of care and compassion hold communities to-gether despite lockdowns and social distancing. In Part III, on collective action, communities, and mutual aid, eight chapters investigate various bottom-up initiatives in the region to support communities and slow the spread of COVID-19. It is of considerable importance that these analyses of everyday strategies of collective care and resistance adopt an intersectional sensitivity to how the uneven impacts of the outbreak, as well as unequal opportunities to access mutual support, have been con-ditioned by existing structures of oppression. These chapters allow us to imagine an alternative system driven by empowered communities. In this regard, Chapter 18 by Padawangi provides an overview of various potentials that collective actions can bring against the capitalist mode of production amid the COVID-19 pandemic. To do so, this chapter sees COVID-19 as an opportunity to challenge 'normalcy' by looking into different collective movements in Indonesia from food-sharing in neighbourhoods to online protests and political participation.

Chapters 19 and 20 demonstrate challenges and possibilities for com-munities to respond to the multiple crises resulting from COVID-19. In Chapter 19, Sangsuradej investigates Myanmar's complex situation resulting from the pandemic and a series of political crises, including the 2021 coup. While the pandemic revealed the deep-rooted political, economic, and ethnic divides of the country, Sangsuradej finds that ur-ban community groups played a key role in preventing the spread of the virus in disadvantaged areas. Similarly, in Chapter 20, Perkasa shows how community groups mobilised themselves to manage and control the spread of the virus by introducing health protocols in response to government mismanagement in Surabaya, Indonesia. For Perkasa, the idea of community-based mutual help, known in Indonesia as *gotong royong*, was a key element to prevent further adverse effects from COVID-19.

In Chapter 21, Lim demonstrates how COVID-19 was utilised by the Singaporean state to legitimate the state's interventions regarding food security issues. He also points out that, despite the rhetoric of food security, the state insufficiently addressed lived food insecurity issues as more households faced difficulties in accessing sufficient, safe, and nutritious food. In such circumstances, community-led food-sharing initiatives were the pivotal point to support vulnerable groups in many parts of Southeast Asia. Chatinakrob, in Chapter 22, analyses the 'happiness-sharing pantries' campaign in Thailand, a platform allowing community members to donate food for whoever needed it. This is an example of how a local, bottom-up initiative can be a national-level campaign supporting vulnerable groups in society. In the Philippines, a similar initiative also played a key role in aiding vulnerable groups. In Chapter 23, Guazon provides a vivid account of community support for female informal residents despite a draconian lockdown imposed by the state. Guazon also reminds us that researchers need to learn from vulnerable people, who are often only seen as the subject of research.

The remaining chapters also show the role of communities in dealing with various social problems beyond the reach of the state resulting from COVID-19. Chapter 24 by Tengku Nur Qistina examines how civil society and NGOs responded to domestic violence issues in Malaysia that the government did not adequately address. In Chapter 25, Hanung argues that already-marginalised groups in Southeast Asia, namely LGBTIQ people, were more severely affected by COVID-19, but community-led initiatives were crucial to empower the groups and build resilience in terms of economy, well-being, and advocacy. The various community-led initiatives introduced in Part III to tackle COVID-19 pandemic indicate the possibility that community-led initiatives can bring more positive and enduring changes to the region.

References

Al Jazeera. (2021). 'Criticism over Myanmar ASEAN deal with military coup leader', 25 April. https://perma.cc/459G-6SFN[Last accessed 19 June 2021].

Ali, S. Harris; and Keil, Roger. (2006). 'Global cities and the spread of infectious disease: The case of Severe Acute Respiratory Syndrome (SARS) in Toronto, Canada'. *Urban Studies*, vol. 43, issue 3, pp. 491–509. https://doi.org/10.1080/00420980500452458

Amin, Ash. (2004). 'Regions unbound: Towards a new politics of place'. *Geografiska Annaler: Series B, Human Geography*, vol. 86, no. 1, pp. 33–44. https://doi.org/10.1111/j.0435-3684.2004.00152.x

Anderson, Ben; and McFarlane, Colin. (2011). 'Assemblage and geography'. *Area*, vol. 43, no. 2, pp. 124–127. https://doi.org/10.1111/j.1475-4762.2011.01004.x

Barbosa, Eliana Rosa de Queiroz. (2020). 'Academic southernness as affective boldness: A quarantined testimonial'. *Space and Culture*, vol. 23, no. 3, pp. 279–285. https://doi.org/10.1177/1206331220938630

Beck, Ulrich. (1992). *Risk Society: Towards a New Modernity*. UK: SAGE.

Bhan, Gautam; Caldeira, Teresa; Gillespie, Kelly; and Simone, AbdouMaliq. (2020). 'The pandemic, southern urbanisms and collective life'. *Society and Space*, 3 August. https://perma.cc/8NEV-XEC9 [Last accessed 17 June 2021].

Bieber, Florian. (2020). 'Global nationalism in times of the COVID-19 pandemic'. *Nationalities Papers*, pp 1–13. https://doi.org/10.1017/nps.2020.35

BMJ Opinion. (2021). 'Myanmar's doctors are risking their lives in the civil disobedience movement', 21 April. https://perma.cc/R2CY-Q5NJ [Last accessed 19 June 2021].

Brickell, Katherine; Picchioni, Fiorella; Natarajan, Nithya; Guermond, Vincent; Parsons, Laurie; Zanello, Giacomo; and Bateman, Milford. (2020). 'Compounding crises of social reproduction: Microfinance, over-indebtedness and the COVID-19 pandemic'. *World Development*, vol. 136, p. 105087. https://doi.org/10.1016/j.worlddev.2020.105087

Brown, Tim; Craddock, Susan; and Ingram, Alan. (2012). 'Critical interventions in global health: Governmentality, risk, and assemblage'. *Annals of the Association of American Geographers*, vol. 102, no. 5, pp. 1182–1189. https://doi.org/10.1080/00045608.2012.659960

Bunnell, Tim. (2013). 'City networks as alternative geographies of Southeast Asia'. *TRaNS: Trans-Regional and -National Studies of Southeast Asia*, vol. 1, no. 1, pp. 27–43. https://doi.org/10.1017/trn.2012.2

Bunnell, Tim; Goh, Daniel P.S.; Lai, Chee-Kien; and Pow, Choon Piew. (2012). 'Introduction: Global urban frontiers? Asian cities in theory, practice and imagination'. *Urban Studies*, vol. 49, no. 13, pp. 2785–2793. https://doi.org/10.1177/0042098012452454

Bunnell, Tim; and Maringanti, Anant. (2010). 'Practising urban and region-al research beyond metrocentricity'. *International Journal of Urban and Regional Research*, vol. 34, no. 2, pp. 415–420. https://doi.org/10.1111/j.1468-2427.2010.00988.x

Caballero-Anthony, Mely. (2021). 'COVID-19 in Southeast Asia: Regional pandemic preparedness matters'. *Brookings Institution*, 14 January. https://perma.cc/C4NK-37UK [Last accessed 18 June 2021].

Chakrabarty, Dipesh. (2000). *Provincializing Europe: Postcolonial Thought and Historical Difference*. USA: Princeton University Press.

Chang, T.C. (2005). 'Place, memory and identity: Imagining "New Asia"'. *Asia Pacific Viewpoint*, vol. 46, no. 3, pp. 247–253. https://doi.org/10.1111/j.1467-8373.2005.00286.x

Chen, Kuan-Hsing. (2010). *Asia as Method: Toward Deimperialization*. USA: Duke University Press.

Chua, Beng Huat. (2011). 'Singapore as model: planning innovations, knowl-edge experts', in Ananya Roy and Aihwa Ong (eds) *Worlding Cities: Asian Experiments and the Art of Being Global*. UK: Blackwell, pp. 29–54.

Cohen, Maurie J. (2020). 'Does the COVID-19 outbreak mark the onset of a sustainable consumption transition?' *Sustainability: Science, Practice and Policy*, vol. 16, no. 1, pp. 1–3. https://doi.org/10.1080/15487733.2020.1740472

Collier, Stephen J.; and Ong, Aihwa. (2005). 'Global assemblages, anthro-pological problems', in Aihwa Ong and Stephen J. Collier (eds) *Global Assemblages: Technology, Politics, and Ethics as Anthropological Problems*. UK: Blackwell, pp. 3–21.

Connolly, Creighton; Keil, Roger; and Ali, S. Harris. (2020). 'Extended ur-banisation and the spatialities of infectious disease: Demographic change, infrastructure and governance'. *Urban Studies*, vol. 58, no. 2, pp. 245–263. https://doi.org/10.1177/0042098020910873

Cowen, Deborah. (2014). *The Deadly Life of Logistics: Mapping Violence in Global Trade*. USA: University of Minnesota Press.

Davies, Sara E. (2019). *Containing Contagion: The Politics of Disease Outbreaks in Southeast Asia*. USA: John Hopkins University Press.

Do, Binh; Nguyen, Ninh; D'Souza, Clare; Bui, Huu Duc; and Nguyen, Thi Nguyen Hong. (2021). 'Strategic responses to COVID-19: The case of tour operators in Vietnam'. *Tourism and Hospitality Research*. https://doi.org/10.1177/1467358421993902

Dodds, Klaus; Broto, Vanesa Castan; Detterbeck, Klaus; Jones, Martin; Mamadouh, Virginie; Ramutsindela, Maano; Varsanyi, Monica; Wachsmuth,

David; and Woon, Chih Yuan. (2020). 'The COVID-19 pandemic: territorial, political and governance dimensions of the crisis'. *Territory, Politics, Governance*, vol. 8, no. 3, pp. 289–298. https://doi.org/10.1080/21622671.2020.1771022

Doucette, Jamie; and Park, Bae-Gyoon (eds) (2019). *Developmentalist Cities? Interrogating Urban Developmentalism in East Asia*. Netherlands: Brill.

The Economist. (2020a). 'Not even Singapore has been able to avoid a lockdown', 11 April. https://perma.cc/U2DR-G4DQ [Last accessed 20 June 2021]

The Economist. (2020b). 'The pandemic has exposed South-East Asia's poor governance', 24 October. https://perma.cc/3EHE-BBT2 [Last accessed 20 June 2021]

The Economist. (2021a). 'A worrying new wave of COVID-19 is hitting South-East Asia', 15 May. https://perma.cc/RGF6-6LTQ [Last accessed 20 June 2021]

The Economist. (2021b). 'Singapore's migrant workers have endured interminable lockdowns', 19 June. https://perma.cc/6YGF-GY3Y [Last accessed 20 June 2021]

Elegant, Naomi Xu. (2020). 'These Asian countries have masterfully limited COVID outbreaks. Here's how they did it'. *Fortune*. 28 December. https://perma.cc/KGM8-RGEN [Last accessed 18 June 2021].

Everts, Jonathan. (2020). 'The dashboard pandemic'. *Dialogues in Human Geography*, vol. 10, no. 2, pp. 260–264. https://doi.org/10.1177/2043820620935355

Firman, Tommy; Surbakti, Indra M.; Idroes, Ichzar C.; and Simarmata, Hendricus A. (2011). 'Potential climate-change related vulnerabilities in Jakarta: Challenges and current status'. *Habitat International*, vol. 35, no. 2, pp. 372–378. https://doi.org/10.1016/j.habitatint.2010.11.011

Foo, Lee-Peng; Chin, Mui-Yin; Tan, Kim-Leng; and Phuah, Kit-Teng. (2020). 'The impact of COVID-19 on tourism industry in Malaysia'. *Current Issues in Tourism*. https://doi.org/10.1080/13683500.2020.1777951

Forester, John. (2020). 'Kindness, planners' response to vulnerability, and an ethics of care in the time of Covid-19'. *Planning Theory and Practice*, vol. 21, no. 2, pp. 185–188. https://doi.org/10.1080/14649357.2020.1757886

Gills, Barry. (2020). 'Deep restoration: From the Great Implosion to the Great Awakening'. *Globalizations*, vol. 17, no. 4, pp. 577–579. https://doi.org/10.1080/14747731.2020.1748364

Goffman, Ethan. (2020). 'In the wake of COVID-19, is glocalization our sustainability future?' *Sustainability: Science, Practice and Policy*, vol. 16, no. 1, pp. 48–52. https://doi.org/10.1080/15487733.2020.1765678

Goh, Daniel P.S.; and Bunnell, Tim. (2013). 'Recentering Southeast Asian cities'. *International Journal of Urban and Regional Research*, vol. 37, no. 3, pp. 825–833. https://doi.org/10.1111/j.1468-2427.2013.01208.x

Gössling, Stefan; Scott, Daniel; and Hall, C. Michael. (2020). 'Pandemics, tourism and global change: a rapid assessment of COVID-19'. *Journal of Sustainable Tourism*, vol. 29, no. 1, pp. 1–20. https://doi.org/10.1080/0966 9582.2020.1758708

Greer, Scott L.; King, Elizabeth J.; Massard da Fonseca, Elize; and Peralta-Santos, Andre. (2020). 'The comparative politics of COVID-19: The need to understand government responses'. *Global Public Health*, vol. 15, no. 9, pp. 1413–1416. https://doi.org/10.1080/17441692.2020.1783340

Gutierrez, Jason. (2020). '"Will we die hungry?" A teeming Manila slum chafes under lockdown'. *New York Times*, 15 April. https://perma.cc/GJH4-8BWC [Last accessed 17 June 2021].

Hae, Laam; and Song, Jesook. (2019). 'Introduction: Core location, Asia as method, and a relational understanding of places', in Jesook Song and Laam Hae (eds) *On the Margins of Urban South Korea: Core Location as Method and Praxis*. Canada: University of Toronto Press, pp. 3–20.

Hall, C. Michael; Scott, Daniel; and Gössling, Stefan. (2020). 'Pandemics, transformations and tourism: Be careful what you wish or'. *Tourism Geographies*, vol. 22, no. 3, pp. 577–598. https://doi.org/10.1080/14616688 .2020.1759131

Harvey, David. (2020). 'Anti-capitalist politics in the time of COVID-19'. *Jacobin*, 20 March. https://perma.cc/L5EG-4G4W [Last accessed 17 June 2021].

Higgins-Desbiolles, Freya. (2020). 'Socialising tourism for social and ecological justice after COVID-19'. *Tourism Geographies*, vol. 22, no. 3, pp. 610–623. https://doi.org/10.1080/14616688.2020.1757748

Huang, Yasheng; Sun, Meicen; and Sui, Yuze. (2020). 'How digital contact tracing slowed Covid-19 in East Asia'. *Harvard Business Review*, 15 April. https://perma.cc/XS8S-VHAM [Last accessed 17 June 2021].

Human Rights Watch. (2021a). *Thailand: Events of 2020*. https://perma .cc/4RAB-24T7 [Last accessed 19 June 2021].

Human Rights Watch. (2021b). *Cambodia: Events of 2020*. https://perma.cc /D3VY-MJS7 [Last accessed 19 June 2021].

Jon, Ihnji. (2020). 'A manifesto for planning after the coronavirus: Towards planning of care'. *Planning Theory*, vol. 19, no. 3, pp. 329–345. https://doi .org/10.1177/1473095220931272

Kanai, J. Miguel; Grant, Richard; and Jianu, Radu. (2018). 'Cities on and off the map: A bibliometric assessment of urban globalisation research'. *Urban Studies*, vol. 55, no. 12, pp. 2569–2585. https://doi.org/10.1177/004209 8017720385

King, Nicholas B. (2002). 'Security, disease, commerce: Ideologies of postcolonial global health'. *Social Studies of Science*, vol. 32, no. 5–6, pp. 763–789. https://doi.org/10.1177/030631270203200507

Kitchin, Rob. (2020). 'Civil liberties or public health, or civil liberties and public health? Using surveillance technologies to tackle the spread of COVID-19'. *Space and Polity*, vol. 24, no. 3, pp. 362–381. https://doi.org/10.1080/135 62576.2020.1770587

Kouřil, Peter; and Ferenčuhová, Slavomíra. (2020). '"Smart" quarantine and "blanket" quarantine: the Czech response to the COVID-19 pandemic'. *Eurasian Geography and Economics*, vol. 61, no. 4–5, pp. 587–597. https://doi.org/10.1080/15387216.2020.1783338

Kuddus, Rohana. (2020). 'Lemongrass and prayer'. *New Left Review*, vol. 122, pp. 35–41. https://perma.cc/XXA3-RXB2 [Last accessed 23 June 2021].

Lawreniuk, Sabina. (2020). 'Necrocapitalist networks: COVID-19 and the 'dark side' of economic geography'. *Dialogues in Human Geography*, vol. 10, no. 2, pp. 199–202. https://doi.org/10.1177/2043820620934927

Lees, Loretta; Shin, Hyun Bang; and López-Morales, Ernesto. (2016). *Planetary Gentrification*. UK: Polity.

Li, Audrey Jiajia. (2020). 'Singapore's divisions are deepening'. *Financial Times*, 28 July. https://perma.cc/N8DF-F3JV [Last accessed 23 June 2021].

Lin, Weiqiang and Yeoh, Brenda S.A. (2020). Pathological (im)mobilities: Managing risk in a time of pandemics'. *Mobilities*, vol. 16, no. 1, pp. 96–112. https://doi.org/10.1080/17450101.2020.1862454

Lowy Institute. (2021). *Covid Performance Index: Country Rankings*. https://perma.cc/3XU9-DV3A [Last accessed 25 June 2021].

Mandhana, Niharika; Solomon, Feliz; and Jeong, Eun-Young. (2020). 'How one Singapore sales conference spread coronavirus around the world'. *Wall Street Journal*, 21 February. https://perma.cc/8DTG-86VX [Last accessed 18 June 2021].

Maroko, Andrew R.; Nash, Denis; and Pavilonis, Brian T. (2020). 'COVID-19 and Inequity: a Comparative Spatial Analysis of New York City and Chicago Hot Spots'. *Journal of Urban Health*, vol. 97, no. 4, pp. 461–470.

McCann, Eugene. (2020). 'Spaces of publicness and the world after the Coronavirus'. *Society and Space*, 1 June. https://perma.cc/GE7C-8BCS [Last accessed 18 June 2021].

McFarlane, Colin. (2010). 'The comparative city: Knowledge, learning, urbanism'. *International Journal of Urban and Regional Research*, vol. 34, no. 4, pp. 725–742. https://doi.org/10.1111/j.1468-2427.2010.00917.x

Meagher, Dominic. (2020). 'What's the secret to Southeast Asia's Covid success stories?' *The Interpreter*, 28 July. https://perma.cc/LC4K-M4GA [Last accessed 18 June 2021].

OECD. (2021). *Economic Outlook for Southeast Asia, China and India 2021: Reallocating Resources for Digitalisation*. OECD Development Centre. https://doi.org/10.1787/711629f8-en

Oldekop, Johan A.; Horner, Rory; Hulme, David; Adhikari, Roshan; Agarwal, Bina; Alford, Matthew; Bakewell, Oliver; Banks, Nicola; et al. (2020). 'COVID-19 and the case for global development'. *World Development*, vol. 134, pp. 1–4. https://doi.org/10.1016/j.worlddev.2020.105044

Ong, Aihwa. (2008). 'Scales of exception: Experiments with knowledge and sheer life in tropical Southeast Asia'. *Singapore Journal of Tropical Geography*, vol. 29, no. 2, pp. 117–129. https://doi.org/10.1111/j.1467-9493.2008.00323.x

Ong, Aihwa. (2011). 'Worlding cities, or the art of being global', in Ananya Roy and Aiwha Ong (eds) *Worlding Cities: Asian Experiments and the Art of Being Global*. UK: Blackwell, pp. 1–26.

Ong, Aihwa. (2016). *Fungible Life: Experiment in the Asian City of Life*. USA: Duke University Press.

Our World in Data. (2021). *COVID-19 Vaccine Doses Administered per 100 People*. https://perma.cc/X7JA-KVDJ [Last accessed 27 June 2021].

Park, Sehoon; Shin, Hyun Bang; and Kang, Hyun Soo (eds). (2020). *Exporting Urban Korea? Reconsidering the Korean Urban Development Experience*. UK: Routledge.

Pepinsky, Thomas. (2021). 'What state-party relations mean for COVID-19 management in Southeast Asia'. *Brookings Institution*, 7 January. https://perma.cc/TGR5-J55U [Last accessed 27 June 2021].

Pineda, Victor Santiago; and Corburn, Jason. (2020). 'Disability, urban health equity, and the coronavirus pandemic: Promoting cities for all'. *Journal of Urban Health*, vol. 97, no. 3, pp. 336–341. https://doi.org/10.1007/s11524-020-00437-7

Pow, Choon Piew. (2014). 'License to travel: Policy assemblage and the "Singapore model"'. *City*, vol. 18, no. 3, pp. 287–306. https://doi.org/10.1080/13604813.2014.908515

Radil, Steven M.; Pinos, Jaume Castan; and Ptak, Thomas. (2021). 'Borders resurgent: Towards a post-Covid-19 global border regime?' *Space and Polity*, vol. 25, no. 1, pp. 132–140. https://doi.org/10.1080/13562576.2020.1773254

Radio Free Asia. (2020). 'Unemployed Southeast Asian migrants in Thailand struggle as COVID-19 shuts down economy', 3 March. https://perma.cc/9BF4-FHHU [Last accessed 18 June 2021].

Ratcliffe, Rebecca. (2020). 'How have Thailand and Cambodia kept Covid cases so low?' *The Guardian*, 16 December. https://perma.cc/44LB-67YR [Last accessed 18 June 2021].

Ren, Xuefei. (2020). 'Pandemic and lockdown: A territorial approach to COVID-19 in China, Italy and the United States'. *Eurasian Geography and Economics*, vol. 62, no. 4–5, pp. 423–434. https://doi.org/10.1080/15387216.2020.1762103

Reuters. (2020). '"Shoot them dead" – Philippine leader says won't tolerate lockdown violators', 2 April. https://perma.cc/9DUJ-B7PP [Last accessed 18 June 2021].

Rimmer, Peter J.; and Dick, Howard. (2009). *The City in Southeast Asia: Patterns, Processes and Policy*. Singapore: NUS Press.

Robinson, Jennifer. (2006). *Ordinary Cities: Between Modernity and Development*. UK: Routledge.

Robinson, Jennifer. (2011). 'Cities in a world of cities: The comparative gesture'. *International Journal of Urban and Regional Research*, vol. 35, no. 1, pp. 1–23. https://doi.org/10.1111/j.1468-2427.2010.00982.x

Robinson, Jennifer. (2016). 'Thinking cities through elsewhere: Comparative tactics for a more global urban studies'. *Progress in Human Geography*, vol. 40, no. 1, pp. 3–29. https://doi.org/10.1177/0309132515598025

Roy, Ananya. (2009). 'The 21st-century metropolis: New geographies of theory'. *Regional Studies*, vol. 43, no. 6, pp. 819–830. https://doi.org/10.1080/00343400701809665

Roy, Ananya. (2011a). 'Postcolonial urbanism: Speed, hysteria, mass dreams', in Ananya Roy and Aihwa Ong (eds) *Worlding Cities: Asian Experiments and the Art of Being Global*. UK: Blackwell, pp. 307–335.

Roy, Ananya. (2011b). 'Slumdog cities: Rethinking subaltern urbanism'. *International Journal of Urban and Regional Research*, vol. 35, no. 2, pp. 223–238. https://doi.org/10.1111/j.1468-2427.2011.01051.x

Roy, Ananya. (2016). 'Who's afraid of postcolonial theory?' *International Journal of Urban and Regional Research*, vol. 40, no. 1, pp. 200–209. https://doi.org/10.1111/1468-2427.12274

Roy, Ananya; and Ong, Aihwa (eds). (2011). *Worlding Cities: Asian Experiments and the Art of Being Global*. UK: Blackwell.

Roy, Arundhati. (2020). 'The pandemic is a portal'. *Financial Times*, 3 April. https://perma.cc/FSD4-SGKU [Last accessed 17 June 2021].

Russell, Martin. (2020). *Coronavirus in South-East Asia: Health, Political and Economic Impact*. European Parliamentary Research Service, June 2020. https://perma.cc/ZA9L-KB3U [Last accessed 25 June 2021].

Sheppard, Eric; Leitner, Helga; and Maringanti, Anant. (2013). 'Provincializing global urbanism: A manifesto'. *Urban Geography*, vol. 34, no. 7, pp. 893–900. https://doi.org/10.1080/02723638.2013.807977

Shin, Hyun Bang. (2021). 'Theorising from where? Reflections on de-centring global (Southern) urbanism', in Colin McFarlane and Michele Lancione (eds) *Global Urbanism: Knowledge, Power and the City*. UK: Routledge, pp. 62–70.

Simone, AbdouMaliq. (2004). *For the City Yet to Come: Changing African Life in Four Cities*. USA: Duke University Press.

Song, Jesook; and Hae, Laam (eds). (2019). *On the Margins of Urban South Korea: Core Location as Method and Praxis*. Canada: University of Toronto Press.

Springer, Simon. (2020). 'Caring geographies: The COVID-19 interregnum and a return to mutual id'. *Dialogues in Human Geography*, vol. 10, no. 2, pp. 112–115. https://doi.org/10.1177/2043820620931277

Thiri Shwesin Aung; Fischer, Thomas B.; and Wang, Yihan. (2021). 'Conceptualization of health and social vulnerability of marginalized populations during Covid-19 using quantitative scoring approach'. *Journal of Immigrant and Refugee Studies*. https://doi.org/10.1080/15562948.2021.1882023

Thompson, Nathan. (2021). 'Southeast Asia had COVID-19 under control. What went wrong?' *Foreign Policy*, 26 May. https://perma.cc/XJT5-BCZ3 [Last accessed 19 June 2021].

Truong, Mai. (2020). 'Vietnam's COVID-19 success is a double-edged sword for the Communist Party'. *The Diplomat*, 6 August. https://perma.cc/V6NB-5XDT [Last accessed 19 June 2021].

Wasdani, Kishinchand Poornima; and Prasad, Ajnesh. (2020). 'The impossibility of social distancing among the urban poor: The case of an Indian slum in the times of COVID-19'. *Local Environment*, vol. 25, no. 5, pp. 414–418. https://doi.org/10.1080/13549839.2020.1754375

Wells, Peter; Abouarghoub, Wessam; Pettit, Stephen; and Beresford, Anthony. (2020). 'A socio-technical transitions perspective for assessing future sustainability following the COVID-19 pandemic'. *Sustainability: Science, Practice and Policy*, vol. 16, no. 1, pp. 29–36. https://doi.org/10.1080/1548 7733.2020.1763002

Wilkinson, Annie. (2020). 'Local response in health emergencies: Key considerations for addressing the COVID-19 pandemic in informal urban settlements'. *Environment and Urbanization*, vol. 32, no. 2, pp. 503–522. https://doi.org/10.1177/0956247820922843

PART I:
URBANISATION, INFRASTRUCTURE, ECONOMIES, AND THE ENVIRONMENT

2. The urbanisation of spatial inequalities and a new model of urban development

Creighton Connolly

Changing patterns of urbanisation strongly influenced the initial outbreak and severity of the COVID-19 pandemic and form the focus of my first section here. The second section outlines how the pandemic highlighted deep existing inequalities and shortfalls in governance that have been associated with the current model of global urban development. As Nixon, Surie, and McQuay (2020) have argued, the COVID-19 pandemic 'brought urban governance to a critical juncture in Asia'. Subsequently, I evaluate how East and Southeast Asian cities are being redesigned in the wake of the pandemic and the role of participatory urban governance in creating healthier and more socio-ecologically just cities.

Urbanisation and infectious disease

Previous research has shown that dramatic changes in demographic and social conditions, including an exponential increase in global transport, have been responsible for much of the global emerging infectious disease problem (Ali and Keil 2006). Diseases like SARS were associated with the rise of globalisation, as interconnected global cities like Toronto and Hong Kong were severely affected (Ali and Keil 2008). This is because decreasing travel times allowed for the quicker spread of microbes and viruses before governance and healthcare systems could identify and control them.

The COVID-19 pandemic, however, was a story of peri-urban and rural–urban connections, as seen in large industrial centres like Wuhan, northern Italy, and parts of Germany, which are connected through global and regional supply chains. We saw more peri-urban and regional connections between a larger network of cities, which make it much

How to cite this book chapter:
Connolly, Creighton. 2022. 'The urbanisation of spatial inequalities and a new model of urban development'. In: Shin, Hyun Bang; Mckenzie, Murray; and Oh, Do Young (eds) *COVID-19 in Southeast Asia: Insights for a post-pandemic world*. London: LSE Press, pp. 37–45. DOI: https://doi.org/10.31389/lsepress.cov.b License: CC BY 4.0.

more difficult to contain disease outbreaks (Connolly, Ali, and Keil 2020). In general, cities are inherently connected with their peripheries through daily flows of people and goods. People commute into and out of the city each day for work; food and other essentials are often produced in peri-urban or rural areas and transported into the city. There are thus plenty of opportunities for the spread of microbes, bacteria, and different forms of nature through these activities and networks.

Urban density has been widely accused in popular media for the severity of the pandemic in places like New York City. Research has shown, however, that density alone cannot be a predictor of the spread of infectious diseases and depends on other factors such as the state of development, adherence to social distancing measures, and the extent of access to public health infrastructure (Florida 2020). It is also important here to distinguish between 'density' and 'overcrowding', where the former refers to high concentrations of people within an area and the latter to the lack of separation or space between people (often caused by inequality). For instance, Asian cities like Hong Kong, Seoul, and Taipei are far denser than New York City but have had far fewer cases of COVID-19 per capita.

Recent trends have suggested that the emergence of pathogenetic zoonoses in rapidly developing and urbanising regions has become a paradigmatic component of urbanisation and globalisation processes in the 21st century (Decaro and Lorusso 2020). This has been happening in tandem with the expansion of urban areas into previously uninhabited or non-urbanised peripheries, where there is more contact/interaction between humans and other animal and plant species. As I have argued previously, rapidly expanding infrastructure networks and urban landscapes can themselves play a role in the emergence of potential outbreaks (Connolly, Keil, and Ali 2021). Examples include deforestation on the edges of cities and new agro-industrial transformations of hinterlands, producing new pathways of emergent infectious disease transmission (Yong 2018).

Adler, Florida, and Hartt (2020) have thus proposed using the concept of the mega-region to understand the geography of SARS-CoV-2's spread and its economic toll. As we saw in the early stages of the COVID-19 outbreak, many initial outbreaks were in wider metropolitan regions such as Milan/Lombardy and New York/New Jersey. These regions tend to be connected through travel corridors that extend well beyond the typical daily commuting range, resulting in the potential for diseases to spread much more widely through the urban fabric. In many cities of Asia, transit-oriented development has been an integral part of urban planning strategies that seek to develop polycentric urban regions, including high-density suburbs. This increasing connection within and between urban regions has resulted in SARS-CoV-2's trajectory of filtering down the urban hierarchy over time from mega-regions to large metropolitan regions and then to smaller towns.

As a result of increasing interconnectivity between cities and their hinterlands, travel bans have proved ineffective in containing disease because there will inevitably be some spread of the disease before they are enforced (Bajardi et al. 2011). At best, they can delay the spread of disease; at worst, they can counterintuitively increase the odds that outbreaks will spread by forcing travellers to seek alternative and even illegal transport routes. Yong (2018) has pointed out that they can also 'discourage health workers from helping to contain foreign outbreaks, for fear that they'll be denied reentry into their home country'.

The emergence of SARS-CoV-2 in Wuhan – a city of 11 million people – immediately before the Lunar New Year holiday played a large factor in the rapid spread of the virus. This was due to Wuhan's role as a major travel hub or 'thoroughfare' in central China (Ren 2020). As Ren (2020) has noted, however, the severity of the outbreak in Wuhan was magnified by the delay of officials in China in notifying the public about the novel virus and taking action to control it. As I discuss below, effective governance is crucial in responding to disease outbreaks and requires close cooperation between citizens and the state.

In contrast, cities that worked the quickest and most diligently to control local transmission through contact tracing, identifying sources of infections, quarantining affected individuals, and so on were most effective. While early lockdowns and social distancing measures helped to flatten the infection curve in some places, they were ultimately ineffective if implemented too late. Essential workers for example, were still needed to keep supermarkets, supply chains, and infrastructure running. Moreover, as Ren (2020) has noted in the case of Wuhan, lockdowns also tended to be unequal, affecting less affluent communities in the urban periphery more than those in the core. The plight of lockdowns on precarious and transient migrant workers has also been well documented, with many of these individuals out of work and with few options to travel home (Nixon, Surie, and McQuay 2020).

The lack of infrastructure in rapidly urbanising regions, including Southeast Asia, can also have severe consequences for the rise of epidemics, as rapid growth in cities and urban populations is not accompanied by the appropriate development of transportation and other essential infrastructure (Recio, Chatterjee, and Lata 2020). This includes access to clean water supplies, which are essential for combating the spread of infectious disease but are often lacking in rapidly growing informal settlements (Wilkinson 2020). Housing is also a crucial issue. In Manila, for example, millions of the city's essential but low-paid workers live in crowded, informal (and often illegal) settlements on the periphery, where they are vulnerable to disease outbreaks.

Even in wealthy cities like Singapore, the poorest sectors of the population are often unable to self-isolate owing to dense living conditions and are thus at higher risk of contracting and spreading diseases. Singapore was initially praised for its handling of COVID-19 and even managed to avoid imposing lockdown conditions until mid-April, when a sharp increase in cases among Singapore's migrant worker population emerged (Jamieson 2020). Nine dormitories housing more than 50,000 men, mostly from Bangladesh, India, and China, were declared 'isolation areas' and effectively on lockdown, meaning that about 300,000 workers had restrictions on their movements within their complexes (Han 2020). Most of these worker dormitories were deliberately located on the peripheries of Singapore and could have 12 to 20 workers sharing a room. They were also essentially 'out of sight' (both literally and metaphorically) as a potential source of vulnerability until the issue exploded (Luger 2020). This illustrates the spatial dimension of urban infectious disease outbreaks, as both the edges of the city and those who are most marginalised in society tend to be the most vulnerable (see Connolly, Ali, and Keil 2020; Iswara 2020).

Post-COVID-19 futures of an urbanising world

There has also been significant discussion about how cities and the world are going to change after the COVID-19 pandemic, much of which also relates to density and urban mobilities. Some urban designers have been arguing for a so-called 'Goldilocks density', which refers to an urban population density that is high enough to reap the benefits of sustainability and convenience provided by cities but not so high that people must live in 30-storey apartment blocks that rely on extensive use of public spaces like elevators (Alter 2020). Singapore has been planning to continue with high-density development while using 'smart solutions' to manage crowds (Board 2020). There has also been a widely recognised need to plan cities better to support bike and pedestrian infrastructure, which will make cities not only more carbon neutral but also less vulnerable to future disease outbreaks (Nixon, Surie, and McQuay 2020). This infrastructure, however, needs to be constructed evenly, rather than just serving wealthy or middle-class communities, which has been the case in many cities in recent decades (Madden 2020).

Indeed, as David Madden (2020) has pointed out, the global urban development model over the past few decades 'has catered to the needs of elite individuals … while allowing the deterioration of social services and public institutions and the intensification of inequality'. This is a point that has been recognised by urban designers across Southeast Asia. For example, Thai urban designer Kotchakorn Voraakhorn has asserted that: 'Bangkok should focus more on the public space and green infrastructure that make the city more liveable rather than the temporary infrastructure in the city for tourists' (quoted in Board 2020). Similarly, Malaysia's green building movement has largely focused on middle- to high-income developments targeted at foreigners and wealthy Malaysians. It has been suggested that the wake of the COVID-19 pandemic could be an ideal time to extend this type of development to the affordable market segment, which, in contrast to the glut of luxury properties nationwide, has seen very little supply (Board 2020).

Urban governance proved to be a critical element of how successful cities were in responding to the COVID-19 pandemic, particularly with regard to the role of civil society and community support. Seoul, for example, focused on an approach emphasising transparency, accountability, and solidarity instead of strict movement restrictions (Jagannathan 2020). Hong Kong is another interesting case in this regard, as the organisational capacity and the civic infrastructure established by 2019's protest movements played a central role in the city's response – and ultimate success – in containing the virus's spread (Tufekci 2020). One group set up a website to track cases of COVID-19, monitor hotspots, warn people of places selling fake PPE, and report hospital wait times and other relevant information. Such reliable information is crucial in managing epidemics within a community (Ren 2020; Yong 2018). Civilians also spontaneously adopted the wearing of masks in public, defying the government's ban on masks (in place due to the mass protests). Large groups of volunteers also distributed masks to the poor and elderly and installed hand sanitiser dispensers in crowded (low-income) tenement buildings. When the government at first refused to close the border with mainland China, more than 7,000 medical workers went on strike, demanding border closures and PPE for hospital workers (Ip 2020). These collective actions illustrate how civil society can organise to make up for the governance failures of urban and regional governments in responding to pandemics in real time.

Conclusion

The massive expansion of the global urban fabric over the past few decades has increased exposure to infectious diseases and posed new challenges to the control of outbreaks. As Nixon, Surie, and McQuay (2020) have argued, the pandemic 'revealed the fragile interconnectedness of metropolitan, peri-urban, and rural spaces and the inequalities upon which cities are built and maintained'. Indeed, while the central business districts of Southeast Asia's largest cities are modern, highly connected spaces, the pandemic highlighted the social inequalities and underinvestment in infrastructure services that are visible in more peripheral urban areas. This has made cities and their inhabitants more vulnerable not only to SARS-CoV-2 but also to other forms of social and economic hardship. The unsustainable urban development model that had been pursued in Asia and around the world therefore not only played a role in the outbreak of the COVID-19 pandemic but also had negative consequences for quality of life and socio-ecological justice.

While urban planning and design is already being reformulated to cope better with the next pandemic, urban governance will also be crucial. Urban governments will need to collaborate more effectively, not only with regional and national levels of government but also with residents and civil society groups to make infrastructure, housing, and livelihood opportunities more equitable. Politics in municipalities, between cities and other jurisdictions, and between municipalities, civil society actors, and local communities will be crucial to understanding the role urban health governance plays in an increasingly urbanised and globalised society (Acuto 2020). To this end, the COVID-19 pandemic offered valuable lessons about the need for building socio-ecological justice by strengthening institutions to promote more socially inclusive and environmentally sustainable forms of development. Without this effort, the inequalities that the pandemic exposed will only grow worse in the years and decades to come.

Acknowledgements

I am grateful to Hyun Bang Shin for the invitation to speak at the LSE public event titled 'Post COVID-19 Futures of the Urbanising World', where an earlier version of this chapter was presented. I am also indebted to Professors Roger Keil and S. Harris Ali for their involvement in shaping the ideas that are presented here. Any inconsistencies or oversights in the analysis are my own.

References

Acuto, Michele. (2020). 'COVID-19: Lessons for an urban(izing) world'. *One Earth*, vol. 2, no. 4, pp. 317–319. https://doi.org/10.1016/j.oneear.2020.04.004

Adler, Patrick; Florida, Richard; and Hartt, Maxwell. (2020). 'Mega regions and pandemics'. *Tijdschrift voor economische en sociale geografie*, vol. 111, no. 3, pp. 465–481. DOI: https://doi.org/10.1111/tesg.12449

Ali, S. Harris; and Keil, Roger. (2006). 'Global cities and the spread of infectious disease: The case of Severe Acute Respiratory Syndrome (SARS) in Toronto, Canada'. *Urban Studies*, vol. 43, no. 3, pp. 491–509. https://doi.org/10.1080/00420980500452458

Ali, S. Harris; and Keil, Roger. (2008). *Networked Disease: Emerging Infections in the Global City*. UK: Wiley-Blackwell.

Alter, Lloyd. (2020). 'Urban density is not the enemy, it is your friend'. *Treehugger*, 25 March. https://perma.cc/62HK-QG39 [Last accessed 22 April 2020].

Bajardi, Paolo; Poletto, Chiara; Ramasco, Jose J.; Tizzoni, Michele; Colizza, Vittoria; and Vespignani, Alessandro. (2011). 'Human mobility networks, travel restrictions, and the global spread of 2009 H1N1 pandemic'. *PLOS One*, vol. 6, no. 1, p. e16591. https://doi.org/10.1371/journal.pone.0016591

Board, Jack. (2020). 'COVID-19: Why saving our forests can help stop the next pandemic'. *CNA*, 9 May. https://perma.cc/M3T9-CRG4 [Last accessed 14 January 2021].

Connolly, Creighton; Ali, S. Harris; and Keil, Roger. (2020). 'On the relationships between COVID-19 and extended urbanization'. *Dialogues in Human Geography*, vol. 10, no. 2, pp. 213–216. https://doi.org/10.1177/2043820620934209

Connolly, Creighton; Keil, Roger; and Ali, S. Harris. (2021). 'Extended urbanisation and the spatialities of infectious disease: Demographic change, infrastructure and governance'. *Urban Studies*, vol. 58, no. 2, pp. 245–263. https://doi.org/10.1177/0042098020910873

Decaro, Nicola; and Lorusso, Alessio. (2020). 'Novel human coronavirus (SARS-CoV-2): A lesson from animal coronaviruses'. *Veterinary Microbiology*, vol. 244, p. 108693. https://doi.org/10.1016/j.vetmic.2020.108693

Florida, Richard. (2020). 'The geography of coronavirus'. *Bloomberg CityLab*, 3 April. https://perma.cc/N7C6-4YCA [Last accessed 9 June 2020].

Han, Kirsten. (2020). 'Singapore's new Covid-19 cases reveal the country's two very different realities'. *Washington Post*, 16 April. https://perma.cc/8RF7-DVK6 [Last accessed 8 June 2020].

Ip, Regina. (2020). 'The bitter pill medical workers on strike might have to swallow'. *South China Morning Post*, 9 February. https://perma.cc/FP8Z-FRK8 [Last accessed 14 January 2021].

Iswara, M. Anthony. (2020). 'Southeast Asia needs progress as pandemic exacerbates inequality: UN'. *Jakarta Post*, 3 August. https://perma.cc/2CBS-AQMH [Last accessed 14 January 2021].

Jagannathan, Vijay. (2020). 'Learning from Seoul to control COVID-19: Transparency, accountability, solidarity'. *TheCityFix*, 18 May. https://perma.cc/B8VH-WZYS [Last accessed 14 January 2021].

Jamieson, William. (2020). 'Logistical violence and virulence: Migrant exposure and the underside of Singapore's model pandemic response'. *LSE Southeast Asia Blog*, 14 October. https://perma.cc/5LJ6-6762 [Last accessed 14 January 2021].

Luger, Jason. (2020). 'Seeing Covid-19 through workers, students, and dormitories: Singapore in comparative framing'. *LSE Southeast Asia Blog*, 16 November. https://perma.cc/3JRA-QZAJ [Last accessed 13 January 2021].

Madden, David. (2020). 'Our cities only serve the wealthy. Coronavirus could change that'. *The Guardian*, 2 June. https://perma.cc/5KLC-YEGJ [Last accessed 4 June 2020].

Nixon, Nicola; Surie, Mandakini; and McQuay, Kim. (2020). 'Covid lays bare the flaws in Asia's booming megacities'. *InAsia*, 19 August. https://perma.cc/9C4G-MP6B [Last accessed 28 September 2020].

Recio, Redento; Chatterjee, Ishita; and Lata, Lutfun Nahar. (2020). 'COVID-19 reveals unequal urban citizenship in Manila, Dhaka and Delhi'. LSE COVID-19 Blog, 5 June. https://perma.cc/Z9LA-6X6E [Last accessed 14 January 2021].

Ren, Xuefei. (2020). 'The quarantine of a megacity: China's struggle over the coronavirus epidemic'. *International Journal of Urban and Regional*

Research, 4 February. https://perma.cc/DLW5-WKM5 [Last accessed 13 April 2020].

Tufekci, Zeynep. (2020). 'How Hong Kong did it'. *The Atlantic*, 12 May. https://perma.cc/D799-64C8 [Last accessed 17 May 2021].

Wilkinson, Annie. (2020). 'The impact of Covid-19 in informal settlements – are we paying enough attention?' *Institute of Development Studies*, 10 March. https://perma.cc/2FAJ-ACS6 [Last accessed 14 January 2021].

Yong, Ed. (2018). 'The next plague is coming. Is America ready?' *The Atlantic*, July/August. https://perma.cc/8BU5-BZNL [Last accessed 17 May 2021].

3. Digital transformation, education, and adult learning in Malaysia

Rachel Gong, Ashraf Shaharudin, and Siti Aiysyah Tumin

Malaysia's government has long recognised the value and promise of technology and innovation, having begun in the 1990s to develop a multimedia super corridor (MSC) to be competitive in a globally digitalised economy (Banerjee 1999). While digitalisation refers to the process of restructuring society around digital and communication infrastructures (Brennen and Kreiss 2016), digital transformation involves socio-technological changes that have broader and more profound implications on society and culture, such as the evolution of information dissemination from edited, curated print articles to unregulated, algorithmically recommended TikTok videos.

Despite its incomplete digital transformation, Malaysia emerged as a relatively well-connected country in Southeast Asia. As of 2019, Malaysia was a mobile-first nation, with a 123% mobile broadband penetration rate and a 9% fixed broadband penetration rate. In populated areas, 4G coverage was reportedly at 82% (MCMC 2020), albeit of questionable quality. Basic data plans are generally affordable, and the most popular online activities among internet users are social communications such as texting and social media (Gong 2020).

Efforts to further digitalise Malaysia had begun before the COVID-19 pandemic. A national broadband infrastructure plan had been launched; programmes had been established to incorporate advanced digital technologies into economic sectors such as manufacturing; and various structural institutions, such as the civil service, institutes of higher learning, and legal courts, had begun incorporating digital services, cloud computing, and big data analysis into their workflows. However, the pandemic revealed in Malaysia, as elsewhere, the stark structural

How to cite this book chapter:
Gong, Rachel; Shaharudin, Ashraf; and Tumin, Siti Aiysyah. 2022. 'Digital transformation, education, and adult learning in Malaysia'. In: Shin, Hyun Bang; Mckenzie, Murray; and Oh, Do Young (eds) *COVID-19 in Southeast Asia: Insights for a post-pandemic world*. London: LSE Press, pp. 46–57. DOI: https://doi.org/10.31389/lsepress.cov.c License: CC BY 4.0.

inequalities present in its digital infrastructure and adoption, a problem that had existed since the days of the MSC (Bunnell 2002). While digital technologies enabled elite segments of society to adapt fairly easily and quickly to life under lockdown, many under-served groups were not as fortunate.

In this chapter we assess the ways in which digital technologies, instead of levelling the playing field, may actually increase socio-economic in-equalities, especially with regard to education and adult learning. We consider the segments of society who may be further marginalised in the future, given the changing conditions of learning and work accel-erated by COVID-19, and suggest how future research and policy can tackle these challenges.

Previously, the digital divide described a fundamental gap in terms of access to computers and the internet (DiMaggio et al. 2001). As com-puting power costs decreased and internet infrastructure became wide-spread, digital inequalities became not just about access but also about meaningful connectivity and use (A4AI 2020; Gong 2020; Hargittai, Piper, and Morris 2018). The question is no longer simply whether everyone can connect to the internet, but also how we are connecting and how we are using our connectivity.

In the wake of the COVID-19 pandemic, Malaysia recognised in-ternet connectivity as a public utility (MOF 2020), paving the way for significant improvements in the development of internet infrastructure. While this may address the access component of the digital divide, it does not guarantee inclusive meaningful connectivity or use. During Malaysia's movement control orders to curb the spread of COVID-19, schools and universities were closed. Despite their best efforts to piv-ot to online classes, teachers and students faced challenges in terms of both digital access and digital pedagogy. When offices closed, a di-vide emerged between workers who could work from home and work-ers who had to be physically present to do their (often essential) jobs. Income has been a good predictor of which side of this divide a worker might fall (Siti Aiysyah 2020).

Income has also been a good predictor of the likelihood of non-es-sential workers staying employed during the pandemic (Parker, Minkin, and Bennett 2020). The number of unemployed people in Malaysia rose 41% from 521,400 in September 2019 to 737,500 in September 2020 (DOSM 2019; DOSM 2020c). Online education opportunities increased as part of adult learning initiatives to reskill and upskill job seekers. However, take-up of these programmes remained relatively low (*Malay Mail* 2020).

Widening gaps in education

We turn now to a discussion of the role and impact of digital technologies and the digital divide on education and adult learning. Malaysian school students lost at least 17 out of 43 normal schooling weeks in 2020 due to school closures. Learning was disrupted for around 4.9 million pre-school, primary, and secondary school students (MOE 2020) and around 1.3 million higher education students (MOHE 2020). Different and compounding forms of existing inequalities became apparent with distance learning.

The clearest gap was the lack of digital resources for some students, rendering digital learning almost impossible. Even before the pandemic made distance learning the default mode, students lacking the resources necessary to learn remotely were found to trail their peers in cognitive abilities and be more likely to drop out in the long run (Murat and Bonacini 2020). In 2019, only 6–9% of Malaysian school students owned a personal computer and/or a tablet (Hawati and Jarud 2020). Unequal access to digital devices and the internet tended to follow the rural–urban and household income gaps (Figure 3.1), aggravating prevailing inequalities.

Approximately 77% of school students were unable to effectively learn digitally from home owing to limited digital access (Ashraf 2020). This likely lower-bound estimate was based on both fixed and mobile broadband access, though fixed broadband access has been much rarer and arguably more effective for learning. In 2019, Malaysia's average mobile download speed of 11.0 Mbps was far slower than developed countries such as Canada (59.6 Mbps) and South Korea (59.0 Mbps) (Fenwick and Khatri 2020). States with lower median household incomes had lower fixed broadband subscription rates (Gong 2020), which implied a higher percentage of disadvantaged students in poorer states.

Distance learning requires self-discipline and self-initiative. A time use survey found that German students reduced their daily learning time by about half during school closures (Grewenig et al. 2020). The reduction was larger among low-achieving students as their learning time was replaced with less useful activities such as gaming or consuming social media, potentially further deteriorating their educational

Figure 3.1. Internet subscription and personal computer and laptop ownership by household segment, 2019

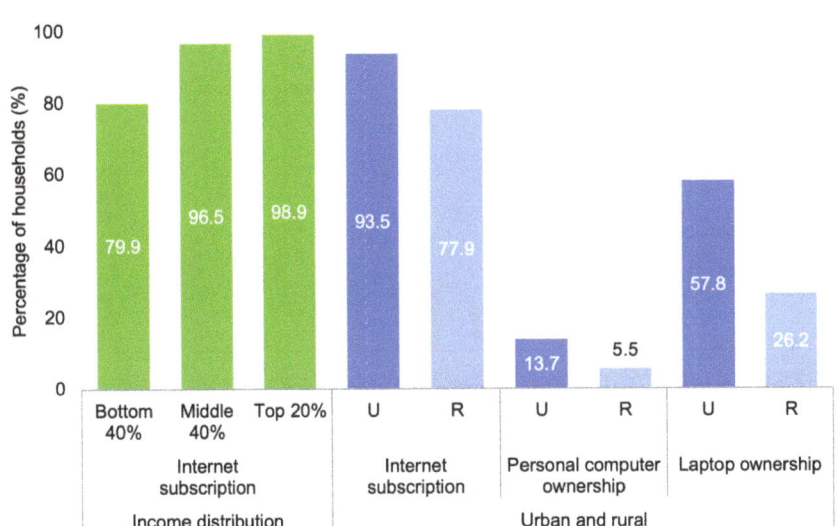

Source: DOSM (2020a).

achievement. This also highlights the discretionary nature of internet use, resulting in different outcomes for users. In 2019, across Malaysia, while 86% of internet users engaged in social networking, only 60% and 56% used the internet to study and read online publications, respectively (Gong 2020).

Researchers discovered that, by April 2020, Google search intensity for online learning resources in the United States had doubled relative to pre-pandemic levels (Bacher-Hicks, Goodman, and Mulhern 2021). However, the demand for online resources was substantially lower in areas with lower income, lower internet access, and more rural schools. Malaysia likely experienced similar inequalities; based on crude observations, during the first lockdown, keyword searches for learning resources were higher in affluent states such as Selangor and Kuala Lumpur.

There was also a gender dimension to distance learning, which raises questions for further research and policy deliberation. In Malaysia, while the proportion of women in the population remained steady from 2012 to 2018, the proportion of internet users who were women declined (Gong 2020). Concurrently, the teaching profession was dominated by women, who disproportionately bore the burden of care work (KRI 2019), which increased during lockdowns.

Figure 3.2. Expenditure on education by decile income group, 2019

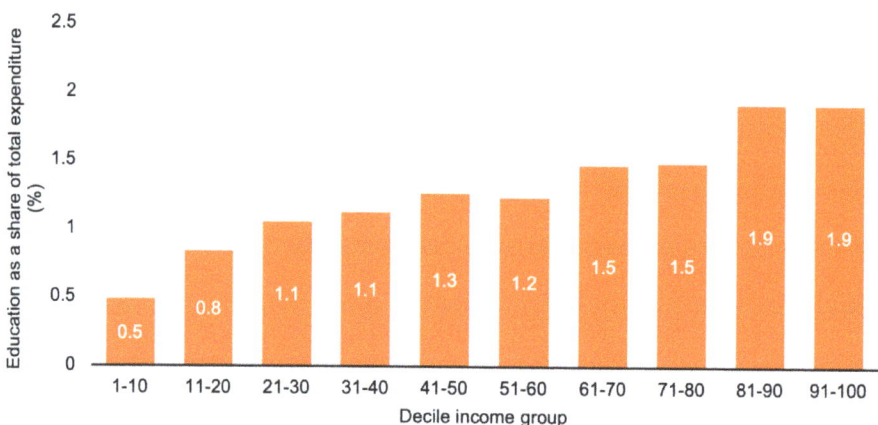

Source: DOSM (2020a).

Meanwhile, boys' disengagement from education was expected to worsen with distance learning (UNESCO 2020). The reduction in learning time due to school closure was larger for boys than for girls (Grewenig et al. 2020). This may have exacerbated the 'lost boys' problem in Malaysia, where boys made up only 30% of higher education enrolment. These 'lost boys' either left school early or did not further their education (KRI 2018).

Without discrediting the benefits of education technology (edutech) for students and teachers alike, for-profit edutech has long-term consequences for how education as a public good is perceived and practised (Williamson, Eynon, and Potter 2020). In 2019, poorer households in Malaysia spent considerably less on education than richer households did, both in absolute terms and as a proportion

of their total expenditures (Figure 3.2) (DOSM 2020a). Further research is needed to understand how the increasing 'platformisation'
of education impacts the education of poor and digitally disadvantaged households. While the pandemic hastened the adoption of digital
technology in education, it is doubtful whether this was an inclusive
digital transformation.

Adult learning and digital exclusion

The lack of digital inclusivity went beyond education. It also affected
adult learning, which was essential given the changing nature of work
due to technological advancements and globalisation (World Bank
2019). COVID-19 might have accelerated the effects of labour market
megatrends such as automation and increased the incentive to substi-
tute capital for labour (Bloom and Prettner 2020). This increased the
importance of adult learning to ensure people remained competitive in
the labour market.

Malaysian policymakers had been actively encouraging reskilling
and upskilling prior to the pandemic. However, pre-pandemic participation in adult learning was generally underwhelming. The training
participation rate among registered employers topped out at 25%,
compared to 49% in Singapore and 77% in Australia (HRDF 2019a).
Only 33% of surveyed manufacturing firms offered formal training,
far lower than peer countries (Nur Thuraya and Siti Aiysyah 2020).
Lack of awareness, inadequate resources, overlapping programmes,
and recognition issues have been cited as the main challenges of adult
learning (HRDF 2019c).

Participation in adult learning was unequal, with young and very
old trainees under-represented. Adult learning at work was also skewed
towards the skilled workforce, compared to the semi-skilled and
low-skilled workforce (Figure 3.3). Unfortunately, COVID-19 exacerbated the vulnerabilities of groups not actively participating in
adult learning. Youth workers were found to be disproportionately
adversely affected by the pandemic (Gonzalez, Gardiner, and Bausch
2020), while lower-skilled workers were most likely to be replaced if
firms decided to automate their business operations during the pandemic (KRI 2020).

The digital divide further increased these inequalities. First, not all
training programmes could be conducted online. In fact, the adoption
rate of e-learning and mobile learning was less than 1% for Human

Figure 3.3. HRDF trainees as a share of total employees, disaggregated by age and skill level, 2018

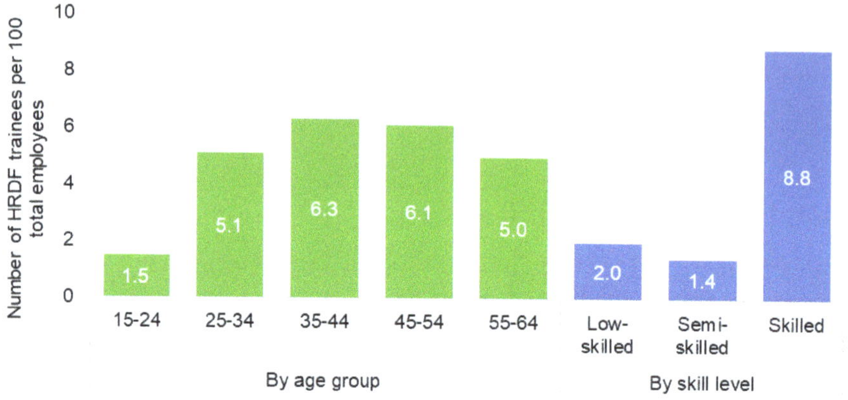

Sources: HRDF (2019c); HRDF (2020); DOSM (2020b).

Resource Development Fund (HRDF) training programmes in 2018 (HRDF 2019b). Training for non-digital technical skills such as machine handling and safe food preparation could not be conducted online because they required practical learning activities.

Second, not all employers were supportive of employee training, as evident in the low training participation rates among employers. In economic downturns, employers face financial constraints in supporting workers' skills development. Additionally, the HRDF only covered selected sectors, and a substantial segment of the workforce not covered by the HRDF (micro-enterprises, workers in the informal sector, and the self-employed) could not afford to invest in adult learning.

Moreover, the lack of digital literacy among the older population has been a significant barrier in accessing online adult learning courses. More mature individuals were not only less likely to use the internet; they were also less likely to use it for learning purposes (Figure 3.4). Online adult learning was likely challenging for lower-income households too, as they faced higher trade-offs between spending on essential goods and investing in adult learning (Rao 2009). Poorer households also faced significant barriers to digital access that limited their adult learning opportunities (Siti Aiysyah 2020).

Reskilling and upskilling were important to help workers navigate the changing nature of work and employment challenges brought on by the pandemic. However, focusing solely on digital skills when many training providers, employers, and workers do not have the capacity

Figure 3.4. Share of internet use by type of activity and age group, 2019 (percentage)

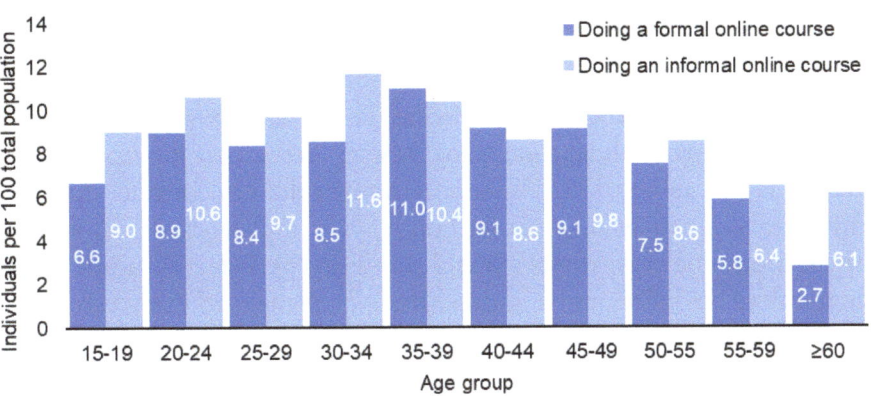

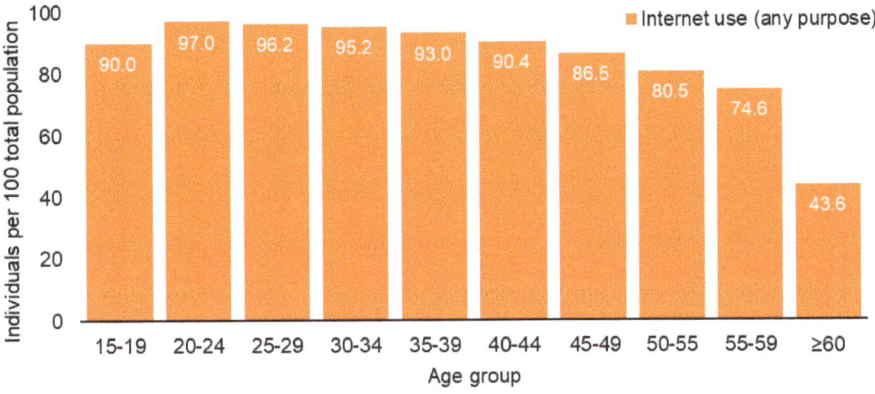

Source: DOSM (2020b).

to do so could further exacerbate existing structural issues in adult learning. Failure to address the digital gap among workers might also perpetuate inequality in the labour market.

Conclusion

The COVID-19 pandemic accelerated digitalisation in many ways, but digital adoption has not been equitable. More research is needed to assess the long-term impacts of the digital divides described in this chapter. While distance schooling is unlikely to fully replace physical schooling for children, online learning is likely to be incorporated into teaching methods. Inclusive education requires an understanding of how digital and analogue inequalities affect educational attainment and subsequent socio-economic opportunities. Improving internet coverage and quality, increasing access to digital devices, and providing digital pedagogy training for teachers must be part of the national socio-economic agenda.

Businesses and governments were proactively encouraging online adult learning during the pandemic to enhance worker resilience. However, many adult learning programmes were costly and had limited participation and impact. These programmes did not consider different adult learning styles, competing family, care, and work demands, and socio-economic constraints (World Bank 2019). Effective adult learning, offline or online, must address these challenges to bring returns to post-schooling human capital investment.

Broadly applying digital solutions to every available situation does not lead to an inclusive digital transformation. Rushed and improperly considered digital adoption is rife with unintended consequences. Diversity of input and research is needed, especially among groups typically under- or ill-served by digital technologies, in order to ensure that digital transformation is beneficial and sustainable for society in the long run.

Acknowledgements

All authors contributed equally to this work.

References

A4AI. (2020). *Meaningful Connectivity: Raising the Bar for Internet Access*. USA: World Wide Web Foundation. https://perma.cc/4MQ9-PK87 [Last accessed 22 April 2021].

Ashraf, Shaharudin. (2020). *Reopening Schools: Giving Access to Education Equitably and Safely*. Malaysia: Khazanah Research Institute. https://perma.cc/VUE4-93X8 [Last accessed 22 April 2021].

Bacher-Hicks, Andrew; Goodman, Joshua; and Mulhern, Christine. (2021). 'Inequality in household adaptation to schooling shocks: Covid-induced online learning engagement in real time'. *Journal of Public Economics*, vol. 193, p. 104345. https://doi.org/10.1016/j.jpubeco.2020.104345

Banerjee, Indrajit. (1999). 'Malaysia's multimedia super corridor: One-stop super shop or highway to progress and prosperity for all?' *Convergence*, vol. 5, no. 3, pp. 106–115. https://doi.org/10.1177%2F135485659900500308

Bloom, David; and Prettner, Klaus. (2020). 'The macroeconomic effects of automation and the role of COVID-19 in reinforcing their dynamics'. *VoxEU*, 25 June. https://perma.cc/PXD8-P557 [Last accessed 22 April 2021].

Brennen, J. Scott; and Kreiss, Daniel. (2016). 'Digitalization', in K.B. Jensen and R.T. Craig (eds) *The International Encyclopedia of Communication Theory and Philosophy*. UK: Wiley-Blackwell, pp. 556–566.

Bunnell, Tim. (2002). 'Multimedia utopia? A geographical critique of high-tech development in Malaysia's multimedia super corridor'. *Antipode*, vol. 34, no. 2, pp. 265–295. https://doi.org/10.1111/1467-8330.00238

DiMaggio, Paul; Hargittai, Eszter; Celeste, Coral; and Shafer, Steven. (2001). *From Unequal Access to Differentiated Use: A Literature Review and Agenda for Research on Digital Inequality*. USA: Russell Sage Foundation. https://perma.cc/G7U8-4477 [Last accessed 22 April 2021].

DOSM (Department of Statistics Malaysia). (2019). *Key Statistics of Labour Force in Malaysia September 2019*. Malaysia: Department of Statistics Malaysia. https://perma.cc/43UL-NY22 [Last accessed 11 January 2021].

DOSM. (2020a). *Households Expenditure Survey Report 2019*. Malaysia: Department of Statistics Malaysia. https://perma.cc/LTT4-FAHA [Last accessed 11 January 2021].

DOSM. (2020b). *ICT Use and Access by Individuals and Households Survey Report 2019*. Malaysia: Department of Statistics Malaysia. https://perma.cc /AK8U-N7LQ [Last accessed 11 January 2021].

DOSM. (2020c). *Key Statistics of Labour Force in Malaysia September 2020*. Malaysia: Department of Statistics Malaysia. https://perma.cc/8A6L-SXXK [Last accessed 11 January 2021].

Fenwick, Sam; and Khatri, Hardik. (2020). *The State of Mobile Network Experience 2020: One Year Into the 5G Era*. UK: Opensignal. https://perma .cc/2U7D-JPPT [Last accessed 22 April 2021].

Gong, Rachel. (2020). *Digital Inclusion: Assessing Meaningful Internet Connectivity in Malaysia*. Malaysia: Khazanah Research Institute. https:// perma.cc/4NUB-4JLG [Last accessed 22 April 2021].

Gonzalez, Susana Puerto; Gardiner, Drew; and Bausch, Jo. (2020). *Youth and COVID-19: Impacts on Jobs, Education, Rights and Mental Well-Being: Survey Report 2020*. Switzerland: International Labour Organization. https://perma.cc/SAL9-HYB4 [Last accessed 22 April 2021].

Grewenig, Elisabeth; Lergetporer, Philipp; Werner, Katharina; Woessmann, Ludger; and Zierow, Larissa. (2020). *COVID-19 and Educational Inequality: How School Closures Affect Low- and High-Achieving Students*.

Germany: IZA Institute of Labor Economics. https://perma.cc/595R-Z874 [Last accessed 22 April 2021].

Hargittai, Eszter; Piper, Anne Marie; and Morris, Meredith Ringel. (2018). 'From internet access to internet skills: Digital inequality among older adults'. *Universal Access in the Information Society*, vol. 18, pp. 881–890. https://doi.org/10.1007/s10209-018-0617-5

Hawati, Abdul Hamid; and Jarud, Romadan Khalidi. (2020). *Covid-19 and Unequal Learning*. Malaysia: Khazanah Research Institute. https://perma.cc/5YHQ-7NSC [Last accessed 22 April 2021].

HRDF (Human Resource Development Fund). (2019a). *HRDF Industry Training Participation Report 2019*. Malaysia: Human Resource Development Fund. https://perma.cc/WB29-TFXW [Last accessed 22 April 2021].

HRDF. (2019b). *Human Capital Report Issue 06: Adoption of E-learning*. Malaysia: Human Resource Development Fund. https://perma.cc/K9AL-CX6U [Last accessed 22 April 2021].

HRDF. (2019c). *Human Capital Report Issue 09: Adult Lifelong Learning*. Malaysia: Human Resource Development Fund. https://perma.cc/AMP7-NKG3 [Last accessed 22 April 2021].

HRDF. (2020). *Industry Training Intelligence Report Issue 03: Training Inequality According to Job Levels*. Malaysia: Human Resource Development Fund. https://perma.cc/NPN6-LP2T [Last accessed 22 April 2021].

KRI (Khazanah Research Institute). (2018). *The School-to-Work Transition of Young Malaysians*. Malaysia: Khazanah Research Institute. https://perma.cc/C69W-XB84 [Last accessed 22 April 2021].

KRI. (2019). *Time to Care: Gender Inequality, Unpaid Care Work and Time Use Survey*. Malaysia: Khazanah Research Institute. https://perma.cc/H456-Z3XW [Last accessed 22 April 2021].

KRI. (2020). *Work in an Evolving Malaysia*. Malaysia: Khazanah Research Institute. https://perma.cc/GBE2-7KBY [Last accessed 22 April 2021].

Malay Mail. (2020). '16,000 participants signed up for MDEC's free online courses, says CEO', 26 June. https://perma.cc/U7JK-UJR9 [Last accessed 22 April 2021].

MCMC (Malaysian Communications and Multimedia Commission). (2020). *Industry Performance Report 2019*. Malaysia: Malaysian Communications and Multimedia Commission. https://perma.cc/64SC-F55X [Last accessed 22 April 2021].

MOE (Ministry of Education). (2020). *Statistik Bilangan Sekolah, Murid and Guru [MS]*. Malaysia: Ministry of Education Malaysia. https://perma.cc/L5NT-P2SM [Last accessed 6 January 2021].

MOF (Ministry of Finance). (2020). *Budget 2021 Speech*. Malaysia: Ministry of Finance. https://perma.cc/58NG-KRT4 [Last accessed 22 April 2021].

MOHE (Ministry of Higher Education). (2020). *Statistik Pendidikan Tinggi 2019 [MS]*. Malaysia: Ministry of Higher Education Malaysia. https://www.mohe.gov.my/en/download/awam/statistik/2019-1 [Last accessed 22 April 2021].

Murat, Marina; and Bonacini, Luca. (2020). *Coronavirus Pandemic, Remote Learning and Education Inequalities*. Global Labor Organization (GLO). https://perma.cc/RF4R-WRU9 [Last accessed 22 April 2021].

Nur Thuraya, Sazali; and Siti Aiysyah, Tumin. (2020). *Leaving No Worker Behind: Deficit in Decent Work*. Malaysia: Khazanah Research Institute. https://perma.cc/E3D3-K4NH [Last accessed 22 April 2021].

Parker, Kim; Minkin, Rachel; and Bennett, Jesse. (2020). *Economic Fallout from COVID-19 Continues to Hit Lower-Income Americans the Hardest*. USA: Pew Research Center. https://perma.cc/CAV4-MYRH [Last accessed 22 April 2021].

Rao, Ramesh. (2009). 'Digital divide: Issues facing adult learners'. *Computer and Information Science*, vol. 2, no. 1, pp. 132–136. https://doi.org/10.5539/cis.v2n1p132

Siti Aiysyah, Tumin. (2020). *Covid-19 and Work in Malaysia: How Common Is Working from Home?* LSE Southeast Asia Blog, 23 November. https://perma.cc/H3PY-UK4G [Last accessed 22 Apr 2021].

UNESCO. (2020). *Addressing the Gender Dimensions of COVID-Related School Closures*. France: UNESCO. https://perma.cc/8VYK-PJWL? [Last accessed 22 April 2021].

Williamson, Ben; Eynon, Rebecca; and Potter, John. (2020). 'Pandemic politics, pedagogies and practices: Digital technologies and distance education during the coronavirus emergency'. *Learning, Media and Technology*, vol. 45, no. 2, pp. 107–114. https://doi.org/10.1080/17439884.2020.1761641

World Bank. (2019). *World Development Report 2019: The Changing Nature of Work*. USA: World Bank. https://perma.cc/9C2X-5ZV6 [Last accessed 22 April 2021].

4. Data privacy, security, and the future of data governance in Malaysia

Moonyati Yatid and Farlina Said

Throughout the course of the spread of COVID-19 in Malaysia, technology was deployed to control, investigate, and mitigate societal well-being beyond public health. Unmanned aerial vehicles like drones were used to monitor society's compliance with lockdown measures (Bernama 2020), e-commerce initiatives were rolled out under the government's economic recovery plan (MDEC 2020), and artificial intelligence-enabled thermal cameras were deployed (*New Straits Times* 2020). However, none of these was more contentious than the technologies used in contact tracing.

From the start of the pandemic, Malaysia introduced several contact-tracing applications driven by both federal and state initiatives. At the federal level, the three main applications were MySejahtera, MyTrace, and Gerak Malaysia. At the state level, there were SELangkah in Selangor and digital surveillance solutions in Sarawak. From August 2020, MySejahtera was mandatory for all business premises, with exemptions only for premises in rural areas or small towns without stable internet connectivity (*The Star* 2020).

In a landscape of evolving digital legislation, the swift implementation of such technologies could outpace efforts for data governance. Thus, the rapid adoption of these technologies could create vulnerabilities in the protection of privacy. As such, this chapter aims to cover the different technologies used in the mitigation of COVID-19 in 2020 with a focus on the contact-tracing applications that were developed. Subsequently, the chapter delves into data privacy and security concerns and concludes with reflections on Malaysia's technological future in data governance.

How to cite this book chapter:
Yatid, Moonyati; and Said, Farlina. 2022. 'Data privacy, security, and the future of data governance in Malaysia'. In: Shin, Hyun Bang; Mckenzie, Murray; and Oh, Do Young (eds) *COVID-19 in Southeast Asia: Insights for a post-pandemic world*. London: LSE Press, pp. 58–66. DOI: https://doi.org/10.31389/lsepress.cov.d
License: CC BY 4.0.

Tech-less contact tracing and the efficacy of application-based contact tracing

Surveillance and public health in Malaysia were not initially so dependent on technology. The country's first case of COVID-19 was discovered on 25 January 2020 thanks to the Ministry of Health's Crisis Preparedness and Response Centre (CPRC) (Ahmad et al. 2020). Common procedures dictated that, from the diagnosis of a COVID-19 case, rapid assessment and rapid response teams would be deployed to collect the patient's socio-demographic information and travel and movement history over the previous 14 days. This established the patient's contact list for tracing (Ahmad et al. 2020). This tech-less contact tracing was the primary method used by the Ministry of Health (MOH) at that time, particularly for district health offices (Boo 2020).

To control rising infections, Malaysia's movement control order (MCO) was initiated on 18 March 2020. Malaysia's MCO had several iterations, corresponding with different standard operating procedures. The 18 March MCO was lifted and replaced by a recovery movement control order (RMCO) on 9 June 2020 in light of a decrease in the number of cases. Technology then began to be used, particularly to assess users' health and risk, to trace possible infections from a specific location, and as a means of delivering updated information and highlighting hotspots. As technology itself is transformative, throughout the MCO and the RMCO, contact-tracing applications in Malaysia learned from competing applications and modified their own processes.

Developers introduced several applications in the months between the MCO and RMCO. The applications differed in terms of ownership, methodology, privacy thresholds, and, where declared, data retention limits. To streamline efforts, an announcement on 3 August 2020 mandated that businesses owners and operators download and register with MySejahtera. With this announcement, and with MySejahtera being the only application tied to short-term economic plan (PENJANA) benefits, certain states such as Penang announced that they would phase out their own applications in favour of MySejahtera, thus consolidating contact-tracing applications into a centralised data collection system. The table below illustrates the different applications rolled out during the MCO; afterwards, PgCare and Gerak Malaysia ceased operation.

These applications had different practices for data retention and data protection. MyTrace, the development of which was led by the Ministry of Science, Technology and Innovation, used Bluetooth and anonymised

Table 4.1. Contact-tracing applications used in various Malaysian states

Application	Developer	Function
MySejahtera	Federal government agencies (National Security Council [NSC], Ministry of Health [MOH], Malaysian Administrative Modernisation and Management Planning Unity [MAMPU], Malaysian Communications and Multimedia Commission [MCMC])	Multi-purpose application intended for individuals to assess health levels, discover hotspots, seek health facilities, and receive latest updates and other materials from the MOH using web-based and QR-scanning functions
MyTrace	Federal government agencies (led by the Ministry of Science, Technology and Innovation [MOSTI])	Bluetooth-enabled contact tracing, with data remaining anonymous and information about potential exposures stored only on one's device
SELangkah	Selangor state government	Location-based and QR code-enabled contact tracing
SabahTrace	Sabah state government	Location-based and QR code-enabled contact tracing
COVIDTRACE	Sarawak state government	Location-based and Bluetooth-enabled contact tracing
Gerak Malaysia (no longer in use as of 2021)	Federal government (MCMC and the Royal Malaysia Police [RMP])	GPS-enabled contact tracing and QR codes to inform authorities of permissions granted to travel
PgCare (no longer in use as of 2021)	Penang state government	Location-based and QR code-enabled contact tracing

data while retaining records of encounters on one's device. Sarawak's COVIDTrace also stated that user data would be anonymised, and geolocation data would not be collected. The information gathered by

COVIDTrace, Selangor's SELangkah, and Sabah's SabahTrace included the individual's name and phone number as well as the date and time of visits to relevant premises. SabahTrace also collected information on the user's body temperature.

MySejahtera is among the examples of centralised data collection tools for which data in transit was said to be encrypted. The data security and governance of MySejahtera were managed by the National Cyber Security Agency (NACSA), an arm of the National Security Council (NSC). Data retention limits for the applications ranged from 21 days to six months, though not all applications declared limits; MyTrace stated the duration of data retention in devices was 21 days (Bedi 2020), while MySejahtera's check-in feature retained data for 90 days (Krishnan 2020). The now-defunct Gerak Malaysia also stated that information on travel would be retained for six months after the MCO ceased. Meanwhile, COVIDTrace stated that, should users revoke consent, their data would be deleted from the system, thus protecting users from future data breaches.

While technology was crucial in mitigating infection rates, the efficacy of contact-tracing applications alone was questionable. For instance, only 4% of all reportedreports of COVID-19 cases in Malaysia were detected by MySejahtera (CodeBlue 2020). Researchers have highlighted, however, that contact tracing could work if it was part of a wider public health strategy and response that encompassed mass testing and strict physical distancing measures at the same time (Browne 2020). The self-assessment tool in MySejahtera detected positive cases with a success rate between 3.1% and 6.5% (Krishnan 2020). In addition, data gathered from the check-in function at a densely populated location could swiftly trace close contacts. A cluster at a large shopping complex resulted in the identification of 221 positive cases from 17,260 screened users, demonstrating an efficacy rate between 15.1% and 37.8% (Krishnan 2020). Such achievements justified the use of contact-tracing applications, as the MOH Director General, Dr Noor Hisham, attested in October 2020 (Palansamy 2020).

Data privacy and security concerns

Privacy has diverse cultural interpretations. Joseph Savirimuthu (2016) has conceptualised privacy through the lenses of jurisdiction, space, and identifiable data. Such concepts were only nascent in Malaysia during the pandemic. Ipsos, a marketing research and consulting firm, surveyed Malaysians in 2019 and revealed a high degree of acceptance of sharing data with the private sector or the government if there was a reward of better services or other benefits (Ipsos 2019). As 'data is the new oil', however, it could be tempting for companies and countries to abuse this receptivity for economic and political gains.

The multitude of applications available to Malaysians and low awareness about the management of data and privacy rights could lead to problems of mining digital platforms for information. In addition, increased surveillance and a culture of exchanging data for benefits could bear social and security-related consequences. Malaysia's data protection and privacy systems have had a poor reputation – in a 2019 study by Comparitech, Malaysia ranked fifth lowest out of 47 countries assessed (Tang 2020). Furthermore, Malaysia had previously suffered from serious data leaks, including the patient records of nearly 20,000 Malaysians (Habibu 2019) as well as 46.2 million mobile subscribers of Malaysian telecommunications companies and mobile virtual network operators (MVNO) (Vijandren 2017). With the Personal Data Protection Act (PDPA) of 2010 falling short of enforcing the mandatory reporting of data breaches, neither the severity of data breaches nor high cyber hygiene levels could be clearly assessed. Malaysia's data governance, however, could be judged by the capability of the government to protect users from data breaches and government efforts to construct standards upholding privacy.

First, heightened responsibility and accountability require appropriate legislation and enforcement. The PDPA possessed loopholes that weakened its protection of personal data beyond commercial purposes. This meant that the regulations did not include the government sector in its scope. While section 203A of the Penal Code provides penalties for any person who leaks information in the performance of their duties, the absence of mandatory data breach reporting rules for the private and public sectors reduced enforcement and transparency.

Additionally, the Act did not specifically address online privacy protections or users' privacy protections. Malaysia's challenges related to protecting privacy would require the reconciliation of cultural interpretations of privacy with technical possibilities. The notion of identity being separate from personal data was not a widespread practice, which could underlie the fundamental delay in the establishment of policy directions in data governance, as concepts and gaps in data classification needed time to become incorporated into policy and law. While international standards such as the EU General Data Protection Regulation (GDPR) had upheld user privacy by adding layers of protection such as anonymisation, pseudonymisation, or encryption, Malaysia's laws and various personal data protection standards did not implement principles of data protection by design. This should be explored further as Malaysia's legislation on the matter develops.

Second, developing industry standards depends on the ability of the industry to uphold principles through various practices. An example of the different practices in security-by-design is the choice between centralised and decentralised data storage, each of which has different cybersecurity implications. The diversity of Malaysia's contact-tracing landscape indicated a variety of practices in data management. Contact-tracing applications in Malaysia utilised both centralised (MySejahtera and SELangkah) and decentralised (MyTrace and partial functions of COVIDTrace) models. MyTrace, for instance, utilised Bluetooth signals and proximity between devices to store information for contact tracing. Bluetooth signals are useful for data collection not directly associated with individuals, as the technology uses unique numbers in place of personally identifiable information. Additionally, MyTrace data was stored on users' devices for up to 21 days, which could assure users that their information was not shared or retained unnecessarily (Bedi 2020). Comparatively, MySejahtera collected data on a secured server with various details about users stored centrally. While MySejahtera's centralised database might have efficiently facilitated contact tracing for the MOH (Yusof 2020), the substantial amounts of information it collected could have unsettled users.

Through the lens of cybersecurity, both models have their weaknesses. For decentralised systems such as MyTrace, the security of the Bluetooth data collection depended on the application operator and the cyber hygiene of the user. In contrast, MySejahtera's centralised system meant that responsibility for data management was in the hands of a single body. Thus, while centralised databases can be more efficient, their weaker anonymity controls and data retention limitations can increase vulnerabilities when sharing information with the application.

As the PDPA and its lacking enforcement measures did not mainstream security-by-design conversations among developers, safeguards should be in place to protect users. Two ideas that can be considered are to collect the minimum data needed and to roll out deletion measures – either for the application or for the data itself. The right to forget should be discussed further in Malaysian social and legislative contexts such that information retained by any data collector can and should be deleted.

Learning from this experience, the government should also provide more transparency for its data processing – and other mechanisms of these applications – in order to gain more trust from citizens. There could also be platforms for citizens to provide open feedback to improve the applications. It is necessary for data to be retained for only a limited timeframe to serve only the specific purpose for which it was collected. In a nutshell, fully transparent and accountable privacy-preserving solutions should be embedded by design to balance the benefits and risks associated with personal data collection, processing, and sharing. Components of an awareness campaign should include channels to contact relative cybersecurity agencies for cybersecurity issues. Thus, the strategy should map out the responsibilities of respective cybersecurity agencies and provide avenues to possible assistance. Another campaign could make cyber hygiene a norm of cyber practices. As washing hands has become the norm to mitigate the risk of COVID-19, similar consistent reminders could relate to standard cyber hygiene practices such as updating applications frequently, reading terms and conditions before agreeing to anything online, being wary of personal information shared, and visiting sites that are secured with necessary certifications.

Concluding reflections and anticipations for the future

The concerns surrounding the privacy and security aspects of technology, which was abruptly and extensively used to combat COVID-19, became more real as possibilities slowly began to look like reality. One example is the case of Singapore, which retracted its promise to safeguard the privacy of its official COVID-19 application users. In March 2020, when Singapore first introduced the TraceTogether application, the government repeatedly and explicitly vowed that the data collected would be used purely for contact-tracing purposes. Ten months later, however, after the application's use became mandatory, it was revealed that the data could also be accessed by police to conduct criminal investigations (Sato 2021). This aligns with warnings made by analysts about the dangers of technological tools being exploited and privacy and security being violated in efforts to heighten surveillance and control.

As with other countries, Malaysia also experienced an increase in technology use during COVID-19, which brought both positive and negative impacts to society. It is safe to say that technology will grow increasingly important in our daily lives, even beyond the pandemic. It is important to remember, however, that the issues of privacy and security should be prioritised: as the internet is borderless, no person, organisation, or country is safe from the attacks of hackers with malicious intentions. While privacy and security concerns related to COVID-19 have largely been discussed in the context of contact-tracing applications, in the near future, other technologies such as vaccine passports could also pose a danger to privacy, particularly as sensitive data travels across borders. The damage of security and privacy violations would be unimaginable; hence Malaysia needs to take steps to protect its citizens at all costs. Transparency in the use of technology, especially in the processing of mass data, and creating platforms for open feedback from citizens, as well as other mechanisms that could instil trust from society, are among the first steps that should be considered. Further, although the political scene in Malaysia has been deemed unstable in recent times – with unpredictable and constantly changing leadership – joint efforts and unity in safeguarding citizens' privacy and security should be made a priority, regardless of who is in power.

References

Ahmad, Noor Ani; Lin, Chong Zhuo; Rahman, Sunita Abd; bin Ghazali, Muhammad Haikal; Nadzari, Ezy Eriyani; Zakiman, Zazarida; Redzuan, Suziana; Taib, Salina Md; et al. (2020). 'First local transmission cluster of COVID-19 in Malaysia: Public health response'. *International Journal of Travel Medicine and Global Health*, vol. 8, no. 3, pp. 124–130. https://doi.org/10.34172/ijtmgh.2020.21

Bedi, Rashvinjeet S. (2020). 'Data from Covid-19 app MyTrace kept on phone, not govt servers, says Khairy'. *The Star*, 8 May. https://perma.cc/9QXN-MFB4

Bernama. (2020). 'COVID-19: MAF to use drones at 12 hotspots during MCO'. *Bernama*, 24 March. https://perma.cc/EPT7-A4ZX

Boo, Su-Lyn. (2020). 'How MySejahtera protects your data and does more than contact tracing'. *CodeBlue*, 12 August. https://perma.cc/P9L9-HG3T

Browne, Ryan. (2020). 'Why coronavirus contact-tracing apps aren't yet the "game changer" authorities hoped they'd be'. *CNBC*, 3 July. https://perma.cc/EG6J-QL5K

CodeBlue. (2020). 'MySejahtera directly tracked just 4% of Covid-19 cases'. *CodeBlue*, 18 November. https://perma.cc/SBK9-ZMY4 [Last accessed 20 May 2021].

Habibu, Sira. (2019). 'Health Ministry investigating leak of patient records'. *The Star*, 19 September. https://perma.cc/4AXM-AFQM [Last accessed 20 May 2021].

Ipsos. (2019). *Global Citizens and Data Privacy: A Malaysian Perspective.* https://perma.cc/5EXR-SH5B [Last accessed 20 May 2021].

Krishnan, Dhesegaan B. (2020). 'MySejahtera app helped Health Ministry detect 9,167 Covid-19 cases nationwide'. *New Straits Times*, 19 November. https://perma.cc/YV8E-3TSZ [Last accessed 20 May 2021].

Malaysia Digital Economy Corporation. (2020). *MDEC Rolls Out Micro and SMES E-commerce Campaign under PENJANA Recovery Plan*, 30 June. https://perma.cc/AP2J-X6VS [Last accessed 20 May 2021].

New Straits Times. (2020). 'TM unveils solution for Covid-19 early detection', 3 April. https://perma.cc/544H-XYHT [Last accessed 20 May 2021].

Palansamy, Yiswaree. (2020). 'Dr Noor Hisham: 1 Utama mall cluster in Selangor at sixth-generation infection'. *Malay Mail*, 20 October. https://perma.cc/4GG5-QBUA [Last accessed 20 May 2021].

Savirimuthu, Joseph. (2016). *Security and Privacy*, vol 3. UK: Routledge.

Sato, Mia. (2021). 'Singapore's police now have access to contact tracing data'. *MIT Technology Review*, 5 January. https://perma.cc/DK5H-NDUZ [Last accessed 20 May 2021].

Tang, Ashley. (2019). 'Study: Malaysia the fifth-worst country for personal data protection'. *The Star*, 16 October. https://perma.cc/49AW-5P9D [Last accessed 20 May 2021].

The Star. (2020). 'My Sejahtera App "a must for all businesses"', 4 August. https://perma.cc/A22G-3U2M [Last accessed 20 May 2021].

Vijandren. (2017). '46.2 million Malaysian mobile phone numbers leaked from 2014 data breach'. Lowyat.net, 30 October. https://perma.cc/UAS5-FE8R [Last accessed 20 May 2021].

Yusof, Teh Athira. (2020). 'MySejahtera app now mandatory for all business'. *New Straits Times*, 3 August. https://perma.cc/WZ82-23SM [Last accessed 20 May 2021].

5. Economic crisis and the panopticon of the digital virus in Cambodia

Sokphea Young

Within Southeast Asia, Cambodia is the most impoverished nation, notwithstanding an economy reliant on garment and manufacturing industries, tourism, and agriculture. The country's garment and manufacturing sector, especially the garment and footwear industry, emerged in the early 1990s after the first general elections organised by the United Nations Transitional Authority in Cambodia. The United States and the European Union supported Cambodia's export-driven economy through their Generalised Systems of Preferences and other trade schemes. The EU, for example, allowed Cambodia to export duty-free and quota-free to its market from 2001 under the Everything but Arms (EBA) scheme. These policies boosted Cambodia's garment sector such that, as of 2019, it employed about 600,000 Cambodians, most of whom were women from rural areas. With the support of the garment industry and other industries, Cambodia managed to significantly reduce poverty and transform its economy to become a lower-middle-income country in 2016. From 2017 to 2019, Cambodia exported on average €4 billion (European Commission 2020) and US$4 billion (United States Census Bureau 2021) of apparel products per year to the EU and US markets, respectively. As such, the manufacturing industry accounted for about 10% of Cambodia's GDP (World Bank 2020).

While these forms of support were significant to the country and its people, the Cambodian government's respect for human rights, particularly freedom of association and freedom of speech, and democracy in general has been dismal, as the country has leaned towards authoritarianism, as evidenced by the dissolution of the most prominent opposition party, the Cambodia National Rescue Party (CNRP), in 2017 as

How to cite this book chapter:
Young, Sokphea. 2022. 'Economic crisis and the panopticon of the digital virus in Cambodia'. In: Shin, Hyun Bang; Mckenzie, Murray; and Oh, Do Young (eds) *COVID-19 in Southeast Asia: Insights for a post-pandemic world*. London: LSE Press, pp. 67–76. DOI: https://doi.org/10.31389/lsepress.cov.e License: CC BY 4.0.

well as the ongoing intimidation and spurious arrests of human rights and environmental defenders, all of which restricted the space of civil society organisations. These restrictions led the EU to partially withdraw its EBA scheme with Cambodia in February 2020, harming workers in related sectors. Many factories were forced to shut down without proper indemnities for the employees.

Coinciding with the imposition of import tariffs by the EU, Cambodia's economy, especially its garment and manufacturing, was doubly punished by the emergence of coronavirus (SARS-CoV-2), which spread across the world. Not only did the pandemic severely disrupt the global supply chain and markets of garment and manufacturing industries, leaving many jobless, but it also affected the entire country's socio-economic conditions. The government's lack of proper remedial measures for the impacts of the pandemic sparked dissatisfaction, which in turn led to activism. Amid the country's shift towards authoritarianism, as seen in the 2018 election, and the restrictions imposed by the government to contain the virus, many were forced to stay at home and were thus compelled to subscribe to digital platforms for study, work, communication, and activism. This pushed those who were affected by the EU's sanctions and the pandemic to carry out online activities to advocate for better solutions rather than stage offline (on-street) protests.

In this chapter, I seek to understand online activities and activism during the pandemic and examine the adverse consequences of avoiding offline activities over the same period. This chapter argues that the endeavour, either by the state or individuals, to avoid offline activities to contain the virus adversely induced a new virus – digital surveillance – that infiltrated everyone's digital devices. More than the panopticon of COVID-19, the symptoms of which are easily observable, this new form of digital virus embodies itself in every smartphone device without showing any symptoms. While social media was a COVID-19-free platform for ordinary citizens and activists to connect and express their concerns during the pandemic, it became an invisible hand of surveillance of the authoritarian ruling system.

This chapter is written based on my ongoing observation of Cambodia's sociopolitical and technological developments, employing digital ethnography and collecting data from relevant social media pages and profiles. The quantitative data presented in this chapter was acquired from Google, focusing on the 'news' media outlets it has captured.

The remainder of this chapter begins with a discussion about conceptualising digital media in the context of surveillance as a new form of digital virus, an expression of the pandemic that has been less familiar to us. It then illustrates how COVID-19 induced Cambodians to subscribe to social media and digital devices before providing evidence on how the latter could strengthen an authoritarian surveillance system.

The virus and digital technology panopticon

The digital community has been recognised as a modern tool of human development and evolution. Many have been impressed by this evolution, as digital devices can process data and circulate images and voices from one community to another. Kittler (2010, p.11) has argued that 'machines take tasks – drawing, writing, seeing, hearing, word-processing, memory and even knowing – that once were thought unique to humans and often perform them better'. Given this capability, digital devices like smartphones and cloud devices have become modern panoptic tools incubated by our everyday lives. These devices and the internet have been replacing our basic needs. Drawing on Foucault's (2012) conception of the panoptic prison cell, I argue that these devices gradually ingrain themselves in our bodies and minds without warning; health applications are exemplary in this sense. It is a virus that affects us without giving us symptoms. With our unintentional consent, this digital virus has extracted our personal data for buyers' commercial and political purposes. Zuboff (2019) has rightly illustrated that access to the digital community exposes oneself to significant risks. At risk is the loss or co-optation of privacy rights, rendering personal data (our private space, in essence) to corporate giants. Having submitted to machine learning, it has been increasingly difficult to hold the state and politicians accountable, particularly through activism. More often than not, for the sake of profit, the corporate capitalist media have allowed surveillance and authoritarian states to use their data to gain legitimate power, as in the US presidential and UK parliamentary elections, and to censor opponents.

Drawing on how activists and the state interact in China, MacKinnon (2010) has introduced the concept of 'networked authoritarianism', which is a political tactic that creates selective social openings for transparency but at the same time monitors and stifles dissent (He and Warren 2011). This networked authoritarianism in the digital era is framed by the notion of a networked society whose key social structures and activities are organised and linked electronically (Castells 2010). The networked authoritarian Chinese government, for instance, allows people to use the internet to submit grievances or unjust activities, but the government also monitors who reports or submits the grievances. In China, only specific applications or types of social media platforms are allowed to be used, and this makes it easier for the ruling regime to scrutinise and surveil users in order to curb outrageous dissent. The use of these digital communication technologies, therefore, has undesirable side effects, one of which is exposure to the surveillance system (Howard and Hussain 2013), a critical concern for digital activism in non-democratic political systems that appear to have adopted the Chinese authoritarian style of panoptic surveillance, of which Cambodia is an example.

Cambodia's online community and activism amid the pandemic

The foregoing theorisation of how digital communication and technologies carry risks has been eminent in the experiences of Cambodia and other countries during the pandemic. Following the government's instructions not to mobilise or make physical contact, especially in education and offices, the pandemic forced millions of Cambodians to subscribe to digital devices and communication platforms. By September 2020, about 67% of Cambodians (11.28 million of about 16 million) had subscribed to Facebook (NapoleonCat 2020), making this social media site a popular means of communication among Cambodian people, particularly the youth. This figure had climbed from about 9.73 million subscribers before the pandemic, in December 2019, only gradually increasing to 9.78 million users by January 2020, by which time COVID-19 had not spread widely in the country. With the pandemic starting to affect the country in early February 2020, the number of subscribers surged rapidly, to 10.52 million in March and 10.95 million in May the same year (see Figure 5.1). Young adults and children were among the new subscribers, with an age distribution of 7.8% ages 13–17, 31.4% ages 18–24, and 47.5% 25–34 as of March 2020 (NapoleonCat 2021). Likewise, the number of smartphone subscribers also increased, as these devices were required to access social media sites such as Facebook, Telegram, and YouTube. ITU (2021) reported that the number of mobile cellular phone subscribers in Cambodia increased from 19.42 million in 2018 to 21.42 million in 2019. Compared

Figure 5.1. Facebook users in Cambodia before and during the COVID-19 pandemic (millions)

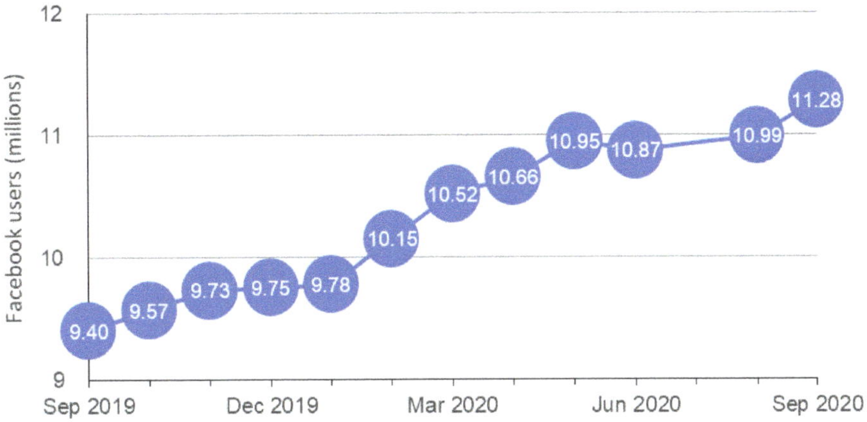

Source: Author's compilation from NapoleonCat (2020).

with a total population of 16 million, this data suggests that many Cambodians could afford at least two phones (Young 2021a). Given the low quality of education, the higher percentage of young subscribers raised critical concerns for data and privacy issues as well as the users' rights. These young adults and children subscribed to the internet and social media for online education, watching livestreamed lectures or pre-recorded video instructions. Based on my field observations, albeit under the supervision of their parents or guardians, many of these users were known to be addicted to YouTube, Facebook, TikTok, and online games and exposed to inappropriate content instead of accessing teaching materials.

Not only did the pandemic compel ordinary Cambodians to go online; it also negatively affected Cambodia's economy (coinciding with the partial withdrawal of the EBA programme). Coupled with the decline of purchase orders in the apparel and footwear industries, Cambodia's GDP growth in 2020 was predicted to be between –1% and –2.9%, with about 1.76 million jobs at risk (World Bank, 2020, p.3). The World Bank (2020) emphasised that the poverty rate in the country was to increase by 20% in 2020. Some factories closed down, as they were affected by either the impact of COVID-19 on global supply chains or the withdrawal of the EU's EBA scheme. This raised concerns for affected populations, especially garment and manufacturing workers, who then sought government intervention and assistance. Given the government's restrictions on physical movement, the ability

Figure 5.2. Online news reports on Cambodia related to selected search terms before and during the COVID-19 pandemic[1]

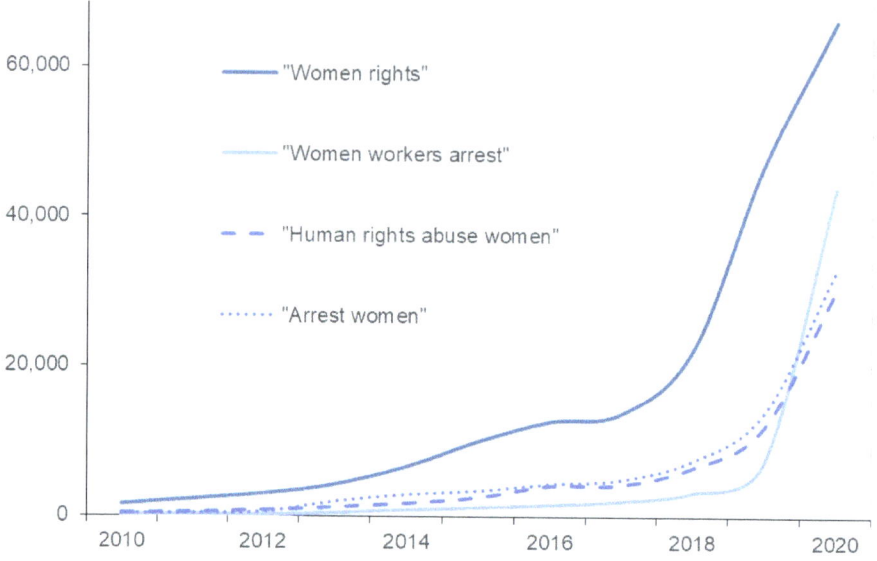

Source: Author's collection of data from Google Search.

to lobby the government and concerned stakeholders was limited to online activities. Workers and other advocates began to use social media platforms including Facebook to express grievances, such as a lack of indemnities (as factories were shut down) and dissatisfaction with the government's failure to remedy job losses and cuts due to COVID-19. Coming from either individuals or media outlets, news on job losses and cuts and people's dissatisfaction with government measures were widely observed in Google searches.

As I traced the development of news on women workers on Google (see Figure 5.2), I found that results for 'women rights Cambodia' were often reported by local and international media outlets: the number of mentions increased from 47,000 in 2019 to 66,100 in 2020. While digital and social media have become platforms for disgruntled women to frame and amplify their concerns to the public, it has not been an ideal solution. Querying the term 'women workers arrest' in Cambodia, I found that the frequency of the term exploded from 7,170 times in 2019 to 43,800 times in 2020. This signified that many women workers or activists were arrested, detained, or harassed by authorities. For instance, one female worker, who was a member of a union, was arrested because of a post on Facebook that criticised her employer for dismissing 88 workers without following government guidelines and instructions not to cut jobs but rather reduce workers' wages (Kelly and Grant 2020). Following her post, the employer who saw the post decided to re-employ the workers, and she immediately deleted her post from Facebook, but the employer still filed a complaint against her, accusing her of creating fake news to defame the company and buyers. The ability to notice who was posting what or putting news on Facebook from their smartphone has indicated the effectiveness of both private companies and government surveillance systems. Both companies and the government may have worked together to censor online activities. The government's Anti-Cybercrime Office has been playing an important role in this effort. In one instance, the prime minister of Cambodia, who had been in power for more than three decades (Young 2021b), claimed that smartphones allowed the government to track and trace anyone effectively (Young 2021c). He claimed, 'If I want to take action against you, we will get [you] within seven hours at the most' (Doyle 2016). For anyone who dares to speak out against the supreme leaders or the government, the consequence is predictable based on that statement.

While many Cambodians moved their activities online to contain and prevent the spread of the virus, political activists, environmental and human rights defenders, workers, and protesters also resorted to online activities. As they went online, they submitted to a new form of authority that I call a 'surveillance virus', which infects users at all times. As in Figure 5.3, it appears that the pandemic caused a surge in spurious arrests of political activists, environmental and human rights defenders, workers, and protesters. The accumulation of the arrest in 2019 and 2020 was induced by two important reasons. First, authorities arrested those activists with whom they were still disgruntled even two years after the 2017 dissolution of the opposition party (CNRP) prior to the 2018 elections. The election allowed the ruling party to take control of all national assembly seats and Prime Minister Hun Sen to remain in power (Young 2021b). Second, the arrests were made in response to those who supported the attempt of CNRP leader Sam Rainsy, who had lived in exile since 2016, to return to Cambodia in 2019. As of September 2020, the number of people arrested by authorities had increased to 55, alarming the international community's concerns over the country's tendency to practise authoritarianism during the pandemic. In tandem with the preceding reasons, the arrests in 2020 were linked to criticisms made by activists and citizens on how the government handled and contained the pandemic. By March 2021, as

Figure 5.3. Activists arrested in Cambodia before and during the
COVID-19 pandemic

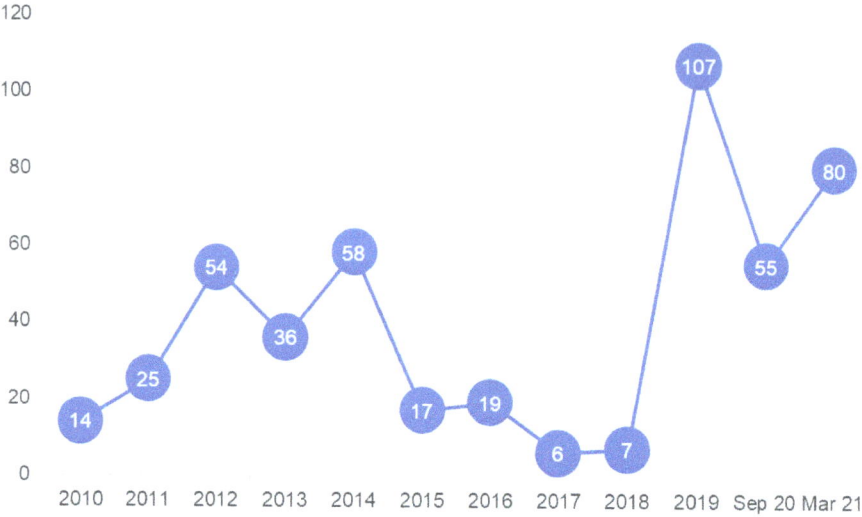

Source: modified from Young and Heng (2021).

many as 80 activists and ordinary citizens had already been arrested or
detained for criticising and expressing their opinions about the efficacy of the Chinese-made COVID-19 vaccines (Sinopharm and Sinovac)
that were preferred and being rolled out by the government. The government claimed that they were arrested because their opinions and
statements (through text and video) on Facebook and TikTok 'gravely
affect[ed] social security' (Finney 2021). Some of the arrests were publicly reported by the Facebook page of the government's Anti-Cyber
Crime Office (ACCO). The ACCO was the surveillance unit actively
censoring and screening online news and posts, including 'fake' news,
on social media. The arrests were enabled by the 'networked authoritarianism' highlighted by MacKinnon (2010) in China: the government
allowed online grievance submissions but tackled critical ones, as they
undermined the ruling regime's authority and legitimacy. Cambodian
activists' and citizens' critiques of how the government handled the pandemic, socio-economic issues, and other social issues during the crisis
have been subject to scrutiny and surveillance. Social media-mediated
devices have become invisible tools of the ruling system.

Conclusion

In this chapter, I have demonstrated how COVID-19 not only affected
Cambodia's economy but also pushed many Cambodians to go online,

subscribing to digital platforms. Digital media platforms have been believed to help contain the spread of COVID-19, but such endeavours apparently allowed users to become infected by a new form of virus, digital surveillance, whose symptoms cannot be diagnosed or known by users, only by the government. This digital virus has surrounded users, placing them in the panoptic prison cell of the surveillance system. The users only realise that they are in the cell when the observers or guards (the government, in this instance) take action against them, as illustrated by the women workers and activists in the present study and beyond. This new type of virus tightened the authoritarian surveillance system to effectively monitor the antagonistic behaviour of citizens and activists that could undermine the ruling system's legitimacy.

Note

1. I used key terms to search on Google and classified the results of the search by year. To ensure that all search results were about Cambodia, 'Cambodia' was always added to individual terms when searched on Google: 'Women workers arrest Cambodia', for example. These search results were limited to 'news' rather than 'all' results in the Google search engine. I then grouped these results by year of publication.

Acknowledgements

The author received financial support for this chapter's research from the European Research Council-funded project entitled PHOTODEMOS (Citizens of Photography: The Camera and the Political Imagination), grant number 695283, at University College London.

References

Castells, Manuel. (2010). *The Information Age: Economy, Society, and Culture*, vol 1: *The Rise of the Network Society*, 2nd edn. UK: Wiley-Blackwell.

Doyle, Kevin. (2016). 'Cambodian leaders' love-hate relationship with Facebook'. BBC, 7 January. https://perma.cc/5LL4-ANEQ [Last accessed 20 January 2021].

European Commission. (2020). *Countries and Regions*, 18 June. https://perma.cc/D4YG-9M4N [Last accessed 26 July 2020].

Finney, Richard. (2021). 'Cambodian activist arrested for criticizing Chinese COVID-19 vaccine'. *Radio Free Asia*, 15 March. https://perma.cc/G4FU-R3EW [Last accessed 25 April 2021].

He, Baohang; and Warren, Mark E. (2011). 'Authoritarian deliberation: The deliberative turn in Chinese political development'. *Perspectives on Politics*, vol. 9, no. 2, pp. 269–289. https://doi.org/10.1017/S1537592711000892

Howard, Philip N.; and Hussain, Muzammil M. (2013). *Democracy's Fourth Wave? Digital Media and the Arab Spring*. UK: Oxford University Press.

ITU (International Telecommunication Union). (2021). *Mobile-Cellular Subscription 2020*, 18 January. https://perma.cc/MDT9-SSVY [Last accessed 25 February 2021].

Kelly, Annie; and Grant, Harriet. (2020). 'Jailed for a Facebook post: Garment workers' rights at risk during Covid-19'. *The Guardian*, 16 June. https://perma.cc/GX5G-VEM7 [Last accessed 20 January 2021].

Kittler, Friedrich. (2010). *Optical Media*. UK: Polity.

MacKinnon, Rebecca. (2010). *Networked Authoritarianism in China and Beyond: Implications for Global Internet Freedom*. USA: Stanford University Press.

NapoleonCat. (2020). *Facebook Users in Cambodia*: September 2020. https://perma.cc/CE6S-JV3R [Last accessed 26 July 2020].

NapoleonCat. (2021). *Facebook Users in Cambodia*: March 2020. https://perma.cc/CF7M-4N4R [Last accessed 1 February 2021].

United States Census Bureau. (2021). *Trade in Goods with Cambodia*. https://perma.cc/6VQM-4KU4 [Last accessed 15 January 2021].

World Bank. (2020). *Cambodia Economic Update: Cambodia in the time of COVID-19*. USA: World Bank.

Young, Sokphea; and Heng, Kimkong. (2021). *Digital and Social Media: How Cambodian Women's Rights Workers Cope with the Adverse Political and Economic Environment amid COVID-19*. Sweden: Raoul Wallenberg Institute.

Young, Sokphea. (2021a). 'Citizens of photography: Visual activism, social media and rhetoric of collective action in Cambodia'. *South East Asia Research*, vol. 29, no. 1, pp. 53–71. https://doi.org/10.1080/0967828X.2021.1885305

Young, Sokphea. (2021b). *Strategies of Authoritarian Survival and Dissensus in Southeast Asia: Weak Men versus Strongmen*. Singapore: Palgrave Macmillan.

Young, Sokphea. (2021c). 'Internet, Facebook, competing political narratives, and political control in Cambodia'. *Media Asia*, vol. 48, no. 1, pp. 67–76. https://doi.org/10.1080/01296612.2021.1881285

Zuboff, Shoshana. (2019). *The Age of Surveillance Capitalism: The Fight for the Future at the New Frontier of Power*. USA: Profile Books.

6. Property development, capital growth, and housing affordability in Malaysia

Keng-Khoon Ng

Many governments and state agencies in the global South have shifted towards the operation of 'property states' (Haila 2015), 'cities for profits' (Shatkin 2017), or 'neoliberal policies' (Chen and Shin 2019). In Malaysia, retirement and second-home properties have been promoted by the government to lure foreigners to buy relatively cheap freehold properties in cities such as Kuala Lumpur, Penang, Melaka, and Johor Bahru. This development tendency, however, has added pressure to the provision of affordable housing because developers have been more keen to develop international property projects than less profitable products of local housing.

From 18 March 2020, Malaysia imposed a series of entry and movement restrictions in response to the COVID-19 pandemic. These restrictions brought uncertainty and new challenges to the (future) operation of international property market. Adopting an urban political economy perspective, this chapter discusses the property-related policy responses taken by Malaysian governments while reflecting on prevailing concerns over housing affordability. Though long-standing impacts on the landscape of housing in Malaysia are hard to predict, the COVID-19 crisis revealed the inevitable risks of fuelling capital growth through the proliferation of speculative, high-priced international real estate projects with little relevance to society.

Constitutionally, housing development in Malaysia is governed by a series of legal Acts and policies authorised by the Ministry of Housing and Local Government. The federal government's role in housing planning and supply, however, is complemented by the various responsibilities that rest upon state governments and local authorities. While housing is a matter governed by both federal and state governments,

How to cite this book chapter:
Ng, Keng-Khoon. 2022. 'Property development, capital growth, and housing affordability in Malaysia'. In: Shin, Hyun Bang; Mckenzie, Murray; and Oh, Do Young (eds) *COVID-19 in Southeast Asia: Insights for a post-pandemic world*. London: LSE Press, pp. 77–85. DOI: https://doi.org/10.31389/lsepress.cov.f License: CC BY 4.0.

the latter definitely enjoys more executive power where actual housing development projects are concerned. In short, housing- and land-related development has remained under the state's authority in Malaysia.

Housing development in Malaysia occurs through a dynamic relationship between state and market. Since the 1980s, housing had become a private enterprise predominantly undertaken by private developers. For example, the Ninth Malaysia Plan (2006–2010) clearly stated that the 'private sector [acts] as the engine of growth while [the] public sector takes up the roles of facilitator and regulator and civil society and others as partners in development' (Economic Planning Unit 2006). Notwithstanding a small number of houses produced directly by the state, housing has remained a private sector-led activity in Malaysia.

How does the government make sure there is a sufficient housing supply for low-income (defined as below the 40th percentile of the income distribution) and middle-income (defined as the 40th to 80th percentiles) households? In practical terms, two basic rules enforced since 1982 are worth mentioning: (1) private developers must dedicate at least 30% of a project's units to low-cost housing, and (2) they must allocate at least 30% of the units for Bumiputera (i.e. Malay and other indigenous groups of Malaysia) buyers with discounted prices under the Bumiputera Lot Quota Regulation (a pro-Bumiputera affirmative action policy). However, the provision of affordable housing for middle-income households, especially those in urban areas, was not adequately addressed by existing housing policy. In addition, one of the root causes of this housing mismatch issue was the proliferation of international property development.

The proliferation of international property development

Land has moved to the centre of urban politics in contemporary Malaysia. While land has remained largely a national asset, land-based developments have been pursued aggressively by both federal and state governments as a key fiscal policy to accelerate economic growth. Despite the contributions of international property investment to Malaysia's fairly rapid economic development, it has neither provided improvements towards the democratisation of urban transformation processes nor increased the provision of affordable housing. Undertaking international property development, with speculative, high-growth investment as an inherent feature, has indeed been an exploitation of land.

The proliferation of international residential property development was bound up with the Malaysia My Second Home programme (MM2H), which provides a special long-term visa (renewable every 10 years) for foreigners to reside in Malaysia. This investment migration programme was introduced by the Ministry of Tourism, Arts, and Culture in 2002, with 42,000 participants having been approved as of 2021. To encourage property-buying, for example, MM2H participants are allowed to partially withdraw from the required fixed deposit from the second year onwards (50,000 Malaysian ringgit for those aged 50 and above or 150,000 Malaysian ringgit for those under 50) for expenses related to purchasing property. It is important to note that, in 2020, the federal government lowered the minimum price threshold to avail of this benefit from RM1 million to RM600,000 (in the condominium/apartment segment) in an attempt to solve property overhang. A total of 31,661 unsold residential units were recorded by the end of the first half of 2020 for all of Malaysia; the states of Johor (with 6,166 unsold units) and Selangor (with 4,865 unsold units) had the most severe property oversupply (NAPIC 2020). To what extent has MM2H accelerated capital growth in residential property? Could it have actually worsened the problems of property oversupply and housing unaffordability?

Despite the fact that there is no government or market data enabling us to answer these questions, the whole idea of MM2H is to capitalise on offshore investments, privileged lifestyles, and the ability to hold long-term visas for small-scale investors. In line with Aihwa Ong's (1999) concept of 'flexible citizenship', MM2H elucidated such intentions by maximising capital accumulation through strategies of migration and border-crossing flexibility. It is interesting to note that, in the first decade of MM2H (2002 to 2012), most of the second-home participants were retirees seeking a high-quality lifestyle with a relatively low cost of living compared to their homelands (see Ono 2015; Toyota and Xiang 2012; Wong and Musa 2014). In the last decade, however, both local and foreign developers have taken advantage of this policy to scale up lucrative international property projects. As MM2H has not been recognised as a discrete housing category, there has not been a distinct type of housing provider or developer for this kind of real estate development. Also, there has not yet been a specific housing policy guide or control the development of MM2H projects.

For example, Iskandar Malaysia regularised the formation of an international zone in Iskandar Puteri (formerly known as Nusajaya) to allow more than 25,000 residential units to be built for a speculative market of seamless border-crossing living between Singapore and Southern Johor (see Ng and Lim 2017; Ng 2020). The formation and legislation of such an international zone enabled local authorities to charge higher property taxes for foreign homebuyers. Most crucially, all the housing projects located in the international zone were permitted to have 100% foreign ownership. In other words, there was no requirement to provide the 30% quota for Bumiputera lots or the 30% quota for low-income housing in the international zone. It is important to note that the establishment of the international zone thus suspended these two policy requirements that had laid a foundation for housing equality in Malaysia since 1982.

In Iskandar Puteri, a series of exclusive facilities such as international boarding schools, a world-class theme park, a private yacht marina, healthcare centres, and hotels were developed to create a lifestyle matching international standards. Forest City by Country Garden Pacificview is another housing mega-project where a well-capitalised Chinese developer ventured into the emerging market of international property in Johor (see Koh, Zhao, and Shin 2021). This project took its cue from Beijing's promulgation of the Belt and Road Initiative to lure homebuyers from China and the neighbouring regions. These high-priced housing projects, however, did not make any direct contribution to the provision of affordable housing for Malaysians.

To this end, the MM2H programme highlights the dynamics of migration policy and economic development under a strong authoritarian state that shaped private housing markets to channel opportunities for land-based developments. In other words, MM2H can be best understood as a result of contingent overlaps of the capitalist interests of the state and real estate developers.

The COVID-19 outbreak in Malaysia caused an unprecedented disruption to the international property market and the operation of the MM2H programme. As a result, new applications for MM2H were suspended with no clear indication as to when the programme could resume. This sudden decision disrupted international property sales. Furthermore, movement restrictions triggered by the pandemic reshuffled the MM2H holders' privileges of border-crossing and visiting their Malaysian homes. For example, the Johor–Singapore border closures had a far-reaching impact on everyday border-crossing practices, not to mention the existing business of international property. Although MM2H visa holders could apply for entry permission to return to Malaysia, the government enforced entry restrictions on foreigners who were travelling from countries that had recorded over 150,000 COVID-19 cases. In addition, all passengers travelling into Malaysia were required to serve a two-week quarantine at dedicated quarantine centres.

Several MM2H pass holders and consultants reported to local news media their dissatisfaction over a lack of clear directions and considerations given by the Malaysian authorities (see Davison 2020; James 2020; *The Star* 2020; Thomas 2020). In brief, they wished for MM2H visa holders to be treated equally as citizens because they had been contributing a large amount of direct investment to the country's economy. From the perspective of developers, the president of the Real Estate and Housing Developers Association Malaysia opined:

> With the Malaysia My Second Home (MM2H) programme put on hold and MCO reinstated, the developers have no other choice but to price the new projects at a very competitive price to survive the pandemic. (Chew and Lim 2021)

To an extent, the statement reflects that property prices could still be adjusted to match the income level of local buyers instead of merely focusing on residential products with higher profit margins.

Taken together, all these perspectives reveal not only the instability of the MM2H programme but also the vulnerability of excessive international property projects in the country. For the government, perhaps the time is ripe to think more rigorously about this investment migration program in terms of risk management, investor relations, and inclusiveness. For the real estate developers, the COVID-19 pandemic exposed underlying concerns over the 'sustainability' of the business model and growth strategies of international property development. What still makes these high-priced residential projects attractive when the selling point of cross-border mobility can no longer be taken for granted? Given that the COVID-19 pandemic might realistically take several years to bring under control globally, the market response towards international property in the post-coronavirus era remains uncertain. For property investors, the up-and-down market sentiments over high-priced residences should ultimately be seen as a high-risk investment because luxury property supply has simply exceeded market demand in Malaysia.

How helpful has the 2021 national budget been for Malaysians to buy homes?

Housing affordability is a salient issue in Malaysia, especially for urban dwellers. Between 2002 and 2016, the country's overall housing affordability worsened significantly, with Kuala Lumpur, Selangor, and Johor ranked in the 'seriously unaffordable' category (KRI 2019). Although there were more than 31,000 unsold units available on the market in 2020, these units were simply unaffordable for the majority of Malaysians.

How did the government help Malaysians attain homeownership amid the COVID-19 pandemic? Reintroduced under the Short-Term Economic Recovery Plan by the federal government in June 2020, the Home Ownership Campaign provided a stamp duty exemption on instruments of transfer (for properties below RM1 million) and an exemption on instruments for securing loans (for properties between RM300,000 and RM2.5 million), as well as a 10% price reduction limited to those developers who registered for the scheme. On 6 November 2020, a series of initiatives targeted at increasing homeownership were announced as part of the 2021 national budget. An extension of the full stamp duty exemption on instruments of transfer and loan agreements was granted for first-time homebuyers buying new-launch or sub-sale properties priced up to RM500,000.

How helpful were these stamp duty exemption schemes? Put simply, they only benefited home buyers who managed to secure housing loans from banks. Banks were likely to tighten lending standards because people's debt-servicing capacity was deemed deteriorated due to potential retrenchment and recession, thus making it relatively difficult for people to participate in the schemes and own their first home.

In the 2021 budget, the Ministry of Finance allocated RM500 million to build 14,000 housing units for those in the bottom 40% of the income distribution and RM315 million for the construction of 3,000 housing units by Syarikat Perumahan Negara Berhad, the state-owned, national housing developer, as part of the Rumah Mesra Rakyat programme. The government also offered a rent-to-own scheme for 5,000 PR1MA units limited to first-time home buyers. While Malaysians recognised these positive attempts to build more affordable housing, there was still a lack of immediate action taken by the government to solve pressing housing concerns. For example, governments should expand the rent-to-own scheme by inviting more private developers to join the initiative. In return, the developers could receive special incentives in the form of tax rebates or social responsibility credits. Also, there was the possibility to convert underutilised public buildings or abandoned shopping malls into short-term solutions for the urban poor or the homeless.

Moreover, there was a worrying tendency for private and government-linked developers alike to focus on the luxury housing market (Lim and Ng 2020). Particularly for the case of Medini Iskandar Malaysia, developers were exempted from building low-cost housing as part of corporate social responsibility requirements. In other cases, developers preferred to pay penalties to local governments instead of meeting their responsibilities. In this regard, local governments should tighten the requirements for private developers to build affordable housing. In short, while Malaysia has actively promoted the MM2H programme and the international property market, the government must also put effort into determining the right balance between capital growth and housing affordability.

Conclusions

Housing development serves Malaysia in two ways. On the one hand, housing provision is premised on increasing home affordability, especially for low- and middle-income groups. On the other hand, the real estate market is an integral part of the government's fiscal policy – which is legislated through an influx of foreign investments and property taxes. In other words, housing production in Malaysia is operated under highly competitive – if not complex – negotiations between a home-owning democracy and a capitalist economy.

Housing has increasingly been regularised into a new geography of profit and politics in Asia (Chen and Shin 2019). To turn property development into a rent-seeking mechanism, the government began to intervene in housing policies and market-oriented practices. Two strategies – control and exploitation – have allowed the government to expand its authority over the public and private realms of property development. These two strategies, however, not only lead to conflicts of interest between the state and non-state actors but they also increasingly collide with social justice and political integrity.

In Malaysia, both COVID-19 and housing affordability remain huge challenges. On the one hand, the coronavirus crisis exposed new operational issues and policy concerns associated with the MM2H programme. On the other hand, the vulnerability of the international property market has been attributed to negative market sentiments arising from movement restrictions. During such challenging times, the government should pay more attention to the local housing supply/demand mismatch and the reordering of state–business relationships in property development. International property development is a contested field of capital accumulation built upon market speculation. To avoid irresponsible market speculation, the government should introduce stronger measures to combat housing built for profit, not for living.

References

Chen, Yi-Ling; and Shin, Hyun Bang (eds). (2019). *Neoliberal Urbanism, Contested Cities and Housing in Asia*. USA: Palgrave Macmillan.

Chew, Rachel; and Lim, Chelsea J. (2021). 'Impact of MCO 2.0 on the property market'. *Edge Property*, 22 January. https://perma.cc/DZ85-G4M3 [Last accessed 18 June 2021].

Davison, Andy. (2020). 'Writing on the wall: Is the MM2H programme doomed?' *ExpatGo*, 29 September. https://perma.cc/V5RV-TQBC [Last accessed 10 November 2020].

Economic Planning Unit. (2006). *The Ninth Malaysia Plan, 2006–2010*. Malaysia: Economic Planning Unit. https://perma.cc/XQL2-7GYU [Last accessed 26 May 2021]

Haila, Anne. (2015). *Urban Land Rent: Singapore as a Property State*. UK: Wiley-Blackwell.

James. (2020). 'MM2H visa holder stranded abroad and confused'. *Free Malaysia Today*, 22 May https://perma.cc/8LTW-29NN [Last accessed 26 October 2020].

KRI (Khazanah Research Institute). (2019). *Rethinking Housing: Between State, Market and Society*. Malaysia: Khazanah Research Institute. https://perma.cc/N8AD-ANR7 [Last accessed 14 November 2020].

Koh, Sin Yee; Zhao, Yimin; and Shin, Hyun Bang. (2021). *The Micropolitics of Speculative Green Urbanism at Forest City, Iskandar Malaysia*. UK: London School of Economics Department of Geography and Environment Discussion Paper Series No. 21. https://perma.cc/H95Y-PMXA [Last accessed 26 May 2021].

Lim, Guanie; and Ng, Keng-Khoon. (2020). 'Housing policy in Johor: Trends and prospects', in Francis E. Hutchinson and Serina Rahman (eds) *Johor: Abode of Development?* Singapore: ISEAS Yusof Ishak Institute, pp. 424–446.

NAPIC (National Property Information Centre). (2020). *Residential Unsold Status H1 2020*. https://perma.cc/A96R-NZKC [Last accessed 10 November 2020].

Ng, Keng-Khoon. (2020). 'Johor Bahru's urban transformation: Authority and agency revisited', in Francis E. Hutchinson and Serina Rahman (eds.)

Johor: Abode of Development? Singapore: ISEAS Yusof Ishak Institute, pp. 407–423.

Ng, Keng-Khoon; and Lim, Guanie. (2017). 'Beneath the veneer: The political economy of housing in Iskandar Malaysia, Johor'. *Trends in Southeast Asia*, December, Singapore: ISEAS Yusof Ishak Institute.

Ong, Aihwa. (1999). *Flexible Citizenship: The Cultural Logics of Transnationality*. USA: Duke University Press.

Ono, Mayumi. (2015). 'Commoditization of lifestyle migration: Japanese retirees in Malaysia'. *Mobilities*, vol. 10, no. 4, pp. 609–627. https://doi.org/10.1080/17450101.2014.913868

Shatkin, Gavin. (2017). *Cities for Profit: The Real Estate Turn in Asia's Urban Politics*. USA: Cornell University Press.

The Star. (2020). 'MM2H visa holders hoping for clear directions', 9 June. https://perma.cc/PKX8-JNZM [Last accessed 26 October 2020].

Thomas, Jason. (2020). 'Country's economy, image at stake in MM2H freeze, say consultants'. *Free Malaysia Today*, 7 July. https://perma.cc/3P37-YGNT [Last accessed 10 November 2020].

Toyota, Mika; and Xiang, Biao. (2012). 'The emerging transnational "retirement industry" in Southeast Asia'. *International Journal of Sociology and Social Policy*, vol. 32, no. 11/12, pp. 708–719. https://doi.org/10.1108/01443331211280737

Wong, Kee Mun; and Musa, Ghazali. (2014). 'Retirement motivation among "Malaysia My Second Home" participants'. *Tourism Management*, vol. 40, 141–154. https://doi.org/10.1016/j.tourman.2013.06.002

7. Business process outsourcing industry in the Philippines

Maddy Thompson

In 2019, the business process outsourcing (BPO) industry was the second largest contributor to the Philippines' economy, providing US$26 billion to the Philippine economy in 2019 (Rosales 2020) and employing at least 1.3 million people in over 1,000 firms, mainly located in urban regions (Reed, Ruehl, and Parkin 2020). BPO workers provide services for overseas corporations including facilitating travel and insurance cover, customer support for technology, and telehealth services. During the COVID-19 pandemic, the Philippine government exempted the BPO industry from closure during quarantine periods owing to the industry's importance for economic and geopolitical relations. BPO workers were thus exposed to a heightened risk of infection so that overseas economic activities could continue. COVID-19 did not just disrupt the BPO industry and the overseas corporations it served; it also highlighted and reproduced endemic levels of global inequality and exploitation.

This chapter discusses the growth of the BPO industry in the Philippines with a specific focus on the healthcare information management sector pre-COVID-19 before examining the various responses that COVID-19 precipitated. The final section reflects on possibilities for the future of the BPO industry and its workers. Throughout, it is argued that BPO work in the Philippines is a recent example of the ways in which colonial lines of exploitation are redrawn in a digital world.

BPO in the Philippines

The Philippines' BPO industry began in earnest in the 1990s, its growth facilitated by 'overly optimistic' government support (Soriano and Cabañes 2020, p.1). The industry was oriented to the country's former

How to cite this book chapter:
Thompson, Maddy. 2022. 'Business process outsourcing industry in the Philippines'. In: Shin, Hyun Bang; Mckenzie, Murray; and Oh, Do Young (eds) *COVID-19 in Southeast Asia: Insights for a post-pandemic world*. London: LSE Press, pp. 86–96. DOI: https://doi.org/10.31389/lsepress.cov.g License: CC BY 4.0.

colonial power, the USA, and also served Europe, Japan, New Zealand, and Australia (BIEN 2019). Its contribution to the Philippine economy was second only to remittances brought in via migration, and, as of 2020, the Philippines had the world's largest concentration of call centre workers, although India had the bigger BPO market share (Reed, Ruehl, and Parkin 2020). Where India successfully marketed key cities as hubs of innovation to attract highly skilled BPO activities, the Philippines largely took on back-end processing work ripe for automation. Only around 15% of Filipino BPO workers were employed in highly skilled roles before the COVID-19 pandemic, and Manila's overall ranking of second on the Tholons list of top super cities for digital innovation (see Table 7.1) reflected the size of the BPO industry rather than a culture of digital innovation (Tholons 2019).

BPO expansion has been connected to the mass emigration of overseas Filipino workers (OFWs) and the Philippines' legacy of colonialism (Soriano and Cabañes 2020; Thompson 2019). As a nation dependent on migration, higher education has tended to reflect Western practices, with most courses instructed in English (Ortiga 2017). Keeping in touch with migrant family members has also made many Filipinos skilled

Table 7.1. Top super cities for digital innovation according to Tholons (2019)

Rank	City	Country
1	Bangalore	India
2	Manila	Philippines
3	Sao Paulo	Brazil
4	Mumbai	India
5	Dublin	Ireland
6	Toronto	Canada
7	Delhi	India
8	Hyderabad	India
9	Singapore	Singapore
10	Buenos Aires	Argentina
11	Krakow	Poland
12	Cebu City	Philippines
...	...	...
95	Davao City	Philippines

in digital and distanced communication (McKay 2016). In some BPO sectors, the connections between OFWs and BPO workers were more apparent. The healthcare information management sector, for example, emerged in response to heightened demand for healthcare-related insurance processing activities generated by the USA's 2010 Affordable Care Act (also known as Obamacare) and relied on vast numbers of under- and unemployed nurses whose dreams of migration had 'turned sour' (Ortiga and Macabasag 2021). Global North markets had long encouraged the Philippines to train nurses beyond demand to provide migrant workers (Ortiga and Macabasag 2021), but during the 2010s, faced with increasing pressures on healthcare systems, rising anti-migration sentiment, and technological advances, outsourcing healthcare via digital platforms became increasingly attractive (Thompson 2019). Incorporating this ready-made, low-cost, highly skilled workforce into the digital health economy allowed profit margins in the global North to increase while restricting the material benefits migration could entail for individuals and their families.

The Philippines' BPO industry has been relatively inclusive. Women have long dominated call centre activities, comprising 53.2% of the workforce in 2019 (BIEN 2019), while BPO has been one of the few industries where Filipino LGBTQ+ workers have found safe employment.[1] Transgender women in particular entered the industry in the thousands through the early 2000s, mainly in call centre roles (David 2015). Nonetheless, workers have had variable employment experiences. For permanent employees, BPO roles offer relatively high pay, working benefits (e.g. health insurance), and safe, air-conditioned working environments (Thompson 2019). As the industry grew, however, pay and conditions declined, with an estimated two-fifths of the workforce employed on 'floating'/'no-work-no-pay' status by 2020 (Rabino 2020). Floating workers had their working benefits removed (BIEN 2017). Such status has been particularly problematic for marginalised groups and those with caring responsibilities, groups that made up the majority of BPO workers in 2020. Additionally, in 2019, an estimated 1.5 million Filipinos were digital freelancers, using digital platforms to sell their services. Wood et al. (2019) have found that these online freelancers had few legal labour rights, as rating systems and global competition created a highly competitive and uncertain industry. Despite the lowering of labour standards, the comparatively high pay compared to non-digital employment meant that Filipinos viewed BPO and freelance work as 'good' (Soriano and Cabañes 2020).

Responding to COVID-19

The Philippines imposed a nationwide 'enhanced community quarantine' from 16 March 2020 (Ocampo and Yamagishi 2020). Although the nationwide lockdown was later relaxed, urban areas, home to BPO offices, were most affected and experienced stricter and more prolonged periods of quarantine. BPO was one of the few industries exempted from closure, demonstrating its importance to the country's economic and geopolitical interests. However, quarantine restrictions, including the closure of public transport combined with insufficient working-from-home conditions for many employees, meant BPO businesses were unable to maintain normal staffing levels, particularly at the onset of the pandemic. Concurrently, global travel restrictions and national lockdowns elsewhere increased short-term demand for travel and insurance services, while other businesses pulled out (Macaraeg 2020; Oxford Business Group 2020). COVID-19 thus caused significant disruptions to the industry.

Responses from the foreign businesses impacted varied. Some sought to facilitate homeworking, shipping IT equipment to workers' homes (Sharwood 2020). As the average Manila household had four to five people and a 'poor yet expensive internet connection' (Ocampo and Yamagishi 2020, p.8), homeworking was unsuitable for many. Others provided on-site accommodation to allow workers with quarantining family members or those without caring duties to continue to work (dela Peña 2020). Workers reported that 'accommodation' included sleeping at workstations or sharing hotel rooms without the separation of infected workers from healthy ones (Macaraeg 2020). Though permanent employees were entitled to sick pay, many had their contracts changed to floating status during the pandemic, removing their access to working benefits (Salgado 2020). Workers who were absent to self-isolate or care for family members or who were otherwise physically unable to work thus went unpaid (Macaraeg 2020). As BPO workers were often the primary breadwinners in their household, periods of no pay had the potential to plunge families into poverty.

COVID-19 both intensified and made more visible the exploitation of BPO workers in the Philippines (see Lawreniuk 2020 for a similar argument in relation to Cambodian garment workers). Those unable to work were made disposable and left without financial security. Those who could work were placed in dangerous settings without proper precautions. The make-up of BPO workers in the Philippines placed vulnerable groups – women and LGBT+ groups – at heightened risk of exposure to exploitative conditions. Furthermore, as many BPO workers were infected and BPO offices were identified as hubs of community transmission nationwide (BIEN 2020), public harassment and discrimination towards BPO workers and returning OFWs occurred (Guadalquiver 2020). BPO workers and migrants, previously perceived as national heroes for their 'service' to the country (Soriano and Cabañes 2020), were transformed into vectors of disease.

The pandemic also made visible the global interconnections that shape BPO. In March 2020, Australian consumers were informed that '[d]ue to increased containment measures announced by the Philippines Government overnight, Telstra's contact centre workforce has been reduced. … [T]here will be longer wait times for customers' (Sharwood 2020). By both blaming the Philippine government and omitting concern for the workers, companies like Telstra absolved themselves of responsibility for their overseas employees (see also Brydges and Hanlon 2020).

The future of BPO in the Philippines

Global responses to COVID-19 included economic protectionism and the tightening of borders. Some foreign companies quickly began re-shoring BPO activities, taking advantage of newly unemployed workforces in places with a wider penetration of broadband and home office equipment and where impacts of future lockdowns were more predictable (Reed, Ruehl, and Parkin 2020). The early rapid termination of contracts revealed the exploitation that globalisation had produced, exposing vulnerable workers and their families to increasing precarity. Other businesses were investing further into automation and artificial intelligence, reducing reliance on human-based workforces for low-skilled work (Chen, Marvin, and While 2020). The simultaneous 'throttling' of labour migration caused by COVID-19 (Abel and Gietel-Basten 2020) meant that remittances from migrants were disrupted, and many migrants were forced to return to the Philippines (Abrigo et al. 2020). Increased competition from returning migrants likely further exacerbated the erosion of labour standards within the BPO industry.

Longer term, business analysts have predicted that shifts in the acceptability of homeworking and the need for companies to cut costs due to economic downturns could create gains in the outsourcing industry (CBI 2020). These gains are likely to be most prevalent for freelance work (Dagooc 2020) and could see the further reduction of tax revenues and workers' rights (Wood et al. 2019). Sectors that might survive would be those where automation was less of a threat. The healthcare information management (HIM) sector, for example, could see longer-term gains owing to the more skilled nature of the work (Rosales 2020). The HIM sector expanded rapidly over the 2010s, and before COVID-19 this growth was expected to continue, as shown in Table 7.2. Revised figures in November 2020 indicated that, while the growth might be less than expected, the industry was still set to grow (IBPAP 2020).

With a world-leading reputation, the Philippines was well-placed to capitalise on the growth in digital health provision that COVID-19 had precipitated. Indeed, within the first six months of the pandemic, digital health industry insiders estimated there had been the equivalent of five to 10 years' expansion in digital health (British Chamber of Commerce 2020), with telehealth operations in particular growing worldwide to maintain both COVID-19-related and non-COVID-19-related care activities (Baynham and Hudson 2020). While there have been no guarantees that the transformation to digital health will be permanent, the cost-saving benefits will make it an attractive option for healthcare providers. Furthermore, industry insiders believed that COVID-19

Table 7.2. Forecasted growth rate of BPO market sectors, 2019–2022

Sector	Forecasted percentage change (prediction intervals)	
	Employees	Revenue
Contact centre and business processing	2.8–6.7	3.3–7.4
IT	2.7–6.2	3.2–6.7
Global in-house centres	2.7–4.7	3.2–5.2
Healthcare	6.8–10.2	7.3–10.8
Animation and game development	6.8–11.7	7.3–12.3
Total IT BPO market	3.0–7.0	3.5–7.5
Total IT BPO market (revised 2020 prediction in light of COVID-19)	2.7–5.0	3.2–5.5

Sources: IBPAP (2019; 2020).

had precipitated a cultural shift, transforming patient and healthcare providers' perceptions as to the acceptability of digital health technologies (British Chamber of Commerce 2020). While this might allow further growth of the HIM sector in the Philippines, there will be an urgent need to question the ethical dimensions of shifting healthcare provision online and overseas.

Tracking the accelerated move to digitally facilitated healthcare, early attention focused on the ability of big data to map COVID-19 (Brice 2020; Desjardins, Hohl, and Delmelle 2020; Rosenkrantz et al. 2021), concerns about security and surveillance (Datta 2020), misinformation (Stephens 2020), and the impact of COVID-19-specific technologies on urban spaces (Chen, Marvin, and While 2020; James et al. 2020; Zeng, Chen, and Lew 2020). Questions of global justice, however, have largely been absent. There is a pressing need to examine how shifts towards digital health in the global North impact the global South. Increases in outsourcing benefit the Philippines but simultaneously exacerbate its vulnerability and dependency on foreign markets. Workers may have access to more stable work, but, with highly uneven healthcare provision in the Philippines, having trained healthcare professionals serving the needs of places with better standards of health raises critical ethical concerns.

Conclusion

BPO workers in the Philippines were put at risk to avoid 'longer wait times' for consumers in the global North. Looking ahead, it seems likely labour standards in the Philippines' BPO industry will continue to decline, while insufficient infrastructure to facilitate large-scale home-working could prompt mass withdrawal of FDI, putting the future of the BPO industry and the livelihoods of its workers at risk. While early responses to COVID-19 described a global 'resurgence of reciprocity' (Springer 2020, p.112), BPO work shows how COVID-19 intensified and made visible enduring forms of global exploitation. Left unchecked, corporate responses to COVID-19 would further heighten inequalities in an already unequal world.

Note

1. Unfortunately, no quantitative data exists regarding the numbers of LGBT+ BPO workers, although qualitative research by Emmanuel David (2015) suggests that, in some offices, over half of staff are transgender.

Acknowledgements

I would like to thank Deirdre McKay for her helpful comments and encouragement with this work, as well as the ever-helpful and constructive comments from the editors at the LSE, Hyun Bang Shin, Murray Mckenzie, and Do Young Oh.

References

Abel, Guy J.; and Gietel-Basten, Stuart. (2020). 'International remittance flows and the economic and social consequences of COVID-19'. *Environment and Planning A: Economy and Space*, vol. 52, no. 8, pp. 1480–1482. https://doi.org/10.1177/0308518X20931111

Abrigo, Michael R.M.; Uy, Jhanna; Haw, Nel Jason; Ulep, Valerie Gilbert T.; and Francisco-Abrigo, Kris. (2020). *Projected Disease Transmission, Health System Requirements, and Macro-economic Impacts of the Coronavirus Disease 2019 (COVID-19) in the Philippines*. Philippines: Philippine Institute for Development Studies Discussion Paper Series No. 2020-15. https://perma.cc/75E6-NJHE [Last accessed 19 May 2021].

Baynham, David; and Hudson, Mary. (2020). 'Rollout of video consultation across general practice'. *Technology in the NHS*, 26 March. https://perma.cc/X5UZ-UMLC [Last accessed 8 July 2020].

BIEN (BPO Industry Employees Network). (2017). *BPO Workers Protest against Floating Status, Attacks on Job Security in SITEL*, 4 July. https://perma.cc/SC5S-7SHL [Last accessed 10 August 2020].

BIEN. (2019). *Work Flexibilisation and Its Impact on BPO Women Workers in Metro Manila*. https://perma.cc/3RFS-NCEU [Last accessed 27 August 2020].

BIEN. (2020). *BIEN Sounds Alarm over COVID19 Outbreaks in Many BPOs*, 13 August. https://perma.cc/2X4R-NPK8 [Last accessed 20 January 2021].

Brice, Jeremy. (2020). 'Charting COVID-19 futures: Mapping, anticipation, and navigation'. *Dialogues in Human Geography*, vol. 10, no. 2, pp. 271–275. https://doi.org/10.1177/2043820620934331

British Chamber of Commerce. (2020). *The Changing Economic Outlook: Healthcare Industry in South East Asia*. https://perma.cc/MP6A-PHVV [Last accessed 11 August 2020].

Brydges, Taylor; and Hanlon, Mary. (2020). 'Garment worker rights and the fashion industry's response to COVID-19'. *Dialogues in Human Geography*, vol. 10, no. 2, pp. 195–198. https://doi.org/10.1177/2043820620933851

CBI. (2020). *Outsourcing Greatly Affected but More Relevant after COVID-19*, 22 April. https://perma.cc/75Q9-8TDS [Last accessed 7 August 2020].

Chen, Bei; Marvin, Simon; and While, Aidan. (2020). 'Containing COVID-19 in China: AI and the robotic restructuring of future cities'. *Dialogues in Human Geography*, vol. 10, no. 2, pp. 238–241. https://doi.org/10.1177/2043820620934267

Dagooc, Ehda M. (2020). '"Gig economy" to rise after ECQ'. *The Freeman*, 14 April. https://perma.cc/X7LF-4WQJ [Last accessed 12 August 2020].

Datta, Ayona. (2020). 'Self(ie)-governance: Technologies of intimate surveillance in India under COVID-19'. *Dialogues in Human Geography*, vol. 10, no. 2, pp. 234–237. https://doi.org/10.1177/2043820620929797

David, Emmanuel. (2015). 'Purple-collar labor: Transgender workers and queer value at global call centers in the Philippines'. *Gender and Society*, vol. 29, no. 2, pp. 169–194. https://doi.org/10.1177/0891243214558868

Desjardins, Michael R.; Hohl, Alexander; and Delmelle, Eric M. (2020). 'Rapid surveillance of COVID-19 in the United States using a prospective space-time scan statistic: Detecting and evaluating emerging clusters'. *Applied Geography*, vol. 118, p. 102202. https://doi.org/10.1016/j.apgeog.2020.102202

Guadalquiver, Nanette. (2020). 'Bacolod folks told not to discriminate vs. BPO workers'. *Philippine News Agency*, 11 August. https://perma.cc/6GQU-PZMH [Last accessed 27 August 2020].

IBPAP (IT and Business Process Association of the Philippines). (2019). *The Philippine IT-BPM Industry Growth Forecast (2019–2022)*. https://perma.cc/4B5U-PGVV [Last accessed 28 April 2021].

IBPAP. (2020). *Recalibration of the Philippine IT-BPM Industry Growth Forecasts for 2020–2022*. https://perma.cc/4B5U-PGVV [Last accessed 28 April 2021].

James, Philip; Das, Ronnie; Jalosinska, Agata; and Smith, Luke. (2020). 'Smart cities and a data-driven response to COVID-19'. *Dialogues in Human Geography*, vol. 10, no. 2, pp. 255–259. https://doi.org/10.1177/2043820620934211

Lawreniuk, Sabina. (2020). 'Necrocapitalist networks: COVID-19 and the "dark side" of economic geography'. *Dialogues in Human Geography*, vol. 10, no. 2, pp. 199–202. https://doi.org/10.1177/2043820620934927

Macaraeg, Pauline. (2020). 'Double whammy: BPO employees get exposed to COVID-19, lose income'. *Rappler*, 19 May. https://perma.cc/A9EA-CBE3 [Last accessed 7 August 2020].

McKay, Deirdre. (2016). *An Archipelago of Care: Filipino Migrants and Global Networks*. USA: Indiana University Press.

Ocampo, Lanndon; and Yamagishi, Kafferine. (2020). 'Modeling the lockdown relaxation protocols of the Philippine government in response to the COVID-19 pandemic: An intuitionistic fuzzy DEMATEL analysis'. *Socio-Economic Planning Sciences*, vol. 72, p. 100911. https://doi.org/10.1016/j.seps.2020.100911

Ortiga, Yasmin Y. (2017). 'The flexible university: Higher education and the global production of migrant labor'. *British Journal of Sociology of Education*, vol. 38, no. 4, pp. 485–499. https://doi.org/10.1080/01425692.2015.1113857

Ortiga, Yasmin Y.; and Macabasag, Romeo Luis A. (2021). 'Temporality and acquiescent immobility among aspiring nurse migrants in the Philippines'. *Journal of Ethnic and Migration Studies*, vol. 47, no. 9, pp. 1976–1993. https://doi.org/10.1080/1369183X.2020.1788380

Oxford Business Group. (2020). *What Does the Covid-19 Outbreak Mean for the Philippines' BPO industry?* https://perma.cc/3FH8-C8RX [Last accessed 7 August 2020].

dela Peña, Kurt. (2020). 'Groups urge gov't, companies to prioritize BPO workers' welfare amid pandemic'. *Rappler*, 24 March. https://perma.cc/SJ9Q-WHHP [Last accessed 11 August 2020].

Rabino, Agatha Hazel. (2020). 'Four in 10 BPO workers are in floating, no work-no pay status during lockdown'. *Manila Today*, 6 June. https://perma.cc/YL9D-PNSS [Last accessed 10 August 2020].

Reed, John; Ruehl, Mercedes; and Parkin, Benjamin. (2020). 'Coronavirus: Will call centre workers lose their "voice" to AI?' *Financial Times*, 23 April. https://perma.cc/SB4C-5ZAU [Last accessed 11 August 2020].

Rosales, Elijah Felice. (2020). 'PHL seen bagging more BPO jobs'. *Business-Mirror*, 8 July. https://perma.cc/LGK8-LY3Z [Last accessed 12 August 2020].

Rosenkrantz, Leah; Schuurman, Nadine; Bell, Nathaniel; and Amram, Ofer. (2021). 'The need for GIScience in mapping COVID-19'. *Health and Place*, vol. 67, p. 102389. https://doi.org/10.1016/j.healthplace.2020.102389

Salgado, Ritchie. (2020). 'BPO workers lament company's lack of compassion amid COVID-19'. *Bulatlat*, 1 May. https://perma.cc/6D4A-AEVK [Last accessed 12 August 2020].

Sharwood, Simon. (2020). 'Philippines sends all workers home, outsourced call centres for Acer and telcos suffer degraded service'. *The Register*, 18 March. https://perma.cc/4M2G-XDFG [Last accessed 11 August 2020].

Soriano, Cheryll Ruth R.; and Cabañes, Jason Vincent A. (2020). 'Entrepreneurial solidarities: Social media collectives and Filipino digital platform workers'. *Social Media + Society*, April–June 2020, pp. 1–11. https://doi.org/10.1177/2056305120926484

Springer, Simon. (2020). 'Caring geographies: The COVID-19 interregnum and a return to mutual aid'. *Dialogues in Human Geography*, vol. 10, no. 2, pp. 112–115. https://doi.org/10.1177/2043820620931277

Stephens, Monica. (2020). 'A geospatial infodemic: Mapping Twitter conspiracy theories of COVID-19'. *Dialogues in Human Geography*, vol. 10, no. 2, pp. 276–281. https://doi.org/10.1177/2043820620935683

Tholons. (2019). *Innovation at Scale: Digital Nations and Super Cities.* https://perma.cc/9UMS-LQNK [Last accessed 12 August 2020].

Thompson, Maddy. (2019). 'Everything changes to stay the same: Persistent global health inequalities amidst new therapeutic opportunities and mobilities for Filipino nurses'. *Mobilities*, vol. 14, no. 1, pp. 38–53. https://doi.org/10.1080/17450101.2018.1518841

Wood, Alex J.; Graham, Mark; Lehdonvirta, Vili; and Hjorth, Isis. (2019). 'Networked but commodified: The (dis)embeddedness of digital labour in the gig economy'. *Sociology*, vol. 53, no. 5, pp. 931–950. https://doi.org/10.1177/0038038519828906

Zeng, Zhanjing; Chen, Po-Ju; and Lew, Alan A. (2020). 'From high-touch to high-tech: COVID-19 drives robotics adoption'. *Tourism Geographies*, vol. 22, no. 3, pp. 724–734. https://doi.org/10.1080/14616688.2020.1762118

8. Global precarity chains and the economic impact on Cambodia's garment workers

Katherine Brickell, Theavy Chhom, Sabina Lawreniuk,
and Hengvotey So

In the first year of the COVID-19 pandemic, Cambodia's emergency health response was widely heralded by the international community as a success (Heng 2020; Hyder and Ly 2020; Ratcliffe 2020). As of January 2021, the country had recorded only 460 COVID-19 cases and zero deaths. Yet its achievements in mitigating the worst health impacts of the pandemic during this period did not insulate its population of 16 million people from the economic fallout wrought by COVID-19. Far from it: Cambodia's deep integration into and reliance upon the faltering global market left at least 1.76 million jobs at risk (World Bank 2020) in Cambodia's three most important economic sectors: garments, tourism, and construction.

In this chapter, we focus attention on Cambodia's garment industry, which prior to the pandemic had a large and highly feminised labour force, nearing one million workers, 80% of whom were women (ILO 2018). We present an analysis of the economic impact of COVID-19 on workers from January 2020, when the pandemic first took hold in China, up until February 2021. Drawing on original research from our UKRI GCRF-funded ReFashion study (www.ReFashionStudy.org), we understand and contextualise the data on workers' experiences within the broader debate surrounding global value chains, and we advance the idea of global precarity chains.

Global value chains bring attention to links and relationships between different sectors along the chain of production, including 'all aspects of the process of production, distribution and retailing across global supply networks' (Barrientos 2001, p.83). Mainstream thinking in academic and policy circles has represented these chains as conducive to new development opportunities for firms and regions in the global South

How to cite this book chapter:
Brickell, Katherine; Chhom, Theavy; Lawreniuk, Sabina; and So, Hengvotey. 2022. 'Global precarity chains and the economic impact on Cambodia's garment workers'. In: Shin, Hyun Bang; Mckenzie, Murray; and Oh, Do Young (eds) *COVID-19 in Southeast Asia: Insights for a post-pandemic world*. London: LSE Press, pp. 97–107. DOI: https://doi.org/10.31389/lsepress.cov.h License: CC BY 4.0.

(Selwyn 2019). However, there exists considerable empirical evidence that these global value chains adversely 'generate new forms of worker poverty' (Selwyn 2019, p.71) for those undertaking the 'nimble finger' work of garment production (Elson and Pearson 1981). Bolstering export-oriented growth, women in the global South have been enrolled in labour-intensive patterns of low-skilled and low-paid garment work that is associated with casualisation, excessive hours, and weak social protection (Nadvi 2004). Under these conditions, women workers 'effectively provide a subsidy to production under supply chains and pay the price of government strategies that rely on precarious jobs' (Kidder and Raworth 2004, p.13).

Precarious jobs are generally understood as those which are insecure, dangerous, and/or characterised by poor working conditions and pay. Capitalism 'works to divide and differentiate populations' (Bhattacharyya 2018, p.147), leading certain individuals and groups to 'suffer from failing social and economic networks of support and become differentially exposed to injury, violence, and death' (Butler 2009, p.25). In this chapter we show the significance of what we call 'global precarity chains' for understanding lived experiences of workers in (pre-)COVID-19 times. It begins with a contextual reading of Cambodia's development trajectory vis-à-vis the garment industry, before turning to two workers' experiences of navigating this political economy during the first year of the COVID-19 pandemic. The chapter evidences, first, the precarious location of Cambodia's garment industry in the value chain and its long-term exposure to shocks like the pandemic; second, the dependency on debt that evolved in response to precarious work in the industry prior to COVID-19 but escalated during the pandemic among poorly paid, suspended, and terminated garment workers; and, third, the precarious nature of development more widely in Cambodia, epitomised by the struggle to diversify economically and create alternative livelihoods outside the garment industry. These were significant issues that predated the pandemic and extended beyond its bounds, calling into further question the ability of Cambodia's elected development pathway to create decent work for all through integration into volatile and exploitative global precarity chains.

Precarious development in Cambodia

It is by now almost a truism to attribute the 'miracle' (World Bank 2018) of Cambodia's transition to the heady growth of its garment manufacturing sector, catalysing a remarkable three-decade turnaround from post-conflict state to 'Asia's new tiger economy' (ADB 2016). It is easy to overlook that this take-off occurred as much by accident as design: a feat of industrial serendipity rather than strategy, as Cambodia's re-entry to the global marketplace in the mid-1990s coincided with regional volatility in the wider garment supply chain. Here, the 'business-friendly investment regime' (Bargawi 2005, p.5) pursued by the Cambodian government following the signing of the Paris Peace Accords in 1991 caught the eye of other Asian garment exporters, whose growth at the time was impeded by quotas restricting access to the US market. Preferential trade access bestowed on Cambodia, first by the US in 1997 and then by the EU in 2001, accelerated the reshoring of garment production from original East Asian outsourcing hubs to these new frontiers in a neat spatial fix for manufacturers. Where, in 1995, Cambodia had 20 factories, employing 18,000 workers and generating exports worth US$27 million (Bargawi 2005, p.9), in 2018 there were more than 600, with a workforce nearing 1 million, generating a combined export value of US$8 billion annually (ILO 2018).

For much of the intervening period, Cambodia's economy outpaced other post-conflict societies globally (Hill and Menon 2014), with 10 years of GDP growth averaging double-digit figures to 2008 and securing graduation to lower-middle-income status in 2015. Over a similar timeframe, the national poverty rate fell dramatically, from 47.8% in 2007 to 13.5% in 2014 (World Bank 2017, p.12). It has been hard to refute the unbridled optimism of initial accounts of the industry's success in pioneering Cambodia's development. Early analyses hailed the 'wonderful job opportunity' (Yamagata 2006, p.3) the sector afforded to women, their labour steering a 'blistering' (World Bank 2017, p.43) trajectory emulating historical precedent, where 'the textile and apparel industries have led industrialization at the early stage of development in many countries of the world' (Yamagata 2006, p.4).

Voices from the factory floor, however, offer a competing narrative that challenges the industry's developmental credentials. As further trade liberalisation fostered increasing international competition in an already densely crowded garments market, downwards pressure on unit prices has been exacted on industry profits. Where forecasters have long divined that such falls 'should be readily absorbable by Cambodian exporters' (Bargawi 2005), in practice it is workers who have borne cuts to balance to the books. Between 2001 and 2011, as GDP growth and consumer inflation soared, real wages in the sector fell by 22%, locked in at rates below reproduction requirements (Selwyn 2019). A sponta-neous eruption of mass labour unrest at the end of 2013 evidenced the scale of mounting discontent. Dispelled with lethal violence by state security forces, the prospect of further collective action has since been thwarted by 'authoritarian innovations' (Ford, Gillan, and Ward 2020) in labour governance that stymie and criminalise the organisation of independent trade union activity. Flexibilisation and intensification of work patterns resulted, with employers resorting to the increasing use of three- and six-month fixed-duration contracts and escalating pro-duction targets to extract ever greater margins from an increasingly exploited workforce (Human Rights Watch 2015).

Yet, beyond GDP growth and job creation, it is not clear how the industry has contributed to wider national development objectives. Cambodian manufacturing remains stubbornly located at the 'down-stream, mass market' (Bargawi 2005, p.5) section of the garment value chain, focused on so-called 'cut–make–trim' operations that turn ready-made fabrics and fibres into packaged products, shipped ready to hang on retail shelves. It is an activity where the share of value added to the final output is already relatively low, further reduced by reliance on im-ports for inputs like textiles, threads, and trimmings. The Cambodian government's business-friendly policies including tax breaks for im-ports and tax holidays for new firms lured investment but permit-ted the industry to get away with injecting little cash into the coffers of the national budget in return. Unlike Cambodia's competitors in the sector, such as Bangladesh, there is no protection for domestic firms. The resulting high proportion of foreign ownership, hovering around 90% since the 1990s, means that 'a significant part of the profits are repatriated' (Ear 2013, p.93).

As the garment sector has grown to dominate Cambodia's share of employment and exports, its shallow integration and weak contribu-tion to the national economy have prompted repeated calls to devel-op and diversify beyond cut–make–trim manufacturing, incorporating higher-value-added segments or sectors (World Bank 2017). Yet the continued growth of garments, rebounding even following the 2008 crash, provided little incentive to work at levelling up. As such, repeat-ed warnings went unheeded. Heading into 2020, then, Cambodia's post-conflict recovery resembled a paper tiger: GDP and jobs had yield-ed only a 'mirage of development' (Crossa and Ebner 2020, p.1218), shielding a precariously lopsided and trade-dependent economy and seeming particularly prone to external crisis.

Precarious work and precarious debt

COVID-19 provided this long-anticipated shock, and its impacts exposed the precarious foundations of development in Cambodia. The global garment industry was severely impacted by the pandemic. Cambodia's precarious location within the wider supply chain brought sustained damage from different waves of the outbreak (Lawreniuk 2020). First came upstream delays of raw material delivery due to manufacturing disruptions in China. Then, dramatic falls in demand from consumer lockdowns in Europe and the US led to the subsequent cancellation of orders by international retailers. The consequence of this was the temporary suspension or firing of garment workers in factories where production was interrupted or permanently ceased, with more than 100 factories closed. The ramifications of this situation were acute for women in Cambodia. Outside the agriculture sector, there was a pronounced segregation of occupations by sex, with women in a narrow range of traditional 'female' occupations, including trade, crafts, sewing, and the entertainment industry (UNIFEM et al. 2004, p.43). Women remained under-represented in managerial and technical roles in the country (ILO 2020), and there were high levels of inequality in higher education attainment (UNDP 2019). Cambodia's precarious development therefore left garment factory workers with few options to make a viable living outside the garment industry, whose legacies of precarious work rendered day-to-day existence a challenge even for those who were able to return to work.

This acute lack of alternatives to garment work and markedness of gender inequality in Cambodia are evident in garment worker Lida's experiences of the gendered burdens of managing household finances.[1] Lida had been married since 2008 and began factory work soon after. After three years, the couple had their first baby, and she moved to live with her mother-in-law because of childcare needs. At this time, her son had an allergy to powdered milk, and she stopped working to breastfeed him. Several years later, Lida started searching and applying for a job at a garment factory to make ends meet. She struggled juggling factory work and childcare. Furthermore, her husband failed to contribute any of his salary to support the family. COVID-19 led to Lida's suspension from her garment job for several months at the end of 2020. During the suspension, she received US$40 per month from a government support fund and US$30 per month from the factory. In 2021, the situation only worsened:

The factory announced that they had cancelled product orders; therefore, they don't have much work for all workers. They decided to change the shift patterns, meaning that I can only work between 10 to 14 days for the whole of January. At the same time, the factory opened up job announcements for new workers. I don't understand ... I always think of finding another job, but I don't have any ability or capacity. I think that I can sell vegetables in the village or at the market, but I don't have any support from my husband, so it is not easy to do. I can only dream, but I can't find a way to follow my dream.

The reduction in working hours put Lida in a precarious financial position, and the factory's decision to hire new workers made her feel discriminated against. Her teammates made complaints about her slow work rate on the normally fast-paced production line. Other workers began to resent her lack of ability, as it placed a further burden on them to work harder and compensate in order to reach production targets. At the same time, Lida felt compelled to accept these conditions given the lack of alternative options. The consequences of completely losing her garment job therefore weighed upon her heavily:

Nowadays, I feel like I am a single mother. I need to handle all my family burdens and support my two children. I am so depressed about this. I am afraid to lose my job because if I lost my job, I will have no money to support my family. I seem to have mental health problems ... I keep thinking all night about these worries.

Lida's experiences of anxiety and depression were shared more widely among garment workers and, for many women, were exacerbated by the burdens of debt they were carrying. This was the case for Chantou, who was orphaned at an early age. In 2018, 58-year-old Chantou had taken out a bank loan of US$6,000 to pay for her disabled sister's healthcare costs in her rural homeland. Although garment workers pay into a contributory health insurance scheme, their dependents are not covered. The garment sector's limited contributions to the national budget, despite its contribution to record GDP growth, had stalled the development of wider healthcare provision and other social protections. Healthcare costs expended by family members could be financially ruinous for workers. Prior to her May 2020 suspension, Chantou had been paying US$150 from her US$230 salary as a factory security guard to repay the outstanding US$4,000 loan. Once suspended, her source of repayment dried up:

I begged them not to suspend me. I begged them for work because I had no money to repay the loan. They did not agree ... I had no money to pay the private loans ... I was screaming and crying loudly. I have endured hunger. I am having to endure eating salt and fermented fish until I have a full salary ... I borrowed more money from the money lenders for four months consecutively, and my monthly borrowing was US$100, combined with cash support of US$70 per month from the factory and the Ministry to repay the private loan.

Chantou's account illuminates the pandemic's toll on garment workers whose lives were trapped by a downward cycle of debt commitments, where they were forced to take out new loans with higher interest rates to repay existing debts. While Chantou returned to work after four months, she encountered partial and irregular payments of her wages, which again made loan repayments difficult. She held a deep-seated fear that she would soon lose the residential land she had secured as collateral for the loan.

COVID-19's economic impact, then, was not only limited to income loss; it also entrenched households' growing reliance on debt to finance everyday consumption and survival. The lack of affordable healthcare in Cambodia is a key structural reason for reliance on credit (Van Damme et al. 2004). Rather than improving people's developmental prospects through driving entrepreneurship, microfinance loans are typically used for daily expenditures on household costs (Bylander 2014; Bylander 2015). This reliance on debt to smooth immediate needs is, as Selwyn (2019) has expounded, a longer-term product of the industry's super-exploitation of workers, where wage rates fail to meet basic reproduction requirements. As Brickell et al. (2020, p.2) have explained, even:

> prior to the pandemic, the microfinance sector's expansion in Cambodia temporarily papered over gaps in public service provision experienced strongly in rural areas, where liquidity was used to deal with household cash-flow uncertainties linked to education, health, and food.

As a result, the economic fallout of the COVID-19 pandemic was a major risk to borrowers, the majority of whom, like Chantou, were reliant on labour wages to repay loans (Green and Estes 2019). Media coverage in Cambodia suggests that the sacrifices that Chantou was making to repay the debts were not unusual. As journalist Gerald Flynn (2020) has written, 'debts to MFIs [microfinance institutions] are a more immediate threat than the virus', with workers facing a decision between eating or repaying loans.

Although microfinance loans assist workers like Chantou in the short term, the long-term burden of newly acquired loans from the COVID-19 shutdowns, on top of existing ones, would only aggravate over-indebtedness and the severity of sacrifices needed to repay them. The World Health Organization (2021), for example, expressed concern that the economic impact of COVID-19 would worsen inequalities and fuel malnutrition for billions in Asia. These inequalities are intensely gendered; the pressures of COVID-19 in Cambodia manifested in precarities tied to women's predominant status in the garment industry and as household managers responsible for social reproduction.

Conclusion: from paper tiger to papering over the cracks

In this chapter, we have introduced the experiences of two Cambodian workers grappling with the economic consequences of the pandemic on a global garment industry in turmoil. The most severe hardships presented by COVID-19 fell on workers inhabiting the most vulnerable positions in the global value chain. To try to cope amid a global crisis, garment workers in Cambodia turned to credit borrowing to paper over the cracks and meet urgent survival needs. In doing so, their fates became intimately connected with the global financial institutions seeking a high return from the unfettered growth of Cambodia's microfinance sector (Bateman 2017). Garment workers' lives are, more than ever, embedded within cross-cutting global precarity chains tied to the manufacturing and finance sectors. Their experiences underscore, first, the vulnerability of the Cambodian economy given its reliance on export earnings coming from the garment sector and, second, that, if decent work for all is to have any hope of being possible in practice, then the country needs to address its structural gender inequalities, which hinder women's educational and career progress outside the garment industry. The COVID-19 pandemic did not make value chains newly precarious but rather exposed and compounded long-standing vulnerabilities that women had already been confronting on a daily basis years before its devastating arrival.

Note

1. All names of garment workers in this chapter are pseudonyms. Their stories arise from 60 semi-structured interviews we conducted with workers between January and February 2021. Given this, the chapter reflects on the indirect economic impacts of the pandemic, as experienced through the first year of the crisis. All worker interviews were conducted in Khmer by Cambodian members of the research team and later transcribed into English. They were recruited to participate in the study with the assistance of independent labour unions and the Ministry of Labor in Cambodia.

Acknowledgements

We are grateful to the garment workers who participated in our ReFashion study in Cambodia. The research was funded by UKRI GCRF (EP/V026054/1). Access requests to underlying research materials should be addressed to rdm@royalholloway.ac.uk.

References

Asian Development Bank. (2016). *Here Comes Cambodia: Asia's New Tiger Economy*. https://perma.cc/KZT9-MEJE [Last accessed 3 February 2021].

Bargawi, Omar. (2005). *Cambodia's Garment Industry: Origins and Future Prospects*. UK: Overseas Development Institute. https://perma.cc/C3MH-PBT6 [Last accessed 26 May 2021].

Barrientos, Stephanie. (2001). 'Gender, flexibility and global value chains'. *IDS Bulletin*, vol. 32, no. 3, pp. 83–93. https://doi.org/10.1111/j.1759-5436.2001.mp32003009.x

Bateman, Milford. (2017). *The Rise of Cambodia's Microcredit Sector: An Unfolding Calamity*. European Association of Development Research and Training Institutes General Conference, Bergen, 21–23 August 2017.

Bhattacharyya, Gargi. (2018). *Rethinking Racial Capitalism: Questions of Reproduction and Survival*. UK: Rowman and Littlefield.

Brickell, Katherine; Picchioni, Fiorella; Natarajan, Nithya; Guermond, Vincent; Parsons, Laurie; Zanello, Giacomo; and Bateman, Milford. (2020). 'Compounding crises of social reproduction: Microfinance, over-indebtedness and the COVID-19 pandemic'. *World Development*, vol. 136, pp. 1–4. https://doi.org/10.1016/j.worlddev.2020.105087

Butler, Judith. (2009). *Frames of War: When is Life Grievable?* UK: Verso.

Bylander, Maryann. (2014). 'Borrowing across borders: Migration and microcredit in rural Cambodia'. *Development and Change*, vol. 45, no. 2, pp. 284–307. https://doi.org/10.1111/dech.12080

Bylander, Maryann. (2015). 'Depending on the sky: Environmental distress, migration, and coping in rural Cambodia'. *International Migration*, vol. 53, no. 5, pp. 135–147. https://doi.org/10.1111/imig.12087

Crossa, Mateo; and Ebner, Nina. (2020). 'Automotive global value chains in Mexico: A mirage of development?' *Third World Quarterly*, vol. 41, no. 7, pp. 1218–1239. https://doi.org/10.1080/01436597.2020.1761252

Ear, Sophal. (2013). 'Cambodia's garment industry: A case study in governance'. *Journal of Southeast Asian Economies*, vol. 30, no. 1, pp. 91–105. https://doi.org/10.1355/ae30-lf

Elson, Diane; and Pearson, Ruth. (1981). '"Nimble fingers make cheap workers": An analysis of women's employment in Third World export manufacturing'. *Feminist Review*, vol. 7, no. 1, pp. 87–107. https://doi.org/10.1057/fr.1981.6

Flynn, Gerald. (2020). 'Garment workers cornered by job loss, virus fears and looming debt'. *VOD*, 16 April. https://perma.cc/SLG3-47JC [Last accessed 3 February 2021].

Ford, Michele; Gillan, Micheel; and Ward, Kristy. (2020). 'Authoritarian innovations in labor governance: The case of Cambodia'. *Governance* (pre-print). https://doi.org/10.1111/gove.12559

Green, Nathan; and Estes, Jennifer. (2019). 'Precarious debt: Microfinance subjects and intergenerational dependency in Cambodia'. *Antipode*, vol. 51, no. 1, pp. 129–147. https://doi.org/10.1111/anti.12413

Heng, Kimkong. (2020). 'What lies behind Cambodia's surprise coronavirus success?' *Nikkei Asia*, 2 June. https://perma.cc/EZB5-W853 [Last accessed 3 February 2021].

Hill, Hal; and Menon, Jayant. (2014). 'Cambodia: Rapid growth in an open, post-conflict economy'. *The World Economy*, vol. 37, no. 12, pp. 1649–1668. https://doi.org/10.1111/twec.12206

Human Rights Watch. (2015). *'Work Faster or Get Out': Labour Rights Abuses in Cambodia's Garment Industry*. USA: Human Rights Watch. https://perma.cc/LG6S-2SJD [Last accessed 26 May 2021].

Hyder, Ziauddin; and Ly, Nareth. (2020). 'What explains Cambodia's effective emergency health response to Covid-19?' *World Bank Blogs*, 19 November. https://perma.cc/GMV3-XXMF [Last accessed 3 February 2021].

International Labour Organization. (2018). *Living Conditions of Garment and Footwear Sector Workers in Cambodia*. Switzerland: International Labour Organization Cambodia Garment and Footwear Sector Bulletin Issue 8. https://perma.cc/J2DM-3ERZ [Last accessed 3 February 2021].

International Labour Organization and Organisation for Economic Co-operation and Development. (2020). *Social Dialogue, Skills and COVID-19*. Switzerland: International Labour Organization. https://perma.cc/E35J-SC3X [Last accessed 3 April 2021].

Kidder, Thalia; and Raworth, Kate. (2004). '"Good jobs" and hidden costs: Women workers documenting the price of precarious employment'. *Gender and Development*, vol. 12, no. 2, pp. 12–21. https://doi.org/10.1080/13552070412331332150

Lawreniuk, Sabina. (2020). 'Necrocapitalist networks: COVID-19 and the "dark side" of economic geography'. *Dialogues in Human Geography*, vol. 10, no. 2, pp. 199–202. https://doi.org/10.1177/2043820620934927

Nadvi, Khalid. (2004). 'Globalisation and poverty: How can global value chain research inform the policy debate?' *IDS Bulletin*, 35, pp. 20–30. https://doi.org/10.1111/j.1759-5436.2004.tb00105.x

Ratcliffe, Rebecca. (2020). 'How have Thailand and Cambodia kept Covid cases so low?' *The Guardian*, 16 December. https://perma.cc/Q24E-DFND [Last accessed 12 February 2021].

Selwyn, Benjamin. (2019). 'Poverty chains and global capitalism'. *Competition and Change*, vol. 23, no. 1, pp. 71–97. https://doi.org/10.1177/102452 9418809067

United Nations Development Programme. (2019). *Human Development Report 2019*. USA: United Nations Development Programme. https://perma.cc/673M-VJCZ [Last accessed 12 February 2021].

United Nations Development Fund for Women (UNIFEM); World Bank; Asian Development Bank; United Nations Development Programme; and Department for International Development of the United Kingdom. (2004). *A Fair Share for Women: Cambodia Gender Assessment*. Cambodia: United Nations Development Fund for Women. https://perma.cc/8ZZ5-2CZB [Last accessed 26 May 2021].

Van Damme, Wim; Van Leemput, Luc; Por, Ir; Hardeman, Wim; and Meessen, Bruno. (2004). 'Out-of-pocket health expenditure and debt in poor households: Evidence from Cambodia'. *Tropical Medicine and International Health*, vol. 9, no. 2, pp. 273–280. https://10.1046/j.1365-3156.2003.01194.x

World Bank. (2017). *Cambodia – Sustaining Strong Growth for the Benefit of All*. USA: World Bank. https://perma.cc/WBM8-9PBQ [Last accessed 12 February 2021].

World Bank. (2018). *Riding the Wave: An East Asian Miracle for the 21st Century*. USA: World Bank. https://perma.cc/V55Y-ZYE3 [Last accessed 16 May 2021].

World Bank. (2020). *Cambodia Economic Update: Cambodia in the time of COVID-19*. USA: World Bank. https://perma.cc/E3RM-VWX3 [Last accessed 12 February 2021].

World Health Organization. (2021). *UN Agencies Warn Economic Impact of COVID-19 and Worsening Inequalities Will Fuel Malnutrition for Billions in Asia and the Pacific*. https://perma.cc/F5RN-MDFD [Last accessed 12 April 2021].

Yamagata, Tatsufumi. (2006). 'The Garment Industry in Cambodia: Its Role in Poverty Reduction through Export-Oriented Development'. *Cambodian Economic Review*, vol. 2, pp. 81–136.

9. The dual structure of Vietnam's labour relations

Joe Buckley

Vietnam's public health response to the COVID-19 pandemic was feted as one of the best in the world. Thanks to rapid actions including closing schools and borders and extensive tracking, tracing, and quarantining, the death toll was kept to a minimum, and the country was the world's fastest growing economy in 2020 (World Bank 2020). Other social and political aspects of the pandemic in Vietnam, however, were less remarked upon. This chapter focuses on one of them: labour politics.

I use Daubler's (2018, p.155) conception of the 'dual structure' of Vietnam's labour relations to understand labour activism and campaigning in the country during COVID-19. Daubler has argued that the 'dual structure' is an effective system: the state-led Vietnam General of Confederation of Labour (VGCL) pushes for national-level changes, while self-organised wildcat worker activism holds employers accountable at the enterprise level. I argue that we saw this structure in action with regard to COVID-19. Wildcat strikes arose for the first time in years as workers demanded, first, safe workplaces and, second, fair wages, social security payments, and benefits in the face of the economic impact of the pandemic. Complementing these actions were the VGCL's activities at the national and regional levels: helping to distribute protective equipment and material aid, participating in discussions over the financial support package, and taking a strong stance during the annual minimum wage negotiations. The two parts of the structure combined to form an effective labour response to the pandemic.

I first explain the context of labour relations in Vietnam and Daubler's conceptualisation of the dual structure before applying the model to labour politics during COVID-19. Data for the chapter is drawn from

How to cite this book chapter:
Buckley, Joe. 2022. 'The dual structure of Vietnam's labour relations'. In:
Shin, Hyun Bang; Mckenzie, Murray; and Oh, Do Young (eds) *COVID-19 in Southeast Asia: Insights for a post-pandemic world*. London: LSE Press, pp. 108–117.
DOI: https://doi.org/10.31389/lsepress.cov.i License: CC BY 4.0.

reports in the Vietnamese labour press, especially the newspapers *Lao Động* (*Labour*) and *Người Lao Động* (*Labourer*).

The dual structure of Vietnam's labour relations

Vietnam is a one-party state with little freedom of association.[1] The state-led VGCL is the country's only legal trade union federation. It is subordinate to the ruling Communist Party at the national level, and enterprise-level unions are often dominated by employers, with human resource managers or similar acting as union branch presidents (Do and van den Broek 2013). Although the organisation does not often genuinely represent workers and is more or less entirely ineffective when it comes to organising campaigns for major social and political change, this does not mean it is totally useless. There have been interesting experiments with collective bargaining (Quan 2015), for example, and the VGCL does at times disagree with and take stronger pro-labour positions than the Ministry of Labour, Invalids, and Social Affairs (MOLISA) (Schweisshelm and Do 2018).

The country has also become famous for large numbers of wildcat strikes,[2] especially since 2006 (Siu and Chan 2015). The VGCL does not lead strikes; rather, they are organised by workers themselves. Strikes are overwhelmingly, although not exclusively, in industrial sectors. They are largely over immediate workplace issues, such as wages and working conditions, but have also had some important impacts on national politics, including forcing policy changes and reforms of labour relations institutions (Buckley 2021). They are often successful (Schweisshelm and Do 2018). Authorities have undertaken many attempts to stop strikes by building 'harmonious labour relations' (*quan hệ lao động hài hoà*). While still significant, strike numbers have been decreasing since 2011, as will be seen below.

A lot of the literature on labour relations in Vietnam – and here I am defining labour relations narrowly, excluding literature on the wider sociology and political economy of work – begins with the implicit normative assumption that what is needed is a tripartite system, in which unions representing workers, the state, and employers peacefully negotiate with each other to solve issues and improve workers' wages and conditions. The most well-known example of this approach is perhaps the influential report from Lee (2006), although there are several more recent examples (see, e.g., Quan 2015; Tran and Bales 2017). From this perspective, the problem to be solved is how and to what extent this system can be built in Vietnam and whether the VGCL can be reformed to become an organisation that is genuinely representative of workers.

Daubler (2018), however, has a different perspective. Instead of seeing Vietnam's existing labour relations as a deviation from the tripartite ideal, he has conceptualised them as having a 'dual structure' (Daubler 2018, p.155). By this he means that the VGCL undertakes 'the less conflict-ridden everyday issues and the distribution of benefits', while wildcat strikes apply 'pressure in the workplace', pursuing 'higher wages and improvements in working conditions'. Crucially, for Daubler (2018, p.158), the structure works: 'this is a fairly gratifying state of affairs … although it has its shortcomings there is no real reason for fundamental changes'. I contend that we effectively saw this dual structure in action during the COVID-19 pandemic. The rest of the chapter will outline how this worked in the COVID period.

Wildcat strikes

The year 2011 was the high-water mark for wildcat strikes in Vietnam, with nearly 1,000 recorded; different sources put the number at somewhere between 857 (Siu and Chan 2015, p.71) and 993 (Schweisshelm and Do 2018, p.128). While still significant, strike numbers fell substantially after then, and in 2019 the VGCL recorded only 121 strikes. Owing to the COVID-19 outbreak, however, the trend reversed slightly in 2020, with 126 strikes recorded. This is shown in Figure 9.1.

An increase of five strikes, therefore, is very modest, and it is a rise from a low base, but it is a rise nonetheless. Towards the beginning of 2020, when the SARS-CoV-2 virus was first detected in Vietnam, many strikes were demanding health and safety in workplaces. For example, the Praegear Vietnam strike of February 2020 involved workers demanding that the Taiwanese-owned sporting goods factory in southern Long An province implement measures to protect them against coronavirus. In response, local union officials organised training and talks by medical experts, and the company introduced measures such as free masks, temperature checks, and spraying disinfectant. Other companies in the same region followed suit (Ky Quan 2020). The mid-February strike at Vast Apparel, a Taiwanese-owned garment factory in central Quang Nam province, occurred over concerns that a Chinese employee who was being quarantined was staying too close to the factory. Officials explained to workers the tests that had been performed and his move-

Figure 9.1. Recorded strikes according to VGCL data, 2015–2020

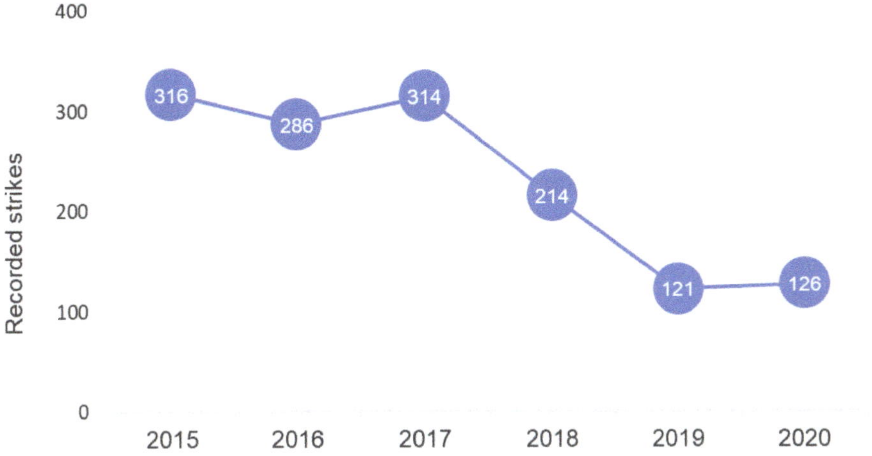

Sources: Internal VGCL data provided to author; Thu Hang (2018); Hoang Manh (2019); T.E.A. (2020); Hoang Manh (2021).

ments prior to returning to the factory before workers ended the strike (Ngoc Phuc 2020). The same week, workers at JY, a Korean-owned stuffed toy factory in northern Ha Nam province, protested against Chinese employees being allowed to return to work without being tested for coronavirus. Authorities said that they had actually been tested but asked the company to provide masks to workers (The Anh 2020).

Later in the year, when the economic impact of the pandemic began to be felt, striking workers shifted to demanding fair wages, social security payments, and benefits. At Tomiya Summit Garment Export, a Japanese-owned factory in southern Dong Nai province, 250 workers went on strike at the end of April 2020 to oppose the company sacking them without providing support for finding other jobs. The company said it needed to cut the labour force because of the impacts of COVID-19, but, in response to the strike, it announced that it would reduce working hours but not the number of workers (Ha 2020). The September 2020 strike at Luxshare-ICT, a Chinese-owned electronics factory in north-eastern Bac Giang province, came at an embarrassing time for the company, as Apple was considering contracting the factory to make some of its products. Workers had a number of demands, including related to salaries, bonuses, working hours, and leave allowances. The vast majority of the demands were met (Bao Han 2020a). Before a December 2020 strike and occupation at My Tu, a Korean-owned garment factory in southern Binh Duong province, the factory had been laying off workers due to COVID-19. Workers discovered that the factory had been deducting social security contributions from salaries but not paying these into the social security fund, meaning workers would not have been able to claim unemployment benefits. There was also doubt about whether the remaining workers would be paid December salaries or bonuses. On 11 December, workers went on strike to demand these and occupied the factory overnight on 15 December. The company then promised to resolve all social security payments by the end of December (Tam An 2020).

Distributing material aid

Strikes were complemented by the VGCL's activities, the second part of the dual structure. At the most basic and immediate level, the VGCL provided material aid. This included donating financial gifts or food packages to workers in need and giving personal protective equipment to workers and their workplaces, as well as checking that these were being used properly. In addition, the VGCL organised information sessions for workers and employers about COVID-19 preventative measures. A campaigning effort organised and coordinated by the VGCL to get landlords to voluntarily freeze or decrease rents for workers who had suffered a loss of income also had some success (FES Vietnam 2020).

Vietnam's flagship economic policy during COVID-19 was a 62 trillion Vietnamese dong (US$2.6 billion) support package, initially from April to June 2020 and then extended until the end of the year with another 18.6 trillion VND (US$798 million). This provided tax breaks and low-interest loans to affected businesses and monthly financial support to those who needed it. Recipients had to be in one of seven groups, including the unemployed, informal workers whose income had significantly decreased, poor and near-poor families, and household businesses. Payments were modest, and the roll-out of the relief encountered substantial issues, as strict bureaucratic conditions that were difficult for many people to meet were attached. For example, many informal migrant workers in Hanoi, such as street vendors and motorbike taxi drivers, were told that, in order to receive the support, they needed a business licence and other documents verifying their residence, income, and nature of work, which they did not have (Lan Phuong and Tat Dinh 2020). Nevertheless, the payments were a lifeline for many. The package was not the VGCL's initiative, but they had a hand in its development. They also played an important role in highlighting the issues that were stopping the money from getting to those who needed it and making suggestions for how that could be improved (Cuoc Song An Toan 2020).

Minimum wage negotiations

The VGCL also took a strong pro-labour stance during minimum wage negotiations in summer 2020. Vietnam's National Wage Council was established in 2013 as a mechanism to negotiate annual minimum wage rises. The council has a tripartite structure, with delegates from the Vietnam Chamber of Commerce and Industry (VCCI), the VGCL, and MOLISA. It meets every summer to decide on minimum wage increases for the following year; they are applied from 1 January.

In normal years, negotiations follow a familiar pattern. The VGCL says that workers are facing hardships from low wages and proposes a relatively large increase. The VCCI says that employers are facing difficulties and thus cannot afford a large increase in minimum wages. They propose a much smaller increase. The council meets and eventually agrees on an amount that falls somewhere between the two proposals. In summer 2019, when the council decided on minimum wage levels for 2020, the amount agreed was celebrated as the first time that minimum wages would cover 100% of workers' basic living costs (Anh Thu 2019).

Negotiations in summer 2020, however, were different. The VCCI said that, given all the hardships which businesses were facing due to the economic impact of the COVID-19 pandemic, there should be no increase in minimum wage levels in 2021; to do so would put too much financial pressure on employers. The VGCL opposed the VCCI, saying that workers had also faced severe hardship and loss of income and therefore needed higher minimum wages in 2021. MOLISA, supporting the VCCI, very quickly proposed that the council take a vote on the issue. The VGCL resisted, saying that no real discussions or negotiations had taken place. The vote went ahead anyway, but the VGCL delegates refused to take part, decrying it as illegitimate; they were aware that, with the MOLISA representatives voting with the VCCI, the vote would be lost even if they took part. The council therefore decided not to raise minimum wages in 2021 (Van Duan 2020). The VGCL did have one suggestion accepted into the official decision, however: the possibility that minimum wages could be raised on 1 July 2021, six months later than usual. The council said that this possibility should be considered at a later date once the full economic impact of the COVID-19 pandemic was known (Bao Han 2020b). At the time of writing, in early 2021, the VGCL had returned to this suggestion, arguing that workers had suffered enough and that employers could afford a minimum wage increase in July 2021, as Vietnam saw economic growth of 2.9% in 2020 (Bao Han 2021).

Conclusion

This chapter has argued that Daubler's (2018, p.155) conception of the dual structure of Vietnam's labour relations is a useful way to understand the labour response to the COVID-19 pandemic in the country. Wildcat strikes demanded safe workplaces and fair wages and benefits at the enterprise level. Complementing these were the VGCL's activities at national and regional levels, including distributing material aid and successfully pushing for and improving government policies to support workers through the pandemic and its economic impacts. In addition to these, even though the VGCL failed to secure a minimum wage increase for 2021, their strong stance against MOLISA and the VCCI meant that the debate continued, opening the door to a potential wage increase later in the year. The two parts of the dual structure thus combined to form a fairly effective response.

The dual structure was by no means perfect. It could not stop workers experiencing significant hardships that were similarly felt around the world. And, despite its best efforts, the VGCL failed to achieve a minimum wage increase in January 2021, even though it succeeded in publicising the issue widely and raising the possibility of an increase in July 2021. As Daubler himself has noted, the dual structure has its shortcomings. Perhaps it would also be less useful in mounting campaigns for major changes. During the COVID-19 pandemic, however, the dual structure was able to provide an effective emergency response, blunting the worst impacts of the pandemic for many workers.

Notes

1. There was no formal freedom of association before January 2021, which saw some limited reforms (see Buckley, forthcoming). This chapter, however, focuses on 2020, before the reforms came into effect.

2. Here I use the term wildcat strike to mean a strike that is not led by a trade union.

References

Anh Thu. (2019). 'Lương tối thiểu vùng năm 2020: "Chốt" tăng 5,5% so với năm 2019' ['2020 regional minimum wages: "Bolted" at a 5.5% increase compared to 2019']. *Lao Động*, 12 July. https://perma.cc/ZMS5-2WGF [Last accessed 13 January 2021].

Bao Han. (2020a). 'Vì sao 5.000 công nhân Công ty TNHH Luxshare – ICT ngừng việc tập thể?' ['Why did 5,000 Luxshare – ICT workers strike?']. *Lao Động*, 14 September. https://perma.cc/6LMZ-9799 [Last accessed 13 January 2021].

Bao Han. (2020b). 'Lương tối thiểu 2021: Cần ghi nhận những đề xuất xác đáng của Tổng LĐLĐVN' ['2021 minimum wage: the VGCL's reasonable suggestions must be noted']. *Lao Động*, 25 August. https://perma.cc/H36U -GXT7 [Last accessed 13 January 2021].

Bao Han. (2021). 'Kiến nghị tăng lương tối thiểu từ 1.7: Giảm áp lực cho doanh nghiệp' ['Petitioning to raise minimum wages from 1 July: Reducing pressure on enterprises']. *Lao Động*, 6 January. https://perma.cc/4EPZ-ZU8G [Last accessed 13 January 2021].

Buckley, Joe. (2021). 'Freedom of association in Vietnam: A heretical view'. *Global Labour Journal*, vol. 12, no. 2, pp. 79–94. https://doi.org/10.15173/glj .v12i2.4442

Cuoc Song An Toan. (2020). 'Tiếp thu kiến nghị của Tổng Liên đoàn về tháo gỡ khó khăn, vướng mắc của gói 62.000 tỷ' ['Receiving the VGCL's ideas about how to solve difficulties and problems with the 62 trillion dong package']. *Cuộc Sống An Toàn*, 29 June. https://perma.cc/5WBD-MADJ [Last accessed 14 January 2021].

Daubler, Wolfgang. (2018). 'Trade union pluralism in Vietnam – Coping with informal associations', in Rudolf Traub-Mertz and Tim Pringle (eds) *Trade Unions in Transition: From Command to Market Economies*. Germany: Friedrich-Ebert-Stiftung, pp. 149–162. https://perma.cc/2A3W-FJTG [Last accessed 13 January 2021].

Do Quynh Chi; and van den Broek, Di. (2013). 'Wildcat strikes: A catalyst for union reform in Vietnam?' *Journal of Industrial Relations*, vol. 55, no. 5, pp. 783–799. https://doi.org/10.1177/0022185613491685

FES Vietnam. (2020). 'Trade union in Vietnam in the context of the Covid-19 pandemic'. *Friedrich-Ebert-Stiftung Vietnam*, 25 May. https://perma.cc /XDE7-TBVA [Last accessed 13 January 2021].

Ha Anh Chien. (2020). 'Cty cho nữ công nhân lớn tuổi nghỉ việc bằng tờ thông báo nhỏ như gang tay' ['Company fires older women workers with a small piece of paper']. *Lao Động*, 28 April. https://perma.cc/463S-NQ6X [Last accessed 13 January 2021].

Hoang Manh. (2019). 'Các cuộc ngừng việc, đình công trong toàn quốc giảm 35%' ['Nationwide work stoppages and strikes reduced by 35%']. *Dân Trí*, 14 March. https://perma.cc/D8DJ-HRQA [Last accessed 16 March 2019].

Hoang Manh. (2021). '126 cuộc ngừng việc tập thể trong năm 2020' ['126 collective work stoppages in 2020']. *Dân Trí*, 9 January. https://perma.cc/T8NG-D4GL [Last accessed 10 January 2021].

Ky Quan. (2020). 'Long An: Doanh nghiệp vào cuộc bảo vệ người lao động trước dịch bệnh Corona' ['Long An: Enterprise gets involved in protecting workers in the face of coronavirus']. *Lao Động*, 6 February. https://perma.cc/G98G-K5D4 [Last accessed 14 January 2021].

Lan Phuong; and Tat Dinh. (2020). 'Hanoi overlooks street vendors in Covid-19 incentive'. *VnExpress International*, 23 June. https://perma.cc/P7GC-7D2K [Last accessed 14 January 2021].

Lee, Chang-Hee. (2006). *Industrial Relations and Dispute Settlement in Viet Nam*. Vietnam: International Labour Organization in Viet Nam. https://perma.cc/A786-BREM [Last accessed 13 January 2021].

Ngoc Phuc. (2020). 'Công nhân đã làm việc trở lại sau khi nghe giải thích về quy trình cách ly người Trung Quốc' ['Workers return to work after hearing an explanation the process of quarantining a Chinese national']. *Sài Gòn Giải Phóng*, 19 February. https://perma.cc/W4WL-D7KA [Last accessed 14 January 2021].

Quan, Katie. (2015). 'One step forward: Collective bargaining experiments in Vietnam and China', in Anita Chan (ed.) *Chinese Workers in Comparative Perspective*. USA: Cornell University Press, pp. 174–192.

Schweisshelm, Erwin; and Do Quynh Chi. (2018). 'From harmony to conflict – Vietnamese trade unions on the threshold of reform', in Rudolf Traub-Mertz and Tim Pringle (eds) *Trade Unions in Transition: From Command to Market Economies*. Germany: Friedrich-Ebert-Stiftung, pp. 109–147. https://perma.cc/FD8N-DECQ [Last accessed 13 January 2021].

Siu, Kaxton; and Chan, Anita. (2015). 'Strike wave in Vietnam, 2006–2011'. *Journal of Contemporary Asia*, vol. 45, no. 1, pp. 71–91. https://doi.org/10.1080/00472336.2014.903290

Tam An. (2020). 'CÔNG TY TNHH MỸ TÚ: Hàng trăm công nhân lo mất trắng quyền lợi' ['MY TU: Hundreds of workers worry about losing their rights and interests']. *Người Lao Động*, 20 December. https://perma.cc/AF3D-VBC2 [Last accessed 13 January 2021].

T.E.A. (2020) 'Số cuộc ngừng việc tập thể giảm gần 50%' ['Collective work stoppages reduce by nearly 50%']. *Lao Động*, 7 January. https://perma.cc /CYT3-9KH3 [Last accessed 13 January 2021].

The Anh. (2020). 'Vụ phản đối công nhân Trung Quốc vì sợ Covid-19: Lãnh đạo huyện giải thích' ['Opposing Chinese workers due to COVID-19 fears: District leaders explain']. *Dân Việt*, 17 February. https://perma.cc/H743 -H6A3 [Last accessed 14 January 2021].

Thu Hang. (2018). 'Đã có 314 cuộc đình công và ngừng việc tập thể' ['There were 314 strikes and collective work stoppages']. *Thanh Niên*, 12 January. https://perma.cc/XU3U-ZLYU [Last accessed 2 June 2018].

Tran Thi Kieu Trang; and Bales, Richard. (2017). 'On the precipice: Prospects for free labor unions in Vietnam'. *San Diego International Law Journal*, vol. 19, no. 1, pp. 71–94. https://perma.cc/RB3W-VTAR [Last accessed 14 January 2021].

Van Duan. (2020). 'Không tăng lương tối thiểu vùng năm 2021' ['No 2021 regional minimum wage increase']. *Người Lao Động*, 6 August. https://perma .cc/8Y2E-WZ3D [Last accessed 13 January 2021].

World Bank. (2020). *Taking Stock, December 2020. From COVID-19 to Climate Change: How Vietnam Can Become the Champion of Green Recovery*. USA: World Bank. https://perma.cc/7UHH-NEMK [Last accessed 13 January 2021].

10. Southeast Asian haze and socio-environmental–epidemiological feedback

Thomas E. L. Smith and Helena Varkkey

While the fire and haze season for Indonesia and Malaysia was mild in 2020 despite 'moderate' meteorological outlooks, there were a number of reasons to expect that the socio-economic impacts of COVID-19 would increase the prevalence of agricultural and land clearance fires and the resultant haze pollution. Furthermore, there was mounting evidence revealing that particulate matter in the haze produced by the fires may have increased transmission rates of COVID-19, exacerbated the symptoms of the disease and severity of infection, and increased overall mortality. We explore the reasons why COVID-19-related lockdowns and economic recessions might have led and will continue to lead to the increasing use of fire in Southeast Asia's peatlands in the short and long terms. We then discuss the role that haze pollution (as well as historic population exposure to this pollution) might have played in exacerbating the COVID-19 crisis through interactions between air pollution and the virus. Finally, we speculate that a novel feedback loop may exist that has exacerbated both the severity of the pandemic and the risk of fire-related haze events.

Haze in 2020 and the situation in 2021

The Southeast Asian 'haze season' usually refers to a regional air pollution crisis generally occurring from late August through November, driven by deforestation and agricultural fires, predominantly in Indonesia (Varkkey 2015). Beyond its immediate effects in Indonesia, the haze often travels across borders to affect Singapore, Malaysia, and sometimes further afield. There have also been increasingly regular haze events in northern Southeast Asia caused by agricultural burning in the 'golden

How to cite this book chapter:
Smith, Thomas E. L.; and Varkkey, Helena. 2022. 'Southeast Asian haze and socio-environmental–epidemiological feedback'. In: Shin, Hyun Bang; Mckenzie, Murray; and Oh, Do Young (eds) *COVID-19 in Southeast Asia: Insights for a post-pandemic world*. London: LSE Press, pp. 118–127.
DOI: https://doi.org/10.31389/lsepress.cov.j License: CC BY 4.0.

triangle' border region of Thailand, Laos, and Myanmar (Greenpeace Southeast Asia 2020).

Much of the haze originating from Indonesia is produced by fires on carbon-rich tropical peatlands. Under pristine forested and waterlogged conditions, peatlands rarely catch fire. Small-, medium-, and large-scale developers, however, often drain peatlands to prepare them for small-holdings and commercial plantations. This process dries out the surface peat layer such that it becomes highly combustible. Furthermore, fire is sometimes used intentionally as a cheap and efficient way to clear the land (Varkkey 2015). Once ignited, peatland fires are difficult to suppress and may smoulder for weeks or months (Hu et al. 2018).

Predicting the timing, extent, and severity of the haze season is complex given that the fires are a function of the weather and longer-term climate variabilities (e.g. El Niño) as well as land and water management. In March 2021, the NOAA's El Niño–Southern Oscillation forecast suggested that El Niño (associated with hot and dry conditions in Southeast Asia) would be unlikely during 2021 (NOAA 2021), reducing the risk of widespread fires that had plagued previous El Niño-exacerbated dry seasons, such as those in 2015 and 2019 (Figure 10.1).

Figure 10.1. A true-colour satellite image with fire hotspot detections (red) over parts of Malaysia, Indonesia, Singapore, and Brunei during the height of the 2019 haze season, on 14 September 2019

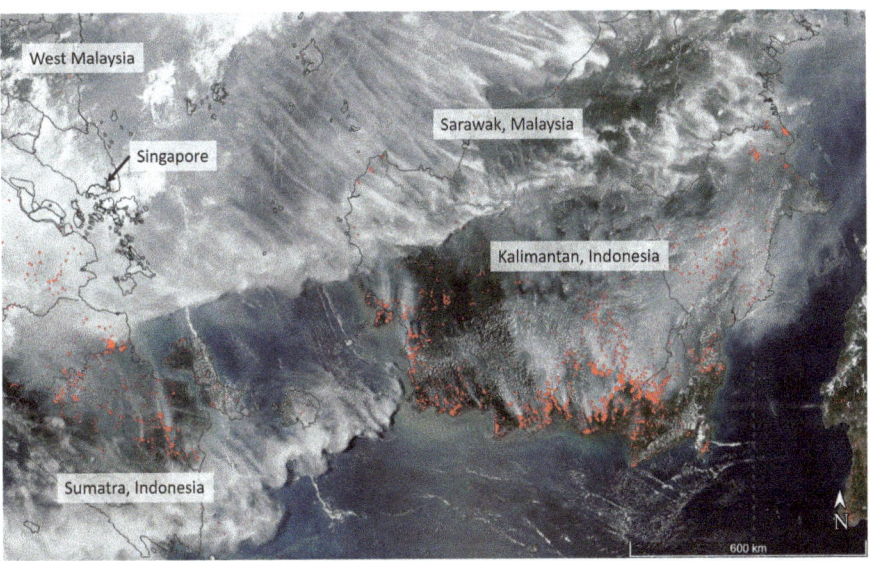

Source: NASA Worldview (2019).
Note: Visible plumes of smoke shroud much of Kalimantan, while plumes from fires on Sumatra are driven by the wind northwards towards Singapore and the Malay Peninsula.

However, the Singapore Institute of International Affairs (SIIA), which releases annual 'Haze Outlook' reports, warned that the impacts of the COVID-19 pandemic could increase the risk of a severe transboundary haze incident, in spite of the low probability of El Niño (SIIA 2020).

COVID-19 and tropical peatland fires

By the end of March 2021, Indonesia had the highest number of COVID-19 cases and deaths in East and Southeast Asia, with 1,470,000 confirmed cases and 39,865 deaths as of 24 March 2021. With only 2.12% of the population vaccinated by the end of March 2021, the disease seemed likely to remain a public health crisis in the region throughout 2021, including the haze season later in the year. The potential influence of the pandemic on tropical peatland fires can be broken down into three critical COVID-19 impacts:

1. The reallocation of government budgets for environmental protection and fire prevention to the COVID-19 response and the deregulation of environmental laws to encourage economic recovery;
2. Lockdown and physical distancing measures inhibiting the deployment of government, NGO, and private sector personnel responsible for environmental protection, community engagement, and fire prevention; and
3. The economic impacts of the pandemic and associated lockdowns on certain plantation companies who might use fire and illegal encroachment to raise profitability.

First, in April 2020, the Indonesian Ministry of Environment declared a reallocation of 1 trillion rupiah (US$111 million) from its budget to help forest communities and farmers affected by COVID-19 (PPID 2020). The consequences of the reallocation included a 50% budget cut for the ministry's fire-fighting teams that were responsible for finding and fighting fires; this in turn led to a 34% reduction in the area of fire patrolling (Ungku and Christina 2020).

And, while the mandate of the Peatland Restoration Agency, a key agency in the fight against peatland fires, was extended for a further four years, several new laws and policies were passed in 2020 that accelerated environmental deregulation in the name of economic recovery and food security. For example, the Omnibus Law on Job Creation included the scrapping of a provision that required the maintenance of a minimum 30% watershed and/or island area as forest area and the shortening of a requirement for plantation companies to develop 30% of their concession areas from three to two years. A new 'food estate' programme, in turn, allowed protected forest areas to be cleared in the process of establishing millions of hectares of new farmland. Such de-regulations put fire-prone peatlands at risk of accelerated development (Jong 2021).

Second, lockdowns and social distancing rules compounded budget cuts, further inhibiting patrol efforts. It was not just government per-sonnel who were stating that COVID-19 restrictions 'hamper … our access to the flames' (Ungku and Christina 2020), but also stakeholders in the private sector who were finding it difficult to assess the situation on the ground, even on their own plantations (Jong 2020). NGOs, of-ten responsible for encouraging more sustainable peatland livelihoods through outreach, fire-free programmes, and demonstration projects, shifted their focus to online activities at a crucial time of the year, and the effectiveness of online activities was highly dependent on reliable internet access, which was often lacking (Ungku and Christina 2020).

Finally, Indonesia's economy contracted for the first time in 20 years in the second quarter of 2020, shortly after COVID-19 hit, and there were concerns of a prolonged recession (Ing 2021). Key sectors linked to fires and haze came into the COVID-19 pandemic on the heels of an already challenging financial year. In particular, palm oil saw especially low commodity prices in 2019 (Khoo 2019), influenced by issues like the European Union's decision to phase out palm oil-based biofuels by 2030.

There were concerns that the associated unemployment and econom-ic pressures will drive smallholders as well as some plantation com-panies to shift to cheaper and less sustainable practices. Smallholders surveyed in Indonesia reported an average 5% decline in selling prices of fresh fruit bunches (FFB), which affects turnover cost efficiency and fertiliser input expenses, with probable long-term knock-on effects for attainable FFB yield (Nurkhoiry and Oktarina 2020).

While larger, more publicly visible transnationals (e.g. Sime Darby, Wilmar, or Golden Agri Resources) made commitments to compli-ance with sustainable certification schemes such as the Roundtable for Sustainable Palm Oil (RSPO) to maintain sustainability practices at all times, this was not the case for less prominent small- and medium-sized companies that had not yet made such commitments. In the face of COVID-19-related economic pressures, such companies might have been more inclined to infringe upon environmental regulations to off-set immediate losses and increase short-term profitability, including the use of fire and illegal encroachment into tropical peat swamp forests (Suwiknyo 2020).

These economic pressures, combined with government cutbacks and movement restrictions, might have decreased the likelihood of effective policing, prosecutions, and convictions, raising the possibility of a more severe transboundary haze event should there be a strong El Niño dry season. The likelihood of a longer-term economic downturn suggested that the impacts of COVID-19 would reach far beyond 2020 and 2021.

How might haze exacerbate the pandemic?

While COVID-19 might have increased the risk of a significant haze incident, there was growing evidence suggesting that air pollution both decreased base-level immunity to the disease and increased mortality rate from it.

A growing body of literature has found statistically robust correlations between air pollution and COVID-19 cases, hospital admissions, and deaths (Cole, Ozgen, and Strobl 2020). In a US study, an increase in concentrations of fine particulate matter ($PM_{2.5}$) of just 1 µgm^{-3} was associated with a 15% increase in COVID-19 deaths (Wu et al. 2020), while a similar study from England found that an increase in the long-term average $PM_{2.5}$ concentrations of 1 µgm^{-3} could explain a 12% increase in COVID-19 cases (Travaglio et al. 2021). These results were especially concerning for the Southeast Asian haze season because concentrations of $PM_{2.5}$ can reach hundreds to thousands of µgm^{-3} during haze events, many times higher than the concentrations investigated in the aforementioned studies.

Understanding the precise pathological mechanism for the correlation has remained a work in progress, although Acute Respiratory Distress Syndrome (ARDS), which has long been linked to polluted air, has been a major cause of COVID-19 related deaths. One notable finding from both the US and UK studies (Travaglio et al. 2021; Wu et al. 2020) was that high rates of COVID-19-related deaths correlated not only to contemporaneous air pollution conditions but also to prolonged exposure to polluted air over time. For example, those living in US counties that had experienced worsening air pollution over the previous 15 to 20 years had a substantially higher mortality rate. $PM_{2.5}$ particles, the particles in air pollution that are small enough to be inhaled into the lungs and even enter the bloodstream, have the long-term effect of weakening human respiratory, cardiovascular, and immune systems. In the context of COVID-19, someone with already weakened lungs and respiratory tracts has a higher risk of not only becoming infected but also suffering worse symptoms (Wu et al. 2020). Both acute and chronic exposure to haze, therefore, decrease the base-level immunity of the population to COVID-19 and increase the risk of death.

Perhaps most worryingly, there was also evidence to suggest that particulate matter may have also acted as a vector for the relatively tiny virus (Barakat, Muylkens, and Su 2020; Setti et al. 2020), offering a surface to which the virus could cling. Frontera et al. (2020) have suggested that viruses travelling on the surfaces of air pollution particles were able to survive longer and travel further (> 2 m) through the air, potentially increasing the basic reproduction number (R), i.e. the spread, of the disease. The minute nature of the haze pollution particles as a host for the virus (as opposed to larger droplets of saliva) was also linked to deeper penetration into the human respiratory system, causing a more severe infection (Frontera et al. 2020). While COVID-19 lockdowns led to a notable decrease in aerosol optic depth (AOD, representing density of particulate matter) over Southeast Asia, it was found that, in areas with extensive forest fires and agricultural burning, AODs remained at very high levels, even during lockdown periods (Kanniah et al. 2020).

A novel socio-environmental–epidemiological feedback mechanism?

The impact of air pollution on the virus's spread and severity is likely to have been scaled with the concentration of particulate matter in the air and the density of people exposed to both the disease and air pollution (Cole, Ozgen, and Strobl 2020; Frontera et al. 2020). Major haze incidents in Southeast Asia are conducive to this effect, with hazardous levels of particle concentrations coinciding with densely populated urban centres.

From this, we may deduce that there is the potential for a novel socio-environmental–epidemiological reinforcing feedback loop (Figure 10.2), whereby environmental air pollution from fires might have led to an increase in the spread and severity of disease, which might in turn have drawn resources away from environmental protection enforcement and fire prevention, which might have further increased the risk of more fires. This vicious cycle might not have been unique to

Figure 10.2. The socio-environmental–epidemiological feedback loop

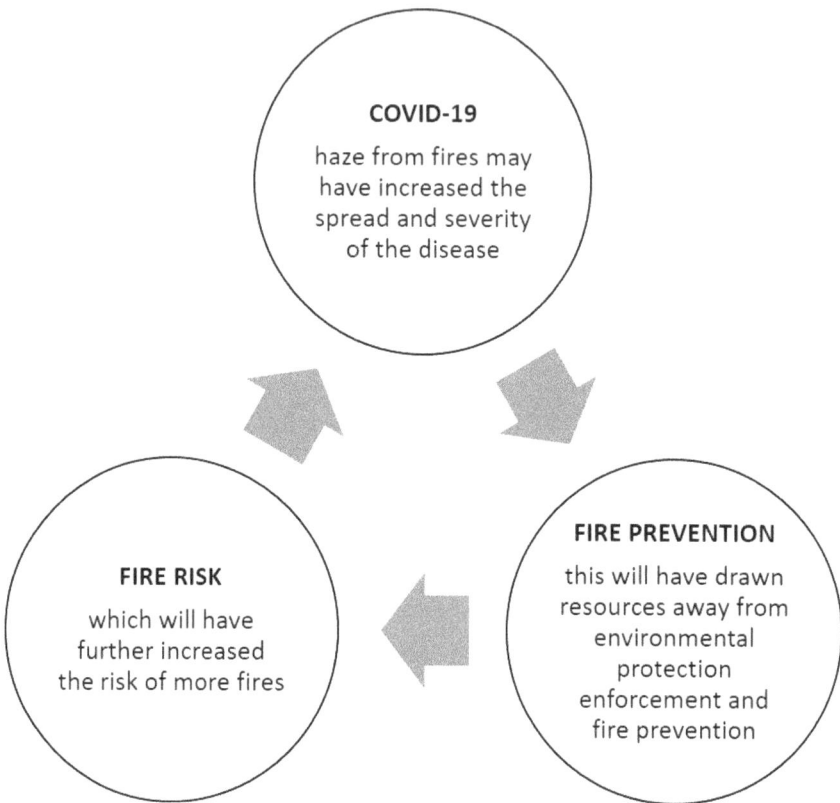

Southeast Asia and haze, possibly also playing a role in exacerbating COVID-19 and air pollution crises in other deforestation fire-affected regions, such as Russia and Brazil.

Beyond the COVID-19 pandemic, tropical peat swamp forests in Southeast Asia also present suitable conditions for the potential emergence of novel zoonotic infectious diseases in the future (Harrison et al. 2020; Morand and Lajaunie 2021). This is due to their high biodiversity, the presence of many potential vertebrate and invertebrate vectors, and high levels of habitat disruption and wildlife harvesting. Morand and Lajaunie (2021) found that increases in outbreaks of zoonotic and vector-borne diseases similar in nature to COVID-19 from 1990 to 2016 were heavily linked to deforestation in tropical countries. In particular, and of important relevance to haze crises, deforestation for oil palm plantations was singled out as a driver of outbreaks of vector-borne diseases (Morand and Lajaunie 2021). Combined with the high likelihood of fires in these areas (and the potential for these fires to exacerbate a pandemic's health effects, as discussed above), any future outbreaks will likely have dire impacts on the public health and livelihoods of remote local communities around peatland areas, most of whom have limited medical facilities and high dependence on external trade (Harrison et al. 2020).

Hence, both in terms of the mitigation of the COVID-19 pandemic and reducing the potential for the emergence of future pandemics, it remains extremely important for governments to continue to prioritise environmental protection and fire prevention, especially in tropical peatlands, throughout and beyond this time of crisis.

Acknowledgements

We acknowledge the use of imagery from the NASA Worldview application (https://worldview.earthdata.nasa.gov), part of the NASA Earth Observing System Data and Information System (EOSDIS).

References

Barakat, Tarek; Muylkens, Benoit; and Su, Bao-Lian. (2020). 'Is particulate matter of air pollution a vector of Covid-19 pandemic?' *Matter*, vol. 3, no. 4, pp. 977–980. https://doi.org/10.1016/j.matt.2020.09.014

Cole, Matthew A.; Ozgen, Ceren; and Strobl, Eric. (2020). 'Air pollution exposure and Covid-19 in Dutch municipalities'. *Environmental and Resource Economics*, vol. 76, pp. 581–610. https://doi.org/10.1007/s10640-020-00491-4

Frontera, Antonio; Martin, Claire; Vlachos, Konstantions; and Sgubin, Giovanni. (2020). 'Regional air pollution persistence links to COVID-19 infection zoning'. *The Journal of Infection*, vol. 81, no. 2, pp. 318–356. https://doi.org/10.1016/j.jinf.2020.03.045

Greenpeace Southeast Asia. (2020). *Maize, Land Use Change, and Transboundary Haze Pollution*, 26 May. https://perma.cc/5VKG-E4JV [Last accessed 26 August 2020].

Harrison, Mark E.; Wijedasa, L.S.; Cole, L.E.S.; Cheyne, S.M.; Choiruzzad, S.A.B.; Chua, L.; Dargie, G.C.; Ewango, C.E.N.; et al. (2020). 'Tropical peatlands and their conservation are important in the context of COVID-19 and potential future (zoonotic) disease pandemics'. *PeerJ*, vol. 8, p. e10283. https://doi.org/10.7717/peerj.10283

Hu, Yuqi; Fernandez-Andez, Nieves; Smith, Thomas E.L.; and Rein, Guillermo. (2018). 'Review of emissions from smouldering peat fires and their contribution to regional haze episodes'. *International Journal of Wildland Fire*, vol. 27, pp. 293–312. https://doi.org/10.1071/WF17084

Ing, Lili Yan. (2021). 'Economic outlook 2021: Beware of prolonged recession'. *Jakarta Post*, 5 January. https://perma.cc/N7AX-WV8D [Last accessed 30 January 2021].

Jong, Hans N. (2020). 'COVID-19 may worsen burning and haze as Indonesia enters dry season'. *Mongabay*, 6 July. https://perma.cc/D7G4-PA2W [Last accessed 26 August 2020].

Jong, Hans N. (2021). 'Indonesia renews peat restoration bid to include mangroves, but hurdles abound'. *Mongabay*, 5 January. https://perma.cc/5MNF-TPW2 [Last accessed 30 January 2021].

Kanniah, Kasturi Devi; Kamarul Zaman, Nurul Amalin Fatihah; Kaskaoutis, Dimitris G.; and Latif, Mohd Talib. (2020). 'COVID-19's impact on the atmospheric environment in the Southeast Asia region'. *Science of the Total Environment*, vol. 736, p. 139658. https://doi.org/10.1016/j.scitotenv.2020.139658

Khoo, Daniel. (2019). 'Palm oil price at 6-month low'. *The Star*, 14 May. https://perma.cc/2J7F-N7YU [Last accessed 26 August 2020].

Morand, Serge; and Lajaunie, Claire. (2021). 'Outbreaks of vector-borne and zoonotic diseases are associated with changes in forest cover and oil palm expansion at global scale'. *Frontiers in Veterinary Science*, vol. 8, p. 661063. https://doi.org/10.3389/fvets.2021.661063

NOAA. (2021). ENSO: *Recent Evolution, Current Status and Predictions*, 26 April. https://perma.cc/UDL4-6G5H [Last accessed 24 March 2021].

Nurkhoiry, Ratnawati; and Oktarina, Sachnaz Desta. (2020). 'How does COVID-19 impact oil palm management practises in Indonesia?' *International Journal of Oil Palm*, vol. 3, no. 2, pp. 56–67. https://doi.org/10.35876/ijop.v3i2.49

PPID (Pejabat Pengelola Informasi dan Dokumentasi). (2020). *KLHK Alokasikan Rp 1,01 Triliun untuk Bantu Masyarakat dan Petani Hutan Terdampak Corona*, 16 April. https://perma.cc/67WH-CEGJ [Last accessed 26 August 2020].

Setti, Leonardo; Passarini, F.; De Gennaro, G.; Barbieri, P.; Perrone, M.G.; Piazzalunga, A.; Borelli, M.; Palmisani, J.; Di Gilio, A.; Piscitelli, P.; and Miani, A. (2020). 'The potential role of particulate matter in the spreading of COVID-19 in northern Italy: First evidence-based research hypotheses. *medRxiv*. https://doi.org/10.1101/2020.04.11.20061713

SIIA (Singapore Institute of International Affairs). (2020). *SIIA Haze Outlook 2020*. Singapore: Singapore Institute of International Affairs. https://perma.cc/5YHJ-EWSU [Last accessed 6 June 2021].

Suwiknyo, Edi. (2020). *Ratusan Perusahaan Sawit Langgar Ketentua, Ekonomi*, 13 May. https://perma.cc/ZCX4-9WRX [Last accessed 26 August 2020].

Travaglio, Marco; Yu, Yizhou; Popovic, Rebeka; Selley, Liza; Leal, Nuno Santos; and Martins, Luis Miguel. (2021). 'Links between air pollution and COVID-19 in England'. *Environmental Pollution*, vol. 268, p. 115859. https://doi.org/10.1016/j.envpol.2020.115859

Ungku, Fathin; and Christina, Bernadette. (2020). 'Coronavirus cuts force Indonesia to scale back forest protection'. *Reuters*, 25 June. https://perma.cc/CHE5-PB6S [Last accessed 26 August 2020].

Varkkey, Helena. (2015). *The Haze Problem in Southeast Asia: Palm Oil and Patronage*. UK: Routledge.

Wu, Xiao; Nethery, Rachel C.; Sabath, Benjamin; Braun, Danielle; and Dominici, Francesca. (2020). 'Exposure to air pollution and COVID-19 mortality in the United States: A nationwide cross-sectional study'. *Science Advances*, vol. 6, no. 45, p. eabd4049. https://doi.org/10.1126/sciadv.abd4049

PART II:
MIGRANTS, (IM)MOBILITIES,
AND BORDERS

11. Logistical virulence, migrant exposure, and the underside of Singapore's model pandemic response

William Jamieson

At the outset of the COVID-19 pandemic, Singapore was lauded for its early declaration of a public health emergency, its assiduous testing regime and track and trace system, and its quarantining of positive cases. However, the initial exemplarity of its pandemic response had been savagely undermined by April 2020 (Chew et al. 2020). Outbreaks in migrant worker dormitories had gone undetected and had to be contained by stringent lockdowns. As the infection spread, it quickly became apparent that it was nigh on impossible for migrant workers to effectively socially distance in their dorms, quartered 15–20 to a room, as well as sharing toilets, kitchens, and dining areas (Koh 2020). Migrant workers were decanted from their dormitories to disperse dense populations of healthy workers from infected dorms and quarantine infected workers. These temporary measures took equally utopian and dystopian turns; some workers were lodged in their own Housing Development Board flats, which are state-administered public housing usually out of reach for this segregated class of worker; some others were relocated to ocean liners, with separate ships for the healthy and for the infected, inverting the bygone practice of plague ships into a parody of the city-state's own attitude towards its workers: out of sight, out of mind. While these measures were eventually effective, Singapore's overall number of infections swelled to 56,000 by late August 2020; over 90% of those cases were from migrant worker dormitories (CNA 2020; Han 2020).

This chapter seeks to locate the unique exposure of migrant workers to disease during the pandemic within the city-state's peculiar political economy and the construction of the migrant worker as an already pathological subject requiring containment, both spatially and logistically. Migrant workers are not only a stigmatised source of cheap labour

How to cite this book chapter:
Jamieson, William. 2022. 'Logistical virulence, migrant exposure, and the underside of Singapore's model pandemic response'. In: Shin, Hyun Bang; Mckenzie, Murray; and Oh, Do Young (eds) *COVID-19 in Southeast Asia: Insights for a post-pandemic world*. London: LSE Press, pp. 131–140. DOI: https://doi.org/10.31389/lsepress.cov.k
License: CC BY 4.0.

Figure 11.1. Tuas View Dormitory

Source: Robert John (2019).

within the city-state, their presence configured through recurrent moral panics by the state and the media, but also the subjects of a covert and problematic model of logistical citizenship that the Singaporean state requires for its reproduction. The initial exemplarity of Singapore's pandemic response was starkly unmasked to reveal what Yea (2020) has termed the 'institutionalised neglect' of its migrant workers; a study in 2017 found migrant workers at higher risk of infectious disease than the general population, owing to a combination of socio-economic status, countries of origin, and living conditions, as well as language and financial barriers to healthcare (Sadarangani, Lim, and Vasoo 2017). Singapore as a model global city has been undergirded by stark disparities in its subjects of governance: citizen, expat, and migrant worker (Yeoh 2006). While others have rightly responded to the exposure of the condition of migrant workers during the pandemic as an appalling disparity that needed to be ameliorated, this chapter will identify the mechanisms through which the vulnerability of migrant workers in Singapore stemmed from the haphazard construction of logistical citizenship, a biopolitical category the city-state relies upon to achieve its vaunted model of governance. This chapter aims to contribute towards critical geographies of logistics by centring the biopolitics of citizenship. It begins with an outline of Singapore's logistical state, followed by a discussion of the evolving governance of migrant workers in Singapore. It then concludes with an analysis of Singapore's implicit model of logistical (non-)citizenship, a model of logistical violence that has in turn ripened into logistical virulence.

Singapore as a logistical state

Recent scholarship has identified logistics as a critical practice that no longer only buffers the friction of global trade but has 'remade geographies of capitalist production and distribution on a global scale' (Cowen 2014, p.10), reconceptualising labour and citizenship within its spaces (Chua et al. 2018). Singapore's rise as a logistical state was intimately tied to the shifting cartographies of global production and circulation in the second half of the 20th century, leveraging its colonial legacy as an entrepot, already a prominent oil and rubber hub (Barr 2019). In labelling Singapore a logistical state, I build on Cowen's (2014) notion of the 'logistics city' – a new urban form central to the development of logistics in the 21st century – to refer to forms of governance that manage and mitigate the demands of logistical operations of paramount importance to self-styled global city 'nodes' such as Singapore, which this chapter will examine through the city-state's management of migrant labour. These forms of governance, as will be demonstrated, depended on a patchwork of formal and informal policy mechanisms, where state-created zones of private contracting and subcontracting engineer systems allow for greater exploitation of labour, while the most flagrant excesses of this system can be dismissed as design failures. These ad hoc systems were engineered not just to limit the liability of the state but to ensure that key logistical systems and infrastructures are maintained without incident. While not the only dimension of the logistical state, as many other theorists of logistics have noted, the disciplining and regulating of labour in logistical operations has been tied to the inherent vulnerability of these systems (Cowen 2014). Following Chua (2017), I demonstrate that this logistical violence has entailed a concomitant logistical vulnerability in the form of a logistical *virulence*. Canny social and economic policies positioned the nascent city-state as a key manufacturing and logistical node in the region, with its swift development through the 1970s and 1980s powered by nimble switches along manufacturing value chains, outsourcing lower-value manufacturing to nearby Malaysia and Indonesia. The introduction of the Central

Provident Fund (a mandatory savings and pensions programme), government-linked companies and banks, and sovereign wealth funds, as well as the vigorous pursuit of foreign direct investment and multi-national companies, formed the public face of Singapore's logistical-developmental trajectory, culminating in the paradoxical policy imaginary of a 'Singapore Model' (Chua 2011).

As Barr (2019) has noted, however, the role that low-paid migrant labour played in this transition has been almost comically underplayed: between 2004 and 2015 the number of foreign workers more than doubled, from 621,400 to 1,368,200, or 40% of the population. Foreign workers have served as a buffer, shielding the average Singaporean from the worst excesses of periodic unemployment (as employment passes can simply be revoked or reduced on an annual basis) and from the worst kinds of work and working conditions. The migrant worker, without any substantive political rights to reside or organise in Singapore, has been intimate with almost every facet of the production and reproduction of the logistical city-state:

> Such foreign workers have built Singapore's factories, schools, skyscrapers, roads and railway lines [and] provided seemingly unlimited domestic service … It is no exaggeration to say that Singapore's reliance upon cheap, vulnerable foreign labour has been at least as important to the country's economic development as more celebrated aspects of the political economy, such as its highly educated citizen workforce. (Barr 2019)

Low-wage migrant workers are unable to vote and are not allowed to collectively organise for better working conditions. They are excluded from the Employment Act, covered instead under the Employment of Foreign Manpower, and, owing to the lack of any fixed minimum wage in Singapore, are paid far lower than their Singaporean counterparts. Currently, Singapore has a foreign worker population of 1.2 million, with nearly half classified as either foreign domestic workers or construction workers on work permits, the lowest-paid category of employment visa (MOM 2020). The fluctuating population of 300,000-odd migrant construction workers come from across South and Southeast Asia to make more money than they would at home. They fill the gap for dangerous and poorly paid labour that very few Singaporeans have to contemplate in facilitating the perpetual construction of the critical infrastructure of the logistical state, as well as its skyline and countless condominiums.

Singapore's successful brand of global city has been underwritten by overwhelming disparities between the subjects of its governance.

In particular, the migrant worker has been *the* political subject of the logistical state. The distinction is important, as its citizens and expats (high-paid migrant labour) can vote and are accorded rights the migrant worker cannot access. While they are more intimately acquainted with the material production and reproduction of the city-state, they rarely encounter the state itself: migrant workers cannot apply directly for a work permit from the Ministry of Manpower but instead have to pay an agent to obtain one on their behalf for thousands of dollars. The agent then acts as a liaison between the Ministry of Manpower (more commonly referred to with the Freudian acronym MOM) and construction companies; the average Bangladeshi worker paid SG$6,400 in agent fees in 2015 (TWC2 2018), not including an additional fee for the construction company to employ them. Workers seeking adequate compensation for workplace injuries and abuses are stymied by labyrinthine layers of bureaucracy that insulate contractors from subcontractors and can take years to rectify (TWC2 2016).

The data on workplace injuries in the construction industry offers a grim if oblique view of the working conditions of the workers at most risk of injury; while the average ratio for recorded injuries to fatalities across 28 EU member states in 2015 was 474:1 (varying from 373:1 in Sweden to 1428:1 in the Netherlands), for Singapore it was 82:1 (TWC2 2018). This strongly suggests that injuries are persistently unrecorded, with several cases reported by Transient Workers Count Too (TWC2) and the Humanitarian Organization for Migration Economics demonstrating the extent to which doctors collaborate with construction companies to send injured labourers back to work. For the Ministry of Manpower, these events are aberrations that result from the informal nature of the migrant labour market, emerging as a natural consequence of competition and the desire for agents to obtain the best deals for the construction companies.

However, these aberrations and excesses have redirected attention from the inequalities structured into the migrant labour market itself and the political subjectivity cultivated by it. Bal (2017) has aptly noted how these cases have been seized upon by the Ministry of Manpower as opportunities to theatrically perform their impartiality and concern, whereas the motivation for the specific kinds of exploitation and abuse faced by migrant workers has stemmed from the legal apparatus controlling migrant labour, such as the foreign worker levy. A complex legal and social system has thus kept migrants at risk to lubricate the capital circuits of the logistical state. Air and seaports, as well as dedicated petrochemical infrastructure, that have fortified Singapore's ongoing logistical relevance, were built and maintained by migrant workers that could not organise, conforming to Cowen's (2014) hypothesis regarding the logistical recasting of labour and citizenship.

Logistical citizenship

Migrants' working and living conditions, seemingly the product of no grand design but rather an impromptu interlocking of design failures, redraw the lines of exploitation and precarity, prompting the question of whether these constitute the emergent conditions of a kind of 'logistical citizenship'. Cowen's (2014) above-mentioned claim that shifts in circulation and logistics entailed a subsequent redrawing of the relations of the state to security, labour, and citizenship merits revisiting. The fragility of just-in-time supply chains necessitated new forms of governance and control commensurate with these territories of circulation (Cowen 2014). The circulatory concerns of the logistical state point towards the desire to obscure not simply the labour that goes into its seamless functioning on the surface but to quarantine the very specific forms of political subjectivity it has constructed in the form of its class of migrant workers. By designing a class of workers insulated from the responsibility of the state through nested transnational chains of agents, middlemen, dormitory companies, contracting, and subcontracting, the state has inadvertently manufactured a political subject conditioned by the practice of logistics. This was made explicit following the security emergency of the 2013 Little India riot.

Singapore's 'bifurcated' regime of migrant labour, according to Yeoh (2006), is premised on a differential politics of inclusion and exclusion: for skilled, highly paid migrants, productivity and loyalty are rewarded with permanent residency and paths to citizenship; for the unskilled, no such route exists, and no matter how long they stay they will ultimately be 'transgressors' to be excluded (Yeoh 2006, p.36). This bifurcation was made a matter of formal government intervention in the aftermath of the Little India riot. In 2013, a migrant construction worker relaxing in Little India, a district comprising the most central migrant worker dormitories and residences that also acts as a leisure hub for many other South Asian migrant workers, was run over and killed by a coach driver. The death prompted an immediate backlash from other workers nearby, resulting in a riot the likes of which Singapore had not seen since the race riots of 1969 (Lee et al. 2015). The riot ruptured the veneer of state-manufactured multi-ethnic harmony, with the politically invisible class of migrant workers becoming problematically present in the national consciousness.

The government was quick to dismiss the riot as an isolated, local event unrelated to the working and living conditions of the workers and focused instead on the predominantly South Asian workers' problematic consumption of alcohol and occupation of Little India on Sundays, as well as the perception of the neighbourhood as an 'area of "disamenity"' (Subramaniam 2017, p.58). Alcohol was temporarily banned in Little India, and in the months and years to come the state would pursue a 'decentralisation' strategy, which saw the construction of additional migrant worker dormitories – gated facilities designed to accommodate tens of thousands of workers (Tan and Toh 2014).

The construction and development of this new model of 'all-inclusive' migrant worker dormitory was developed as an explicit response to an unprecedented crisis of security for 21st-century Singapore. Their haphazard attempts to wean migrant workers off the downtown core and leave them content and entertained at the periphery perversely mimicked the spatial contours of quarantine, and the discourse around the problematic presence of migrant workers within the city framed their transgression as a matter of public hygiene. While the permanent yet provisional presence of these migrant workers in the city was always regarded as a nuisance at best and a public health emergency at worst, what the riot and the immunological response to it made explicit was the pathologising of this class of worker by the state.

Conclusion: logistical virulence

The unbearable presence of Singapore's brand of logistical citizenship is a constitutive source of political and social unease because it points to the cracks within the Singapore model itself: beyond leveraging inequality, logistical citizenship is the political subject governed by the principles of logistics itself. Citizenship is informally rescaled by logistics to the raw input of labour-power, rendered 'efficient' by an opaque transnational market, and its presence is deemed pathological and in need of socio-spatial quarantine. While not an explicitly formulated class of citizen (beyond the regulations necessary for cultivating cheap and provisional sources of labour), what logistical citizenship holds for the political economy of the Singaporean state is not the jurisgenerative Roman spectre of Agamben's (1998) *homo sacer*, the bare life that can be exposed to death, but the exact kind of labour-power required by the considerable political-economic machinery of the logistical state. What has been legislated through logistical citizenship is not the calibration of the state of exception upon the expendable figure of bare life but the disciplining and governance of a product – labour – in the lubrication of capital circuits specific to chokepoints in global markets like shipping, petrochemicals, and construction. The pathological sociality of logistical citizenship needs to be contained and subject to legal-economic displacement so that the state's formal citizens do not encounter the true political-economic terms of their enduring prosperity.

The implicit logic of the sequestration was again made explicit by repeated coronavirus outbreaks in migrant worker dormitories; while citizens and permanent residents were subject to an exemplary response in pandemic control, those in the logistical state were exposed to exponential viral reproduction, with their mobility rendered pathological (Lin and Yeoh 2021). Here we find the perverse limit of the Singaporean state's ongoing experiment with an 'elastic notion of the scale of the nation and its citizenship' (Ong 2006, p.178). It is no accident that the city-state's over-leveraging of low-paid migrant labour and desire to segregate it according to an implicit socio-immunological principle configured ideal circuits for viral reproduction. As Wallace et al. (2020) have noted, the COVID-19 pandemic was conditioned by the circuits of capital themselves and the shifting economic geography of land use, agriculture, and enclosure and then reproduced globally by ubiquitous transport infrastructure. By linking logistical violence with virulence, we can then locate the outbreak of coronavirus in Singapore's migrant worker dormitories within the precarious construction of logistical citizenship itself.

Acknowledgements

I would like to thank the editors of this collection for putting together such a timely collection of articles on the impact of the coronavirus pandemic on Southeast Asia, and for their support and incisive comments that improved the chapter in numerous ways; any mistakes that remain are my own. I would also like to thank Robert John, who was the photographer of Figure 11.1.

References

Agamben, Giorgio. (1998). *Homo Sacer: Sovereign Power and Bare Life*. Translated by D. Heller-Roazen. USA: Stanford University Press.

Bal, Charan. (2017). 'Myths and facts: Migrant workers in Singapore'. *New Naratif*, 9 September. https://perma.cc/G8F3-ZWZD [Last accessed 28 January 2020].

Barr, Michael. (2019). 'Foundations laid, directions set'. *New Naratif*, 27 January. https://perma.cc/KUP7-EBJZ [Last accessed 18 February 2019].

Chew, M.H.; Koh, F.H.; Wu, J.T.; Ngaserin, S.; Ng, A.; Ong, B.C.; and Lee, V.J. (2020). 'Clinical assessment of COVID-19 outbreak among migrant workers residing in a large dormitory in Singapore'. *Journal of Hospital Infection*, vol. 106, pp. 202–203. https://doi.org/10.1016/j.jhin.2020.05.034

Chua, Beng Huat. (2011). 'Singapore as model: Planning innovations, knowledge experts', in Ananya Roy and Aihwa Ong (eds) *Worlding Cities: Asian Experiments and the Art of Being Global*. UK: Wiley-Blackwell, pp. 27–54. https://doi.org/10.1002/9781444346800.ch1

Chua, Charmaine. (2017). 'Logistical violence, logistical vulnerabilities'. *Historical Materialism*, vol. 25, pp. 167–182. https://doi.org/10.1163 /1569206X-12341544

Chua, Charmaine; Danyluk, Martin; Cowen, Deborah; and Khalili, Laleh. (2018). 'Introduction: Turbulent circulation: Building a critical engagement with logistics'. *Environment and Planning D: Society and Space*, vol. 36, pp. 617–629. https://doi.org/10.1177/0263775818783101

Cowen, Deborah. (2014). *The Deadly Life of Logistics*. USA: University of Minnesota Press.

Han, Kirsten. (2020). 'The cost of "Singapore Inc."? A coronavirus outbreak among migrants'. *The Nation*, 17 August. https://perma.cc/F6QY-AVM6 [Last accessed 15 May 2021].

Koh, David. (2020). 'Migrant workers and COVID-19'. *Occupational and Environmental Medicine*, vol. 77, no. 9, pp. 634–636. https://doi.org/10.1136 /oemed-2020-106626

Lee, Wei Feng; Ooi, Chee Kheong; Phua, Dong Haur; Wong, Ming Hai Eric; Chan, Wui Ling; and Ng, Yih Yng. (2015). 'The Little India riot: Experience of an emergency department in Singapore'. *Singapore Medical Journal*, vol. 56, pp. 677–680. https://doi.org/10.11622/smedj.2015188

Lin, Weiqiang; and Yeoh, Brenda. (2021). 'Pathological (im)mobilities: Managing risk in a time of pandemics'. *Mobilities*, vol. 16, pp. 96–112. https://doi.org/10.1080/17450101.2020.1862454

MOM (Ministry of Manpower). (2020). *Foreign Workforce Numbers*. https:// perma.cc/L5LZ-XD7P [Last accessed 29 April 2021].

Ong, Aihwa. (2006). *Neoliberalism as Exception: Mutations in Citizenship and Sovereignty*. USA: Duke University Press.

Sadarangani, Sapna P.; Lim, Poh Lian; and Vasoo, Shawn. (2017). 'Infectious diseases and migrant worker health in Singapore: A receiving country's perspective'. *Journal of Travel Medicine*, vol. 24, no. 4, pp. 1–9. https://doi.org/10.1093/jtm/tax014

Subramaniam, Gurubaran. (2017). 'Evidence-based approaches to place management: Finding common ground in historic ethnic districts'. *Urban Solutions*, vol. 11, pp. 50–59.

Tan, Amelia; and Toh, Yong Chuan. (2014). 'Cinema, cricket field at Singapore's biggest dormitory'. *Straits Times*, 10 August. https://perma.cc/P5T9-GVXA [Last accessed 2 December 2019].

TWC2. (2018). 'Recruitment cost in some cases about 20 times monthly salary', 22 November. https://perma.cc/2X77-H28L [Last accessed 7 January 2021].

TWC2. (2016). 'Workers who find their doctors and lawyers adding to their problems', 18 September. https://perma.cc/J9KH-RS4U [Last accessed 7 January 2021].

Wallace, Rob; Liebman, Alex; Chaves, Fernando Luis; and Wallace, Rodrick. (2020). 'COVID-19 and circuits of capital'. *Monthly Review*, 1 May. https://perma.cc/4RXJ-RFJ8 [Last accessed 27 August 2020].

Yea, Sallie. (2020). 'This is why Singapore's coronavirus cases are growing: A look inside the dismal living conditions of migrant workers'. *The Conversation*, 29 April. https://perma.cc/47A3-JUDG [Last accessed 25 August 2020].

Yeoh, Brenda. (2006). 'Bifurcated labour: The unequal incorporation of transmigrants in Singapore'. *Tijdschrift voor economische en sociale geografie*, vol. 97, pp. 26–37. https://doi.org/10.1111/j.1467-9663.2006.00493.x

Yeoh, Grace; and Smalley, Ruth. (2020). 'Recovered from COVID-19, migrant workers live on a cruise ship and in an HDB flat'. *CNA*, 23 May. https://perma.cc/A9Q3-GBZB [Last accessed 6 August 2020].

12. The new normal, or the same old? The experiences of domestic workers in Singapore

Laura Antona

While extensive and far-reaching, the COVID-19 pandemic did not impact all nations – or all people – equally. Within Singapore, a country that was lauded, at least initially, for its exemplary approach to controlling the pandemic (Teo 2020), the ways in which the virus ultimately spread through the city-state exposed existing inequalities and injustices in its migrant worker populations, with construction workers' dormitories becoming the epicentre of the nation's outbreaks.

This chapter engages directly with these injustices to demonstrate how migrant domestic workers were impacted by the global pandemic, particularly by the 'circuit-breaker' measures enforced by the Singaporean state.[1] As such, it argues three core points. First, that many domestic workers were subjected to increased surveillance and bodily control during the COVID-19 pandemic, with the home space becoming the centre of this. Second, that many migrant workers experienced a removal of their rights and increased immobility. Finally, this chapter argues that, for many domestic workers, there was very little change to their circumstances, with the notion of the 'new normal' requiring further interrogation. Indeed, this chapter ultimately suggests that the experiences of populations who ordinarily experience prolonged confinement need further consideration if we are to achieve more just and equitable futures for all post-COVID-19.

Significantly, this chapter was written while I was living under restrictions in the UK during the COVID-19 pandemic. As such, the interviews and informal conversations on which it is based were conducted online with domestic workers, activists, and NGO workers/volunteers with whom I had existing relationships following prolonged ethnographic fieldwork between June 2016 and December 2017. Knowing

How to cite this book chapter:
Antona, Laura. 2022. 'The new normal, or the same old? The experiences of domestic workers in Singapore'. In: Shin, Hyun Bang; Mckenzie, Murray; and Oh, Do Young (eds) *COVID-19 in Southeast Asia: Insights for a post-pandemic world*. London: LSE Press, pp. 141–149. DOI: https://doi.org/10.31389/lsepress.cov.l License: CC BY 4.0.

about these individuals' lives and perspectives prior to the outbreak of the global pandemic, I build on this more recent dialogue and use this chapter to detail *how*, and in some cases *if*, the COVID-19 pandemic impacted the domestic worker population of Singapore. All of the names included in this chapter are pseudonyms.

Increased bodily surveillance and tensions in the home

Unlike labour that takes place in more public settings, both the intimacy and spatiality of domestic labour mark it as distinct, often leaving domestic workers under heightened scrutiny from their employers. This is particularly acute for live-in domestic workers, who not only have to work and rest in the home of their employer but are often overworked and experience increased vulnerability to abuse (Anderson 2000; Constable 1997; Ehrenreich and Hochschild 2002; Huang and Yeoh 2007; Parreñas 2001). In Singapore, as in many other national contexts, domestic workers are only able to migrate under an employer-sponsored scheme, rendering employers responsible for workers' salaries, accommodation, food, and well-being (MOM 2021). In addition to their bodily maintenance, employers are also made to be responsible for domestic workers' bodily control, with it being argued that the state legislates this in such a way as to leave them vulnerable to intense surveillance (Chok 2013; MOM 2021). While conducting ethnographic fieldwork prior to the COVID-19 pandemic, I encountered many domestic workers who had either been monitored by CCTV or watched closely by family members to ensure that they did not rest and worked to the standard required by their employers (Antona 2019). This often became a point of tension and distress.

While many domestic workers are used to a high degree of surveillance, the pandemic further intensified this. Indeed, following the introduction of circuit-breaker measures, one of the key changes addressed by the domestic workers I interviewed was the sustained presence of their employer (and employer's family) in the home. One domestic worker, Benilda, said very simply in an exasperated tone: 'It just means I am being watched all the time.' She explained that, because she did not have a bedroom of her own, instead sleeping on the floor of her employer's child's room, she had no privacy or space to rest. While she would ordinarily have the house to herself on weekdays, meaning she could sit at the table to relax or could call her children at convenient times, she explained that she felt unable to do this in front of her employer and so would not sit down all day. She also added that she would make smaller portions of food for herself, fearful that her employer would think she was taking too much.

These sentiments were shared by many others, who also expressed their frustrations with having less rest and an increased workload. Rose, another domestic worker I interviewed, said that the amount of cleaning and cooking increased dramatically, especially as the family was no longer eating any meals out. She explained: 'They always eating, the children playing, making mess, I get so tired from all the work.' Rose also said that she would be able to cope more easily if she was not constantly being watched and could take some time off: 'It's more pressure to be watched as well.'

In addition to the increased bodily surveillance and workload, and perhaps as a result of this, many domestic workers also described heightened tensions in the home. As mentioned, both the intensive bodily surveillance enacted by many employers and the intimacy of domestic labour often produce friction between employer and employee, with domestic workers remaining highly vulnerable to mistreatment, abuse, and being overworked. During the pandemic, activists, NGOs, politicians, advocates, and survivors across the world spoke out about the increase in domestic violence and abuse (Bradbury-Jones and Isham 2020; End Violence Against Children 2020; Women's Aid 2020). Indeed, it has been widely shown that increased societal and household stress – whether it be produced socially, economically, politically, or otherwise – often results in higher rates of domestic violence (Aoláin, Haynes, and Cahn 2011; Bradley 2018; Tyner 2012). While none of the domestic workers that I spoke to said that they had experienced any physical violence during this period, many attested to increased working hours and more stressful living/working environments. In addition, HOME (the Humanitarian Organization for Migration Economics), an NGO that supports domestic workers in Singapore and operates a helpline, verified a 25% increase in calls after the government introduced circuit-breaker measures (*The Star* 2020). FAST (the Foreign Domestic Worker Association for Social Support and Training), another NGO that supports domestic workers in Singapore, also reported increased tensions within home spaces, suggesting that the number of domestic workers fleeing their employers' homes had doubled in the months of March and April 2020 (Yang 2020).

It is evident, then, that in many circumstances an employer's continued presence in the home caused increased tensions during the pandemic. With more domestic workers seeking support from NGOs and their embassies and in some circumstances fleeing their employer's homes, it is clear that the circuit-breaker measures detrimentally impacted the working and living conditions in the home space for many of these labourers. While Rose's and Benilda's increased discomfort and hardship were, thankfully, short-lived – as their employers returned to work (and their employers' children to school) following the relaxation of the circuit-breaker measures in June 2020 – many other homes were permanently impacted, causing domestic workers to flee these spaces and return to their 'home' nations.

Removal of rights and decreased mobility

While often defined by their mobile status, many migrant labourers, including domestic workers, were rendered immobile by the COVID-19 pandemic in many respects. Indeed, the pandemic enforced stillness at multiple scales: within national borders, within urban regions, and within the micro scale of the home. In Singapore, particularly when the circuit-breaker measures were in place, many domestic workers were unable to travel to and from their home countries. One domestic worker, Maya, had been hoping to travel to Indonesia to visit her children during the summer of 2020, having not seen them for four years, prior to renewing her employment contract. She explained how upset she was at deciding not to travel back, instead renewing her contract and delaying a visit for another two years. Maya explained that she felt she had no choice in her decision, as she could not risk getting stuck in Indonesia; her wages were vital for providing her children with education.

Beyond being confined within the national borders of Singapore, many domestic workers also discussed the tightened societal controls and their enforced confinement to their employer's home. Indeed, domestic workers were encouraged not to leave their employers' homes on their weekly day off, requiring them to rest in their place of work.[2] Margielyn was just one domestic worker who expressed her upset with this, explaining: 'Even if I can't meet with friends, staying in all day always means more work.' Like others, Margielyn said she understood the need for the circuit-breaker measures but felt unable to get any rest without a room of her own. Being bound to the home in the presence of her employer meant that she would be asked to do small 'favours' or jobs regularly, ultimately requiring her to work every day. While being restricted to the home space was a shared experience of Singaporean citizens and migrants alike, the lack of freedom to move around the city also resulted in a removal of many domestic workers' rights to rest and time off from work. Even after the circuit-breaker measures were lifted, Margielyn explained that her employer would not allow her outside on her day off. She stated: 'Ma'am thinks I will meet with friends and bring back the virus, so she don't allow me out.' The lack of trust within this relationship, paired with her employer's unequal positioning of power and the bodily controls that they were able to exert, meant that Margielyn, like many other domestic workers who would ordinarily be given a weekly rest day, continued to be subjected to confinement long after Singaporean citizens were allowed more freedom and mobility.

Alongside these experiences of heightened immobility, some domestic workers were, conversely, forced to move out of Singapore. During the circuit-breaker period, the Singaporean state affirmed that it would carry out inspections of key sites to ensure that migrant labourers did not break any social distancing measures (Zhuo 2020). If caught doing so, the state did not, however, impose the same punishment as it did to citizens. Instead of being fined, migrant workers were liable to have their work passes revoked and be blacklisted, meaning they would be unable to work in Singapore again (Zhuo 2020). A volunteer from HOME suggested that the population's unease, or perhaps disdain, towards migrants might have impacted the state's decision to further stratify the rights and positioning of citizens vis-à-vis non-citizens. Interestingly, this rule was applied not only to domestic workers and other foreign workers in Singapore but also to White 'expats', or 'professionals', who did not adhere to circuit-breaker regulations (Low 2020).

It can, therefore, be argued that the COVID-19 pandemic resulted, even if temporarily, in a reconfiguring of both mobility and migration within Singapore and Southeast Asia more broadly. Rather than leaving Singapore for a holiday or ending a period of employment and feeling certain that returning for new work would be simple, domestic workers had to make decisions on whether to remain in the city-state for a prolonged period or to return to their 'home' countries with no certainty that they could return when desired. This decision, for Maya and others, proved particularly distressing. Indeed, while domestic workers' ability to move to and from Singapore was always mediated by the state and their ability to freely move around the city was always controlled by their employers, the additional circuit-breaker measures further decreased their mobility and freedoms, leading to an increased workload and a restriction of their rights.

The new normal or the same old?

Alongside the aforementioned concerns, several domestic workers, interestingly, reported that they had experienced no significant changes to their lives in Singapore since the global pandemic had begun. In interviews, comments such as 'no sister, nothing change' and 'things are quite OK, the same really' led me to question how this could be the case when so much attention had been on how quickly and greatly the world had transformed. While none of these domestic workers were entirely happy in their employment, their working environments had not deteriorated or worsened during this period. In interviews, it transpired that none of these women had been given a day off prior to the circuit-breaker measures, when their employers would have regularly been at home. As such, their already heavily restricted mobility, the dynamic/relationships within the home and the surveillance they were under were not impacted.

While discourse during the pandemic largely focused on the ways in which labour practices and people's relationships with space changed both profoundly and quickly, it was striking that these domestic workers' experiences had remained unaffected. Upon reflection, however, it became clear that it was an individual's prior experience of freedoms that made their enforced confinement so starkly felt. For many domestic workers, being forced to live and work in the same space, confined to the same few rooms for months or even years, is the norm and an employment decision that they make because the financial opportunities and gains are so much more significant than any other options they have.

Conclusion

When considering the impacts of the COVID-19 pandemic on the daily lives of domestic workers in Singapore, and particularly when reflecting on comments and sentiments about a lack of change to some individuals' lives, it is clear that their situation was unique. While it became evident through interviews that the imposed circuit-breaker measures had heightened certain tensions in the home spaces in which domestic workers lived and worked, the issues described were not entirely new. Indeed, domestic workers that I interviewed through the course of my extended ethnographic fieldwork for my PhD thesis commented widely on their level of surveillance and a relentless workload, as well as a lack of free time, rest, and basic rights. Rather than being a 'new normal', then, it became evident that, for most domestic workers, the issues that arose during the pandemic were, in fact, more of the 'same old'.

While it is important for policymakers, activists, NGOs and others to recognise the increased surveillance and household tensions that domestic workers were subjected to, as well as their more limited rights and mobility, it is also important to re-examine the structures and systems in place within Singapore that have maintained this form of labour migration. With increased concern about both the immediate and longer-term physical and mental health consequences of enforced confinement (as there has been globally with lockdowns and circuit-breaker measures), it is important to reflect on those individuals whose daily lives are ordinarily heavily confined. Live-in domestic workers, particularly those with minimal or no days of rest, regularly experience isolation and confinement for extended periods, sometimes years. When taking into account a domestic worker's inability to choose when and what they eat, the physically and emotionally arduous labour that they perform without rest, the social isolation they are forced to endure (particularly for those people who are not allowed to use their mobile phones and can only speak to their family and friends at limited times), and their precarious status, which renders them dependent upon their employer, it is clear that their mental and physical well-being should be a much more significant societal priority. Rather than remaining concerned only by the changes that the COVID-19 pandemic and lockdowns/circuit-breakers brought to Southeast Asia and the world at large, it is also important to reflect on those whose daily lives were not altered during this period. Only then might we be able to work towards a more equitable future for all.

Notes

1. Similar to 'lockdown' measures in many other countries around the globe, circuit-breaker measures were introduced in Singapore on 7 April 2020, by the state, in order to control the spread of COVID-19. This period saw the closure of schools, workplaces and non-essential shops, as well as mandated social distancing/isolation, in order to minimise the spread of the virus.

2. While the Employment of Foreign Manpower Act (MOM 2021) states that domestic workers in Singapore are entitled to one weekly day off and 'adequate' daily rest, this ruling was ultimately not enshrined in law and can be circumvented if there is written agreement by the employee and employer.

Acknowledgements

My foremost thanks go to the migrant domestic workers who informed this writing and who continue to graciously give up their free time to talk to me about their ongoing experiences. I would also like to give particular thanks to Hyun Bang Shin, who, as my former PhD supervisor, continues to support my work and provide me with mentorship. Finally, I would like to thank Do Young Oh, Murray Mckenzie and the other editors from the LSE Press, for their suggested revisions and support in the production of this chapter.

References

Anderson, Bridget. (2000). *Doing the Dirty Work? The Global Politics of Domestic Labour*. USA: Zed Books.

Antona, Laura. (2019). 'Making hidden spaces visible: Using drawing as a method to illuminate new geographies'. *Area*, vol. 51, no. 4, pp. 697–705. https://doi.org/10.1111/area.12526

Aoláin, Fionnuala Ní; Haynes, Dina Francesca; and Cahn, Naomi. (2011). *On the Frontlines. Gender, War, and the Post-Conflict Process*. UK: Open University Press.

Bradbury-Jones, Caroline; and Isham, Louise. (2020). 'The pandemic paradox: The consequences of COVID-19 on domestic violence'. *Journal of Clinical Nursing*, vol. 29, no. 13–14, pp. 2047–2049. https://doi.org/10.1111/jocn.15296

Bradley, Samantha. (2018). 'Domestic and family violence in post-conflict communities. International human rights law and the state's obligation to protect women and children'. *Health and Human Rights Journal*, vol. 20, no. 2, pp. 123–136. https://perma.cc/UA3U-E45X [Last accessed 23 May 2021].

Chok, Stephanie. (2013). *Labour Justice and Political Responsibility: An Ethics-Centred Approach to Temporary Low-Paid Labour Migration in Singapore*. Unpublished thesis (PhD), Murdoch University.

Constable, Nicole. (1997). *Maid to Order in Hong Kong. Stories of Migrant Workers*. USA: Cornell University Press.

Ehrenreich, Barbara; and Hochschild, Arlie Russell. (2002). *Global Woman: Nannies, Maids and Sex Workers in the New Economy*. UK: Granta Publications.

End Violence Against Children. (2020). *Protecting Children During COVID-19*. Campaign webpage. https://perma.cc/FP7R-4B53 [Last accessed 21 April 2021].

Huang, Shirlena; and Yeoh, Brenda S.A. (2007). 'Emotional labour and transnational domestic work: The moving geographies of "maid abuse" in Singapore'. *Mobilities*, vol. 2, no. 2, pp. 195–217.

Low, Dominic. (2020). 'Robertson Quay incident: Seven fined, work passes for six revoked'. *Straits Times*, 26 June. https://perma.cc/6YUX-FXZT [Last accessed 21 April 2021].

MOM (Ministry of Manpower). (2021). Employment of Foreign Manpower Act (Chapter 91A). Employment of Foreign Manpower (Work Passes) Regulations 2012. Singaporean governmental statute, created 8 November 2012, updated 21 April 2021. https://perma.cc/Y7YV-REXC [Last accessed 21 April 2021].

Parreñas, Rhacel Salazar. (2001). *Servants of Globalization: Women, Migration, and Domestic Work*. USA: Stanford University Press.

Teo, Joyce. (2020). 'Coronavirus: WHO praises Singapore's containment of COVID-19 outbreak'. *Straits Times*, 10 March. https://perma.cc/75JE -5KMW [Last accessed 21 April 2021].

The Star. (2020). 'Singapore's domestic workers face "hidden plight" due to COVID-19', 15 May. https://perma.cc/X7QU-87KS [Last accessed 21 April 2021].

Tyner, James. (2012). *Space, Place, and Violence: Violence and the Embodied Geographies of Race, Sex, and Gender*. UK: Routledge.

Women's Aid. (2020). *A Perfect Storm: The Impact of the Covid-19 Pandemic on Domestic Abuse Survivors and the Services Supporting Them*. UK: Women's Aid.

Yang, Wong. (2020). 'Coronavirus: More maids running away during circuit breaker, say advocacy groups'. *Straits Times*, 18 May. https://perma.cc/K93S -3MAT [Last accessed 21 April 2021].

Zhuo, Tee. (2020). 'Coronavirus: MOM will revoke work passes of migrant workers in large gatherings if they refuse to disperse'. *Straits Times*, 25 March. https://perma.cc/G6HJ-Z5EF [Last accessed 21 April 2021].

13. Questioning the 'hero's welcome' for repatriated overseas Filipino workers

Maria Carmen (Ica) Fernandez, Justin Muyot,
Maria Karla Abigail Pangilinan and Nastassja Quijano

As the world entered its second year of the COVID-19 pandemic, global inequalities around access to healthcare, vaccines, and therapeutics, as well as border closures and lockdowns, heightened existing inequalities between the global South and the reopening North. An emerging area of engagement has been the immobilising effect of the pandemic on migrant labour, specifically on citizens who were repatriated back to their home countries, and the communities that received them. The experience of the Philippines, which had the slowest recovery in Southeast Asia as of 2021, and its repatriated migrant workers provided early evidence of this phenomenon.

Domestically known as overseas Filipino workers (OFWs),[1] temporary migrant workers have been hailed as *bagong bayani* (modern-day heroes) for contributions to their respective households and the Philippine economy. In exchange for higher incomes and foreign currency, OFWs made the difficult decision to part from their families for prolonged periods of time in foreign lands or aboard sea vessels. As of April 2021, the Department of Labor and Employment reported 627,576 OFWs affected by pandemic closures who had been forced to repatriate (PNA 2021). Official records tallied at least 2.2 million OFWs scattered worldwide out of 108.1 million Filipinos as of 2019 (PSA 2020), although migrant workers have been historically estimated at around 10% of the population (San Juan 2009).

The Philippines was the world's fourth largest destination of remittances in 2019 (World Bank 2020), reaching US$30 billion (1.56 trillion Philippine pesos), or about 8% of the Philippines' US$377

How to cite this book chapter:
Fernandez, Maria Carmen; Muyot, Justin; Pangilinan, Maria Karla Abigail; and Quijano, Nastassja. 2022. 'Questioning the 'hero's welcome' for repatriated overseas Filipino workers'. In: Shin, Hyun Bang; Mckenzie, Murray; and Oh, Do Young (eds) *COVID-19 in Southeast Asia: Insights for a post-pandemic world*. London: LSE Press, pp. 150–161. DOI: https://doi.org/10.31389/lsepress.cov.m License: CC BY 4.0.

billion (PHP 19.52 trillion) economy (BSP 2020). The effects of remittances have been felt not only by OFW families; they have shaped the Philippine built environment as well. A settlement called 'Little Italy' south of Manila features a village of largely empty Italian-style villas constructed by its OFW population, thanks to decades of remittances from domestic and service workers, nurses, and au pairs (Onishi 2010). Shopping malls were once the pre-pandemic leisure area of choice for 'balikbayans' ('home-comers') on holiday, consistent with the country's consumption-driven economy. OFWs also comprised a sizeable portion of the condominium market, although banks have expressed concern regarding furloughed workers defaulting on mortgage payments (Dass 2020).

The global role of OFWs was highlighted early in the pandemic, as heavily affected countries such as the United States and the United Kingdom employed more than 165,000 Filipino registered nurses on the frontlines.[2] However, other OFWs were not as 'lucky'. Of the 327,000 OFWs repatriated in 2020, around 70% were land-based workers from badly hit industries such as logistics, construction, and the oil sector, while the rest were sea-based (DFA 2021).[3]

Thus, OFWs from affected sectors were forced to return and found themselves unemployed under one of the longest and most stringent COVID-19 lockdowns in the world. Despite such draconian efforts, the Philippines recorded more than one million confirmed cases as of April 2021, the second highest in the ASEAN region (CSIS 2021). Intermittent lockdown cycles halted approximately 75% of economic activities and rendered nearly half of the country's adult labour force jobless, leaving repatriated OFWs scrambling to retrain during the worst recession since the tail end of the Marcos dictatorship (Social Weather Stations 2020).

All evidence points to how the pandemic magnified persistent inequality and lack of opportunities in the Philippines – the same factors that had driven Filipino labour migration reaching back to the early 1900s, when Filipinos were first hired as temporary plantation workers across the United States; in the 1970s, when male construction and oil refinery workers left en masse for the Middle East; and again in the 1980s as more women pursued opportunities abroad as domestic, administrative, and healthcare workers (Orbeta and Abrigo 2009). How do we begin to understand these multiple layers of displacement, (im) mobility, and uncertainty?

Layers of vulnerability: double displacement and migrant work

As of 2019, the preferred destinations of OFWs were Saudi Arabia (22.4%), the United Arab Emirates (13.2%), Hong Kong (7.5%), Taiwan (6.7%), and Kuwait (6.2%), with the largest proportion of workers coming from the regions in and around the capital, namely Calabarzon at 20.7%, Central Luzon at 13.3%, and Metro Manila at 9.7% (PSA 2020). Observers have argued that the Philippines' labour export policy was originally intended only as a stopgap measure, and so the lack of in-country opportunities has been a form of displacement where citizens are forced to move elsewhere by 'push' factors such as persistent unemployment and underemployment, political instability, cyclical environmental disasters, or armed conflict (Asis 2017). However, unlike the decision to leave the Philippines for work, being displaced yet again from their jobs abroad and returning during the COVID-19 pandemic was not a voluntary choice.

The desire to provide more for the household has often been mentioned as a reason for choosing to work abroad, the higher wages contributing to the once-burgeoning middle class (Ducanes and Abella 2008). A study on 2007 and 2008 patterns of income and expenditure compared Filipino households with and without OFWs. Households with OFWs, compared to those without, sourced about PHP 28,000 (US$630) more of their income from remittances, while sourcing PHP8,700 (US$195) to PHP15,000 (US$335) less from domestic wages and salaries (Ducanes 2015). The study demonstrated that remittances from a household member working abroad more than made up for the effects of an OFW leaving a domestic job or another household member leaving a job to take over household responsibilities. The same study reported that households with OFWs had higher expenditures in education and in health. Lastly, the study estimated that households able to send a member overseas had odds of climbing out of poverty two to three times greater than similar households who could not.

Precarity has remained an issue. Using 2015 data, Albert, Santos, and Vizmanos (2018) found that 19% of OFWs belonged to the lower-income cluster (i.e. between the poverty line and twice the poverty line) while 37% belonged to the lower-middle-income cluster (i.e. between two and four times the poverty line). Even OFWs categorised as middle class or lower-middle class have been economically vulnerable as many of these families are single-income households who might slide back to poverty if the breadwinner dies or becomes unemployed (Bird 2009). Even prior to the pandemic, remittances had usually been spent on basic needs, education, and healthcare. Several surveys run by the Central Bank of the Philippines showed that 97% of OFW families depended on remittances for food and basic household needs; only 38% were able to put away savings, while a paltry 6% were able to funnel earnings into investments (BSP 2019).

With future employment uncertain, more than half of households with OFWs faced the risk of sliding into poverty. Deployment figures in 2020 decreased to around 1.4 million from around two million in 2019. The sudden shift from hypermobility to pandemic immobility had a disproportionate impact on specific sectors. Managers and technical professionals (who might have been able to redeploy easier as companies pivoted to digital work platforms) comprised a smaller share of the migrant worker population. At least 39.6% of the total number of OFWs in 2019 held elementary occupations requiring manual labour, of whom 88.3% were women. The next largest cohort of OFWs, those employed in the global service and sales industries (18%), were equally affected by layoffs (PSA 2020).

In the absence of a systematic review of pandemic impacts on migrant workers, anecdotal and partial reports indicated that permanent and temporary job losses affected OFW household allocations for food and education. Data from the Department of Education showed that only 27% of private school students who enrolled in 2019 returned for the 2020–2021 school year (Ramos 2020) – indicating that families were forced to cut a costly investment in economic mobility despite the mixed quality of the Philippine public school system.

The economic slump offered limited options to returning OFWs that sought alternative sources of income in the Philippines. In the domestic labour market, the number of employed persons decreased to around 40 million in 2020 from around 42 million in 2019 (PSA 2020). Nevertheless, the challenges faced by those forced home paled in comparison to the difficulties of those who had lost their jobs but had not been able to repatriate. By the second half of 2020, labour secretary Silvestre Bello III announced that an estimated 80,000 OFWs were stranded abroad (Terrazola 2020). Reports that circulated on social media showed images of displaced workers forced to sell blood to secure money for food (Casilao 2020), photos of organ donation scars, and even suicides among stranded cruise ship workers, whose former places of work were moored, immobile, in harbours around the world.

By the end of 2020, at least six cruise ship suicides had been Filipino (Carr 2020).

Repatriated OFWs and lacklustre public sector response

Although the Philippines' Department of Foreign Affairs and Department of Labor and Employment had existing capacity to facilitate repatriation and assistance in host countries, the COVID-19 experience exposed the limits of existing government mechanisms. Previous economic shocks that resulted in job loss and mass repatriation of OFWs – such as the Gulf War in the 1990s or recent events in Libya, Syria, and Lebanon – were contained and had minimal impact on domestic affairs. With COVID-19, however, repatriation requirements no longer ended once OFWs were brought back to the country. It extended until OFWs were able to get back to their home provinces amid lockdowns and multiple quarantine arrangements. Asis (2020) has noted that, unlike previous repatriations, COVID-19 needed not only a 'whole-of-government approach, but a whole-of-nation approach, which hinges on joint efforts between government and nongovernment entities'. Without this interlocking and collaborative approach, haphazard policies affecting migrant workers that were not fit for purpose unnecessarily extended the discomfort of an unemployed cohort in cycles of transit and forced immobility, facing risks greater than other citizens who had the option to stay indoors.

The suffering was marked by stretches of movement and immobility: at sea or in their previous host countries, upon arrival in Manila, and yet another two-week quarantine upon arrival in their communities of origin. The final leg from Manila to their home provinces was facilitated through the now-suspended Balik Probinsya and Hatid Probinsya programmes (return and bringing back to the provinces), which rendered close to 593,000 individuals, including OFWs, stranded on Metro Manila's streets, under its overpasses, and in its sports arenas for weeks or even months while waiting to be brought home (CNN Philippines 2020a; NDRRMC 2021). The lack of coordination between the national government and the receiving communities meant that impoverished provinces and municipalities were forced to set up rudimentary systems for testing, quarantine, and basic financial assistance for those displaced. One consequence included stranded individuals from the provinces of Sulu, Basilan, and Tawi-Tawi in the southernmost region of the Philippines being dropped off by a government vessel at the wrong port, Cagayan De Oro, nearly 500 km away from the intended destination (Maulana 2020).

Upon reaching their hometowns, repatriates had to contend with the dual stigma of losing their jobs and disinformation regarding COVID-19 transmission. Reports told the tale of returning OFWs experiencing discrimination or animosity from neighbours due to misconceptions that they were potential vectors of the disease (Heinrich Böll Stiftung 2020). This prompted a flurry of local orders and a congressional bill criminalising discrimination against frontline workers, confirmed or suspected cases, and returning OFWs (Cepeda 2020). A widely shared photo showed a tarpaulin congratulating a repatriate for testing negative for COVID-19 – a family's public announcement for all the neighbours to see (Laureta-Chu 2020).

Initial COVID-19 repatriation programmes offered by the Overseas Workers' Welfare Agency were limited to its regular menu of capacity-building activities, job placements, livelihood packages, and individual loans, for which about US$14 million (PHP 700 million) had been allocated before the pandemic (DBM 2020; OWWA 2020). When demand for emergency repatriation soared, the government disbursed USD$103.6 million (PHP 5 billion) to almost 500,000 OFWs to cover quarantine and transportation expenses as well as some cash aid. In March 2021, OWWA sought an additional US$202 million (PHP 9 billion) since they claimed that their agency budget was about to run out that year (*Business Mirror* 2021). The Philippine government also promised to support unemployed OFWs by matching them with 60,000 jobs in special economic zones (Philippine Economic Zone Authority 2020) and in the construction sector through the infrastructure-led growth strategy of the Duterte administration called 'Build, Build, Build' (CNN Philippines 2020b). However, no detailed plans related to these initiatives had been released by the first half of 2021.

Other policy choices met criticism from repatriates and the public alike. A knee-jerk decision to institute a deployment ban for healthcare workers in April 2020 was lifted eight months later. In May 2020, President Duterte announced the suspension of a policy that required OFWs to pay higher state health insurance premiums. This announcement came on the heels of protests from OFWs who had lost their jobs and could no longer act as 'cash cows', as well as a corruption controversy involving the embattled state health insurer, PhilHealth (Lopez

2020). By early 2021, reports surfaced regarding a thriving black market for vaccines, first for presidential guards, then for elites, and potentially for workers desperate for 'vaccine passports' so they could return to work abroad (Cabato 2021)

In the face of continued restrictions and incoherent, oft-changing policies, the onus to support returning workers fell on provincial and city governments, together with the private sector, to kickstart economic activity in their respective localities. However, the magnitude of the local and international repatriation and reintegration problem coupled with staggering unemployment required resources for social services and livelihood support that not all local governments possessed. In the last quarter of 2020, the Philippines was ravaged by eight different typhoons barely weeks apart, depleting strained local disaster funds used for both pandemic and typhoon response (Torres 2020). Some affluent provinces and cities were able to offer jobs by purchasing agricultural produce and personal protective equipment (PPE) from local businesses, entering into service contracts with transportation providers, and enabling e-commerce platforms to thrive in their areas.

In the absence of publicly funded safety nets, the burden of survival was carried by neighbours, relatives, and fellow Filipinos through various mutual aid arrangements. The Catholic Church and various faith-based groups launched their own OFW-focused programmes, acknowledging the dual economic and social costs to affected families. Local microfinance institutions reported that OFWs resorted to loans to pay for basic necessities and secure start-up capital. Along with other displaced workers, repatriates were forced to start small online businesses, usually food-based, and find forms of alternative livelihood such as motorcycle delivery. The ventures that emerged were small but quickly absorbed OFWs and other affected local workers.

Conclusions: quo vadis?

Ultimately, the pandemic exposed the Philippines' vulnerability as an unequal society kept afloat by remittances while underinvesting in human capital and community infrastructure. The Migrant Workers and Overseas Filipinos Act of 1995 states that the government 'does not promote overseas employment as a means to sustain economic growth and achieve national development'. However, exporting labour will remain the reality until long-standing recommendations to shift the structure of the Philippine economy away from remittances are implemented

– an unlikely scenario with current calls from the Duterte administration to create a Department of OFWs.

Global evidence has pointed to how post-COVID economic recovery hinges on how well governments are able to address the health crisis. Based on the challenges faced by repatriated OFWs, the existing public sector response can be described as fragmented at best. At worst, it has displayed a vacuum in leadership that has resulted in poor prioritisation and haphazard execution of support programmes (Quijano, Fernandez, and Pangilinan 2020). Inconsistent messaging, coupled with harsh lockdown–release cycles and different punishments for elite rulebreakers and regular citizens, translated into dismal public health communication despite the Philippine government's sizeable investment in state broadcasting and online platforms – including so-called 'troll armies', which have instead been used to stifle dissent (Billing 2020).

Nevertheless, the pandemic forced local governments and private actors to try to creatively piece together long-overdue reforms to create and sustain local jobs as well as support families battling multiple rounds of economic displacement. Early evidence has pointed to the promise of digital and neighbourhood-level economic and food security initiatives as a survival measure, although many have been simply biding their time until borders open again. But, even as target countries in the global North reopened, redeployment proved more difficult thanks to suspended flights and stricter, costlier requirements because domestic efforts to battle the pandemic were unsuccessful. Thus, the romanticised rhetoric of OFWs as long-suffering heroes is no longer tenable – this time, it is the old saviours that need saving.

Notes

1. Alternative terms include overseas contract workers (OCWs) and overseas Filipinos (OFs), although the latter also captures Filipinos who have migrated and have since taken foreign citizenship.

2. A Filipina nurse was the first to administer the coronavirus vaccine jab in the UK (Baker 2020; Batalova 2020), and nearly a third of nurses who died of COVID-19 in the US during the first year of the pandemic were Filipino despite comprising only 4% of the country's nursing population (Shoichet 2020).

3. The Philippines is presently the world's largest source of seafarers. Prior to the pandemic, a third of all global cruise ships were staffed by Filipinos (Maritime Industry Authority 2020).

References

Albert, Jose Ramon G.; Santos, Angelo Gabrielle F.; and Vizmanos, Jana Flor V. (2018). *Profile and Determinants of the Middle-Income Class in the Philippines*. Philippines: Philippine Institute for Development Studies Discussion Paper Series No. 2018-20. https://perma.cc/M39M-2CZB [Last accessed 28 April 2021].

Asis, Maruja M.B. (2017). 'The Philippines: Beyond labor migration, toward development and (possibly) return'. *Migration Information Source*, 12 July. https://perma.cc/TJP6-PD3Z [Last accessed 1 May 2021].

Asis, Maruja M.B. (2020). *Repatriating Filipino Migrant Workers in the Time of the Pandemic*. Philippines: IOM Migration Research Series No. 63. https://perma.cc/K3N2-XLK6 [Last accessed 1 May 2021].

Baker, Carl. (2020). *NHS Staff from Overseas: Statistics*, 4 June. https://perma.cc/VA46-EHPF [Last accessed 26 April 2021].

BSP (Bangko Sentral ng Pilipinas). (2019). *Consumer Expectations Survey: Fourth Quarter 2019*. https://perma.cc/AA8K-WK5S [Last accessed 1 May 2021].

BSP. (2020). *Overseas Filipinos Remittances*. https://perma.cc/GJ5W-WG3H [Last accessed 11 January 2021].

Batalova, Jeanne. (2021). 'Immigrant health-care workers in the United States'. *Migration Information Source*, 14 May. https://perma.cc/3B4S-XZTJ [Last accessed 26 April 2021].

Billing, Lynzy. (2020). 'Duterte's troll armies drown out COVID-19 dissent in the Philippines'. *Rappler*, 22 July. https://perma.cc/MGG6-BGER [Last accessed 16 January 2021].

Bird, Kelly. (2009). 'Philippines: Poverty, employment, and remittances – some stylized facts', in BSP International Research Conference on Remittances, Mandaluyong City, 30–31 March 2009, no. 11. https://perma.cc/GQ7R-EVTU [Last accessed 28 August 2020].

Business Mirror. (2021). 'OWWA seeks P9.2-billion funds as OFW hosting cost rises'. 11 March. https://perma.cc/XBM6-HJBX [Last accessed 26 April 2021].

Cabato, Regine. (2021). 'A black market for illegal coronavirus vaccines is thriving in the Philippines'. *Washington Post*, 16 July. https://perma.cc/525G-WVMA [Last accessed 16 January 2021].

Carr, Austin. (2020). 'The cruise ship suicides'. *Bloomberg Businessweek*, 30 December. https://perma.cc/7FWR-DPY3 [Last accessed 16 January 2021].

Casilao, Joahna Lei. (2020). 'Stranded OFWs in Saudi forced to sell their blood to survive'. *GMA News*, 24 June. https://perma.cc/S8P3-5DSK [Last accessed 6 August 2020].

CSIS (Center for Strategic International Studies). (2021). *Southeast Asia Covid-19 Tracker*. https://perma.cc/F3NA-6LEX [Last accessed 26 April 2021].

Cepeda, Mara. (2020). 'House OKs bill penalizing discrimination vs COVID-19 frontliners, patients, repatriates'. *Rappler*, 2 June. https://perma.cc/MW68-2SYF [Last accessed 1 May 2021].

CNN Philippines. (2020a). 'PH temporarily bans deployment of health workers abroad amid COVID-19 outbreak'. 26 May. https://perma.cc/3LZU-P6Z4 [Last accessed 31 August 2020].

CNN Philippines. (2020b). 'Gov't pledges construction jobs to thousands of returning OFWs'. 26 May. https://perma.cc/B37N-GSFV [Last accessed 31 August 2020].

CNN Philippines. (2021). 'LOOK: Lack of physical distancing among locally stranded individuals at crowded Rizal Memorial'. 25 July. https://perma.cc/BYE4-R27D [Last accessed 2 May 2021].

Dass, Jojo. (2021). 'OFWs in a bind with condo payments due to pandemic'. *Rappler*, 8 August. https://perma.cc/HS4B-SKF4 [Last accessed 2 May 2021].

DBM (Department of Budget Management). (2020). General Appropriations Act Volume 1. https://perma.cc/V3GA-YEZS [Last accessed 22 August 2020].

DFA (Department of Foreign Affairs – OFW Help). (2021). *DFA Repatriates 327,511 Overseas Filipinos in 2020*. Facebook, 3 January. https://perma.cc/SE53-DLA9 [Last accessed 14 January 2021].

Ducanes, Geoffrey. (2015). 'The welfare impact of overseas migration on Philippine households: Analysis using panel data'. *Asian and Pacific Migration Journal*, vol. 24, no. 1, pp. 79–106. https://doi.org/10.1177/0117196814565166

Ducanes, Geoffey, and Abella, Manolo. (2008). 'Overseas Filipino workers and their impact on household employment decisions'. *ILO Working Papers No. 5*, 25 March. https://perma.cc/MX6T-7QWJ [Last accessed January 2021].

Heinrich Böll Stiftung. (2020). 'Filipino seafarers find their future – and lives – adrift', 26 June 2020. https://perma.cc/D62H-Z4AZ [Last accessed January 2021].

Laureta-Chu, Krizette. (2020). 'LOOK: Returning OFW's family puts up congratulatory tarpaulin of negative COVID-19 test to avoid discrimination'.

Manila Bulletin, 16 July. https://perma.cc/FFD2-UV7Q [Last accessed 1 May 2021].

Lopez, Melissa Luz. (2020). 'Duterte suspends higher PhilHealth premiums for OFWs, makes payments voluntary – Roque'. CNN Philippines, 4 May. https://perma.cc/5G4R-CSNF [Last accessed 1 May 2021].

Maulana, Nash. (2020). 'LSIs mistakenly ferried to CDO'. *Manila Standard*, 9 July. https://perma.cc/RN9X-3VAX [Last accessed 22 August 2020].

NDRRMC (National Disaster Risk Reduction and Management Council). (2021). *National Task Force Coronavirus Disease 2019 Situational Report No. 390.* https://perma.cc/FV8F-ZHGC [Last accessed 26 April 2021].

Onishi, Norimitsu. (2010). 'Toiling far from home for Philippine dreams'. *New York Times*, 18 September. https://perma.cc/N23D-6TBX [Last accessed 2 May 2021].

Orbeta Jr., Aniceto; and Abrigo, Michael. (2020). 'Philippine international labor migration in the past 30 years: Trends and prospects'. Philippines: Philippine Institute for Development Studies Discussion Paper Series No. 2009-33. https://perma.cc/HHN5-EW8W [Last accessed 22 August 2020].

OWWA (Overseas Workers Welfare Administration). (2020). *Reintegration.* https://perma.cc/XH24-Y4GK [Last accessed 2 May 2021].

Patino, Ferdinand. (2020). 'DOLE receives over 600k applications for displaced OFWs' cash aid'. *Philippine News Agency*, 9 November. https://perma.cc/47B3-3L4Y [Last accessed 16 January 2021].

Philippine Economic Zone Authority. (2020). *PEZA to Launch DOLLAR Program's Job Fair for Repatriated OFWs, Those Laid Off Workers Due to Pandemic*, 8 July. https://perma.cc/TZ74-D558 [Last accessed 22 August 2020].

PNA (Philippine News Agency). (2021). 'More than 500K pandemic-hit OFWs sent home'. https://perma.cc/252M-39R4 [Last accessed 26 April 2021].

PSA (Philippine Statistics Authority). (2020a). *2019 Survey of Overseas Filipinos*, 4 June 2020. https://perma.cc/URE6-FAAJ [Last accessed 31 August 2020].

PSA. (2020b). *Employment Situation in October 2020*, 3 December. https://perma.cc/4DZ5-XXQC [Last accessed 1 May 2021].

PSA. (2021). *2020 Annual Preliminary Estimates of Labor Force Survey (LFS).* https://perma.cc/J5RR-7EPB [Last accessed 28 April 2021].

Quijano, Nastassja; Fernandez, Maria Carmen; and Pangilinan, Maria Karla Abigail. (2020). 'Misplaced priorities, unnecessary effects: Collective suffering and survival in pandemic Philippines'. *Asia Pacific Journal*, vol. 18, no. 15, pp. 6. https://perma.cc/T7BK-LLKJ [Last accessed 1 May 2021].

Ramos, Christia Marie. (2020). 'Only 27% have enrolled in private schools, says DepEd'. *Inquirer. net*, 21 July. https://perma.cc/NC5M-Z2UY [Accessed 22 August 2020].

San Juan, Epifanio. (2009). 'Overseas Filipino workers: The making of an Asian-Pacific diaspora'. *The Global South*, vol. 3, no. 2, pp. 99–129. https://doi.org/10.2979/gso.2009.3.2.99

Shoichet, Catherine. (2020). 'COVID-19 is taking a devastating toll on Filipino American nurses'. CNN, 24 November. https://perma.cc/4EJJ-7GXT [Last accessed 16 January 2021].

Social Weather Stations. (2020). *SWD July 3–6, 2020 National Mobile Phone Survey – Report No. 16: Adult Joblessness Rises to Record-High 45.5%*, 16 August. https://perma.cc/NT99-BHME [Last accessed 22 August 2020].

Terrazola, Vanne Elaine. (2020). 'Nearly half a million OFWs displaced, infected by COVID-19 – DOLE'. *Manila Bulletin*, 1 October. https://perma.cc/K5RK-KPSN [Last accessed 16 January 2021].

Torres, Estrella. (2020). 'Heavy cost of coronavirus response drains local governments' disaster budgets'. *Philippine Center for Investigative Journalism*, 3 September. https://perma.cc/L89X-Z6D6 [Last accessed 16 January 2021].

World Bank. (2020). *Migration and Remittances Data*, April 2020. https://perma.cc/KJ8X-PHL7 [Last accessed 30 April 2021].

14. Exposing the transnational precarity of Filipino workers, healthcare regimes, and nation states

Francesca Humi

Following the outbreak of COVID-19, academics and researchers across social science fields highlighted the ramifications of the pandemic for the movement of people across borders, ranging from the implications of the pandemic on global remittance flows to the geographies on grief, intimacy, and loss (Abel and Gietel-Basten 2020; Maddrell 2020). These pieces of preliminary research highlighted the inherent international and globalised state of the world in the 21st century. The experience of one group, however, emerged as an ideal subject of study and poignant symbol of the impact of the pandemic on the most vulnerable, those at the frontlines, and those whose existence has been inherently diasporic and fragmented – in short, those whose lives intersected with all things most impacted by the COVID-19 health, social, and economic crises. That is, the globalised Filipino healthcare community.

This chapter examines the precarity of Filipino healthcare workers caught in between nation states' duties of care by focusing on those in the Philippines and the UK and by drawing on studies of Filipino labour migration and COVID-era commentary on Filipino healthcare workers in the two countries. This study posits that the Filipino experience is indicative of how migrant labour is controlled and exploited under globalised capitalism and by modern nation states in both the pre- and post-COVID worlds,[1] and calls for voices from the community to be given due consideration and audience.

The global Filipino nation

In 2013, over 10 million Filipinos lived abroad, about 10% of the country's total population (Commission on Filipinos Overseas 2013)

How to cite this book chapter:
Humi, Francesca. 2022. 'Exposing the transnational precarity of Filipino workers, healthcare regimes, and nation states'. In: Shin, Hyun Bang; Mckenzie, Murray; and Oh, Do Young (eds) *COVID-19 in Southeast Asia: Insights for a post-pandemic world*. London: LSE Press, pp. 162–171. DOI: https://doi.org/10.31389/lsepress.cov.n License: CC BY 4.0.

without accounting for second-, third-, or fourth-generation Filipinos around the globe. Migration flows from the Philippines have been shaped by experiences of colonialism and economic intervention from international organisations (Parreñas 2001, p.10). But the migration pattern of medical professionals has been particularly steeped in colonial legacies. American colonial rule in the Philippines from 1898 to 1946 established nursing as a medical profession through training programmes and teaching hospitals (Choy 2003, p.19). This was part of the US's mission of 'benevolent assimilation', which positioned health and education as a means to achieve self-rule (Choy 2003, pp.20–21). It was also specifically designed to bring Filipino nurses to the US away from the Philippines (Choy 2003, p.5). In 2020, about 20,000 Filipinos worked for the UK's National Health Service (NHS), the largest group after British and Indian workers (Baker 2020). Although this presence originated in the US colonial period, the 1990s saw the first major wave of Filipino nurses and other high-skilled workers migrating abroad, including to the UK, facilitated by Philippine government bodies and programmes (Choy 2003, p.1).

The Filipino experience can be taken as representative of a fragile, globalised system relying on the mobile and docile labour of migrants for their work both in their destination country and 'back home', where they provide remittances as well as stability for the Philippines' 'export-based economy' (Parreñas 2001, p.11). Though the Filipino nation has become disconnected due to physical boundaries and political borders – and, more recently, a global pandemic – it is connected through an imagined global community, to borrow Benedict Anderson's (1983) concept of the nation, and through shared occupations and similar socio-economic status (Parreñas, 2001, p.12). This is an archipelagic experience – by virtue of its geography and diaspora – shifting the focus from the national to a more dispersed and fragmented one, still connected through an imagined bond (David 2018, p.335).

The impact of COVID-19 on this global Filipino nation has been documented by journalists, commentators, and academics alike. Galam (2020) has emphasised the role of community care among Filipino migrants in the UK, which stepped in where governments took a step back. Many have lauded the heroism demonstrated by Filipino healthcare workers and mourned the devastating toll the pandemic had on the community because of this and of broader structural issues from defunding of public health services to immigration regimes and legacies of racism and colonialism (Chikoko 2020; Day 2021).[2] For many in the community, it felt like Filipino healthcare workers were receiving long-awaited recognition (Isidro 2020), but the complex and at times tragic realities for Filipino healthcare workers have warranted further exploration.

The failure of two 'hero' narratives

While the global economy's exploitation of and dependency on Filipino labour have earned Filipino migrants the titles of 'servants of globalisation' (Parreñas 2001) and 'manufactur[ed] heroes' (Guevarra 2009) forming an 'empire of care' (Choy 2003), the crises caused by COVID-19 have cast new light on this phenomenon. Shortly after the pandemic outbreak, the Philippine government halted the deployment of healthcare workers abroad even if they had signed contracts to return to work abroad, while asking them to 'volunteer' at home for 500 Philippine pesos (about US$10) a day (Magsambol 2020). The ban was partially lifted in April 2020 (Calonzo 2020), but in 2021 the Philippine government offered healthcare workers to Germany and the UK in exchange for vaccines (Morales 2021). The government's decisions to call on 'healthcare warriors' (Magsambol 2020) to save the country from public health disaster and then offer them as a bartering tool for vaccines demonstrated the pressure exerted by the global economy and its reliance on workers' willingness to sacrifice themselves for the benefit of society.

In the UK, as early as May 2020, Filipinos were the single largest nationality to die from coronavirus among NHS staff. They accounted for 22% of COVID-19 deaths among nurses, despite Filipino nurses comprising only 3.8% of the nursing workforce (Kearney et al. 2020). By April 2021, at least 71 Filipino health and social care workers had died after contracting COVID-19, according to the data collected by the Kanlungan Filipino Consortium (hereafter Kanlungan) – a charity working to support the Filipino migrant community in the UK (Day 2021).

Filipino healthcare workers were placed at the intersection of two separate, but overlapping, hero narratives. Healthcare workers in the UK and around the globe were hailed as heroes and applauded as model citizens during the pandemic (Mohammed et al. 2021, p.4). In the Philippines, the push to work abroad was bolstered by popular narratives of the overseas Filipino worker (OFW) as a 'modern-day hero' who endures tremendous hardship to form the backbone of the Philippines' economy (Almendral 2018; Rocamora 2018). Their remittances, which contributed about 10% of the country's gross domestic product in 2019 (World Bank 2019), represented education and material stability for people at home. As a Facebook tribute to Dondee, a Filipino NHS nurse who died from COVID-19 in April 2020, pointed out, '[h]e was the breadwinner of his family back home and helping 3 of his nieces/nephews to college' (Fernandez 2020).

Workers like Dondee may have been attributed the status of hero but

Figure 14.1. A Filipino woman with groceries delivered by Kanlungan volunteers in London, April 2020

Source: Courtesy of Kanlungan.

it did not provide him or his family with a changed material reality. Such attribution was, in fact, a tactic to deflect responsibility from politicians (Mohammed et al. 2021, p.8). Being an NHS hero receiving doorstep

Figure 14.2. Posters appealing for donations and volunteers for Kanlungan's COVID-19 community outreach project in a Filipino grocery store window in London, April 2020

Source: Courtesy of Kanlungan.

claps[3] from the British public and the prime minister did not translate into adequate pay rises, sufficient personal protective equipment, or secure immigration status for staff (Campbell 2021; UK Government and Parliament Petitions 2020; UK Government and Parliament Petitions 2021), nor did it translate into better protection from the Philippine government, as its offer to exchange workers for vaccines revealed (Morales 2021). Community groups and charities, such as Kanlungan, responded to the health and economic impact of the crisis on communities who were either not able to access or not eligible for COVID-19 government support owing to their immigration status[4] by filling in these gaps in welfare provision with emergency grocery delivery, mental health support, and the dissemination of COVID-19 guidelines in community languages (Galam 2020, pp.452–453; Kanlungan Filipino Consortium 2021).

The situation faced by Filipino health and social care workers exposed the failure and emptiness of these two narratives. Celebrating Filipino healthcare workers for their sacrifices and contributions, such as – ironically – administering the first COVID-19 vaccine in the UK (Chikoko 2020), may have made them heroes, but this public discourse did not translate into material and economic security. For Filipinos 'at home', the crisis demonstrated the need to fundamentally question the hero narrative surrounding OFWs. The hardship faced by OFWs must be recognised and appreciated, but a new narrative must be forged, one of empowered immigration through informed decision-making for migrants about their work and immigration, systematic access to adequate support services and knowledge about labour rights, and sustained agency. As Cielito Caneja (2020, p.2), a Filipino nurse in London, stated: 'Please do not call me a hero. … I am a nurse delivering my oath and this is what we do, day in and day out. Long before the pandemic.'

Calls for change amid uncertain post-COVID futures

The tragedy of the Filipino is transnational. Whether they were abroad – dying from caring for the sick – or in the Philippines – experiencing loss of income, being killed in the streets for breaking lockdown rules, or being 'red-tagged' as communists (Talabong 2020; *UN News* 2021) – for many Filipinos, the present has become dire and the future deeply uncertain.

The pandemic required studies of the Filipino global nation and other diasporas to be re-evaluated. Much like the climate emergency, the long-term disruptive impact of the pandemic will lead to a reassessment of global migration, healthcare and welfare regimes, and the further fragmentation of imagined global communities. The crises generated by the pandemic proved again the precarious position of both nation states and migrant workers caused by global capitalism. Nation states faced a near collapse of healthcare provision without the constant supply of migrant workers, while migrant workers were caught in between nation states, with neither able to properly care for them (Galam 2020, p.442; Ghosh 2020, p.92). On a micro scale, politicians, academics, and civil society at large must ask themselves, as Cielito, the Filipino nurse in London, asked, 'who cares for the carers?' (Caneja 2020, p.3).

Finally, the pandemic brought attention to issues that migrants' rights activists and community members had been campaigning on for years (Galam 2020, p.442). It has been bittersweet to consider that public and academic interest in these issues expanded only after such tragedy had occurred. Much of the COVID-19 era's activism was trauma-responsive: the international Black Lives Matter and Stop Asian Hate movements, conversations in the UK about violence against women in the wake of Sarah Everard's murder, and reckonings with systemic racism and inequalities in public health as non-White people continued to bear the brunt of the pandemic. There is an urgent need to listen to community members and resource their leadership in academic research and political decision-making, as opposed to making them the subject to/of research and relying on trauma to mobilise and beg for political capital. COVID-19 revealed injustices in the immigration, healthcare, education, and many other public systems. Let us not wait until the next global crisis to take these experiences seriously.

Notes

1. A literal 'post-COVID' world may never occur. Much like the 'post' in postcolonialism is used to emphasise the impact of colonialism and empire on the contemporary moment, my use of 'post' in this chapter is an acknowledgement that any future occurring after the outbreak in late 2019–early 2020 will be shaped by the pandemic and the global response to it.

2. A more general repertory of news coverage relating to healthcare workers as heroes during the pandemic can be found in Mohammed et al. (2021).

3. During the first lockdown, people across the UK, including Prime Minister Boris Johnson and other senior politicians, took part in weekly claps on their doorsteps to show appreciation and support for health and social care workers.

4. In the UK, under what is known as the 'hostile environment' policy, migrants have no recourse to public funds, unless they have been granted indefinite leave to remain.

Acknowledgements

I am indebted to my Kanlungan colleagues and the Filipino community who inform, guide, and support me in my work to highlight the experiences of our *kababayan*. Thank you.

References

Abel, Guy J.; and Gietel-Basten, Stuart. (2020). 'International remittance flows and the economic and social consequences of COVID-19'. *Environment and Planning A: Economy and Space*, vol. 52, no. 8, pp. 1480–1482. https://doi.org/10.1177/0308518X20931111

Almendral, Aurora. (2018). 'Why 10 million Filipinos endure hardship abroad as overseas workers'. *National Geographic*, December. https://perma.cc/8P3M-JQXE [Last accessed 14 April 2021].

Anderson, Benedict. (1983). *Imagined Communities: Reflections on the Origin and Spread of Nationalism*. UK: Verso.

Baker, Carl. (2020). *NHS Staff from Overseas: Statistics*. UK: House of Commons Library. https://perma.cc/4H8Y-KWQU [Last accessed 13 April 2021].

Calonzo, Andreo. (2020). 'Philippines relaxes ban on nurses leaving for jobs overseas'. *Bloomberg*, 14 April. https://perma.cc/HNF4-7S3C [Last accessed 15 April 2021].

Campbell, Denis. (2021). 'NHS staff should get 5% payrise next year, says thinktank'. *The Guardian*, 21 March. https://perma.cc/7EMZ-W8B5 [Last accessed 14 April 2021].

Caneja, Cielito. (2020). 'The Coronavirus Collective: Who cares for the carers?' *Sushruta Journal of Health Policy and Opinion*, vol. 13, no. 3, pp. 1–3. https://doi.org/10.38192/13.3.11

Commission on Filipinos Overseas. (2013). *Stock Estimates of Overseas Filipinos as of Dec. 2013*. https://perma.cc/LE7Y-8VE5 [Last accessed 15 April 2021].

Chikoko, Cryton. (2020). 'How Britain could truly honour its Filipino frontline workers'. *Each Other*, 18 December. https://perma.cc/Y28C-ZUXQ [Last accessed 15 April 2021].

Choy, Catherine C. (2003). *Empire of Care: Nursing and Migration in Filipino American History*. USA: Duke University Press.

David, Emmanuel. (2018). 'Transgender archipelagos'. *Transgender Studies Quarterly*, vol. 5, no. 3, pp. 332–354. http://dx.doi.org/10.1215/23289252 -6900724

Day, Aasma. (2021). 'Why so many Filipino health workers are dying of Covid-19'. *Huffington Post*, 14 April. https://perma.cc/H8EX-Y2AM [Last accessed 18 April 2021]

Fernandez, Alejandro. (2020). *I still can't believe it* 😢😭 *So sad to get a phone call early this morning from our common friend. I* […]. Facebook, 8 April. https://perma.cc/FWN4-7NJ6 [Last accessed 18 April 2021].

Galam, Roderick. (2020). 'Care and solidarity in the time of Covid-19: The pandemic experiences of Filipinos in the UK'. *Philippine Studies: Historical and Ethnographic Viewpoints*, vol. 68, no. 3–4, pp. 441–464. https://doi.org /10.1353/phs.2020.0028

Ghosh, Ambar K.; and Chaudhury, Anasua B.R. (2020). 'Migrant workers and the ethics of care during a pandemic', in Ranabir Samaddar (ed.) *Borders of an Epidemic: Covid-19 and Migrant Workers*. India: Maharniban Calcutta Research Group, pp. 91–97.

Guevarra, Anna R. (2009). *Marketing Dreams, Manufacturing Heroes: The Transnational Labor Brokering of Filipino Workers*. USA: Rutgers University Press.

Isidro, Charissa. (2020). 'They've filled essential health-care roles for decades. Now, the coronavirus is killing them'. *The Daily Beast*, 14 November [online]. https://perma.cc/B4GL-VYQ3 [Last accessed 18 April 2021].

Kanlungan Filipino Consortium. (2021). COVID19 Filipino Response. https:// perma.cc/SP7C-2REW [Last accessed 14 April 2021].

Kearney, Lesa; Lennane, Simon; Woodmand, Ella; Kursumovic, Emira; and Cook, Tim. (2020). 'At least 23 nationalities among NHS staff killed by covid'. *HSJ*, 19 May. https://perma.cc/PN8H-KH22 [Last accessed 18 April 2021].

Maddrell, Avril. (2020). 'Bereavement, grief, and consolation: Emotional-affective geographies of loss during COVID-19'. *Dialogues in Human Geography*, vol. 10, no. 2, pp. 107–111. https://doi.org/10.1177/2043820620934947

Magsambol, Bonz. (2020). 'DOH asks for volunteer health workers vs coronavirus, to be paid P500 a day'. *Rappler*, 27 March. https://perma.cc/A8N4 -C6SZ [Last accessed 10 June 2020].

Mohammed, Shan; Peter, Elizabeth; Killackey, Tieghan; and Maciver, Jane. (2021). 'The "nurse as hero" discourse in the COVID-19 pandemic: A post-structural discourse analysis'. *International Journal of Nursing Studies*, vol. 117, pp. 1–11. https://doi.org/10.1016/j.ijnurstu.2021.103887.

Morales, Neil J. (2021). 'Philippines offers nurses in exchange for vaccines from Britain, Germany'. *Reuters*, 21 February. https://perma.cc/N9BD -P6VX [Last accessed 14 April 2021].

Parreñas, Rhacel S. (2001). *Servants of Globalization: Women, Migration and Domestic Work*. USA: Stanford University Press.

Rocamora, Joyce Ann L. (2018). 'OFWs: Modern-day heroes still'. *Philippine News Agency*, 27 August. https://perma.cc/T5LZ-MTUL [Last accessed 11 April 2021].

Talabong, Rambo. (2020). 'QC officials maul, drag fish vendor for not wearing face mask'. *Rappler*, 28 April. https://perma.cc/EU2T-V7FF [Last accessed 14 April 2021].

UK Government and Parliament Petitions. (2020). *Give Non-British Citizens Who Are NHS Workers Automatic Citizenship*. https://perma.cc/9RVL-5PR3 [Last accessed 20 August 2020].

UK Government and Parliament Petitions. (2021). *Offer Indefinite Leave to Remain to All NHS and Social Care Workers*. https://perma.cc/6PX3-A95Z [Last accessed 14 April 2021].

UN News. (2021). *Philippines: UN Rights Office Appalled over Simultaneous Killings of 'Red-Tagged' Activists*. 3 March. https://perma.cc/N828-9H98 [Last accessed 18 April 2021].

World Bank. (2019). *Personal Remittances, Received (% of GDP) – Philippines, 2019*. https://perma.cc/SP4R-J466 [Last accessed 20 August 2020].

15. The economic case against the marginalisation of migrant workers in Malaysia

Theng Theng Tan and Jarud Romadan Khalidi

The plight of migrant workers in many countries has been in the spotlight since the beginning of the global COVID-19 outbreak. Owing to their low-income, precarious jobs and poor living standards, migrant workers became one of the most vulnerable populations amid the pandemic.

Migrant workers in Malaysia were no exception. In 2020, there were at least two million migrant workers, mostly from Indonesia and Bangladesh, making up 14% of Malaysia's total employed persons (DOSM 2021; MOHA 2020). Many were known to live in overcrowded accommodation in unsanitary conditions, either provided by unscrupulous employers or sourced by workers themselves, making it impossible to maintain good hygiene and practise physical distancing during the pandemic. Moreover, the Malaysian Trades Union Congress also reported violations of migrant workers' rights by their employers during the pandemic. This included unfair terminations, unpaid wages, workers being required to continue working in non-essential jobs, and workers' uncertainty about their employment status due to limited contact with employers (ILO 2020). Those who lost their jobs would have also lost their work passes, making them undocumented and at risk of being arrested.

Unfortunately, the Malaysian government did little to address the vulnerabilities faced by these workers. Although the government gazetted the Workers' Minimum Standard of Housing and Amenities Bills, which require all employers to provide standard accommodation to their migrant workers, this took place only in August 2020, and most employers were unable to comply with the regulation immediately, especially in a difficult economic climate (*Straits Times* 2020c). Overall, fewer than 10% of documented migrant workers lived in regulation-compliant housing by December 2020 (Bernama 2020).

How to cite this book chapter:
Tan, Theng Theng; and Khalidi, Jarud Romadan. 2022. 'The economic case against the marginalisation of migrant workers in Malaysia'. In: Shin, Hyun Bang; Mckenzie, Murray; and Oh, Do Young (eds) *COVID-19 in Southeast Asia: Insights for a post-pandemic world*. London: LSE Press, pp. 172–182. DOI: https://doi.org/10.31389/lsepress.cov.o License: CC BY 4.0.

Furthermore, when major immigration raids took place in May 2020 to detain undocumented workers, concerns were raised that more migrant workers would have been scared into hiding, making testing and treatment, as well as tracing the spread of coronavirus, even more challenging (*Straits Times* 2020b). Given migrant workers' precarious living conditions, the government's actions did little to contain migrant workers' exposure to coronavirus. It is no surprise that, by the end of 2020, migrants accounted for more than 40% of all confirmed COVID-19 cases in Malaysia, despite constituting only 10% of the country's population (MOH 2020; authors' calculation).

On the job front, government assistance was lacking as well. One of the most prominent initiatives was a 25% cut for the migrant worker levy due between April and December 2020 to alleviate the financial burden on hard-hit small- and medium-sized enterprises. Unfortunately, this was likely not helpful as the levy cut amounted to discounts of only 103–463 Malaysian ringgit, roughly US$25–115, per worker (Tan, Nazihah, and Jarud 2020). Even after restrictions on movement were gradually lifted, the government repeatedly urged employers to prioritise locals in their hiring practices as part of measures to alleviate soaring unemployment among Malaysians. This policy was also justified as an effort to wean Malaysia off its reliance on low-wage migrant workers and encourage automation in the long run (Minderjeet 2020).

In a global public health and economic crisis, it is only humane to treat everyone with care and dignity, regardless of nationality or social class. Migrant workers deserve protection by the simple virtue that they are human, and basic protection should be part of their human rights. Unfortunately, human rights arguments often fall on deaf ears, with many still calling for governments to prioritise their citizens over migrants.

However, even from a pure economic perspective, an ideology that puts the welfare of citizens first must give way to inclusive protection measures. Although some may argue that, given limited resources, governments have an obligation to prioritise their citizens over migrants, there are several strong economic arguments against the marginalisation of migrant workers.

Neglecting migrant workers hurts locals too

The pandemic laid bare the pervasiveness of economic externalities beyond what was previously thought. In the case of migrant workers in Malaysia, the economic consequences of neglecting their welfare manifested in at least two ways.

First, the failure to manage migrant workers' exposure to coronavirus strained the public healthcare system and led to the extension of movement restrictions. In November 2020, a cluster linked to the migrant workers at Top Glove Corp's congested dormitories became the largest COVID-19 cluster in Malaysia as of April 2021 (Malaysiakini 2021; *Straits Times* 2020a). After more than 3,000 workers tested positive within a month, coronavirus spread beyond the workers' circle to the community, forced the company to shut its factories, and caused the area to be placed under an extended period of lockdown (Hazlin 2020; Teh and Dhesegaan 2020). On a national scale, by early January 2021, the number of confirmed locally transmitted cases among non-citizens had risen drastically by more than 30,000. This contributed to the pressure that eventually brought the country's healthcare system to 'breaking point', forcing the government to lengthen movement restrictions within the country (Ahmad 2021). Clearly, any outbreak – whether involving poor migrant workers or rich Malaysians – would indiscriminately affect the larger population by straining the public healthcare

Figure 15.1. Migrant workers are important to Malaysia's economy

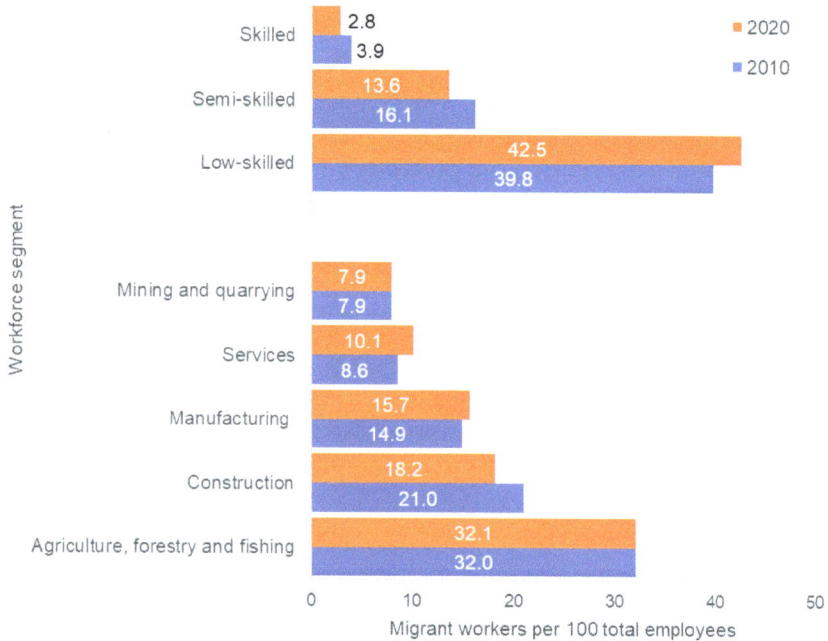

Source: DOSM (2011), DOSM (2015), DOSM (2021) and authors' calculation.
Note: Migrant workers made up a large proportion of workers in different sectors and among the low-skilled workers.

system and throwing more businesses into deeper waters as lockdown became inevitable.

Second, in terms of migrant workers' job security, inadequate support to protect workers' jobs also had a spillover effect on the survival of industries and businesses. Malaysia's economy had long been heavily reliant on the migrant workforce. In 2020, migrant workers made up more than 30% of the workforce in the agriculture sector, and just below 20% in both the construction and manufacturing sectors (Figure 15.1). Almost half of the low-skilled workers in Malaysia were of foreign origin. For semi-skilled jobs, where the majority of jobs were, more than one in 10 were migrant workers. Overall, an estimated 22% of establishments in Malaysia hired migrant workers in 2018 (MOHR 2019).

As such, without adequate support to protect migrant workers' jobs, Malaysia effectively unplugged its economy's access to a large swathe of the labour force. This served an extra blow to businesses that were already grappling with the economic consequences of the pandemic. As firms struggled to stay afloat, this in turn complicated the effort to reduce unemployment.

The difference between migrant and local workers

When migrant workers became absent from the labour market – whether due to sickness or job loss – hiring local workers to replace them was not easy simply because migrant and local workers are not perfect substitutes.

Between 2010 and 2020, most of the migrant workers who entered the labour market had at most a secondary education (Figure 15.2). By contrast, the Malaysian labour force was becoming more educated: there were fewer people with only a primary education or less and over two million more who were tertiary educated. This partly explains why, within the same decade, most migrant workers tended to go into lower-skilled jobs, whereas Malaysians were mostly hired in skilled and semi-skilled occupations.

In other words, given their distinct education profiles, migrant and local workers generally do not do the same jobs. Lower-educated migrant workers often take on lower-skilled jobs that are deemed dirty, dangerous, and difficult (3D), which are also jobs that Malaysians usually shun. Indeed, in a survey conducted by the Malaysian Employers Federation (MEF), around 78% of 101 member companies reported that the main reason for recruiting migrant workers was a 'shortage of local workers to fill vacancies' (MEF 2014). Although this survey was

Figure 15.2. Migrant and local workers occupied different occupational spaces

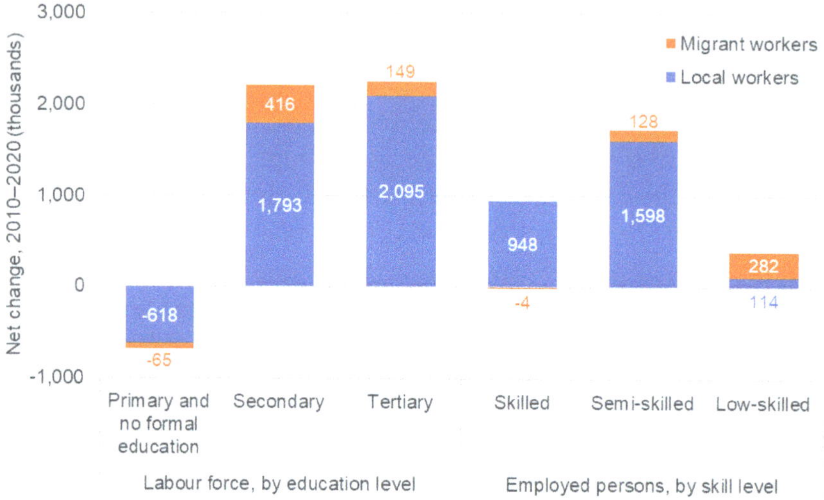

Sources: DOSM (2011), DOSM (2015), DOSM (2021) and authors' calculation. Note: Between 2010 and 2020, migrant workers mostly went into low-skilled occupations due to their lower education backgrounds.

not nationally representative, it gives a broad sense of the struggle that firms faced in hiring local workers.

Therefore, by neglecting migrant workers' health and requiring employers to hire only local workers after lockdown, the government was putting employers in a challenging position. For example, following the government's directive to stop hiring migrant workers, market traders at wholesale and wet markets in Selangor found it hard to hire (Soo 2020). The jobs that migrant workers did were often too demanding for locals, such that it took two locals to handle one migrant worker's workload. As such, the market functioned at less than 20% of its full capacity due to the staffing disruption.

Encouragingly, after a petition by some employers, the government announced in August 2020 that employers could hire migrant workers who had previously been laid off. This was indeed a move in the right direction. After all, migrant and local workers had been occupying different occupational spaces. Expecting this to change overnight – even amid a global economic crisis – was unrealistic.

The march towards automation

Last but not least, the pathway to a successful structural transformation of the economy that will benefit all Malaysians does not depend solely on reducing Malaysia's reliance on migrant workers. Although there has been a wealth of economic research on the short-term impact of immigration on the employment and wages of locals, immigration's long-term effects on Malaysia's choice of production technology and the growth potential of its economy have remained under-investigated. One view holds that current low-cost, labour-intensive production strategies – made possible by the relative abundance of migrant workers – may actually have been slowing down Malaysia's adoption of the latest forms of technology (KRI 2018; Ng, Tan, and Tan 2018). If true, this has significant implications for Malaysia's ability to sustain its economic development and eventually transition to an advanced economy.[1]

Without a doubt, this is a highly consequential research question. Yet it does not imply that removing migrant workers from the labour market would automatically promise a structural transformation of Malaysia's economy that guarantees prosperity and employment security for all. First and foremost, it is naïve to assume that firms would simply upgrade their technology once low-skilled migrant workers are absent from the labour market. For one thing, labour-saving technologies are costly. The adoption of automation or the relocation of production to overseas locations with low-cost labour are luxuries that are often exclusive to large firms only, while other firms might go out of business instead (Sumption and Somerville 2009). This is pertinent in light of the fact that, in 2016, 90% of Malaysian manufacturing firms had fewer than 75 employees each (DOSM 2017). It forces the question of how Malaysia can ensure these firms remain competitive in the face of global technological advancement so that the manufacturing sector can continue to be a reliable source of job creation.

From the workers' perspectives, automation and new technology are bound to replace jobs, and it is Malaysians, not migrant workers, who are at the highest risk of job displacement. Based on findings by KRI (2017a), in the next two decades, 54% of all jobs in Malaysia could be displaced by technology. Four in five of these high-risk jobs are semi-skilled jobs. Malaysians will be most affected because 86% of all semi-skilled jobs are held by Malaysians. In fact, the hollowing-out of semi-skilled jobs by technology has been evident since 2001 (Figure 15.3). The void is only expected to deepen further with rapid progress in technology, more so if the government fully commits itself to the transformation of the country's economic model.

Clearly, the road to economic transformation comes with its own set of labour and industrial challenges that will inevitably put Malaysians'

Figure 15.3. The disappearing middle – percentage point changes in employment share between 2001 and 2020

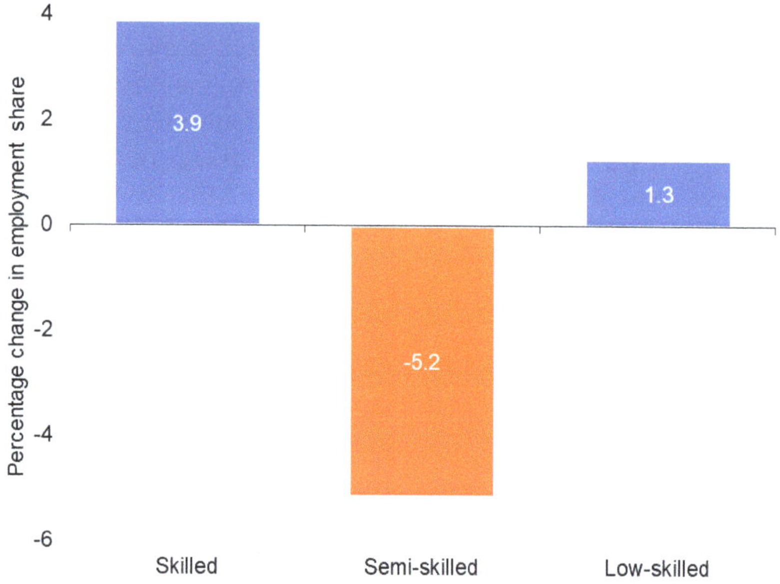

Sources: DOSM (n.d.), DOSM (2021) and authors' calculation.
Note: Unlike jobs on both ends of the skills spectrum, semi-skilled jobs experienced a dip between 2001 and 2020.

jobs at risk. Reducing Malaysia's reliance on migrant workers could be an important policy lever to drive transformation, but it is a foundation of sound labour, industrial, and education policies that will ensure the sustainable creation of quality jobs and prepare all Malaysians for the rapidly evolving employment landscape. This may involve, among other things, strengthening public–private interactions to better inform industrial policies to create an enabling environment for innovation, developing active labour market policies to continually retrain the workforce, and reforming the education system to equip all Malaysians with relevant skills for the future (KRI 2017a; Rodrik and Sabel 2020). As far as employment security is concerned, the question is: has Malaysia invested enough in building the foundation?

Conclusion – becoming better, together

If there is anything that the pandemic has taught us, it is that we are all in this together, and only by caring for one another can we emerge from the crisis safe and strong. From this chapter, it should be clear that neglecting migrant workers incurs significant economic externalities that inevitably hurt the greater population. Furthermore, amplifying the urgency to reduce the reliance on migrant workers in a time like this has only distracted the country from what needs to be fundamentally improved in order to transform Malaysia's economy in the medium to long term.

Nonetheless, economic arguments should not be the only consideration when it comes to the ways in which we treat others. Certainly, the population of migrant workers – whether documented or otherwise – who have contributed significantly to Malaysia's economy are owed a duty of care. Besides stepping up job protection for all migrant workers during the pandemic, Malaysia must commit to protecting migrant workers' rights at all times. This includes overhauling existing regulations to safeguard workers' undisputed access to healthcare services and decent living conditions and holding employers and all authorities along the migrant workers' employment line accountable for any form of mistreatment of workers. These should apply in any other countries that host migrant workers, because how we treat migrant workers will determine not only the fate of our societies but also how our countries are remembered in the annals of history.

Note

1. This section draws from the research findings of KRI (2017a) and KRI (2017b), two of the few studies in Malaysia that thoroughly investigate the impact of automation on the Malaysian employment landscape.

Acknowledgements

This chapter draws from the discussion in Tan, Nazihah, and Jarud (2020), a discussion paper that explains at length the practicality of protecting migrant workers in Malaysia. The authors are grateful for the valuable comments by Allen Ng, Nazihah Mohamad Noor, and Ryan Chua. All errors remain those of the authors.

References

Ahmad, Naqib Idris. (2021). 'PM: Nation's healthcare system is at breaking point'. *The Edge*, 11 January. https://perma.cc/BT8J-VWXE [Last accessed 13 January 2021].

Bernama. (2020). 'Saravanan: Accommodation for over 90% of foreign workers in Malaysia not in compliance with Act 446'. *The Edge*, 3

December. https://www.theedgemarkets.com/article/saravanan-accommo-dation-over-90-foreign-workers-malaysia-not-compliance-act-446 [Last accessed 13 January 2021].

DOSM (Department of Statistics Malaysia). (2011). *Labour Force Survey Report 2010*. Malaysia: Department of Statistics Malaysia.

DOSM. (2015). *Labour Force Survey Report 2015*. Malaysia: Department of Statistics Malaysia.

DOSM. (2017). *Economic Census 2016: Manufacturing*. Malaysia: Department of Statistics Malaysia.

DOSM. (2021). *Labour Force Survey Report 2020*. Malaysia: Department of Statistics Malaysia.

DOSM. (n.d.) *Labour Force Survey (LFS) Time Series Statistics by State, 1982–2019*. Malaysia: Department of Statistics Malaysia. https://perma.cc /M5DH-BEFQ [Last accessed 13 January 2021].

Hazlin, Hassan. (2020). 'World's biggest glove maker shuts 28 Malaysia fac-tories after Covid-19 infections'. *Straits Times*, 23 November. https://perma .cc/4JGB-KWTP [Last accessed 13 January 2021].

ILO (International Labour Organization). (2020). *COVID-19: Impact on Migrant Workers and Country Response in Malaysia*. Switzerland: International Labour Organization. https://perma.cc/4DPW-MELH [Last ac-cessed 13 January 2021].

KRI (Khazanah Research Institute). (2017a). *The Times They Are a-Changin': Technology, Employment, and the Malaysian Economy*. Malaysia: Khazanah Research Institute. https://perma.cc/9EVS-EPA9 [Last accessed 13 January 2021].

KRI. (2017b). *An Uneven Future? An Exploration of the Future of Work in Malaysia*. Malaysia: Khazanah Research Institute. https://perma.cc/HYK4 -RUN5 [Last accessed 13 January 2021].

KRI. (2018). *The State of Households 2018: Different Realities*. Malaysia: Khazanah Research Institute. https://perma.cc/NTP3-WCK7 [Last accessed 29 April 2021].

Malaysiakini. (2021). Covid-19 in Malaysia, 28 April. https://perma.cc/U6U3 -P76G [Last accessed 29 April 2021].

MEF (Malaysian Employers Federation). (2014). *Practical Guidelines for Employers on the Recruitment, Placement, Employment and Repatriation of Foreign Workers in Malaysia*. Malaysia: Malaysian Employers Federation. https://perma.cc/7K3T-85X8 [Last accessed 13 January 2021].

Minderjeet, Kaur. (2020). 'Rethink foreign worker policies now, govt told as massive job losses loom'. *Free Malaysia Today*, 24 April. https://perma.cc /WBZ6-VX2B. [Last accessed 13 January 2021].

MOH (Ministry of Health). (2020). 'Situasi Terkini COVID-19 di Malaysia 31 Disember 2020', 31 December. https://perma.cc/2UUL-HUL4 [Last accessed 13 January 2021].

MOHA (Ministry of Home Affairs). (2020). *Statistik pekerja asing mengikut negara dan tahun*. Malaysia: MOHA. https://perma.cc/FW89-DE8A [Last accessed 13 January 2021].

MOHR (Ministry of Human Resources). (2019). *National Employment Returns (NER) 2018*. Malaysia: MOHR. https://perma.cc/6NN5-Y5W2 [Last accessed 13 January 2021].

Ng, Allen; Tan, Theng Theng; and Tan, Zhai Gen. (2018). *What Explains the Increase in the Labor Income Share in Malaysia?* Japan: Asian Development Bank Institute Working Paper 894. https://perma.cc/DY2H-VTFE [Last accessed 29 April 2021].

Rodrik, Dani; and Sabel, Charles. (2020). *Building a Good Jobs Economy*. UK: HKS Faculty Research Working Paper Series RWP20-001.

Soo, Wern Jun. (2020). 'Told not to hire migrant workers, market traders in KL struggle to handle business on their own'. *Malay Mail*, 18 May. https:// perma.cc/746U-BTES [Last accessed 13 January 2021].

Straits Times. (2020a). 'Malaysia's Top Glove confirms first worker death from Covid-19', 14 December. https://perma.cc/VPA7-25ZS. [Last accessed 13 January 2021].

Straits Times. (2020b). 'Malaysia detains hundreds of foreign workers in major raid on KL Wholesale Market'. 11 May. https://perma.cc/PU23-5UGK [Last accessed 13 January 2021].

Straits Times. (2020c). 'Malaysia employers plead for time to provide standard accommodation for foreign workers'. 7 September. https://perma.cc /WHT6-78XU [Last accessed 13 January 2021].

Sumption, Madeleine; and Somerville, Will. (2009). *Immigration and the Labour Market: Theory, Evidence and Policy*. USA: Migration Policy Institute. https://perma.cc/4G8M-336K [Last accessed 13 January 2021].

Tan, Theng Theng; Nazihah, Muhamad Noor; and Jarud, Romadan Khalidi. (2020). *Covid-19: We Must Protect Foreign Workers*. Malaysia: Khazanah Research Institute. https://perma.cc/C8MU-F64J [Last accessed 13 January 2021].

Teh, Athira Yusof; and Dhesegaan, Bala Krishnan. (2020). 'Teratai cluster: "The virus has spread beyond factory workers' circle"'. *New Straits Times*, 23 November. https://perma.cc/7CHF-4ZUL [Last accessed 13 January 2021].

16. Emergent bordering tactics, logics of injustice, and the new hierarchies of mobility deservingness

Sin Yee Koh

Borders and bordering practices have long been used by nation states to selectively include and exclude migrants and foreigners, whether in-territory or ex-territory. This was no different in the era of the COVID-19 pandemic. On the one hand, travel lockdowns hardened existing external borders, preventing inward and outward mobilities. Under the guise of health security, additional layers of internal and external borders emerged. This accentuated and complicated existing structures that stratified the already selective inclusion and exclusion of 'others'. On the other hand, in juggling pandemic control and economic recovery, some countries introduced new bordering tactics such as travel bubbles, green lanes, and fast lanes to spur the mobilities of those who were considered eligible (Abdullah 2020).

These new and emergent borders and bordering tactics were used by state authorities in an attempt to manage and control the spread of the virus and its implications. Underlying these tactics, however, were certain logics and assumptions about who should be protected, who should be kept away, and who should be allowed in or out, when and where (Ferhani and Rushton 2020; Laocharoenwong 2020). In this reflective chapter, I put forth a twofold argument: first, the COVID-19 pandemic shed light on the enduring logics of injustice that inform existing and emergent borders and bordering tactics; second, as health security becomes intertwined with the governance of mobilities, we will be seeing the emergence of new hierarchies of mobility deservingness that have important political and ethical implications.

To develop this argument, I first outline the metaphorical understanding of borders. I then discuss how Ayelet Shachar's (2020b) conceptualisation of the shifting border can help us understand borders

How to cite this book chapter:
Koh, Sin Yee. 2022. 'Emergent bordering tactics, logics of injustice, and the new hierarchies of mobility deservingness'. In: Shin, Hyun Bang; Mckenzie, Murray; and Oh, Do Young (eds) *COVID-19 in Southeast Asia: Insights for a post-pandemic world*. London: LSE Press, pp. 183–192. DOI: https://doi.org/10.31389/lsepress.cov.p
License: CC BY 4.0.

and the bordering tactics that nation states used during the COVID-19 era. In doing so, I highlight the enduring injustices that underlie and inform such bordering tactics. Finally, I put forth the argument for the emergence of the new hierarchies of mobility deservingness. I conclude by calling for greater attention to the urgent task of considering the political and ethical issues surrounding border(ing)s in the COVID-19 era.

Borders: from lines to time-specific spaces

When thinking of borders, it might be easy to jump straight into using linear metaphors – lines that demarcate, walls that segregate, boundaries that include/exclude, partitions that divide, or gates that open/close. Regardless of which metaphors we use (see Parmar 2020, pp.177–179), the important thing about borders is that they perform these functions *selectively*. The criteria – for inclusion/exclusion, entry/non-entry, permission/restriction – are typically based on selective sets of requirements. Furthermore, these sets of selective criteria may vary across contexts and in time. In the context of the COVID-19 pandemic, we saw rapid shifts in the development of new international travel restrictions and authorised entry on the basis of medical requirements and other conditions for selective groups of people (Figure 16.1).

Of course, none of this was new: borders and bordering tactics had been in use for a long time for different purposes – whether to selectively include/exclude certain groups or to produce certain (economic/political) subjects (Mezzadra and Neilson 2013; Newman 2016). The COVID-19 pandemic, however, gave us more concrete examples of borders as *spaces*, in contrast to lines. For example, we saw the emergence of 'travel bubbles' (Wong 2020), also known as 'travel corridors' and 'corona corridors', as a kind of protected zone of travel – almost like a tunnel. These corridors were theoretically sealed from the point of origin to the destination as well as throughout the journey – including quarantine facilities at the destination. We also saw the emergence of 'green lanes' (Chong 2020), 'fast lanes' (Toh 2020), and 'fast-track entry' (Chang 2020) for less restricted travel depending on multilateral agreements.

What is interesting here is that *the border became a space tied to a specific temporality*. These bubbles and corridors existed only in a specific spatio-temporality (i.e. between an origin country and a destination country during a specified timeframe) created through the mutual agreement of the authorities involved. As people travelled in and through these border(ed) spaces, their mobilities were circumscribed

Figure 16.1. COVID-19-related international travel restrictions (thousands), 8 March 2020 to 12 April 2021

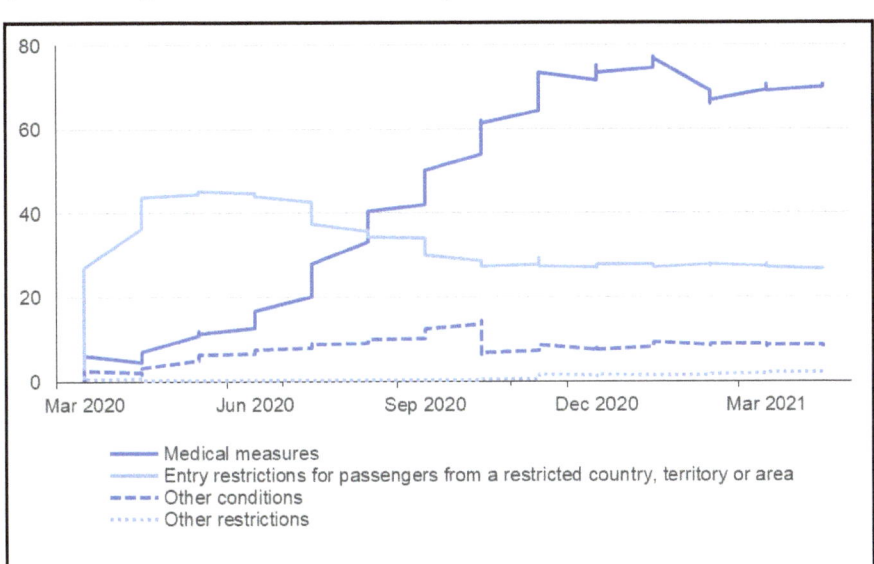

Source: IOM (2021), reproduced with permission by the IOM.
Note: As changes in restrictions were monitored at biweekly and weekly intervals and the dynamic of the measures was at times changing on a more frequent basis, the graph cannot be indicative of the exact date of change in travel restriction policies.

and characterised by different velocities and viscosities. On the one hand, some were able to move from point A to point B with higher speeds, fewer hassles, and fewer additional costs – whether these were financial or opportunity costs. On the other hand, some mobilities were significantly slowed down, subject to multiple starts and stops along the way, suspended, or even entirely prohibited. As Susan Martin and Jonas Bergmann (2021, p.9) have noted, COVID-19-related travel bans and restrictions 'clearly affect[ed] the capabilities of people, regardless of their aspirations, to move from one location to another'. As borders morphed into time-specific spaces that are in constant flux, travel, migration, and mobility also significantly changed.

Shifting borders and enduring injustices

To understand borders and bordering tactics during the COVID-19 era, I turn to Ayelet Shachar's (2020b) *The Shifting Border*. Shachar (2020b, p.4) has argued that the border 'has become a moving barrier, an unmoored legal construct' that is not fixed in place. Indeed, as the border becomes disentangled from a fixed locality, it attains *spatial agility*. Nevertheless – and perhaps because of this unfixed nature – the shifting border can be flexibly used to suit different purposes at different times. In this sense, the border becomes a method (Mezzadra and Neilson 2013) and a means to creatively and flexibly operationalise inclusion and/or exclusion as necessary. Importantly, this carefully calibrated instrument that is the shifting border has been rapidly expanding its reach beyond territorial confines.

In the context of pandemic control, the shifting border offered nation states the ability to contain or keep out those deemed risky in order to protect those deemed worthy of protection. Ann Stoler (2016, p.121), however, has highlighted that 'what and who must be kept out and what and who must stay in are neither fixed nor easy to assess. Internal enemies are potential and everywhere.' During the pandemic, there was similarly no clear and universal answer to the question of '*who gets in*, … *[who] gets out*, and *who gets rescued*' (Ferhani and Rushton 2020, pp.461–462, original emphasis). We saw this fear of the potential enemy manifested in increased health and mobility surveillance, lockdowns resulting in selective im/mobilities, and deportations. In this regard, the shifting border was 'revived as a *dispositif* to protect the state from a virus that [had been] increasingly portrayed as a foreign invader' (Radil, Pinos, and Ptak 2020, p.3), in- and ex-territory.

It is here that the COVID-19 pandemic exposed enduring injustices based on structures of inequality such as race and class that were unequally shouldered by different groups. Those who had been marginalised and scapegoated in pre-COVID-19 times (e.g. migrant workers or asylum seekers) were easily and uncritically turned into 'enemies'. They were contained, detained, fixed in place, kept waiting, stopped in their tracks, and deported (e.g. Sukumaran and Jaipagras 2020; *Straits Times* 2020). Such bordering tactics imposed on the so-called 'enemies', however, disregarded the precarious conditions that made them more at risk to the virus in the first place (Yea 2020). Bordering tactics also disregarded the medium- and long-term vulnerabilities that these groups faced, such as the risk of contracting COVID-19, lack of access to appropriate and affordable care, livelihood insecurity, stigmatisation, and discrimination (see Guadagno 2020). Regardless of prior and potential contributions to and membership of local and national communities, the migrant was made 'disposable, subject to (even more) heightened security, and racialised as the source of pathogenic risk' (Collins 2021, p.80) during the pandemic.

By contrast, those *not* seen as enemies were allowed to move and to cross internal and external borders because they were not considered (health) security threats. As part of state strategies to revive national economies weakened by prolonged lockdowns, we saw nation states taking on a certain degree of calculated risk to partially reopen borders to certain groups. These included business travellers and investors (Ahmad Naqib Idris 2020), medical tourists (Valentina 2020), international students (Adam 2020), and border commuters (*Malay Mail* 2021) – groups who arguably had more capacities and resources to take on the additional (financial and time) costs of pandemic travel and whose mobilities had not been seriously curtailed, compared to the groups who were seen as 'enemies'.

As Meghann Ormond (2021) has highlighted, both routine and exceptional treatments of different groups during the pandemic can reveal 'how embodied "risk" is imagined, evolves, and gets differentially attributed and practiced by national governments'. The bifurcated bordering tactics imposed upon 'enemies' and 'non-enemies' revealed 'the underlying script states follow when they embrace or filter *The Other*' (Kenwick and Simmons 2020, p. E37, original emphasis). The pandemic brought the problematic logic that informs existing and emergent bordering tactics into greater clarity, showing how control regimes that delineate '(im)mobilities of the "past"' (Lin and Yeoh 2021, p.96) continued to shape mobility regimes in the COVID-19 era.

New hierarchies of mobility deservingness

Putting aside legitimate public health considerations that might have justified the pandemic's bordering tactics, it is important to recognise that the shifting border translated into material violence that positioned people in 'new relations of power in political spaces of im/mobility' (Shachar 2020b, p.6; see also Shachar 2020a). Indeed, it has been widely acknowledged that border control and migration governance have been inherently political, both during and before pandemic times (Kenwick and Simmons 2020). As health security becomes intertwined with the (political) governance of mobilities in the COVID-19 era, I argue that we will be seeing the emergence of *new hierarchies of mobility deservingness*.

In their article on Malaysia's healthcare regime, Meghann Ormond and Alice Nah wrote about 'hierarchies of healthcare deservingness' (Ormond and Nah 2020) whereby migrants have been positioned along a hierarchy of differential access to healthcare largely on the basis of moral judgements. There are some parallels that can be drawn here: in the context of the COVID-19 pandemic, those who were deemed fit for travel – that is, deserving of (risk-free) mobilities that did not compromise public health – were allowed to move. On the one hand, this is arguably a relatively objective judgement (i.e. health status on the basis of scientific measurements) in comparison to subjective moral judgements. On the other hand, the seeming neutrality of its 'objective-ness' obscures pre-existing structures of inequality and inequity that might have contributed to an individual's compromised health status in the very first place (e.g. differential access to housing, healthcare, nutrition, economic opportunities, networks, and information). Moreover, frames of deservingness are neither static nor apolitical (Landolt and Goldring 2016).

If the emergent hierarchy of mobility deservingness develops into an accepted norm, those positioned higher in the hierarchy will be able to enjoy greater access to mobility and opportunities to accumulate mobility capital (i.e. resources from previous experiences of mobility *and* the potential to undertake future mobilities; see Moret 2020). Accumulated mobility capital can then be converted into other forms of capital in the future, locally as well as in another transnational locations. As Moret (2020, p.238) has explained, mobility capital 'opens up and solidifies options in more than one place'. The unequal access to mobility capital, in turn, contributes to the exacerbation of inequalities as this new structure of inequity – mobility deservingness – overlaps and interacts with existing ones (e.g. race, class, and citizenship).

Concluding thoughts

In moments of crisis, great uncertainties, or a pivotal moment in history – like the COVID-19 pandemic – we can observe that states display a tendency to add more layers to the 'highly variegated terrain of social protection and vulnerability' (Sheller 2018, p.xi). Protection becomes selective, while non-protection or outright abandonment expands to more groups and individuals. This clearly signals and reminds us that the rights and privileges accorded by nation states are highly discretionary (Koh 2020). One's status and access to rights and privileges are subject to changing circumstances and shifting state priorities (Shachar 2020a). They are not – and cannot – be taken for granted. This applies equally to those of us who belong to groups of relative privilege (e.g.

citizens, permanent residents, privileged migrants) as well as those of us who belong to groups of relative underprivilege (e.g. undocumented migrants). This is because, as borders shift, morph and mutate, we become positioned within these categories, sometimes without even realising it.[1]

The development of new hierarchies of mobility deservingness is important because we know that migration and mobility are ways for people to achieve their aspirations, have a chance at attaining social mobility, or escape vulnerabilities. Furthermore, mobility has implications for residential status and citizenship acquisition later on or for the next generation. This is therefore not just a question of equity and justice for the current generation; it is also about that for future generations. The new hierarchy of mobility deservingness raises political and ethical questions that should be carefully thought through, critiqued, and debated.

Note

1. See Lin and Yeoh (2021) for examples of how different groups in Singapore were recategorised according to their (state-perceived) risks of spreading the COVID-19 virus.

Acknowledgements

An earlier draft of this chapter was presented as an intervention at the 'Migration and Mobility in the COVID-19 Era' panel for the LSE Southeast Asia Week 2020. I thank Professor Hyun Bang Shin and the Saw Swee Hock Southeast Asia Research Centre for the kind invitation, the panellists (Dr Yasmin Y. Ortiga and Professor Johanna Waters) for their insightful interventions, and the audience members for their helpful questions. Thanks also to the International Organization for Migration for permission to reproduce Figure 16.1.

References

Abdullah, Zhaki. (2020). 'Fast lane, green lane, air travel bubble: What you need to know about Singapore's COVID-19 travel measures'. *CNA*, 13 October. https://perma.cc/LF5A-FQ56 [Last accessed 19 April 2021].

Adam, Ashman. (2020). 'Malaysia reopens borders to international students from Jan 1'. *Malay Mail*, 22 December. https://perma.cc/UCM6-LZDP [Last accessed 19 April 2021].

Ahmad Naqib Idris. (2020). 'Govt to speed up approval for entry of business travellers, subject to strict conditions'. *The Edge Markets*, 30 December. https://perma.cc/XD7U-P5ZY [Last accessed 19 April 2021].

Chang, May Choon. (2020). 'Over 1,000 business travellers have benefited from "fast track" entry deal between China, South Korea'. *Straits Times*, 29 May. https://perma.cc/B8XT-2RYG [Last accessed 19 April 2021].

Chong, Clara. (2020). 'Coronavirus: Regional green lanes will take more time than bilateral ones'. *Straits Times*, 8 July. https://perma.cc/3B67-LW5F [Last accessed 19 April 2021].

Collins, Francis Leo. (2021). 'Migration ethics in pandemic times'. *Dialogues in Human Geography*, vol. 11, no. 1, pp. 78–82. https://doi.org /10.1177/2043820620975964

Ferhani, Adam; and Rushton, Simon. (2020). 'The International Health Regulations, COVID-19, and bordering practices: Who gets in, what gets out, and who gets rescued?' *Contemporary Security Policy*, vol. 41, no. 3, pp. 458–477. https://doi.org/10.1080/13523260.2020.1771955

Guadagno, Lorenzo. (2020). *Migrants and the COVID-19 Pandemic an Initial Analysis.* Switzerland: IOM Migration Research Series No. 60. https://perma .cc/3ALR-TPLW [Last accessed 17 January 2021].

IOM (International Organization for Migration). (2021). *Displacement Tracking Matrix (DTM)*, 12 April 2021 [unpublished dataset].

Kenwick, Michael R.; and Simmons, Beth A. (2020). 'Pandemic response as border politics'. *International Organization*, vol. 74, S1, pp. E36–E58. http://dx.doi.org/10.1017/S0020818320000363

Koh, Sin Yee. (2020). 'Noncitizens' rights: Moving beyond migrants' rights'. *Migration and Society*, vol. 3, no. 1, pp. 233–237. https://doi.org/10.3167 /arms.2020.030119

Landolt, Patricia; and Goldring, Luin. (2016). 'Inequality and assemblages of noncitizenship in an age of migration'. *Discover Society*, 5 April. https:// perma.cc/N6CA-DZQL [Last accessed 19 April 2021].

Laocharoenwong, Jiraporn. (2020). 'COVID-19, Health Borders, and the Purity of the Thai Nation'. *Heinrich Böll Stiftung*, 9 October. https://perma .cc/VQJ4-NSE6 [Last accessed 19 April 2021].

Lin, Weiqiang; and Yeoh, Brenda S.A. (2021). 'Pathological (im)mobilities: Managing risk in a time of pandemics'. *Mobilities*, vol. 16, no. 1, pp. 96–112. https://doi.org/10.1080/17450101.2020.1862454

Malay Mail. (2021). *Periodic Commuting Arrangement Scheme Expansion to Include Malaysian Workers Holding Singapore PR from Jan 11*, 9 January. https://perma.cc/GXS3-EFRW [Last accessed 19 April 2021].

Martin, Susan; and Bergmann, Jonas. (2021). '(Im)mobility in the age of COVID-19'. *International Migration Review*. https://doi.org/10.1177/01979 18320984104

Mezzadra, Sandro; and Neilson, Brett. (2013). *Border as Method, or, the Multiplication of Labor*. USA: Duke University Press.

Moret, Joëlle. (2020). 'Mobility capital: Somali migrants' trajectories of (im) mobilities and the negotiation of social inequalities across borders'. *Geoforum*, vol. 116, pp. 235–242. https://doi.org/10.1016/j.geoforum .2017.12.002

Newman, David. (2006). 'The lines that continue to separate us: Borders in our "borderless" world'. *Progress in Human Geography*, vol. 30, no. 2, pp. 143–161. https://doi.org/10.1191/0309132506ph599xx

Ormond, Meghann. (2021). 'Managing internationally mobile bodies in a world on hold: Migration, tourism and biological citizenship in the context of COVID-19', in Gavin J. Andrews, Valorie Crooks, Jamie Pearce and Janey Messina (eds) *COVID-19 and Similar Futures: Pandemic Geographies*. Switzerland: Springer, pp. 119–124.

Ormond, Meghann; and Nah, Alica M. (2020). 'Risk entrepreneurship and the construction of healthcare deservingness for "desirable", "acceptable" and "disposable" migrants in Malaysia'. *Journal of Ethnic and Migration Studies*, vol. 46, no. 20, pp. 4282–4302. https://doi.org/10.1080/136918 3X.2019.1597477

Parmar, Alpa. (2020). 'Borders as mirrors: Racial hierarchies and policing migration'. *Critical Criminology*, vol. 28, no. 2, pp. 175–192. https://doi.org /10.1007/s10612-020-09517-1

Radil, Steven M.; Pinos, Jaume Castan; and Ptak, Thomas. (2020). 'Borders resurgent: Towards a post-Covid-19 global border regime?' *Space and Polity*. https://doi.org/10.1080/13562576.2020.1773254

Shachar, Ayelet. (2020a). Beyond open and closed borders: The grand transformation of citizenship. *Jurisprudence*, vol. 11, no. 1, pp. 1–27. https://doi.org /10.1080/20403313.2020.1788283

Shachar, Ayelet. (2020b). *The Shifting Border: Legal Cartographies of Migration and Mobility*. UK: Manchester University Press.

Sheller, Mimi. (2018). *Mobility Justice: The Politics of Movement in the Age of Extremes*. UK: Verso.

Stoler, Ann Laura. (2016). *Duress: Imperial Durabilities in Our Times*. USA: Duke University Press.

Straits Times. (2020). 'Malaysia turns back Rohingya boat over coronavirus fears'. 18 April. https://perma.cc/F5K9-FTMZ [Last accessed 19 April 2021].

Sukumaran, Tashny; and Jaipragas, Bhavan. (2020). 'Coronavirus: Hundreds arrested as Malaysia cracks down on migrants in Covid-19 red zones'. *South China Morning Post*, 1 May. https://perma.cc/KMF9-VUW8 [Last accessed 19 April 2021].

Toh, Ting Wei. (2020). 'Coronavirus: Fast lanes based on multiple factors in partner countries'. *Straits Times*, 26 June. https://perma.cc/6QD8-DE7G [Last accessed 19 April 2021].

Valentina, Jessicha. (2020). 'Malaysia reopens borders partially to medical travellers'. *Jakarta Post*, 21 July. https://perma.cc/H4CX-A5YX [Last accessed 19 April 2021].

Wong, Tsui-kai. (2020). 'Explainer: What is the Covid-19 travel bubble and what could it mean for Hong Kong?' *Youngpost*, 9 September. https://perma.cc/3BAH-ETPA [Last accessed 19 April 2021].

Yea, Sallie. (2020). 'This is why Singapore's coronavirus cases are growing: A look inside the dismal living conditions of migrant workers'. *The Conversation*, 30 April. https://perma.cc/4KZD-RS2K [Last accessed 19 April 2021].

17. The impacts of crisis on the conflict-prone Myanmar–China borderland

Abellia Anggi Wardani and Maw Thoe Myar

After the outbreak of COVID-19, the Chinese government decided to close the border in Muse, a small town in Myanmar's northern Shan State. Inbound and outbound movements from both countries came to a halt. A chain of truck trailers lining up on the transnational route between China and Myanmar left only one side of the road for vehicles to pass by. The trucks were stuck there for months in a lose–lose situation – leaving meant losing the possibility of trading their goods, whereas staying put meant remaining stranded in a place of uncertainty. During our short visit to Muse in July 2020, it was agonising to see a dozen miles of hope and hard work falling apart. What the experience of the truck drivers, traders, farmers, and consumers in Muse offered was a glimpse of how COVID-19 impacted cross-border economic activities and movement of people in Myanmar's border areas.

Myanmar, undergoing economic development and a tumultuous democratic transition, was prone to socio-economic impacts from the COVID-19 pandemic due to the uneven and underdeveloped provision of health services, a lack of accurate reporting, and low test-and-trace capabilities. The situation became worse in places where institutional and administrative regulations heavily relied on the security situation, such as border areas. The health crisis exacerbated already-uncertain terrain.

This short analysis investigates the impact of COVID-19 on cross-border trade areas in Muse, emphasising how different actors engaged in or governed cross-border trade activities and the pandemic's implications for cross-border trade movement. The chapter aims to highlight specific organisational tinkering with cross-border trade in a conflict-prone area during the COVID-19 pandemic. It builds upon participatory observation during a short trip to Muse in July 2020,

How to cite this book chapter:
Wardani, Abellia Anggi; and Myar, Maw Thoe. 2022. 'The impacts of crisis on the conflict-prone Myanmar–China borderland'. In: Shin, Hyun Bang; Mckenzie, Murray; and Oh, Do Young (eds) *COVID-19 in Southeast Asia: Insights for a post-pandemic world*. London: LSE Press, pp. 193–201. DOI: https://doi.org/10.31389/lsepress.cov.q License: CC BY 4.0.

which was part of a research project on people's livelihoods in conflict-affected areas, and data collected from secondary sources.

Observable impacts on cross-border trade in the conflict-affected Muse area during the COVID-19 pandemic manifested at two levels of analysis: macro and micro. The study gives an overall understanding of border areas using multiple lenses to capture the dynamics of different actors in their political, economic, and social settings. In this analysis, those settings are juxtaposed with the three pillars that support society: the state, markets, and community. The state represents the structures of political governance and, in this case, what can be found in Muse in Myanmar and Ruili in China. Markets include all private economic structures in production and exchange processes, including both large- and small-scale trades. As the third pillar, community consists of people who share a specific locality, government, and cultural and historical heritage. In this chapter, the community comprises people who live in the areas separated by the Shweli River. When any of the three pillars is disturbed, society must find a new balance to reach equilibrium (Hann and Hart 2009; Rajan 2019). Given this complexity, an analysis of the impacts of the COVID-19 pandemic at macro and micro levels in Muse can make a valuable addition to the analysis of conflict-prone borderlands.

The micro-level analysis focuses on small-scale trade as a coping mechanism of grass-roots actors during the border closure. Meanwhile, the macro level covers the values behind COVID-19 regulations and policies that impacted cross-border trade routines. The underlying argument is that small-scale trade, such as peddling, hawking, and smuggling, is among the economic activities most sensitive to changes in border settings and is usually among the first to feel the impact of macro-level policy changes. Simultaneously, small-scale trade is a prerequisite for and inseparable from the development and maintenance of large-scale world trade (Evers and Schiel 1987; Goodhand 2020).

Cross-border trade in an unpredictable environment

Studies on the relationship between borderlands and trade in various regions, especially conflict-prone areas, have increasingly attracted the attention of scholars from diverse disciplinary backgrounds (for the borderland in Vietnam, see Bonnin 2010; for Thailand and Laos, see Phadungkiati 2014; for Myanmar and China, see Grundy-Warr and Lin 2020; for Afghanistan, see Goodhand 2008; for Indonesia, see

Wardani 2020). The border is understood as a contested space with an uncertain temporality. In conflict-prone areas, the border is a vital part of the battle for control and surveillance. Such an understanding invites the assumption that the border as a space embeds domination and power (Foucault 1977). In the case of Muse, where governance has come from entities at many different scales – supra-national, national, regional, and local – the border closure unravelled previously intangible hierarchies of power that had existed only in the abstract for grassroots economic actors.

Literature on the border has often been the province of political scientists and has been disconnected from more in-depth anthropological debate, which suggests that geographical place defines boundaries and then demarcates the identities of the communities around it. In the case of Muse, the border area had been continuously shaped and reshaped by economic exchanges performed by diverse actors. Historically, the two communities on both sides of the border shared the same cultural characteristics and social-psychological environment despite their split nationalities (Dong and He 2018; Ganesan 2017). Therefore, looking at cross-border trade with only a macro-level analysis is insufficient owing to the transnational sociocultural embeddedness that factors into the two countries' cultures and plays a significant role in trade (Hann and Hart 2009). Over the years, such embeddedness has been transformed into social networks of cross-border trade. It has comprised complicated relations and influences between state and non-state actors from both countries, especially given that the area was formerly under the de facto control of ethnic armed groups instead of the Myanmar government (Ganesan 2017). Su (2020) has argued that border control in Muse has served to balance economic development and national security, as informal economies were pushed to formalise in an attempt to safeguard national sovereignty at the border.

Muse, also known as the Muse 105-mile trade zone, is one of the most significant economic corridors between Myanmar and China. Since 1988, the town has seen dramatic increases in connectivity and economic cooperation between the two countries. Considered 'a successful model for border trade gates and routes in Myanmar', Muse has served as a vital point in Myanmar and China's contemporary development strategies (Kudo 2010, p.266). It was also an important spot for a planned infrastructure route worth billions of dollars that promised to connect the Indian Ocean oil trade with China's Yunnan province. Labelled the China–Myanmar Economic Corridor (CMEC), the project was designed to allow China to diversify its energy shipping routes and ease its reliance on the vulnerable Strait of Malacca. The bilateral cooperation on border trade zones thus fostered export and import activities in Muse. Between October 2019 and October 2020, Muse's trade volume – almost US$4.8 billion – accounted for nearly half of Myanmar's total border trade volume (Ministry of Commerce 2020). Indeed, China's political influence in mainland Southeast Asia has intertwined with regional countries' interests, including Myanmar's, to advance their economic and trade positions (Grundy-Warr and Lin 2020). Without this cross-border connection, exchanges of capital, labour, and natural resources between China and its neighbouring countries in mainland Southeast Asia would come to a stop.

The coronavirus outbreak in Wuhan, China, in December 2019 turned the situation in Muse on its head. After the first confirmed cases, in March 2020, the Myanmar government implemented a series of prevention and mitigation measures to contain the spread of COVID-19. It also issued a nationwide order to close public areas and cancel events, including Thingyan (the Burmese New Year festival). Moreover, people were ordered to stay at home, practise social distancing, and temporarily close their businesses. The government took legal action against those who did not obey the laws and prevention measures. Nevertheless, even when COVID-19 cases were soaring in Myanmar, China sought to move forward with the CMEC project and claimed that the pandemic would not deter its initial plans (Nan Lwin 2020).

Coping with COVID-19 in conjunction with trade

At the micro level, two types of trade activities were common in Muse. In addition to legal trade with government-authorised documents or licences, conducted mostly by large-scale traders, informal economic exchanges also significantly increased due to a somewhat loose licensing process, which allowed actors to evade taxes and trade restricted products. Motorcycles and cars were among the best-selling items in this shady border marketplace. A man riding a motorcycle while carrying another motorcycle on top was a common sight along the border route. Sometimes people also used cars to carry several motorcycles. Despite efforts by Myanmar and neighbouring governments to regulate the import and export of automotive products, such illegal practices continued to flourish.

Moreover, the thin line that constituted the border between Myanmar and China became a grey zone in which two currencies, the kyat and yuan, were used interchangeably in economic transactions. Informal currency exchange kiosks were easy to find in the corners of Muse, and at shops buyers were allowed to pay with whichever currency they had.

In Muse, COVID-19 and the governments' measures to contain it also led to the stalling of trade activities. Truck drivers found themselves deadlocked, as they could not pass through the closed checkpoint but still had hope that the border would reopen soon. They mostly relied on local people in nearby villages for food and hygiene necessities to cope with the situation. Some tried to cut their losses by selling the agricultural goods to local traders. Others, failing to do so, decided to throw away what had rotted. Most of the drivers spent the night in their vehicles to guard their products against theft or other damage given that the area had long been a battlefield for ethnic armed groups.

Amid the Myanmar government's certainty that the country was free from coronavirus in the early months of the global outbreak, large numbers of migrants, both legal and undocumented, managed to cross the border with China. This raised questions as to whether these border-crossers had somehow contracted the virus yet remained undetected owing to limited testing in the border area of Muse.

In Muse, some traders operated without proper documents, highlighting rampant corruption practices in the local bureaucracies. Informal trade networks provided ample employment opportunities, attracting locals and migrants who were mostly low-skilled workers (Set Aung 2011). The rise of illegal migration, however, created inevitable tension in the area. In August 2020, 20 illegal migrants from China were arrested by the Myanmar authorities (Pyae Sone 2020). In total, from January to August 2020, 297 Chinese people were arrested.

Moreover, research suggested that Myanmar and China's alleged violent land expropriation process in ethnic minority areas with ceasefire agreements that also happened to be resource-rich, such as Kachin State and northern Shan State, had worsened the situation on the ground (Woods 2011). Policies on smuggling also seemed to fail in preventing illicit trade in the border areas during the pandemic. Despite continuous attempts to secure the border areas, clandestine commerce between people from Myanmar and China continued to exist thanks to the established trade networks among traders who shared long-existing ethnic and kinship relationships (Su 2020). With economic activities restricted by border policies, local traders found themselves stuck between the state's regulations and individual–collective moral convictions, such as cooperation between truck drivers and local villagers, in order to survive during the pandemic.

Regulatory constraints and transnational trade

At the macro level, China imposed cross-border cargo policies to forbid all Myanmar's vehicles and small-scale traders from April 2020 to contain the coronavirus's spread. This move was seen as a one-sided policy instituted without any consultation with the Myanmar government, implying a lack of trust in its ability to control the virus's spread. It also created imbalanced business opportunities for Chinese traders and had protectionist undertones (Bharat 2020). Traders and consumers who had previously engaged in cross-border trading activities in Muse were caught in an unfortunate situation, as the primary operations of import and export halted and border checkpoints closed. As a result, trade volume in the Muse 105-mile trade zone decreased significantly. Traders from both sides were unable to cross, with around 500 trucks stranded along the way to the border. The restrictions put traders and cargo owners at risk of bankruptcy (Bharat 2020). The Chinese government also decided to increase tax rates, making the traders' lives even more difficult.

The border closure impacted not only Myanmar's agriculture and livestock sectors. Most of the raw industrial materials used to power Myanmar's factories were imported from neighbouring countries, especially China. Given its strategic and vital position, the border closure in Muse contributed to the shortage of raw materials and forced factories and industries to close. In Yangon, at least 47 closed or reduced operations due to the lack of raw materials, significantly increasing the unemployment rate (Myo Pa Pa San 2020).

Myanmar's government tried to negotiate with China to resume the flow of goods. Chinese authorities suggested that loaded trucks should not park along the route, to avoid congestion. Moreover, Chinese authorities allowed Chinese drivers with a COVID-19-free health certificate to enter Myanmar to drive the trucks that were already en route to deliver China's exports to prevent Myanmar drivers from entering China. The Chinese drivers would then return the trucks to the Myanmar drivers waiting at the border. The Chinese authority put the driver substitution policy in place in April 2020; then, in October 2020, the Chinese administration decided to triple the associated fees. Concerns remained, however, as only a few trucks out of the hundreds could operate due to the limited number of Chinese drivers. As a result, most trucks were still stuck for more than two months in a lose–lose situation due to China's lessened demand. Despite the Myanmar government's efforts to ease the border area trade restrictions, conditions did not change much.

Moreover, while the influx of migrant workers was not as apparent in Muse as in the border areas with Thailand, the government continuously attempted to tackle trafficking by strengthening law enforcement, albeit with unsatisfactory results. The pressing issues behind these illegal practices were closely linked to inadequate opportunities, insufficient border trade facilities, high-cost licences and documents, and the exploitation of vulnerable people (Set Aung 2011).

The illegal drug trade, human smuggling or trafficking, and illicit labour migrants were also found in Muse. It was arguably common knowledge among the locals that people could buy drugs 'openly' in small shops along the trade routes. It is also worth noting that Muse and the trade routes linked to it fell within areas of prolonged conflict involving seven ethnic armed groups. Muse, as a borderland connecting China and Myanmar with relatively easy access to lucrative foreign markets, often became a favourable option for ethnic armed groups to extort money. Along with neighbouring towns, Muse had been administratively controlled by an ethnic armed group called the United Wa State Army (UWSA) (Ganesan 2017).

The frequent fighting between the Myanmar military and ethnic armed groups impacted the everyday socio-economic situations of the local population and the actors who engaged in trading activities in Muse. Given Myanmar's strategic location in China's Belt and Road Initiative, China and Chinese economic interests influenced geopolitical relations and security in Myanmar's border areas, where ceasefires between conflicting parties were arguably heavily influenced by attempts to enable cross-border economic exchange (Grundy-Warr and Lin 2020). In recent years, China had shown keen interest in brokering peace in the area for at least two reasons: first, to ensure security along the Chinese border and, second, to maintain dominance over the informal political economy of the Northern Alliance, comprising the Wa and Kokang peoples – the latter of which is ethnically Chinese (Ganesan 2017).

Conclusion

The COVID-19 pandemic had a dire impact on the movement of people and goods around the world. In the small yet strategic town of Muse in the Myanmar–China borderlands, cross-border trade was forced to stop, causing significant damage to the local and national economies. Building from social theory, borderlands provide a sphere where the ongoing pandemic directly impacted the three pillars of society: the state, markets, and community, all of which are in constant dialectical relations with one another. Such dialogues are constructed and negotiated through everyday life at the micro level just as much as through policymaking processes at the macro level. The border closure in Muse and the lining up of trucks along the transnational road made power relations visible within communities that shared the same sociocultural background despite being separated by a border. It rendered abstract concepts such as 'the state' and 'politics' far more observable than in ordinary, pre-COVID-19 times for the communities in the borderlands.

Acknowledgements

The fieldwork for this research was financed by the Center for Social Integrity (CSI), Myanmar, as part of a research project on livelihoods in northern Shan State. The CSI also supported the data analysis and writing of this chapter. We acknowledge Muhamad Arif for assistance with editing and for the valuable comments.

References

Aung, Winston Set. (2011). *Informal Trade and Underground Economy in Myanmar: Costs and Benefits*. Thailand: Institute de recherche sur L'Asie du Sud-Est.

Bharat, Shah Suraj. (2020). 'Border trade authorities wary of Myanmar's COVID-19 second wave'. *The Diplomat*, https://perma.cc/J2EY-9TWF [Last accessed 23 January 2021].

Bonnin, Christine. (2010). 'Navigating fieldwork politics, practicalities and ethics in the upland borderlands of northern Vietnam'. *Asia Pacific Viewpoint*, vol. 51, no. 2, pp. 179–192.

Dong, Min; and He Jun. (2018). 'Linking the past to the future: A reality check on cross-border timber trade form Myanmar (Burma) to China'. *Forest Policy and Economics*, vol. 87, pp. 11–19.

Foucault, Michel. (1977). *Discipline and Punish*. UK: Penguin.

Ganesan, N. (2017). 'Changing dynamics in Myanmar's ethnic peace process and the growing role of China'. *Asian Journal of Peacebuilding*, vol. 5, no. 2, pp. 325–339.

Goodhand, Jonathan. (2008). 'War, peace and the places in between: Why borderlands are central', in Michael Pugh, Neil Cooper and Mandy Turner (eds) *Whose Peace? Critical Perspectives on the Political Economy of Peacebuilding*. UK: Palgrave Macmillan, pp. 225–244.

Goodhand, Jonathan. (2020). 'In the world's forgotten borderlands, the drug trade helps people survive – but at a cost'. *The Conversation*, https://perma.cc /5JDF-L5F7 [Last accessed 28 January 2021].

Grundy-Warr, Carl; and Lin, Shaun. (2020). 'COVID-19 geopolitics: silence and erasure in Cambodia and Myanmar in times of pandemic'. *Eurasian Geography and Economics*, vol. 61, no. 4–5, pp. 493–510.

Hann, Chris; and Hart, Keith. (2009). *Market and Society: The Great Transformation Today*. UK: Cambridge University Press.

Kudo, Toshihiro. (2008). 'Myanmar's economic relations with China: who benefits and who pays?' in Skidmore, Monique; and Wilson, Trevor (eds.), *Dictatorship, Disorder and Decline in Myanmar*. Canberra: ANU Press, pp. 87–109.

Kudo, Toshihiro. (2010). *Myanmar's Border Trade with China: Situation, Challenge and Prospects*. Thailand: IDE-JETRO.

Lwin, Nan. (2020). *Myanmar-China Relations: 2020 Review*. The Irrawaddy, https://perma.cc/Y8GA-MLG4 [Last accessed 23 January 2021].

Ministry of Commerce. (2020). *Ministry of Commerce Export/Import Trade Situation of Myanmar in (1-10-2020) to (22-1-2021) Compared to the Same Period of 2018-2019 Fiscal Year*. https://perma.cc/R9AC-B9X3 [Last accessed 21 September 2020].

Phadungkiati, Lada. (2014). *Negotiating Regionalisation: Social Networks and Survival of Informal Cross-Border Traders*. Unpublished thesis (PhD), University of Sydney.

Rajan, Raghuran. (2019). *The Third Pillar*. UK: William Collins.

Sone, Pyae. (2020). '20 More illegal Chinese migrants arrested in Muse'. *Eleven*, https://perma.cc/M7AE-VVC8 [Last accessed 21 January 2021].

Su, Xiaobo. (2020). 'Smuggling and the exercise of effective sovereignty at the China-Myanmar border'. *Review of International Political Economy*, pp. 1–28. https://doi.org/10.1080/09692290.2020.1859400

Than, Tin Maung Maung. (2003). 'Myanmar and China: A special relationship?' *Southeast Asia Affairs*, pp. 189–210.

Wardani, Abellia Anggi. (2020). *'It was kind of safe': The Role of the Market in the Everyday Peacebuilding Processes during the Ambon Conflicts*. Unpublished thesis (PhD), Tilburg University.

Woods, Kevin. (2011). 'Ceasefire capitalism: Military-private partnerships, resources concessions and military state-building in the Burma-China borderlands'. *The Journal of Peasant Studies*, vol. 28, no. 4, pp. 747–770.

PART III:
COLLECTIVE ACTION, COMMUNITIES, AND MUTUAL AID

18. Rethinking urbanisation, development, and collective action in Indonesia

Rita Padawangi

The term 'development' on its own indicates progress towards becoming more advanced. In most of today's urbanisation, however, the term 'urban development' has implied a capitalist mode of production in which planners consider capitalism the most rational way of managing and distributing space in everyone's best interests (Stein 2019). As a result, many urban developments around the world have normalised social inequalities for the sake of economic efficiency in the profit-making scheme of spatial distribution. The COVID-19 pandemic, however, exposed social inequalities that had been 'normalised' in 'normal' times. For example, Singapore won worldwide praise for curbing infection levels in the first month of the pandemic, only to see it spike tremendously by the end of March 2020 (Kurohi 2020; Ng 2020). The initial measures missed migrant workers in dormitories; many were construction workers in Singapore, but their living quarters were segregated from most of the population. Once the virus reached the dormitories, dense living conditions made physical distancing difficult, and towards the end of June 2020 there were more than 40,000 COVID-19 cases among migrant workers in dormitories. There was also panic buying across supermarkets in the early days of the virus's spread in Singapore (Chang 2020), an indication of perceived insecurity in a crisis.

Normalcy implies the status quo, which might include the social inequalities, discrimination, and even oppression that were taken for granted in everyday situations. In the context of capitalist urban development, the constant presumption of economic growth as the main indicator of development has normalised the relegation of other aspects of societal progress to lesser importance (Friedmann 1992). The ready association of gross national product (GNP) per capita with livelihood

How to cite this book chapter:
Padawangi, Rita. 2022. 'Rethinking urbanisation, development, and collective action in Indonesia'. In: Shin, Hyun Bang; Mckenzie, Murray; and Oh, Do Young (eds) *COVID-19 in Southeast Asia: Insights for a post-pandemic world*. London: LSE Press, pp. 205–217. DOI: https://doi.org/10.31389/lsepress.cov.r License: CC BY 4.0.

improvements has been applied almost universally throughout world economies despite the known shortcomings of using income as a measure of progress, as it neglects the human scale and social-environmental interconnectedness across borders. As a result, urbanisation around the world has continued to decrease space for various communities who become collateral to development, such as farmers, fisherfolk, and *adat* (traditional) societies. They are underappreciated when unquantifiable aspects of social-cultural life are converted into quantified economic valuation. Those who are collateral to development comprise everyone on the margins, including the urban poor, who have often been targets of forced evictions (Padawangi 2019a).

The domination of the capitalist urban development paradigm has had both ideological and pragmatic impacts. On the pragmatic side, development strategies have been in favour of the drive to urbanise. Singapore, for example, has achieved accelerated development since the 1960s through an economic restructuring that transformed an agricultural society into an industrial one. Agriculture was significantly reduced, as it contradicted the city-state's land-scarce development strategy. Singapore's position as the wealthiest city-state in Southeast Asia subsequently became a development model for the entire world. The desirability of this development model was further cemented by the global city's image as a cultural hub, formed through the construction of large-scale facilities for arts and culture, in connection with the city's function as an economic hub (Kong 2010; Yeoh 2005).

Yet, cities' economic superiority has relied on footprints beyond their territories, as cities have been dependent on the countryside for resources. Urbanisation has taken up fertile land, rice fields, and forests to extract natural resources through mining as well as building roads, airports, houses, condominiums, and new towns (Spinney 2020). Simultaneously, spaces in the city that attract more investment have often relied on crowding people in high density to maximise profit (Luscombe 2020). In the process, these developments have increased the likelihood of zoonosis and other infectious diseases and have also made urban spaces products to be traded in the market economy (Spinney 2020). Consequently, social inequalities have been apparent in spatial inequalities that limit livelihood improvement opportunities for marginalised groups and affect access to health services and environmental quality.

Activists and scholars have questioned 'normalcy' through the critical rethinking of urbanisation and have thus called for alternative visions of it (Brenner, Marcuse and Mayer 2012; Cabannes, Douglass, and Padawangi 2019; Lefebvre 2003). They have called for increased attention to people's actions to change the city in order to change society (Castells 1983), to 'rethink the economy' by carefully analysing social relations rather than income per se (Friedmann 1992, p.44), and to look at the smallest units of society as social, political, and economic agents (Cabannes, Douglass, and Padawangi 2019). Looking beyond state interventions has been important to examine possible alternatives. In Southeast Asia, excluding Singapore, the state's limitations have been obvious in the mismatch between master plans and everyday realities. With these limits on state capacity, collective actions in civil society have yielded important social dynamics in Southeast Asia. After recent natural disasters, such as typhoons in the Philippines and earthquakes in Indonesia, local and transborder collective actions like aid deliveries and empowerment programmes have been particularly important.

How have collective actions from civil society members and groups responded to the pandemic? What have been their limitations? What could we learn from the dynamics of Southeast Asia's collective action in questioning normalcy in today's urban development? Collective action comprises 'purposive, meaningful, and potentially creative' ways to challenge political establishments (Chesters and Welsh 2011, p.5). Examinations into local efforts to 'counter the alienating forces of capitalist urban growth' (Cabannes, Douglass, and Padawangi 2019, p.16) have been of central importance in understanding how, why, and how far collective action could challenge presupposed notions of 'normal' urban development (Harvey 2020). In Southeast Asia, these collective responses have emerged through existing networks of civil society groups and citizens. From self-imposed area quarantines to food-sharing, crowdfunding, and collective farming, crisis-activated actions have effectively countered the market-driven production of urban space. In addressing the questions on the process of collective action responses, limitations, and connecting collective action with today's urban development, there are two important considerations: first, the perspective of the actors on the ground in social mobilisation during a crisis has been key to understanding the processes behind these responses, and, second, actions that aim to question normalcy and create lasting change require sustainability. These two considerations are elaborated below.

First, since actions on the ground have been of key importance, we need to look at neighbourhoods as a group of households that can make collective decisions on local spatial governance (Beard and

Figure 18.1. Gatekeepers at Kampung Akuarium, Jakarta

Source: Dharma Diani (2020).

Dasgupta 2006). The COVID-19 pandemic provided a window onto the collective abilities of neighbourhoods in making purposive decisions for the public good in the absence of authoritative government responses to protect public health. A case in point is Jakarta, where the pandemic's early months became a stage for political competition: national elites opposed measures by the local governor-cum-political rival at the expense of public health (Jaffrey 2020). Amid this situation, various neighbourhoods took action, from restricting movements through collective guarding to disinfecting public spaces. For example, a poor urban neighbourhood in north Jakarta, Kampung Akuarium, imposed movement restrictions as early as 9 March 2020, before the city implemented official restrictions. Subsequently, residents built a gate and assigned shifts to guard the checkpoint (Figure 18.1). Local initiatives to curb large gatherings and encourage public health measures like mask-wearing occurred in various neighbourhoods across Indonesia (Figure 18.2), showing how collective actions were geared towards protecting shared spaces.

Amid the popularity of the 'cities as engines of economic growth' paradigm (Colenbrander 2016), the pandemic was also a reminder of the importance of food security. In Indonesia, food production has very much been a part of many societies' traditional cultural practices, but capitalist urban development has reduced the space to do so. Traditional fisherfolk in Jakarta Bay, for instance, have been sidelined for real estate-driven reclamation projects (Padawangi 2019b). The fertile island of Java is

Figure 18.2. Mask mandate banner in Kampung Peneleh, Surabaya

Source: Muhamad Rohman Obet (2020).

also the most populated and most industrialised. Even in a place like Bali, where agriculture is still tied to everyday life, the share of agriculture in the province's economy has continued to decline, in contrast with the growing share of tourism-related trade and services (Figure 18.3). Global tourism that is 'good' for the economy has threatened the sustainability of *subak* – the thousand-year-old traditional water management system for irrigation – as agricultural land use has competed with tourism (Salamanca et al. 2015). Such dependency on global tourism became the economy's Achilles' heel during the pandemic.

Therefore, it is unsurprising that a popular collective action during the pandemic was the return to farming. A group of youths called Serikat Tani Kota Semarang (STKS), for example, started cultivating unused land on the fringes of the city during the pandemic. There were also groups of youths in Bali who went back to farming as the urbanised, touristified economy ground to a halt (Firdaus 2020; Muhajir and

Figure 18.3. Selected professions in Bali, 2010–2016

Source: BPS (2016, February data cycle); Graph published in Padawangi (2019b).

Figure 18.4. 'Punk-Pangan' – free vegetable distribution at WALHI, Denpasar

Source: Gilang Pratama (2020).

Suriyani 2020). The return to farming (and fishing) also corresponded with food-sharing initiatives; for example, Denpasar Kolektif (Denpasar Collective), a hardcore punk community, initiated 'Punk-Pangan' (Punks for Food) to regularly distribute free vegetables at the offices of Wahana Lingkungan Hidup (WALHI) (Figure 18.4). The distribution of free vegetables also created space for greater advocacy against laws, projects, and practices considered harmful to the environment, such as the Benoa Bay reclamation and changes to the spatial planning, mining, and 2020 national omnibus 'job creation' laws. WALHI itself is an environmental NGO known for its advocacy activities for environmental issues in Indonesia; hence, the distribution of free vegetables at their offices, interspersed with handwritten advocacy posters on the table where they placed the vegetables, made the pandemic moment into a call for collective action to address wider environmental issues. In the case of STKS, the youths also developed training on the basic techniques of farming and food processing alongside classes on philosophical and sociological concepts that questioned capitalist development, including critical topics such as agrarian social movements, feminism, and ecology (STKS 2020).

These farming movements are examples of collective actions that were both pragmatic and political. By demonstrating society's ability to continue functioning socially, economically, and culturally, they promoted a message of resilience. Compared to the panic buying of basic supplies in cities like Hong Kong, Singapore, and Jakarta at the start of the pandemic, this association between farming and resilience was situated in the pandemic as a critique of 'cities as engines of economic growth' as an unsustainable paradigm that exploits the countryside for resources (Tacoli 1998). In practice, these farmers' collectives ranged from very pragmatic ones – choosing farming after being laid off from service jobs, for example – to ideologically purposive ones – challenging urban development trajectories and promoting ecological-environmental sustainability. Nevertheless, the promotion of resilience in farming as a form of collective action makes farming a 'purposive, meaningful, and potentially creative' way to challenge political establishments (Chesters and Welsh 2011, p.5), especially when they had regularly evicted farmers to develop infrastructure for urban economies.

Second, collective actions transcended beyond local neighbourhoods through peer-to-peer citizens' networks. Where government interventions were lacking and corporations' activities were slowed down, existing networks marshalled food resources from the countryside. Bursts of crowdfunding initiatives in the Philippines, Indonesia, and Singapore during the pandemic constituted collective actions beyond their immediate spatial territories. It is, however, fair to question the sustainability of these initiatives. Nathalie Dagmang (2020), an activist in Manila, said:

It feels frustrating knowing that what we were doing was still inefficient and unsustainable. The government has all the resources, communication channels, control over transportation, and the personnel for checkpoints and local units. They are the ones mandated, by virtue of our votes and taxes, to provide for our needs during calamities such as this. But where are they now?

These initiatives highlighted the lack of state capacity in these countries, and the sustainability of citizens' collective actions depended on their ability to evolve into a structured societal alternative.

On the one hand, the pandemic provided a political opportunity for collective actions that advocated for societal change. Restrictions on physical spaces for gatherings intensified the use of technology as a public sphere. For instance, Kampung Akuarium in Jakarta continued their ongoing land reform process through online meetings with government officials. Protests and discussions occurred online, covering issues such as environmental sustainability, critical thoughts on urbanisation-as-usual, and the distribution of land and agrarian reform. Examples of these online actions included the 'People's Court' (*Sidang Rakyat*) on 1 June 2020, which was facilitated by the Indonesia Legal Aid Foundation to gather testimonies of witnesses from many parts of Indonesia to demand revocation of the new mining law. Online–offline alliances also opened up possibilities to connect distant geographies to build solidarity, such as the crowdfunding initiative to buy rice from cement factory-threatened farmers in Central Java for the urban poor in Jakarta.

On the other hand, overreliance on the online sphere might perpetuate larger social inequalities in access to technology. Furthermore, there were signs of pandemic-induced shrinkage of civic spaces following restrictions on public gatherings, cuts in funding for democracy and human rights advocacy, movement restrictions, and further limitations on freedom of speech (Gomez and Ramcharan 2020). Restrictions in the name of preventing the virus's spread might have also functioned as tools of repression. As the pandemic lingered, citizens' attitudes shouldered the blame. The 'new normal' emerged as a popular term to represent living with the virus as a given reality while minimising its spread. However, the term carries urban-biased assumptions. The eagerness to practise the 'new normal', largely defined by hygiene practices and regulations on social distancing, reduced the role of citizens in pandemic alleviation to merely abiding by the rules. Such a 'new normal', while logically correlated to curbing the spread of the virus, reduced the problem to citizens' attitudes rather than questioning the larger problem of inequality in 'normal' urban development trajectories. While there have been legitimate questions on how citizens' lack of discipline worsened the pandemic, seeing the persistence of the pandemic solely as a problem of discipline increases the appeal of authoritarianism. Celebrating the achievements of countries that took more authoritarian approaches to containing the pandemic weakened the political opportunity to advocate for alternative societal structures and urban development paradigms. COVID-19 thus called into question 'the ability of the democratic model to cope with devastating events' (Belin and De Maio 2020, p.1).

The COVID-19 pandemic demonstrated how collective action could provide alternatives to 'normal' urbanisation through action on the ground, activating networks, and intensifying the use of an online public sphere. These collective actions highlighted alternatives to the 'normal' supply chain, the 'normal' competitive economy, and the 'normal' obsession with skyscrapers and buildings. The ability to collectively act and function autonomously in the local context – socially, economically, and culturally – allowed citizens to continue thriving during a crisis. These actions largely consisted of simple gestures in social relationships, care for the environment, and making economies relevant to the everyday life of the land. The sustainability of these alternatives, however, was also affected by the availability of space, resources, and time. With governments and economic powers actively promoting 'new normal' narratives, existing social inequalities and environmental issues could remain unresolved, potentially affecting spaces for collective actions that need to continue evolving to sustain their momentum.

Acknowledgements

I am grateful to Muhamad Rohman Obet and Nathalie Dagmang, and to the Southeast Asia Neighborhoods Network (SEANNET) in general, for the discussions, sharing of experiences, and solidarity that makes this chapter possible. I thank the Henry Luce Foundation for its funding support for SEANNET. I would also like to thank Ibu Dharma Diani (Kampung Akuarium), Gilang Pratama (Denpasar Kolektif, ForBALI, WALHI Bali), Asfinawati (Yayasan Lembaga Bantuan Hukum Indonesia/YLBHI), and Bosman Batubara (Serikat Tani Kota Semarang/STKS) for the sharing of ideas and their support, as well as for their consistency and resilience. Last but not least, I thank the editors for their feedback and for making this publication possible.

References

Beard, Victoria A.; and Dasgupta, Aniruddha. (2006). 'Collective action and community-driven development in rural and urban Indonesia'. *Urban Studies*, vol. 43, no. 9, pp. 1451–1468. https://doi.org/10.1080/00420980600749944

Belin, Célia; and De Maio, Giovanna. (2020). *Democracy after Coronavirus: Five Challenges for the 2020s*. USA: Brookings Institution. https://perma.cc /SYJ7-S7SZ [Last accessed 1 May 2021].

Brenner, Neil; Marcuse, Peter; and Mayer, Margit. (eds) (2012). *Cities for People, Not for Profit: Critical Urban Theory and the Right to the City*. UK: Routledge.

Cabannes, Yves; Douglass, Mike; and Padawangi, Rita. (eds) (2019). *Cities in Asia by and for the People*. Netherlands: Amsterdam University Press.

Castells, Manuel. (1983). *The City and the Grassroots: A Cross-Cultural Theory of Urban Social Movements*. USA: University of California Press.

Chang, Nicole. (2020). 'COVID-19: Supply chain remains robust, "panic buying" situation has stabilised, says Lawrence Wong'. CNA, 12 February. https://perma.cc/7YY9-SK6G [Last accessed 1 May 2021].

Chesters, Graeme; and Welsh, Ian. (2011). *Social Movements: The Key Concepts*. UK: Routledge.

Colenbrander, Sarah. (2016). *Cities as Engines of Economic Growth: The Case for Providing Basic Infrastructure and Services in Urban Areas*. UK: International Institute for Environment and Development Working Paper. https://perma.cc/G3CE-2SM7 [Last accessed 1 May 2021].

Dagmang, Nathalie D. (2020). 'Responding to Escolta's street vendors: How do we provide relief and security to the economically vulnerable?' *Bulatlat*, 2 May. https://perma.cc/NUH3-RDM6 [Last accessed 1 May 2021]

Firdaus, Febriana. (2020). '"Bali is not only about tourism": Covid-19 prompts rethink for island's residents'. *The Guardian*, 1 August. https://perma.cc /523Z-CHJ7 [Last accessed 1 May 2021].

Friedmann, John. (1992). *Empowerment: The Politics of Alternative Development*. UK: Blackwell.

Gomez, James; and Ramcharan, Robin. (2020). 'COVID-19 shrinks civil space in Southeast Asia'. *Jakarta Post*, 25 April. https://perma.cc/C6RN-YNVN [Last accessed 1 May 2021].

Harvey, David. (2020). 'We need a collective response to the collective dilemma of coronavirus'. *Jacobin*, 24 April. https://perma.cc/Y9QK-A3A7 [Last accessed 1 May 2021].

Jaffrey, Sana. (2020). 'Coronavirus blunders in Indonesia turn crisis into catastrophe'. Carnegie Endowment for International Peace, 29 April. https://perma.cc/YK3T-VQFX [Last accessed 22 January 2021].

Kong, Lily. (2007). 'Cultural icons and urban development in Asia: Economic imperative, national identity, and global city status'. *Political Geography*, vol. 26, no. 4, pp. 383–404. https://doi.org/10.1016/j.polgeo.2006.11.007

Kurohi, Rei. (2020). 'S'pore is gold standard for case detection: Harvard study'. *Straits Times*, 18 February. https://perma.cc/M6WU-R93S [Last accessed 10 July 2020].

Lefebvre, Henri. (2003). *The Urban Revolution*. USA: University of Minnesota Press.

Luscombe, Belinda. (2020). 'Architect Rem Koolhaas says redesigning public spaces was necessary before the pandemic'. *Time*, 14 May. https://perma.cc/9TJR-Z9C8 [Last accessed 1 May 2021].

Muhajir, Anton; and Suriyani, Luh De. (2020). 'Geliat petani muda Bali di tengah pandemic Covid-19'. Mongabay, 12 May. https://perma.cc/2G4C-BX6T [Last accessed 1 May 2021].

Ng, Eileen. (2020). 'Singapore battles virus hotspots in migrant workers' dorms'. *Associated Press*, 10 April. https://perma.cc/EA9S-BX2Z [Last accessed 1 May 2021].

Padawangi, Rita. (2019a). 'Forced evictions, spatial (un)certainties and the making of exemplary centres in Indonesia'. *Asia-Pacific Viewpoint*, vol. 60, no. 1, pp. 65–79. https://doi.org/10.1111/apv.12213

Padawangi, Rita. (2019b). 'Urban development, vulnerabilities, and disasters in Indonesia's coastal land reclamations: Does social justice matter?' in Lisa Reyes Mason and Jonathan Rigg (eds) *People and Climate Change: Vulnerability, Adaptation, and Social Justice*. UK: Oxford University Press, pp. 122–146. https://doi.org/10.1093/oso/9780190886455.003.0007

Salamanca, Albert M.; Nugroho, Agus; Osbeck, Maria; Bharwani, Sukaina; and Dwisasanti, Nina. (2015). *Managing a Living Cultural Landscape: Bali's Subaks and the UNESCO World Heritage Site*. Thailand: Stockholm Environment Institute Project Report 2015-05. https://perma.cc/3GLE-B4Q9 [Last accessed 1 May 2021].

Spinney, Laura. (2020). 'It takes a whole world to create a new virus, not just China'. *The Guardian*, 25 March. https://perma.cc/5XLL-8G7X [Last accessed 9 July 2020].

Stein, Samuel. (2019). *Capital City: Gentrification and the Real Estate State*. UK: Verso.

Serikat Tani Kota Semarang. (2020). *Sekolah di lahan*. https://perma.cc/Z9E9 -9GBJ [Last accessed 9 July 2020].

Tacoli, Cecilia. (1998). 'Rural-urban interactions: A guide to the literature'. *Environment and Urbanization*, vol. 10, no. 1, pp. 147–166. https://doi.org /10.1177/095624789801000105

Yeoh, Brenda. (2005). 'The global cultural city? Spatial imagineering and politics in the (multi)cultural marketplaces of South-East Asia'. *Urban Studies*, vol. 42, no. 5–6, pp. 945–958. https://doi.org/10.1080/00420980500107201

19. Community struggles and the challenges of solidarity in Myanmar

Ponpavi Sangsuradej

Myanmar is not unfamiliar with disaster. The country was hit in 2008 by Cyclone Nargis, which led to 90,000 confirmed deaths and US$10 billion in damage (Hurricanes: Science and Society 2015). Defying the military government's resistance to local and international aid, self-organised Burmese citizens rallied to support residents of the heavily flooded Irrawaddy Delta (Adams 2009). In 2020, Myanmar's elected government oversaw the country's official response to the COVID-19 pandemic, but the self-mobilisation of communities remained prominent. While the Myanmar government framed its efforts against the disease as demonstrating and inspiring national solidarity, many of its responses failed to account for the pervasive social and economic divisions within the country. This chapter primarily covers COVID-19 prevention efforts in Myanmar from the start of the COVID-19 pandemic until September 2020, with some comment on the military coup that began on 1 February 2021 and as of April 2021 was still ongoing. The chapter explores state and community-based responses, including the Myanmar government's uneven and politicised pandemic relief, challenges of urban civil society efforts in informal settlements, and community-level initiatives in rural areas. I argue that community-level responses to the COVID-19 pandemic further highlighted Myanmar's existing socio-economic divides and ethnic conflicts.

A divided nation

After its independence from Britain in 1948, Myanmar was plagued by decades of civil war between ethnic minorities and the Myanmar army (Tatmadaw), which took control of the state in a 1962 coup. This authoritarian rule resulted in further ethnic conflict and economic

How to cite this book chapter:
Sangsuradej, Ponpavi. 2022. 'Community struggles and the challenges of solidarity in Myanmar'. In: Shin, Hyun Bang; Mckenzie, Murray; and Oh, Do Young (eds) *COVID-19 in Southeast Asia: Insights for a post-pandemic world*. London: LSE Press, pp. 218–227. DOI: https://doi.org/10.31389/lsepress.cov.s License: CC BY 4.0.

mismanagement that continued to hinder the country's progress. Although the country saw its first freely elected government in 2015, poverty remained an important issue for Myanmar. The World Bank reported that, in 2017, the poor population in rural areas was 6.7 times higher in absolute terms than in urban areas, where economic development was more prevalent (World Bank 2019). The poorest families lived in the ethnic minority Chin State, suggesting a geographical correlation between poverty and the ongoing ethnic conflicts (World Bank 2019).

Economic and social development projects have been concentrated in urban areas such as the Mandalay and Yangon regions. Urban poverty, however, has remained a concern. For example, Yangon's informal settlements contained as many as 400,000 people, or 8% of the region's population (UN-Habitat 2020a, p.5). The socio-economic divides both within urban areas and between urban and rural settlements were evident in various official and community-based responses to the COVID-19 crisis, thus posing a real challenge to the already-divided nation.

While the general election in November 2020 saw a landslide for the civilian National League for Democracy, Myanmar fell into one of its darkest periods when the military staged a coup on 1 February 2021 and arrested dissidents, politicians, and citizens alike. To oppose the military takeover, people took to the streets as part of a nationwide civil disobedience movement. More than 103,000 government health workers went on strike and joined the movement (*Frontier Myanmar* 2021a). It was undeniable that health workers' strikes hindered the COVID-19 pandemic response, but a common protest refrain was that 'the military is more dangerous than COVID-19' (*Frontier Myanmar* 2021b).

State inefficiency amid public health crisis

Back in March 2020, though Myanmar had only seen five positive COVID-19 cases, the pandemic caused heightened alarm among citizens. With factories closed and lockdown impending, tens of thousands of Burmese migrants were returning from Thailand and Malaysia. The Myanmar government, however, was not ready to cope with such a large number of returnees. Myanmar citizens were alarmed by inconsistent state quarantine procedures. With migrants confused, many of them resisted quarantine enforcement, crossing the Thailand–Myanmar border undocumented or fleeing from the buses before reaching Yangon's Aung Mingalar bus station to avoid checkpoints and mandatory quarantine

(Ye Mon, Hein Thar, and Eaint Thet Su 2020). News channels displayed chaotic scenes of migrants trying to catch taxis and mingling in crowds. Inconsistent enforcement of quarantine exacerbated the anxiety. For example, 2,000 returnees were reportedly restricted to a quarantine facility, while the next day many thousands of newcomers were let go without having to go through the same procedure (Ye Mon, Hein Thar, and Eaint Thet Su 2020). Moreover, different rules and measures were introduced in different regions and states. By 23 March 2020, at least 215 out of Myanmar's 54 million people had tested positive, but COVID-19 testing was only available to those who had symptoms, which worried citizens because of asymptomatic cases (Leong 2020). Questions such as 'who will have to go through state quarantine?', 'why did some get away?', and 'who will get tested?' were whispered. Lack of resources meant insufficient staff and testing kits at border checkpoints (Ye Mon, Hein Thar, and Eaint Thet Su 2020).

The macroeconomic fallout of the COVID-19 pandemic in Myanmar heavily affected the country's households (ADB 2020). From April to May 2020, the Asia Foundation surveyed 750 businesses, which had reportedly laid off 16% of their workforces (Asia Foundation 2020, p.13). Moreover, the government's new social distancing regulations put a burden on vulnerable members of society. The construction industry was heavily hit by the crisis. The government imposed new restrictions of 50 people per construction site, a significant decrease from 1,000 workers during pre-COVID-19 times (Rhoads et al. 2020). This resulted in a huge drop in the employment of day labourers.

One of the main challenges was Myanmar's informal economy. Its large unbanked population became a problem for the government's COVID-19 fund and Economic Relief Plan (CERP), which was aiming for a resilient recovery through tax relief, credit for businesses, and food and cash for households. The CERP received criticism for its non-inclusiveness and inflexible spending targets (World Bank 2020). Two immediate relief efforts targeted vulnerable families: a special handout of five basic commodities (rice, cooking oil, salt, onions, and beans) in April 2020, and a two-instalment cash payment of 40,000 Myanmar kyat (around £22) in July and August 2020 (Htin Lynn Aung 2020). The eligibility criteria, however, were very narrow: a whole family would be excluded if any member owned land or was registered as having formal employment. In Myanmar's traditional households, several generations live together. Owing to these criteria, the entire family would miss out on the government's cash assistance if even one family member was ineligible (Rhoads 2020). These measures deepened the vulnerabilities of those already most affected by the economic impacts of the pandemic.

Self-mobilisation in urban areas and challenges on informal settlements

There were various reactions to the government's calls for public cooperation in the fight against the pandemic. The Myanmar government's response to the COVID-19 pandemic was shaped by its long-term aim of national unity. In contrast to ongoing and historical conflicts among the government, the military, and the wider population, the pandemic presented an invisible and external common enemy that threatened the physical body of the nation and its individuals. Mask-wearing in Myanmar was seen not just as a matter of self-protection but as a demonstration of a commitment to protect others. A sense of solidarity also pushed many civil society organisations to initiate community-based responses to facilitate state-led projects, e.g. assisting government staff in food distribution. Other efforts included food donations by local charities, student blood donation drives, and hotel owners providing free stays to healthcare personnel (Rhoads et al. 2020). This solidarity also manifested in initiatives aimed at addressing the perceived gaps in the government's response. In April 2020, the charity group People to People distributed basic goods to 2,660 trishaw drivers across Yangon who had lost their income during lockdown (Eaint Thet Su 2020). Other charity groups provided assistance, including funeral services and a free 24/7 ambulance service. These types of community efforts were widely publicised on social media. For example, a story of Myanmar citizens donating their electricity subsidy to aid the state's coronavirus fight was widely shared on social media (Kyaw Phyo Tha 2020). However, such solidarity efforts, while popular among urban dwellers who lived in relatively more affluent areas, did not engage with or attempt to address the socio-economic problems that necessitated these campaigns in the first place.

The scale of informal settlements in Yangon posed a challenge to tackling transmission. As reported in 2020, 400,000 people or 8% of Yangon's population lived in 423 informal settlements across the city (UN-Habitat Myanmar 2020a, p.5; see Figure 19.1). These communities had been living under threat of eviction since 2018. Moreover, as more than 70% of informal settlers were not registered on any housing record, the pandemic was a threat to their livelihood, income, and tenure. Relief efforts by the state and NGOs were hindered by a lack of

Figure 19.1. Map of informal settlements in Yangon

Source: UN-HABITAT Myanmar (2020a).
Note: Informal settlement areas are shown shaded orange.

data on the ground (UN-Habitat Myanmar 2020b, p.6). Moreover, according to a survey of the impact of the pandemic on informal settlements, 81% of the surveyed households had at least one member who
had lost their job in the preceding 30 days and 94% reported a decrease
in household income (UN-Habitat Myanmar 2020b, p.12). In addition
to lost income, the lockdown hindered communal projects that would
have been of help during these times. For example, residents of urban

savings groups used to meet daily before the pandemic to deposit savings, which enabled them to save a small amount for recurring costs such as electricity, rent, and food. Some groups even collected savings for community development projects such as sewage works (Rhoads et al. 2020). The ban on assembly, however, prevented regular community gatherings that used to bring together 10 or 20 people (Rhoads 2020).

Civil society actions were key to the prevention of COVID-19 in more disadvantaged areas, especially informal settlements. Community efforts in informal settlements underlined the existing inadequacy of government functions in the community. Local civil society organisations and self-organised *parahita* (voluntary sector) groups used their local knowledge and contacts to act as leading responders. The *parahita* groups provided training and tools to prevent the spread of coronavirus (Rhoads et al. 2020). They also coordinated with local and state governments to distribute food to those who did not meet the criteria for state aid. They distributed water and masks, sprayed disinfectants, and organised waste collection (Rhoads et al. 2020). According to UN-Habitat's survey (2020, p.4), half of the surveyed households feared eviction. As many residents lost their jobs in the informal sector, they decided to take loans for day-to-day expenses.

With an imminent fear of eviction by the government, several informal settlers' groups attempted to prove their worth as 'good citizens' and contribute to national solidarity. The Bawa Pann Daing business group from the informal settlement of Dagon Seikkan township started making masks in response to a shortage thereof (Liu 2020). Comprising 15 women, the self-sufficient venture produced 6,000 hand-sewn cotton masks. The group donated around 5,000 to the community and 800 to the local government. Often seen as society's outcasts, the group's members hoped that their contribution would alleviate the threat of eviction (Liu 2020).

Experiences in rural areas

In contrast to the campaigns by civil society in urban areas, community actions in rural areas were often driven by distrust towards a government that community members felt was neglecting them. The inconsistent quarantine measures mentioned earlier confused not only domestic travellers but also locals. Different states and regions introduced varying rules: quarantine ranged from zero to 21 days in state facilities. Some even required a health certificate for travellers (Ye Mon 2020). Lacking or distrusting official guidance, many villages organised their own informal checkpoints and mandated quarantine procedures to prevent the spread of COVID-19 and ensure their safety. West of the Yangon region, the Phya Tha Dike village tract[1] administrator and village elders decided among themselves to set up a school as a quarantine facility – similar measures were adopted in many areas across the country. The villagers felt it was a crucial step, as people in rural areas were already struggling to access healthcare services (Kyaw Ye Lynn, Ye Mon, and Naw Betty Han 2020). The Phya Tha Dike village had only one qualified healthcare worker, a midwife, and not enough tools and staff if an outbreak were to occur (Kyaw Ye Lynn, Ye Mon, and Naw Betty Han 2020).

Antagonistic feelings rose, especially towards migrants seen as bringing a disease from abroad (Lotha 2020). Many returnees from big cities like Yangon also faced stigmatisation and were forced to quarantine in community facilities far from their villages despite an order from the government that allowed domestic travellers to quarantine in a private home (Pollock and Aung Thet Paing 2020, p.2). Attitudes such as 'we don't know who's infected and who's not' caused fear and rifts in the community, as rumours were spread of returnees ignoring quarantine altogether (Lawi Weng 2020). It was hard to check who followed home quarantine in Burmese households, as private rooms were not always available (Pollock and Aung Thet Paing 2020, p.2).

Even though the villages took inspiration from state quarantine guidelines, there was no guarantee of a consistent standard. In Mon State, more than 36 township facilities operated largely on community initiatives (Kyaw Ye Lynn, Ye Mon, and Naw Betty Han 2020). Some smaller Mon townships, however, later shut down their own community-level quarantine centres and relegated returnees to a more centralised facility in town (Lawi Weng 2020). Throughout this continuous confusion, the state government was not involved (Lawi Weng 2020). These local facilities were initiated by local civil society organisations that donated money for medical supplies and human resources to carry out the project. For example, a volunteer group formed in February 2020 ran a community quarantine facility in Mon State's Ye township at their own initiative (Kyaw Ye Lynn, Ye Mon, and Naw Betty Han 2020). In April 2020, the government ordered that all quarantine schemes organised by wards and villages would need the approval of the regional committee, but this was met with resistance from locals (Kyaw Ye Lynn, Ye Mon, and Naw Betty Han 2020). Although local practices might not have followed government rules, many communities preferred breaking the law to sacrificing their own safety.

Conclusion

Community responses to the COVID-19 pandemic in Myanmar highlighted existing social and economic divides that had long been mishandled by the government. Positive responses seemed to come mainly from relatively affluent urban dwellers, while marginalised informal settlements, densely populated with low hygiene standards and scattered throughout the city, persisted. Dealing with the COVID-19 pandemic should have been an opportunity for the state to realign its view of these communities as being part of society rather than forgotten outcasts.

Community reactions to the central policies of regional and ward quarantine reflected wider political, economic, and ethnic divides and mistrust between the central government and the states. In 2020, Myanmar's governments continued their crackdown on critics, just as was done after 2008's Cyclone Nargis (Adams 2009). Even the democratically elected NLD government attempted to assert broad control over local organisations and threatened the livelihoods of many, especially ethnic minorities across the country. For example, anti-government statements were banned in Kayah State (Zue Zue 2020). Aung San Suu Kyi's aspirations of national solidarity were an illusion for many, as the government continued its oppression, attempting both to eradicate the disease and to stifle criticism of its response.

During the first months of the pandemic, Burmese citizens' reactions to state pandemic policies indicated wider political fractures and mistrust towards the authorities. The violent military coup of February 2021 then obliterated any chance to mend these divides. As of April 2021, nationwide protests and mass civil disobedience were continuing, and over 750 civilian deaths had been reported (*Reuters* 2021). The military's brutal actions utterly severed any link between communities and the state, leaving the fate of the entire nation uncertain.

Note

1. A village tract is the lowest subdivision of the Myanmar government administrative structure.

References

Adams, Brad. (2009). 'The lessons of Cyclone Nargis'. *Human Rights Watch*, 3 May. https://perma.cc/8ZW3-8EF2 [Last accessed 21 August 2020].

Asia Foundation. (2020). *COVID-19 Impact on Businesses: A Survey*, 5 June. https://perma.cc/8283-ZT7R [Last accessed 10 August 2020].

ADB (Asian Development Bank). (2020). *Economic Indicators for Myanmar, September 2020*. https://perma.cc/QN9P-AYQ7 [Last accessed 3 February 2021].

Eaint Thet Su. (2020). 'Charities, civil society lend a helping hand to the needy'. *Frontier Myanmar*, 16 April. https://perma.cc/9UE2-79TE [Last accessed 15 August 2020].

Frontier Myanmar. (2021a). '"More dangerous than COVID-19": Anti-military fury leaves SAC pandemic response in shambles', 25 March. https://perma.cc/V9KB-PGYG [Last accessed 29 April 2021].

Frontier Myanmar. (2021b). 'Striking health staff boycott COVID-19 jabs as the CDM grows', 9 March. https://perma.cc/JZD5-R226 [Last accessed 29 April 2021].

Htin Lynn Aung. (2020). 'Millions of families get first COVID-19 relief payments'. *Frontier Myanmar*, 1 August. https://perma.cc/A47M-Z4GD [Last accessed 15 August 2020].

Hurricanes: Science and Society. (2015). *Cyclone Nargis*. https://perma.cc/L4 WK-T6YL [Last accessed 21 August 2020].

Kyaw Phyo Tha. (2020). 'Myanmar citizens give up power subsidy to aid COVID-19 fight'. *The Irrawaddy*, 8 April. https://perma.cc/3N5J-MMZK [Last accessed 29 April 2021].

Kyaw Ye Lynn; Ye Mon; and Naw Betty Han. (2020). 'Community quarantine: On the rural frontline in the fight against COVID-19'. *Frontier Myanmar*, 17 April. https://perma.cc/U5AF-PHMT [Last accessed 15 August 2020].

Lawi Weng. (2020). 'Myanmar's Mon State consolidates quarantine centers for returning migrants'. *The Irrawaddy*, 6 April. https://perma.cc/4SNR -5N5R [Last accessed 29 April 2021].

Leong, Wai Kit. (2020). 'Enough COVID-19 test kits for Myanmar, says WHO representative'. CNA, 24 March. https://perma.cc/XK95-L9T6 [Last accessed 29 April 2021].

Lotha, Lesly. (2020). In Myanmar, quarantine facilities become first responders for returning migrant women. *UN Women*, 17 September. https://perma .cc/2ZL2-JLYY [Last accessed 29 April 2021].

Liu, John. (2020). 'Yangon's informal settlers stitching together a new community'. *Myanmar Times*, 26 June. https://perma.cc/GZJ2-GFSU [Last accessed 16 August 2020].

Nwet Kay Khin. (2020). 'Hitting where it hurts: Impacts of COVID-19 measures on Myanmar poor'. *Transnational Institute*, 6 July. https://perma.cc /CDC7-HEY2 [Last accessed 3 February 2021].

Pollock, Jacqueline; and Aung Thet Paing. (2020). 'COVID-19: Impact on migrant workers and country response in Myanmar'. *International Labour Organization*, 20 June. https://perma.cc/R745-WTSS [Last accessed 29 April 2021].

Reuters. (2021). 'Fighting erupts in Myanmar; junta to "consider" ASEAN plan', 27 April. https://perma.cc/XBF3-LRDB [Last accessed 29 April 2021].

Rhoads, Elizabeth. (2020). 'COVID-19 pandemic and Myanmar's response'. *The London Burma Reading Group*. Unpublished transcript.

Rhoads, Elizabeth; Thang Sorn Poine; Cho Cho Win; and Kyed, Helene. (2020). *Myanmar Urban Housing Diagnostic and COVID-19 Rapid Assessment*. USA: World Bank. https://perma.cc/ZG77-YB97 [Last accessed 4 August 2020].

UN-Habitat. (2020a). *COVID-19 Discussion Paper on Policy Options for Myanmar*. *Myanmar*: UN-Habitat. https://perma.cc/K396-LZX7 [Last accessed 29 April 2021].

UN-Habitat. (2020b). *Rapid Assessment of Informal Settlements in Yangon: COVID-19 pandemic and its impact on residents of informal settlements*. *Myanmar*: UN-Habitat. https://perma.cc/RC2Q-MTGR [Last accessed 10 August 2020].

World Bank. (2019). *Poverty Report – Myanmar Living Conditions Survey 2017*, 26 June. https://perma.cc/F63F-63SM [Last accessed 29 April 2021].

World Bank. (2020). *Myanmar's Economy Severely Impacted by COVID-19: Report*, 25 June. https://perma.cc/5MM5-K7BD[Last accessed 19 August 2020].

Ye Mon. (2020). 'Inconsistent quarantine rules leave domestic travel uncertain'. *Frontier Myanmar*, 3 June. https://perma.cc/AZ35-JCAM [Last accessed 15 August 2020].

Ye Mon; Hein Thar; and Eaint Thet Su. (2020). 'Alarm as thousands of returning workers ignore quarantine orders'. *Frontier Myanmar*, 27 March. https://perma.cc/BQ45-8DJB [Last accessed 15 August 2020].

Zue Zue. (2020). 'Myanmar's Kayah State angers activists with protest ban'. *The Irrawaddy*, 7 May. https://perma.cc/KU77-JJRM [Last accessed 20 August 2020].

20. Gotong royong and the role of community in Indonesia

Adrian Perkasa

'We are tired with DraSu, all we need is *gotong royong*!' This statement came from Husin Ghozali, alias Cak Conk, who was the owner of Warung Kopi (coffee shop or *warkop*) Pitu Likur in Surabaya, Indonesia. His coffee shop went viral in social media in the last week of July 2020, or the beginning of the new school year in Indonesia. The Indonesian government decided to conduct online learning, or School from Home (SFH), in all levels of education, from elementary to high school, owing to the COVID-19 outbreak. However, many students' parents were unhappy with this decision, especially in many households in the *kampung*s (neighbourhoods) of Surabaya. They felt it brought more difficulties to their families, who were already struggling very hard to cope with the new situation. Then, Cak Conk initiated a plan to help many students in his *kampung*. He invited students to use the Wi-Fi in his coffee shop during SFH (see Figure 20.1). Not only free access to the internet; he also provided a glass of tea or milk for the students who spent their school day there.

Unfortunately, the municipal government of Surabaya complained about Cak Conk's initiative. An official from the *Dinas Pendidikan* (Education Agency) of Surabaya warned students to avoid public spaces such as his *warkop* to prevent increasing numbers of COVID-19 cases. In line with this complaint, several members of the Surabaya Parliament also criticised the *warkop*. They urged the students to stay at home as regulated previously by the government. According to them, Surabaya's municipality would provide free internet in several public spaces in the neighbourhood, such as *Balai RW* (the neighbourhood hall). However, by mid-August 2020, this plan had remained on paper (Kholisdinuka 2020). Moreover, the students still came to Warkop Pitu

How to cite this book chapter:
Perkasa, Adrian. 2022. 'Gotong royong and the role of community in Indonesia'.
In: Shin, Hyun Bang; Mckenzie, Murray; and Oh, Do Young (eds) *COVID-19 in Southeast Asia: Insights for a post-pandemic world*. London: LSE Press, pp. 228–238.
DOI: https://doi.org/10.31389/lsepress.cov.t License: CC BY 4.0.

Figure 20.1. Free Wi-Fi for online schooling … Free: a cup of tea

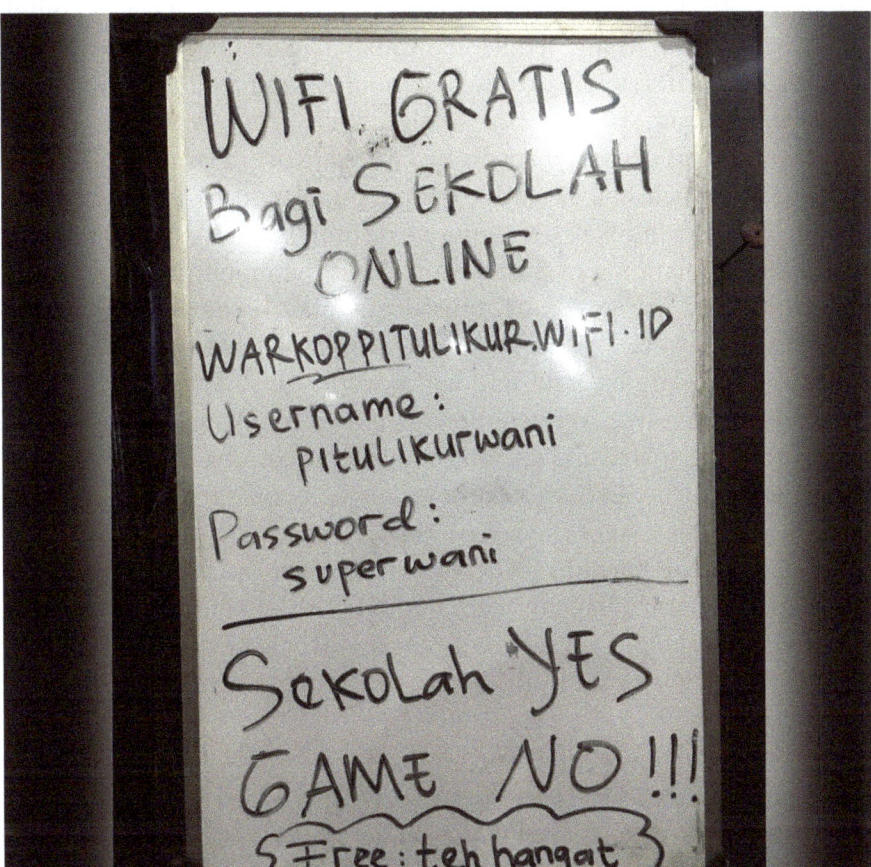

Source: Reproduced with permission of the photographer.

Likur every morning to attend school online. Cak Conk explained to me on the phone at the end of July:

> Actually, I don't have any intention to promote my business. I only heard many parents of my son's friends in the school face difficulties in providing internet for their children. Thus, I just quickly responded by open [sic] my *warkop* for them.

According to him, *kampung* people were tired of the failure of the government to minimise the pandemic's effects on their everyday lives (interview, 26 July 2020). Surabaya, the second biggest city in Indonesia and the capital of East Java province, had become the epicentre of the COVID-19 outbreak in this province. Moreover, this situation was worsening because of the bitter relationship between the mayor of Surabaya, Tri Rismaharini, and the governor of East Java, Khofifah Indar Parawansa. Many people in Surabaya, including Cak Conk, had a particular term referring to this relation: *Drama Surabaya* (Surabaya Drama) or *DraSu*.

This term was derived from *Drama Korea* (Korean Drama/K-Drama) or *DraKor*, which had recently become popular in many parts of the world. The first publicly acrimonious dispute between the two figures was over the planning of Surabaya to limit the mobility of people entering the city. The governor refused this plan because, according to her, large-scale social restrictions had been implemented under the authority of the regional and national governments. A few weeks later, they became involved in hostilities again after Tri Rismaharini told the media that the increasing COVID-19 cases in Surabaya were because many new patients in Surabaya hospitals had come from other towns in East Java. The two of them were engaged in conflict over two mobile polymerase chain reaction (PCR) test labs, which had been loaned from the Badan Penanggulangan Bencana Nasional (National Mitigation Disaster Agency) (Syambudi 2020). In early August 2020, the governor denied the mayor's claim of a decreasing number of COVID-19 cases in Surabaya.

The political rivalry between these two leaders also affected the pandemic's management, especially in hospitals and other healthcare facilities. According to Donny,[1] a doctor at Surabaya's Dr Soetomo Hospital, many difficulties emerged in handling the COVID-19 pandemic because of that rivalry (interview, 26 July 2020). The first and foremost problem, according to him, was that there was a lack of coordination between healthcare facilities managed by the municipality of Surabaya and those managed by the province of East Java. Dr Soetomo Hospital was the COVID-19 referral centre in the Surabaya region operated by the province of East Java. As soon as the COVID-19 outbreak began in Surabaya, many new patients sent directly to this hospital from Surabaya's healthcare facilities bypassed national and regional handling procedures for COVID-19. As a result, the hospital became an epicentre for the virus's spread. The spokesman for Surabaya's disease task force publicly stated several times, however, that the situation in Surabaya was under control (Widianto and Beo da Costa 2020a).

The Ikatan Dokter Indonesia (Indonesian Medical Association) admitted that healthcare workers had felt overwhelmed by the high number of patients and increasing workloads due to the government's pernicious management. Arguably, the world's highest rate of deaths of healthcare workers was in Indonesia (Barker, Walden, and Souisa 2020). Many medics in Surabaya were reportedly infected by the virus. 'It's like a vicious cycle, and the one blames another party and vice versa. The municipal and provincial governments should work together to protect their people. We need *gotong royong*,' Donny stressed to me. Again, there was another person who emphasised the importance of *gotong royong*, loosely translatable as 'communal or neighbourly help', to deal with the pandemic.

People practise *gotong royong* in everyday life and communal activities, from family celebrations such as weddings or engagements to the celebration of religious feasts and national days. It is also not uncommon for *kampung* people in urban areas like Surabaya to still practise *gotong royong*. The case of Cak Conk and his *warkop* has been the best example of how *gotong royong* has been relevant during the pandemic. In previous studies, scholars such as Bowen (1986), Guinness (1986), and Sullivan (1986) have argued that *gotong royong* is a construction from the state, rather than originally embedded in the Indonesian community. Even though this kind of mutual assistance reflects genuine indigenous notions of moral obligations and generalised reciprocity, it has been argued that it has been reworked by the state to become a cultural-ideological instrument for the mobilisation of village labour (Bowen 1986, pp.545–546). Suwignyo (2019, p.407) traced the initial concept of *gotong royong* to the Dutch colonial period and its further development under Japanese occupation and in post-independence Indonesia. According to his research, every government from the 1940s to the 1990s promoted *gotong royong* extensively as a signifier of collective identity. He concluded that *gotong royong* became a form of social engineering and an ingenious linguistic strategy by which elites orchestrated control over citizenship-making.

Nevertheless, the aspirations of Cak Conk and Doctor Donny in Surabaya seemingly contradicted such scholarly arguments. Rather than the state promoting *gotong royong*, the people were urging their government to act with *gotong royong* when facing troubled times during the pandemic. Or, can it be said that Cak Conk's initiative for *gotong royong* was only a particular case or even an exceptional phenomenon?

A recent survey by LaporCOVID-19 and the Social Resilience Lab at Nanyang Technological University showed that the majority of people in Surabaya tended to underestimate the risk of being infected by coronavirus. The economic and social situations also had a significant impact on the lesser perception of risk (LaporCOVID-19 2020). Thus, the *kampung* people who worked as daily labourers or ran a small *warung* like Cak Conk contributed heavily to this lesser perception of risk. Another scholar in Surabaya, Windhu Purnomo, also stressed the similar argument that most of the people in Surabaya only prioritised their economic interests in the traditional market and public spaces (Larasati 2020). These arguments were in line with the state perspective that often blamed people as a main cause of the high number of COVID-19 cases in Surabaya (Meilisa 2020).

To get a broader picture and understand the situation in Surabaya, I am turning my attention to look at bottom-up responses from other *kampung*s. Despite many limitations during this time, I tried to conduct fieldwork in online environments. I interviewed several *kampung* residents in Surabaya whom I had known before, including Cak Conk and Doctor Donny, via WhatsApp video calls. The first *kampung* I decided to scrutinise was Kampung Peneleh (see Figures 20.2 and 20.3). I have had a long and intensive relationship with the residents of this *kampung* for more than a decade. I have also been working as a local principal investigator for the Southeast Asian Neighbourhood Network (SEANNET) in Kampung Peneleh. I worked with several residents of Kampung Peneleh – including Obet, who assisted me with writing field notes from March to August 2020.

In the early period of the outbreak, the *kampung* situation seemed to confirm the results of the LaporCOVID-19 survey. There was a disagreement within the *kampung* in the adoption of new health protocols. A group of youths in a neighbourhood association promoted new hygienic attitudes by spraying disinfectant gas throughout the *kampung* and surrounding areas. However, not everyone, including several elders in the *kampung*, agreed with their initiative. The situation quickly escalated to a physical conflict between a youth neighbourhood association and other groups in the *kampung*. Eventually, after several heads of Rukun Tetangga (RT; the Neighbourhood Associations) mediated, the conflict subsided.

Perhaps one can quickly assess that the above situation displayed how many groups in the community resisted new health protocols. Nevertheless, the root of the dispute within Kampung Peneleh was not about resistance to health protocols after an outbreak. The first and foremost reason why many groups in Kampung Peneleh rejected the plan of fogging or spraying disinfectant was because this activity was fully sponsored by a political candidate who would be running in a mayoral election at the end of the year. This candidate was promoted

Figure 20.2. An entrance to Kampung Peneleh with notification banners to obey health protocols

Source: Image taken by Obet on 13 May 2020. Reproduced with permission of the photographer.

by the coalition of political parties who opposed the incumbent mayor from Surabaya. However, the heads of RT in Kampung Peneleh decided only to follow official protocols from the government.

Figure 20.3. Eid prayer in Kampung Peneleh during the pandemic

Source: Image taken by Obet on 31 July 2020. Reproduced with permission of the photographer.

Indeed, there was further resistance to obey new health protocols in Kampung Peneleh. Several *kyai* (Islamic leaders) and *ustadz* (Islamic teachers) refused a health protocol that requested the closure of the mosque until further notice. According to them, it was heretical to fear the threat of a virus; all Muslims should only fear God. Moreover, the situation became more difficult because the first request from the government coincided with Ramadan, a month full of fasting and praying for Muslims. There is a significant and historical mosque in Kampung Peneleh called Masjid Jamik (Grand Mosque). Before the COVID-19 outbreak, this place was a centre of religious activities during Ramadan not only for people in Kampung Peneleh but also for people from surrounding neighbourhoods. As a consequence, the *kyai* and *ustadz* declined the request of the official health protocols. They were still doing many activities as they usually did in Ramadan before the pandemic.

Later there was a circular letter dated 3 April 2020 from the Nahdlatul Ulama, the biggest Islamic organisation in Indonesia, in response to the COVID-19 outbreak. They issued a decision to slow the spread of coronavirus by avoiding any activities of meeting and gathering of Muslims in large numbers. It called for the implementation of worship during Ramadan, usually done together with the congregation in mosques or other praying halls, to be held at home. Other activities relating to the celebration of the Eid al-Fitr feast after Ramadan were also to defer to the provisions and policies of social restrictions and maintaining physical distance as determined by the government's official health protocols (Surat Edaran PB Nahdlatul Ulama 2020). Likewise, Muhammadiyah, another prominent Islamic organisation in Indonesia, had released a similar statement several days earlier (Surat Edaran PP Muhammadiyah 2020). Although these instructions were not directly implemented in Peneleh, the *kyai* and *ustadz* gradually started following it. Moreover, these figures also participated in promoting the government's instruction for people to stay at home for Eid al-Fitr and not going back to their respective regions or *mudik*. They did it through *gotong royong* with other *kampung* residences, including those who professed other religions such as Christianity, Hinduism, and Confucianism.[2]

Another case came from Kampung Pabean, where the biggest traditional market in Surabaya is located. As expected by previously mentioned scholars like Windhu Purnomo, indeed, many daily workers in that market were not obeying health protocols. However, it was only a slice of reality in the market and the *kampung*, and it was incomplete. Sahib, who was living in this *kampung* and was also a caretaker of the neighbourhood association there, told me another story. Together with the association, he always reminded everyone in the market and the neighbourhood to follow health protocols. In addition, they provided daily workers in the market with a free mask every day. Furthermore, the neighbourhood association of Kampung Pabean was taking care of the poor people who became infected by the virus and were required to self-quarantine at home. They voluntarily supplied provisions to them during the quarantine: Sahib thus argued that 'we should *gotong royong* to take care of ourselves' (interview, 27 July 2020).

Conclusions

There were many bottom-up initiatives led by the people of Surabaya's *kampung*s, but they have been neglected by most scholars. Instead of endorsing these people's initiatives, some scholars have only painted the same picture as the state – a perspective that has seen people's lack of awareness as the leading cause of the increasing numbers of COVID-19 cases in Surabaya. People like Cak Conk and the residents of Kampung Peneleh and Kampung Pabean have effectively incorporated the concept of *gotong royong* as a strategy to face the pandemic. They have urged and challenge the government, especially the municipality of Surabaya and the East Java provincial government, to set aside political enmity and use *gotong royong* to prevent further adverse effects from COVID-19.

As Springer (2020, p.114) has stated, in this challenging moment, people can gather, depending not upon the state and the command of any authority but on their collectivity. As one could see in the people's *gotong royong*, collectivity was vital not only during this time but also for their future as urban dwellers and Indonesian citizens. However, Indonesia's crisis went from bad to worse. Indonesia failed to bring the pandemic under control after March 2020: as of December 2020, there were 563,680 confirmed cases and 17,479 confirmed fatalities, plus another nearly 70,000 suspected cases. It has had by far the most extensive caseload and death toll in Southeast Asia, and the data showed that at the time of writing the situation was intensifying (Widianto and Beo da Costa 2020b). Following Harari's (2020) argument, today's civilisation faces an acute crisis, not only because of coronavirus but also because of the lack of trust among humans. People must trust science, and citizens need to trust public authorities. In addition to that, the state should show that its citizens can trust them. As with scientists, citizens, and public officials, trust and good faith prevail when people can rely on each other to uphold their commitments. Instead of requiring obedience, public authorities can appeal to common goals so that everyone can appreciate the needs that underlie a pledge or policy.

Notes

1. I have changed the names of all informants except Cak Conk and his *warkop*.

2. Indonesia's Ministry of Religion recognised Confucianism as one of six official religions in Indonesia.

References

Barker, Anne; Walden, Max; and Souisa, Hellena. (2020). 'In five days, Dea lost half her family to coronavirus. Now she's fighting COVID-19 alone in isolation'. *ABC News*, 26 June. https://perma.cc/D7JS-Z93S [Last accessed 31 July 2020].

Bowen, John. (1986). 'On the political construction of tradition: Gotong Royong in Indonesia'. *The Journal of Asian Studies*, vol. 45, no. 3, pp. 545–561. https://doi.org/10.2307/2056530

Guinness, Patrick. (1986). *Harmony and Hierarchy in a Javanese Kampung*. Singapore: Oxford University Press.

Harari, Yuval Noah. (2020). 'In the battle against coronavirus, humanity lacks leadership'. *Time*, 15 March. https://perma.cc/VC9D-L4DC [Last accessed 9 January 2021].

Kholisdinuka, Alfi. (2020). 'DPRD Surabaya Desak Pemkot Tambah Subsidi Internet Untuk Anak Miskin'. *Detik News*, 13 August. https://perma.cc/6CHQ-7VBS [Last accessed 3 September 2020].

LaporCOVID-19. (2020). *Persepsi Risiko Surabaya*. https://perma.cc/PQ5M-SV3R [Last accessed 3 September 2020].

Larasati, Aziza. (2020). 'Penyebab Jatim Pusat COVID-19 Kurangnya Disiplin dan Kesadaran Masyarakat'. *Mata-Mata Politik News*, 3 July. https://perma.cc/MJW4-2PY4 [Last accessed 3 September 2020].

Meilisa, Hilda. (2020). 'Khofifah Sebut Tingkat Kepatuhan Protokol COVID-19 Surabaya Raya Rendah'. *Detik News*, 24 June. https://perma.cc/9HBM-9RTK [Last accessed 3 September 2020].

Springer, Simon. (2020). 'Caring geographies: The COVID-19 interregnum and a return to mutual aid'. *Dialogues in Human Geography*, vol. 10, no. 2, pp. 112–115. https://doi.org./10.1177/2043820620931277

Sullivan, John. (1986). 'Kampung and state: The role of government in the development of urban community in Yogyakarta'. *Indonesia*, vol. 41, pp. 63–88. https://doi.org/10.2307/3351036

Suwignyo, Agus. (2019). 'Gotong royong as social citizenship in Indonesia, 1940s to 1990s'. *Journal of Southeast Asian Studies*, vol. 50, no. 3, pp. 387–408. https://doi.org/10.1017/S0022463419000407

Syambudi, Irwan. (2020). 'Perseteruan Risma Dan Khofifah Di Zona Merah Corona'. *Tirto.ID*, 9 June. https://perma.cc/3NMK-LYFV [Last accessed 1 August 2020].

Warkop Pitu Likur. (2020a). 'Hari pertama adek2 kita lagi semangat belajar daring memanfaatkan wifi di warkop PituLikur secara gratis dan free teh hangat juga'. Twitter, 20 July. https://perma.cc/XL62-37H9 [Last accessed 26 July 2020]

Warkop Pitu Likur. (2020b). 'Tetap semangat belajar adek2, walaupun dgn keterbatasan dimasa pandemi ini'. Twitter, 21 July. [Last accessed 26 July 2020]. https://perma.cc/D96N-X6QF[Last accessed 26 July 2020].

Widianto, Stanley; and Beo Da Costa, Agustinus. (2020a). 'Coronavirus patients flood hospitals in Indonesia's second-largest city'. *Reuters*, 28 May. https://perma.cc/7HV6-36GW [Last accessed 1 August 2020].

Widianto, Stanley; and Beo Da Costa, Agustinus. (2020b). 'Death of senior doctor rings alarm bells in pandemic-struck Indonesia'. *Reuters*, 3 December. https://perma.cc/G2UT-G6WA [Last accessed 9 January 2021].

21. Rewriting food insecurity narratives in Singapore

Al Lim

For many, the phenomenon of food insecurity can be reduced to a fundamental fear: what happens if I run out of food? People were made acutely aware of this fear at the start of the COVID-19 pandemic in early 2020, when supermarkets began to run out of essentials. In Singapore, I propose that this fear was rooted in the narrative of scarcity and accelerated by the pandemic's crisis rhetoric. It extended a scarcity narrative developed since Singapore's independence, being an island nation cut off from Malaysia that had to survive with limited resources. Concurrently, this built on the neo-Malthusian logic seen in the Green Revolution of food scarcity as the main framing of the problem of hunger, instead of malnutrition and interconnected social issues. This way, the narrative obfuscated a more important statistic – 10.4% of Singapore's population was still food insecure in 2020 (Nagpaul, Sidhu, and Chen 2020).[1]

This chapter reframes Singapore's narrative of food insecurity away from a misapplied scarcity and securitisation lens, instead connecting food insecurity to the lived experience thereof. Engaging this challenge paves the way for key discussions about how food insecurity is not isolated but intersects with consumption and malnutrition through axes of inequality such as class, gender, climate, and race. Solely increasing food production has not been nor will be the solution to eradicating hunger, especially without attention to its wider social processes. This has vital implications for the current national strategy of ramping up food production and diversifying food sources. In the wake of the pandemic, it has become even more vital to consider the heterogeneity of Singapore's social body to ensure future foodscape policy decisions do not reproduce existing inequalities.

How to cite this book chapter:
Lim, Al. 2022. 'Rewriting food insecurity narratives in Singapore'. In: Shin, Hyun Bang; Mckenzie, Murray; and Oh, Do Young (eds) *COVID-19 in Southeast Asia: Insights for a post-pandemic world*. London: LSE Press, pp. 239–248.
DOI: https://doi.org/10.31389/lsepress.cov.u License: CC BY 4.0.

Constructing the strategic myth of food insecurity

Food insecurity is not food scarcity. Eradicating scarcity or having excessive food supply does not mean that there is no food insecurity, as many may not receive food due to distribution channels, accessibility, or other confounding factors. So, why has this connection between insecurity and scarcity been constructed or accepted in Singapore? One way to account for this is that the scarcity narrative has been built on two powerful logics: the historical trope of Singapore's scarcity thinking since its inception and the neo-Malthusian, Green Revolution rationale.

Scarcity is ingrained in Singapore's ideology. The dominant narrative of scarcity and survival can be traced to modern Singapore's origins (Sadasivan 2014). It is common knowledge in Singapore that the country began as a resource-scarce island that separated from Malaysia in the 1960s and, through a miraculous transformation, became a contemporary economic powerhouse. Part of this involved the state-invoked strategy of militarisation to ensure political tranquillity through perceptions of crises since the country's independence (Chong and Chan 2017, p.367; Tan 2001). The narrative legitimated drastic measures that the state needed to take, especially against those that might have seemed to come against it. Furthermore, crises stoke national sentiments. Consider how a government and population must do whatever it takes to ensure its success in an existential battle. Through the repeated invocation and naturalisation of scarcity-premised crises, this logic has remained dominant in contemporary Singaporean imaginaries.

To be sure, Singapore is a small island city-state and its resource scarcity cannot be wholly dismissed, but what must be explored further is whether the scarcity narrative is still appropriate. Singapore's position as a global city and top-ranked smart city, and its stellar economic profile, has placed the country in a radically different place from the 1960s. The repeated strategy of invoking crises and the rationale of not having any natural resources has simplified a far more complex reality, a process that has served to enhance the state's political position. However, the use of the scarcity narrative in contemporary Singapore has faltered because it no longer stands for a corresponding reality, as the city does not face the same 'scarcity' that it did 60 years ago.

Singapore's historical penchant for scarcity blends with the neo-Malthusian, Green Revolution narrative of scarcity, food production, and demographic constraints. Thomas Malthus (1798) is known for his theory that the geometric-ratio (exponential) increase of the population would far exceed the arithmetic-ratio (linear) increase of food production, resulting in catastrophe when population outstrips food supply. The Malthusian link between population and food scarcity has been leveraged by proponents of the Green Revolution, claiming triumph over hunger and population woes through increased agricultural productivity. This connection was clearly stated when Norman Borlaug (1970) invoked the 'Population Monster' in his Nobel lecture, saying that the Green Revolution had only temporarily stemmed the tide against problems of human reproduction, where the scarcity of resource use remained the ultimate enemy.

However, the link between scarcity and hunger has been socially constructed and tenuous. As Amartya Sen (1983, p.8) has written, the 'mesmerizing simplicity of focusing on the ratio of food to population has persistently played an obscuring role over centuries'. The empirical evidence supports this and exposes the failures of this logic. While food production increased after the Green Revolution's implementation of 'miracle wheat' from its initial phases in Mexico in the 1950s, the number of hungry people increased by more than 11% in the decades of the Green Revolution's major advances (excluding China as an anomaly) (Rosset, Collins, and Lapp 2000). This finding questioned the success of the Green Revolution and challenged how increasing food supply and capacities do not necessarily reduce the problem of hunger and malnutrition. Moreover, critics of the Green Revolution have pointed out that it was a set of misguided technologies forced on developing nations – a form of American cultural imperialism – that disrupted rural patterns, cultivated patterns of dependency for seeds and chemicals, and caused largescale environmental degradation (Beeman and Pritchard 2001). While the Green Revolution has ended, its legacy has far from disappeared (Patel 2013). The notion of not having enough (food scarcity) during COVID-19 powerfully evoked and legitimated the need for increased food production, which has been the case for Singapore, despite little empirical support for the connection between food scarcity and hunger.

The two narratives of scarcity from Singapore's inception and the Green Revolution have combined to produce a strategic myth. This myth was not originally unfounded owing to strategic actions against material and resource constraints. Nevertheless, its continued usage has misapplied the logic of scarcity. The myth – an invocation of present-day food scarcity as food insecurity – no longer conformed to the reality of pandemic-era Singapore or the actions that it has legitimated, such as the heavy focus on agricultural innovation. In other words, the scarcity rationale from the post-independence narrative did not fit its contemporary Singaporean context, and resulting actions of increasing technological production must be critically reconsidered.

'Security' and COVID-19 as catalysts

The securitisation discourse and effects from the COVID-19 pandemic also highlighted the urgency of food scarcity, amplifying this strategic myth. As a catalyst for this narrative, the 'security' aspect sharpened the need for apparent food production or diversifying food sources to address scarcity. The framing of securitisation relied on the construction of an external enemy, using the logic of survival, urgency, and defence as a necessary response to danger or risk (Sahu 2019). This enabled the actors responsible to undertake whatever means necessary to fight the problem. In other words, the discursive focus on external food security relied upon, as security expert Naraghi-Anderlini (2020) has claimed, the belief that the deities of national security can never be questioned.

Ample evidence for securitising food security premised on addressing scarcity can be found in public discourse and reportage of COVID-19 and food insecurity in Singapore. It was imperative to 'secure a supply of safe food for Singapore', according to the Singapore Food Agency (2019). This was reinforced by Minister of Trade and Industry Chan Chun Sing (2020) expressing how Singapore should not 'comprise our ability to secure such supplies from other sources by revealing our national stockpile'. Historically, Singapore had been '*buttressing*' its food security for decades (Ng 2020), and it had now become 'every individual's fight' to maintain it (Tan 2020). The discursive repetition of securitised terms like 'security', 'fighting', 'buttressing', and 'stockpiling' framed Singapore's need to secure its food supply using military terminology. They became part of the country's naturalised and necessary discursive response to the pandemic.

The rhetoric of securitisation, along with uncertainty in the time of COVID-19, complemented a set of strategic acts by the government. The Singaporean state adopted numerous measures to assuage public fears, such as Minister of Trade and Industry Chan Chun Sing posting pictures of 300,000 eggs arriving in March 2020. This emphasised the resilience of stockpiling strategies by national supermarket NTUC FairPrice, which avoided volatile price fluctuations and shortages. To further clarify what went on at the start of the pandemic, the state published an article that claimed that Singapore's food supply was never really at any risk and that it was an inter-agency effort between the Singapore Food Agency, the Ministry of Trade and Industry, Enterprise Singapore, and the Ministry of Foreign Affairs to ensure agri-trade was maintained through diverse and resilient mechanisms (Government of Singapore 2020). These public announcements complemented the Agri-Food and Veterinary Authority of Singapore's (2013) food security roadmap, which primarily focused on diversifying sources of imports, investing abroad, developing industry, producing locally, and stockpiling. The COVID-19 pandemic resulted in an acceleration and expansion of these long-term plans for securitisation, as the state narrative remained resolute in its defence against food scarcity through a security modality.

What about lived food insecurities?

What the strategic myth and scarcity narratives missed was how food insecurity is a lived experience of hunger and malnutrition. It has been apparent that inequality exists in Singapore (Teo 2017a). Specifically, inequality in domestic food consumption and security existed prior to COVID-19. Based on the definition of food security in the World Food Summit (1996), all people at all times should have access to sufficient, safe, and nutritious foods to meet their dietary needs and food preferences for an active and healthy life.[2] This was the working definition that the nationally representative survey of the Lien Centre for Social Innovation (LCSI) used, and the results indicated that 10.4% of Singaporean and permanent resident (PR) households had been severely (3.5%) or moderately (6.9%) food insecure in the previous 12 months (Nagpaul, Sidhu, and Chen 2020).

These statistics were pre-pandemic, and COVID-19 undoubtedly worsened them. Many of those who were food insecure lived in one- or two-room flats, and only 22% of food-insecure households were seeking support, due to social stigmatisation (Nagpaul, Sidhu, and Chen 2020). The pandemic's effects of lockdowns, economic and financial precarity, cabin fever, and compounding stresses increased the intensity and number of households facing food insecurity. Little representative data was available on the long-drawn-out effects of the pandemic, though social isolation served to reinforce the very boundaries preventing food-insecure households from reaching out in the first place. Therefore, the domestic portrayal of food insecurity, where not all people have access to adequate food at all times, was rendered less visible by the strategic myth of scarcity.

The lived experience of food insecurity has also been fundamentally a question of health. Adverse health outcomes due to food insecurity have long been documented, affecting cognitive performance and being linked to higher risks of depression, anxiety, and cardiovascular risks such as hypertension and diabetes (Gundersen and Ziliak 2015; Seligman, Laraia, and Kushel 2011). The reduction in the comprehensive dietary requirements of food insecurity added to existing physical and mental health burdens from the pandemic.

These health tolls have also been unevenly distributed throughout the population along lines of inequality. The strategic myth has homogenised the population as benefiting wholesale from improved food production but has done little to unpack the disadvantages and other myths along axial intersections such as class and the climate disaster, as well as citizenship, gender, and race (Dutta 2015; Teo 2017a; Teo 2017b).

A new narrative of food insecurity

As a direct response to COVID-19, food production capacities ramped up, with urban farms becoming popular in the country. The increase in productive capacities was part of efforts to increase the domestic production of Singapore's nutritional needs from 10% to 30% by 2030 (Teng 2020). This goal, along with the state's diversification strategies, was driven by the notion of scarcity and running out of food. To write against the strategic myth of food-insecurity-as-scarcity became an important endeavour, raising the critical question of: food security for whom?

Singapore does not need another Green Revolution and more scarcity thinking; food insecurity is not a simple, technocratic fix of production and supply. Addressing the problem of food insecurity must simultaneously account for its interconnected social processes, distribution channels, and the people consuming the food. Distributive channels and the 'who' can be illuminated by connecting it to community initiatives such as Eat for Good, Food from the Heart, and Foodbank's Feed the City. They continued to alleviate food insecurity during the lockdown and provided for families in need while supporting local businesses, and they should help to shape directions for addressing national food insecurity as vital stakeholders.

Better health and well-being outcomes for citizens during and beyond COVID-19 are at stake. The pandemic thus played an expository role, bringing into sharp relief and exacerbating social inequalities like extant food security, as well as powerful ideologies like the scarcity narrative that undergird policy decisions. Considering the impact of the scarcity narrative, what narratives can Singapore rewrite? Indeed, with the series of wicked problems currently facing the island nation, what narratives *must* Singapore rewrite? For example, what happens if there is a shift from scarcity to frugality? Both acknowledge resource limits. Where the former evokes anxiety around the possibility of running out of resources, implying the need to securitise, the latter generates less anxiety while still maintaining the need for a more circumspect management of resources. This way, Singapore can mitigate the reproduction of mistakes that technology-as-salvation and neo-Malthusianism have wrought while creating more equitable foodways. Moreover, this chapter posits that being the 'top' in the world does not mean being free of problems, and other cities can undertake similar exercises to reflect on their own strategic myths, extant social inequalities, and the series of wider processes that the pandemic painfully exposed. Thus, to challenge inherited myths is also to enact more caring and careful modes of policymaking.

Notes

1. The statistic was released in a nationally representative survey by the Lien Centre for Social Innovation (LCSI) in August 2020, uncovering the hidden pockets of food insecurity in what the Economist Intelligence Unit (2019) had ranked as the most food-secure country in the world.

2 Compare this definition with how the Economist Intelligence Unit's (2019) ranked Singapore top in food security. The latter's three evaluative measures – affordability, availability, and quality and safety – are external components that pay little attention to the lived experiences of food insecurity. These indicators measure how resistant Singapore's food supply chain is to shocks, whether consumers have a wide variety of food to purchase at stable prices, and if the nutritional quality and safety of food are relatively high. The measures are determined by external factors such as economic tariffs, the amount invested in research and development, and the diversification of foods. While important, the definition can be integrated with a more expansive understanding of food security using the World Food Summit's definition.

Acknowledgements

Special thanks to Professor Sylvia Chant, Professor Michael Dove, Professor Paul Kockelman, Vanessa Koh, Jolene Lum, Isabelle Li, and the editors – Professor Hyun Bang Shin, Dr Murray Mckenzie, and Dr Do Young Oh – for their generous contributions in shaping this chapter.

References

Agri-Food and Veterinary Authority of Singapore. (2013). *AVA's Food Security Roadmap for Singapore, Food for Thought*. Singapore: Singapore Food Agency. https://perma.cc/APY3-A97L [Last accessed 20 September 2020].

Beeman, Randal S.; and Pritchard, James A. (2001). *A Green and Permanent Land: Ecology and Agriculture in the Twentieth Century*. USA: University Press of Kansas.

Borlaug, Norman. (1970). *Acceptance Speech, on the Occasion of the Award of the Nobel Peace Prize in Oslo, Norway*. https://perma.cc/TCA2-T6P3 [Last accessed 21 August 2020].

Chan, Chun Sing. (2020). *Ministerial Community Walkabout at Jurong Spring Division*, 9 February. https://perma.cc/R5CW-RYCL [Last accessed 19 August 2020].

Chong, Alan; and Chan, Samuel. (2017). 'Militarizing civilians in Singapore: preparing for "crisis" within a calibrated nationalism'. *The Pacific Review*, vol. 30, pp. 365–384. http://doi.org/10.1080/09512748.2016.1249906

Dutta, Mohan J. (2015). *Food Insecurity and Health of Bangladeshi Workers in Singapore: A Culture-Centered Study*. Singapore: CARE White Paper Series, National University of Singapore. https://perma.cc/JM95-2JZE [Last accessed 20 August 2020].

Economist Intelligence Unit. (2019). 'Global Food Insecurity Index: Rankings and trends'. *The Economist*. https://perma.cc/76NC-J8PZ [Last accessed 19 August 2020].

Government of Singapore. (2020). *Food Security: It's Not Just about the Eggs*. https://perma.cc/5TKK-RT9M [Last accessed 28 August 2020].

Gundersen, Craig; and Ziliak, James P. (2015). 'Food insecurity and health outcomes'. *Health Affairs*, vol. 34, pp. 1830–1839. http://doi.org/10.1377/hlthaff.2015.0645

Malthus, Thomas. (1798). *An Essay on the Principle of Population, as It Affects the Future Improvement of Society*. UK: Printed for J. Johnson.

Nagpaul, Tania; Sidhu, Dalvin; and Chen, Jinwen. (2020). *The Hunger Report: An In-Depth Look at Food Insecurity in Singapore*. Singapore: Lien Centre for Social Innovation. https://perma.cc/K5B4-5ML6 [Last accessed 16 September 2020].

Naraghi-Anderlini, Sanam. (2020). *The COVID-19 Crisis Response: Putting Women at the Centre*. LSE Institute of Global Affairs, 29 April. https://perma.cc/TGT3-QM2A [Last accessed 19 August 2020].

Ng, Jun Sen. (2020). 'The big read: Singapore has been buttressing its food security for decades. Now, people realise why'. *CNA*, 23 March. https://perma.cc/Z5FL-LJQT [Last accessed 19 August 2020].

Patel, Raj. (2013). 'The long green revolution'. *The Journal of Peasant Studies*, vol. 40, no. 1, pp. 1–63. https://doi.org/10.1080/03066150.2012.719224

Rosset, Peter; Collins, Joseph; and Lapp, Frances Moore. (2000). 'Lessons from the green revolution: Do we need new technology to end hunger?' *Tikkun Magazine*, vol. 15, no. 2, pp. 52–56. https://perma.cc/US4F-P9ET [Last accessed 17 September 2020].

Sadasivan, Viswa. (2014). 'A narrative for winning', in Victor R. Savage (ed.) *Singapore Challenged: The Uneasy and Unchartered Road Ahead*, pp. 13–20. Singapore: National University of Singapore Society. https://perma.cc/7M59-AD7K [Last accessed 26 May 2021].

Sahu, Anjan Kumar. (2019). 'Referent object, securitising actors and the audience: The climate change threat and the securitisation of development in India'. *Cambridge Review of International Affairs*, pp. 1–24. http://doi.org/10.1080/09557571.2019.1707509

Seligman, Hilary K.; Laraia, Barbara A.; and Kushel, Margot B. (2010). 'Food insecurity is associated with chronic disease among low-income NHANES participants'. *The Journal of Nutrition*, vol. 140, pp. 304–310. http://doi.org/10.3945/jn.109.112573

Sen, Amartya. (1983). *Poverty and Famines: An Essay on Entitlement and Deprivation*. UK: Clarendon Press.

Singapore Food Agency. (2019). *About SFA*. https://perma.cc/R3VY-UGYP [Last accessed 19 August 2020].

Tan, Kenneth Paul Andrew Sze-Sian. (2001). 'Civic society and the new economy in patriarchal Singapore: Emasculating the political, feminizing the public. *Crossroads: An Interdisciplinary Journal of Southeast Asian Studies*, vol. 15, pp. 95–122. https://perma.cc/M6TN-XN8U [Last accessed 17 August 2020].

Tan, Audrey. (2020). 'Safeguarding Singapore's food security at the national and household levels during coronavirus pandemic'. *Straits Times*, 8 April. https://perma.cc/N96D-59D7 [Last accessed 19 August 2020].

Teo, You Yenn. (2017a). *This is What Inequality Looks Like*. Singapore: Ethos Books.

Teo, You Yenn. (2017b). 'Poor people don't like oats either', in Kah Seng Loh, Ping Tjin Thum and Jack Meng-Tat Chia (eds) *Living with Myths in Singapore*, pp. 239–248.

Teng, Paul. (2020). 'Assuring food security in Singapore, a small island state facing COVID-19'. *Food Security*, vol. 12, pp. 1–4. http://doi.org/10.1007/s12571-020-01077-0

World Food Summit. (1996). Rome Declaration on World Food Security. Rome: Food and Agriculture Organization of the United Nations. https://perma.cc/P98L-DW4W [Last accessed 20 August 2020].

22. Happiness-sharing pantries and the 'easing of hunger for the needy' in Thailand

Thanapat Chatinakrob

The COVID-19 pandemic directly affected the Thai economy and its growth projections, as Thailand was one of the first countries with cases (WHO 2020). The Thai economy, which relied on global trade, shrank by at least 5% in 2020 (World Bank 2020, p.4; USDA Foreign Agricultural Service 2020, pp.2–6). From March 2020, the service sector also faced a sharp decline in tourism and other related industries, such as transportation, accommodation, and food service activities. It accounted for approximately 15% of GDP (World Bank 2020, pp.8–11). Household welfare was likely to be more severely affected by the pandemic. The number of households living below US$5.50 per day doubled, from 4.7 million in the first quarter of 2020 to an estimated 9.7 million in the second quarter of 2020 (World Bank 2020, pp.26–28). The Thai government came up with strategic preparedness and response plans (WHO 2020, pp.1–3) to tackle the pandemic and provide compensation for its people, but they were not adequate. Fortunately, several community-based initiatives arose as a bottom-up approach in challenging the pandemic. A key part of these stories in Thailand was a campaign called 'happiness-sharing pantries'.

This chapter introduces community-led food-sharing initiatives in response to COVID-19 in Thailand through the happiness-sharing pantries campaign. It also analyses the operation and the effectiveness of this campaign, which was run by charities and local communities in Thailand. It is believed that the campaign not only contributed to the well-being of the needy during the pandemic but also revealed problems with social welfare structures and the social protection system in the country.

How to cite this book chapter:
Chatinakrob, Thanapat. 2022. 'Happiness-sharing pantries and the 'easing of hunger for the needy' in Thailand'. In: Shin, Hyun Bang; Mckenzie, Murray; and Oh, Do Young (eds) *COVID-19 in Southeast Asia: Insights for a post-pandemic world.* London: LSE Press, pp. 249–256. DOI: https://doi.org/10.31389/lsepress.cov.v License: CC BY 4.0.

The happiness-sharing pantries campaign

In March 2020, the happiness-sharing pantries campaign was introduced by the local community in Bangkok (Little Brick Group 2020). It began with the simple idea that people in the community could share food, daily necessities, or even medicines with those who needed them. The pantry used in this campaign was a common pantry or cupboard that almost every house in Thailand already had. The work of happiness-sharing pantries was also uncomplicated. Community members would place donations in a roadside cupboard, and people who were in need would take an appropriate amount of what they needed. It was suggested that people who obtained food would feel happy and people who donated them would feel the same (Thai News Service Group 2020).

It started from only five model pantries located at different places in Bangkok. This campaign aimed to alleviate the economic effects of the COVID-19 pandemic. At first, people believed that this campaign would not work, as the social structure of Thailand differs from other countries (Little Brick Group 2020). There was also a survey conducted by the Little Brick Group (2020) showing that no one would put free food in the pantries. Two weeks after the beginning of the campaign, however, the pantries were still in their original places and thus received substantial attention (Thai News Service Group 2020). The pantries were widely accepted and then increased in number throughout Thailand. Government agencies responded positively to the campaign and placed additional cupboards at the entrances of their offices (Thai News Service Group 2020). Temples, police stations, military camps, hospitals, local markets, and some supermarkets also joined the campaign (Thai News Service Group 2020). At the end of 2020, every province in Thailand had pantries, with most in urban areas and smaller numbers in rural provinces. There were more than 300 official pantries in Bangkok, more than 100 official pantries in Phuket, and more than 50 official pantries in Chonburi (Pattaya), with the total number of official pantries reaching more than 1,400 (Little Brick Group 2020). Table 22.1 lists the approximate number of pantries in each province of Thailand.

Why did the happiness-sharing pantries campaign work in Thailand? At least three key players contributed to this campaign: charities, local communities, and the government. No official source confirmed where the happiness-sharing pantries campaign originated, but one of the most likely sources was a group of 20 people named 'Happiness-Sharing

Table 22.1. The approximate number of happiness-sharing pantries in each province of Thailand, as at 30 December 2020

Region	Number of happiness-sharing pantries
Central (including Bangkok)	692
Northern	157
North-eastern	142
Eastern	130
Western	68
Southern	283
Total	1,472

Source: Happiness-Sharing Pantries by Little Brick Group (2020).

Pantries by the Little Brick Group', which was inspired by the 'Little Free Pantry' launched by Jessica McClard in the United States (Little Brick Group 2020). The Little Brick Group first installed five model pantries at different places in Bangkok. Even though the types and characteristics of the pantries had no formal standard, they had to resist heat and rain. They also required, if possible, a cover to prevent bugs or other animals from getting inside, as well as an accompanying sign that specified their purpose (Little Brick Group 2020). The pantries also needed to be noticeable and placed at accessible locations such as markets, public transportation stops, government service offices, and any other easily reachable community spaces.

The campaign was genuinely a local, bottom-up initiative. At the very first stage, the campaign was initiated by local communities; no government agency contributed to it. Every pantry nationwide was a locally based initiative. Local communities maintained this campaign by promoting feelings of shared ownership (Little Brick Group 2020). Even though each pantry technically belonged to a person in the community and someone had to be responsible for its installation, communities tried to build a consensus that everyone was an owner of the pantry, thus promoting a sense of shared ownership (Little Brick Group 2020). Feelings of shared ownership, sometimes called a sense of community ownership, require the participation of local communities in making decisions at every stage of the process (Bowen 2005, pp.78–86; Lachapelle 2008, pp.53–55). The feeling of shared ownership of happiness-sharing pantries in Thai local communities was promoted in the same way (Gingerella 2020; Thai News Service Group 2020): it became a community event to take part in caring for the pantry, including filling up and taking out the right amount of food.

Setting up any instalments along the roadside in Thailand, however, needs official permission from the local authorities. Any pantry donor had to ask for permission from the relevant local authority in order to abide by the law, namely Section 39 of the Act on the Maintenance of the Cleanliness and Orderliness of the Country, B.E. 2535 (1992). This Act made it mandatory to request permission for any actions that might affect public places, such as installing a happiness-sharing pantry. Submitting such a request drew the attention of local authorities, especially police officers. They recognised the existence of the pantries, however, and even supported the regularity and orderliness of the pantries (Thai News Service Group 2020). For example, many central administration offices – such as the Ministry of Culture and the Department of Rural Roads – and provincial administration offices – such as the provincial governor of Phra Nakhon Si Ayutthaya, Chiang Mai Administration, Chachoengsao City Municipality, and Phetchabun Local Administrative Office – joined the campaign by installing pantries in their own areas.

After the Centre for COVID-19 Situation Administration of Thailand (CCSA) announced the easing of Phase 5 restrictions from 1 July 2020 (National News Bureau of Thailand 2020), most business operations reopened, and the pantry scheme seemed to become less of a priority. People rarely donated food, and some pantries were abandoned. A civil society organisation called the PunSook (Happiness-Sharing) Society, however, was formed to coordinate and sustain the campaign (PunSook Society 2020). This permanent organisation was also supported by many governmental and non-governmental agencies, including the Digital Economy Promotion Agency, the Federation of Thai Industries, the State Railway of Thailand, the Transport Co., Ltd., and the Board of Trade of Thailand (PunSook Society 2020). Therefore, the PunSook Society could sustainably act as an agent between donors and the needy in the post-COVID-19 era.

The COVID-19 situation in Thailand seemed to be under control between July and December 2020, with no new cases. There were new clusters, however, after outbreaks in several provinces, including Samut Sakhon, Rayong, and Chonburi, in late December 2020 and April 2021. This resurgence of new clusters led to the reintroduction of the happiness-sharing pantries campaign to local communities in Thailand.

Social impacts

Whether there was a COVID-19 outbreak or not, the existence of happiness-sharing pantries for the distribution of foods to the needy could decrease economic and social disparities in Thai communities. The pantries require neither minimum nor maximum donations, as the idea of the pantries comes from only sharing small portions of leftover food in any household's kitchen that could be shared with others (Little Brick Group 2020).

Several scholars have realised that the pantries reflect the structural problems of social welfare and the social security system in Thailand (Ariyapruchya et al. 2020; Nattaya 2020). Although the campaign intended to help people who were economically affected by the pandemic, chaos still raged in the community: some groups of people tried to take excessive amounts of supplies out of the pantries. As a result, those people were seen as selfish. On the other hand, this problem remained only somewhat controversial. Some critics believed that donors should give without worrying about what recipients would take, which was more or less what they did.

The scramble for donated items from the pantries exposed social welfare problems in Thai society. This has been called 'the gleaning welfare system': people must mainly be responsible for themselves primarily, and the government would provide only partial assistance since it does not view social welfare as a system for achieving the equity of all citizens. Therefore, the burden of ensuring social security must be borne by the people, who consequently tried to collect as much of the donations as possible to survive, as they did not know whether there would be donations left if they came to the pantries the next day. Interestingly, many experts believe that such behaviour was displayed not only by the poor but by people of all socio-economic classes owing to inequality (Ariyapruchya et al. 2020).

Furthermore, scrambling for donations likely occurred most often in communities where resources were not distributed evenly and fairly and people did not believe that government aid mechanisms were effective enough (Ariyapruchya et al. 2020). Therefore, if the government had a mechanism that could assure that people would be able to live well at a basic level, these people would only need to worry about taking just enough donated items from the pantries for that day such that, if they needed more the following day, they could simply visit again to pick up more items. Scrambling for donations might then be reduced. Otherwise, if they were unsure whether there would be enough donations the next day, they would naturally choose to stockpile. Hence, such behaviours might have derived from the structural social welfare problems that forced them to struggle for survival.

Moreover, the existence of the pantries also demonstrated the ability of people in communities to express their social responsibilities (Ariyapruchya et al. 2020). Many times, people chose not to follow society's rules because of their financial and social status. Whenever people were insecure, they were unable to exercise their social responsibility. Proper picking of donated items thus could not happen. In addition, this could occur in societies with high inequality, especially where the poor are deprived of social rights: whenever these people saw an opportunity to take advantage of donations, they would take it.

It must then be asked whether the happiness-sharing pantries were suitable for Thai society or for solving the problem of hunger for the poor in Thailand. Supporting one another is a common practice in Thai society, and the pantries were a means of solving the problems at hand in helping the needy. It has been observed, however, that the existence of pantries might not have been suitable for the Thai social structure. Even though there were still many pantries in Thailand by the end of 2020, people in communities had already reduced their interest considerably, which might have been because the campaign originated in the United States and European countries, where welfare systems were highly developed. In those contexts, the target groups of the pantries were homeless people or immigrants who did not have access to the social welfare system. In addition, the pantries did not facilitate interpersonal communication, which prevented donors and recipients from knowing each other, resulting in fear of lower social classes. Thai society became a society in which people wanted to help each other but did not help to achieve equality for the poor. It was only temporary help, which did not lead to any long-term solutions. More seriously, if people felt that the existence of the pantries could enable them to live in this kind of community, they would not fight for more important things like universal welfare. The participation of the government in solving problems, such as setting up cameras, arranging staff to guard the pantries, and instituting rules for taking things out of the pantries, led to an additional problem: preventing community learning because people participated as if they were being forced to comply. People became more organised owing to fear but did not learn new behaviours. The government should instead be involved in other duties, such as making the welfare system more accessible. As for the care of the pantries, this should be left to the community.

The happiness-sharing pantries thus seemed to be another weapon to challenge not only the COVID-19 pandemic but also economic and social disparities in Thai communities.

Conclusion

The community-led food and happiness-sharing initiative in Thailand was a mechanism that charities and local communities ran in response to COVID-19. It started from five model pantries and increased in number, reaching more than 1,400 pantries in Thailand. This campaign worked because of the contributions of charities, local communities, and the government. The existence of the pantries, however, reflected structural problems of social welfare and the social security system in Thailand. Communities faced scrambles for food because of the uncertainty, unfairness, and inequality of the welfare system. Therefore, the campaign seemed to help the needy during the pandemic, but only for a limited period of time, as it did not solve the underlying problems of Thailand's social welfare structures.

References

Ariyapruchya, Kiatipong; Nair, Arvind; Yang, Judy; and Moroz, Harry Edmund. (2020). 'The Thai economy: COVID-19, poverty, and social protection'. *East Asia and Pacific on the Rise*, 28 April. https://perma.cc/4N FC-2CNW [Last accessed 15 January 2021].

Bowen, Glenn A. (2005). 'Local-level stakeholder collaboration: A substantive theory of community-driven development'. *Journal of the Community Development Society*, vol. 36, no. 2, pp. 73–88. https://doi.org /10.1080/15575330509490176

Gingerella, Benita. (2020). *Building the Food Pantry of the Future*. https:// perma.cc/F4UL-92VH [Last accessed 15 January 2021].

Lachapelle, Paul. (2008). 'A sense of ownership in community development: Understanding the potential for participation in community planning efforts'. *Journal of the Community Development Society*, vol. 39, no. 2, pp. 52–59. https://doi.org/10.1080/15575330809489730

Little Brick Group. (2020). ตู้ปันสุข กลุ่มอิฐน้อย. Facebook. https://perma.cc /NZH2-4JGU [Last accessed 15 January 2021].

National News Bureau of Thailand. (2020). 'Thailand finalizes Phase 5 restrictions easing plan'. *Thailand Business News*, 29 June. https://perma.cc/2NTV-ZFW9 [Last accessed 2 September 2020].

Nattaya L. (2020). 'Pantries of sharing and Thai social welfares'. *Sanook*, 20 May. https://perma.cc/HT4Q-B7PD [Last accessed 15 January 2021].

PunSook Society. (2020). *PunSook Society*. http://www.punsooksociety.com [Last accessed 2 September 2020].

Thai News Service Group. (2020). 'Thailand: Pantry of Sharing campaign unlocks Thais' spirit of generosity'. *Asia News Monitor*, 13 May. https://perma.cc/5CWC-AER7 [Last accessed 16 May 2021].

USDA Foreign Agricultural Service. (2020). *The COVID-19 Impact on the Thai Economy*. USA: United States Department of Agriculture. https://perma.cc/33VD-C6ZL [Last accessed 16 May 2021].

World Bank. (2020). *Thailand Economic Monitor: Thailand in the Time of COVID 19*. USA: World Bank. https://perma.cc/9BJP-XMV6 [Last accessed 16 May 2021].

WHO (World Health Organization). (2020). *COVID-19 Strategic Preparedness and Response Plan: Country Preparedness and Response Status for COVID-19*. Switzerland: World Health Organization. https://perma.cc/H6HA-RVUZ [Last accessed 16 May 2021].

23. Being-in-common and food relief networks in Metro Manila, the Philippines

Tessa Maria Guazon

In this chapter, I reflect on mutual aid networks in the Philippines during the COVID-19 pandemic, focusing on food relief platforms that were mobilised in the early days of Metro Manila's lockdown in 2020. While mutual aid is commonly understood through the Filipino notion of *bayanihan* (helping each other in times of need), the COVID-19 pandemic shed light on new structures of aid, most of which were greatly bolstered by social media platforms. I explore new articulations of what is commonly understood as *bayanihan*, an often-romanticised aspect of Filipino identity that has been routinely deployed by the Philippine national government in its aid rhetoric during national emergencies. Crises result in altered ways of life. These resulting changes can be understood in the context of 'communities of sense', whereby a community 'recognises a contingent and non-essential manner of being together' (Hinderliter et al. 2009, p.2). This 'contingent being together' is often the outcome of events that, as Jacques Rancière (2009, p.31) has claimed, 'frame a being-in-common', a mode of togetherness or collectivity that is simultaneously palpable and political.

The COVID-19 pandemic greatly affected food and livelihood security in the Philippines, with daily wage earners the most gravely affected. To elucidate ways of being together, I refer to my experience with women who had served as partners on a research project on neighbourhoods in Metro Manila. Before the pandemic, our women partners relied on meagre earnings from odd jobs on the streets of Escolta and adjoining areas. Lockdown and ensuing curfews made it impossible for them to continue earning their keep. A faulty public health system, the slow roll-out of assistance from the national government, and a crackdown on citizen-led initiatives greatly hampered the provision of

How to cite this book chapter:
Guazon, Tessa Maria. 2022. 'Being-in-common and food relief networks in Metro Manila, the Philippines'. In: Shin, Hyun Bang; Mckenzie, Murray; and Oh, Do Young (eds) *COVID-19 in Southeast Asia: Insights for a post-pandemic world*. London: LSE Press, pp. 257–271. DOI: https://doi.org/10.31389/lsepress.cov.w
License: CC BY 4.0.

assistance and aid to the majority of Filipinos. Food relief networks, including community kitchens and community pantries, provided immediate relief to many in need. These initiatives ensured readily available assistance, and, because they were initiated at the grass roots, they were less burdened by bureaucratic processes.

The next paragraphs provide an overview of how the pandemic affected food supplies and aid provision in the Philippines in light of the national government's response to the public health crisis. These contextualise the necessity of citizen-led food relief initiatives. The latter part of the chapter draws heavily from participatory fieldwork for our neighbourhood research project. They reflect on how social ties and relations of togetherness are formed during situations of crisis.

COVID-19 cases in the Philippines surged in the early weeks of March 2021, with more than 5,000 active cases recorded daily (Department of Health 2021). A projection from OCTA Research suggested the numbers could rise to 11,000 new cases per day, which was an ominous sign for the economy (CNN Philippines 2021). Rising cases of COVID-19 infections posed a threat to people's sense of security, specifically with regard to their livelihoods and the provision of basic needs. In interviews aired on both television and radio in 2020, daily wage earners said they would rather leave their homes and brave the virus than die of hunger (Talabong and Gavilan 2020). The national government's task force, together with local government officials, swayed back and forth in the precarious dance of halting the rise of COVID-19 cases through movement restrictions and fully opening the economy to provide jobs.

Filipinos' sense of security was further threatened by the national government's response to the pandemic. The Philippines was placed under a longer lockdown than other countries in the region, rivalling even that of Wuhan province in China, where the first cases of COVID-19 were thought to have emerged. While the government was slow to close the Philippines' borders to travellers from nations with widespread outbreaks, it was quick to deploy its military and police forces to patrol the streets during lockdown. Philippine president Rodrigo Duterte declared a public health emergency on 8 March 2020, and a lockdown took effect in Metro Manila and the rest of the island of Luzon on 16 March. Metro Manila and cities across the archipelago were placed under varying degrees of quarantine: community quarantine, enhanced community quarantine (ECQ), and modified enhanced community quarantine (MECQ). A prolonged city-wide lockdown would inevitably cripple the economy, as it would hinder workers' ability to commute a long distance to work. The so-called 'granular' or zone-specific lockdowns implemented in 2021 seemed ineffectual in stemming the rise of active COVID-19 cases.[1]

With Proclamation No. 1021, Duterte declared the country would be under a year-long state of calamity from 13 September 2020 until 12 September 2021 (Aurelio 2020). According to the president, extending the state of calamity would 'afford the national government as well as local government units ample latitude to continue utilising appropriate funds, including the quick response fund' in their response to the public health crisis. The president was also granted special powers to reapportion the 2020 national budget through the Bayanihan to Heal as One Act. The proposed 2021 budget of 4.5 trillion Philippine pesos was meant to bolster government response to the public health crisis (CNN Philippines 2021).

A lockdown of draconian proportions

The government's response to the crisis was continuously marred by other equally worrying developments, including the misappropriation of funds by officials of the state-run health insurer Philippine Health Insurance Corporation (PhilHealth) (Luci-Atienza 2020); the non-renewal of the franchise and subsequent closure of the largest media company in the country, ABS-CBN (IFJ 2020); the continuing spate of activist killings and the arrest of citizens protesting the government's feeble response to the pandemic; and restrictions imposed on individuals and local media critical of the government.[2] Filipinos grappled with the startling figures of rising COVID-19 cases in the country, the staggering loans the government amassed in 2020, and the great numbers of poor people who continued to face hunger during the pandemic.

Official statistics from 2018 placed poverty incidence in the Philippines at 16.7%, translating to 17,000,000 poor Filipinos (PSA 2020, p.ii). Furthermore, 12.1% of Filipino families did not have sufficient income to buy minimum basic needs, including both food and non-food needs (PSA 2020, p.ii). The National Capital Region (NCR) was recorded as having the lowest poverty incidence among families, while the Autonomous Region in Muslim Mindanao (ARMM) had the highest poverty incidence. Secretary of Agriculture William Dar assured Filipinos there was adequate food supply until the end of 2021 despite restrictions on mobility (Miraflor 2021). The secretary remained overly optimistic, confident in his projection of a 2.5% growth rate even though the price of goods continued to soar.

The Inter-Agency Task Force (IATF) on the COVID-19 pandemic also instituted a government programme focused on a national food policy, Zero Hunger 2021, led by cabinet secretary Karlo Nograles. The Philippines' National Food Policy was launched in October 2020.[3] It endorsed a 'whole-of-nation' approach to eradicating hunger. The Department of Agriculture partnered with the IATF in bringing forward the key policies of the National Food Policy programme, including 'Agriculture 4.0', which aimed for a 'smarter and more efficient industry'. The Zero Hunger task force cites among its accomplishments the creation of the Enhanced Partnership Against Hunger and Poverty, the institutionalisation of the Zero Hunger programme guidelines, the airing of the webinar series *Kasapatan at Ugnayan ng Mamamayan sa Akmang Pagkain at Nutrisyon* (KUMAIN), the Feeding Programs Initiative for the First 1000 Days of Life, the launch of Pilipinas Kontra Gutom, and the draft of the proposed Philippine Multi-Sectoral Nutrition Project for the World Bank (Department of Education 2020).[4] Despite government pronouncements and the recent institutionalisation of the National Food Policy programme, many Filipino families remained impoverished. Food prices continued to rise, with an estimated increase of 6.7% year-on-year as of February 2021, the highest recorded food inflation since December 2018 (Trading Economics 2021).

The pandemic also brought about an unprecedented loss of livelihoods, with informal workers and daily wage earners suffering greatly. The impact of the city-wide lockdown and the government's slow response to curbing COVID-19 cases and the provision of aid was strongly felt by millions of poor Filipinos. This situation was greatly reflected in the life situations of our women research partners in the Southeast Asia Neighbourhoods Network (SEANNET) project, who lived on the streets of Escolta, Manila, and whose struggles to make a living were magnified a thousandfold during the pandemic. I turn to their experiences in the following section.

Survival on the streets of Manila

Together with artists Alma Quinto and Nathalie Dagmang, I worked closely with our women partners on the Manila case study for the SEANNET research project. The Manila share of the project explored the links between art and urban development. We were keen to understand how arts and culture had been enfolded in urban redevelopment programmes and in processes of gentrification. We also wanted to

Figure 23.1. Escolta street party, revellers congregate in front of the historic First United Building, 2017

Source: Photograph by the author.

employ the methods and approaches of the visual arts to understand how processes of urban development marginalise and disenfranchise poor and itinerant communities. Often, art collectives, cultural projects, and residency programmes are benignly subsumed into gentrification processes, but there are also approaches that utilise the arts as a means for disadvantaged communities to be heard. We worked with a core group of six women who lived on the streets of Escolta. They were third- and fourth-generation street dwellers and made a living from informal jobs. We were interested to know how informal settlers adapted to changes in the urban fabric. The social ties these women developed with each other were instrumental to their survival on Manila's streets. We wanted to know how neighbourly attitudes helped them survive the hardships of life on the streets.

Escolta used to be a thriving commercial street, linking the River Pasig to both the walled city, Intramuros, and thriving Binondo, Manila's Chinatown. Manila flourished as a port city thanks to the galleon trade in the 17th and 18th centuries, and even then Escolta housed warehouses and *bodegas* for commercial goods. Manila was heavily bombed under Japanese occupation in World War II, and Escolta fell into ruins. It had a brief revival in the 1950s and 1960s but became derelict by the 1970s, when the city of Manila was overshadowed by rising commercial districts elsewhere in Metro Manila, including Quezon City to the north and Makati to the south. The local government of Manila regarded Escolta as a crucial commercial development corridor. The late 1990s thus saw efforts to revitalise the area. There were campaigns to conserve and reuse historic buildings in the area. There were also plans in the early 2000s for Escolta to adopt a mixed-use development plan, which did not materialise. In the mid-2000s, Escolta and other areas in Metro Manila saw a revival through art and cultural events, trendy shops, hip coffee bars and restaurants, bazaars, and street parties. In Escolta, these events or happenings were centred on the historic First United Building, which housed spaces for creatives and start-up businesses, including 98B, an arts initiative that was at the forefront of these projects. These events attracted many visitors to Escolta, mostly young people who lived in other parts of sprawling Metro Manila.

Our women partners made a living by selling candies, instant noodles, and packed-for-retail food items. Two of them ferried passengers across Escolta, Quiapo, and Binondo in their pedicabs. Sol, a busker, also had a thriving makeshift store under a bank's awning, where she and her son had sheltered for years. Brenda and Susan made a living by selling fruits, drinks, and peanuts. These earnings were augmented by their partners' and children's wages. Escolta vendors relied heavily on their *suki*, or regular customers, for daily earnings, averaging between 150 and 300 Philippine pesos (around US$3 or £2 to around US$6 or £4) on a good day. We witnessed many transitions in their lives in the years we worked with them (i.e. 2017 to 2020). Two moved into rented spaces, which, though still makeshift, were a significant departure from living inside a pedicab or on the streets. One lost a child and found a new partner; another had her son's kidney stones surgically removed; and another's husband recovered from a lingering lung illness. They described their life on the streets as '*pamamangketa*', a means of survival and a manner of reciprocity that allowed them to live through everyday hardships. During our often-compelling sessions, they described the difficulties they faced every day, but they would always claim there was a way to live together and 'be in common': to be with another, to feel each other's pain, and to empathise with each other. They cited attributes such as '*maabilidad*', '*maparaan*', and '*madiskarte*' (creative and resourceful), as well as '*magaling makisama*', '*marunong makisama*', '*may malasakit*' (to be able to relate well with one another, to feel for each other). These life skills entailed close observation, creativity, interdependence, and shared concern.

In the summer of 2018, we conducted a cookout and personal history workshop with our women partners. The workshop components, designed by artist Nathalie Dagmang, started with a trip to Divisoria Market to buy ingredients, followed by cooking together and sharing a meal with our women partners and their children. Our women partners were responsible for convening the participants and arranging our transportation to and from the market and the workshop venue. After our shared lunch, we had a personal history session where our women partners connected life events with historical and day-to-day events in Escolta and the adjoining areas of Quiapo and Binondo. It was interesting to note that the women emphatically mentioned how much they missed cooking their meals, which they could not do because they lived in the discreet spots and corners of Escolta Street. The ability to provide meals was a primary concern for our women partners.

Figure 23.2. Shared lunch during our structured cookout at a rented upper floor of a cafeteria in Escolta, May 2018

Source: Photograph by Eric Guazon.

Figure 23.3. Timeline workshop with our women partners, May 2018

Source: Photograph by Eric Guazon.

Restrictive pandemic policies

In March 2020, the Philippine National Police made 41,000 arrests for violations of enhanced community quarantine (ECQ) regulations (Castañeda 2020). The situation was widespread, with a host of informal workers and daily wage earners severely affected by the lockdown and curfews in Metro Manila. Fear and distrust of local police were prevalent among informal settler communities. Similar concerns often came up in discussions with our women partners: recollections of when belongings were carted off during raids; when children were brought by Department of Public Services personnel to holding centres like Boys Town; and how livelihoods were greatly dependent on illegal fees or *butaw*.

While the National Food Policy had been institutionalised and inaugurated, food provision and food security were matters not easily resolved by the government, especially during lockdown. On 1 April 2020, residents from Quezon City's Sitio San Roque, one of the Philippines' largest informal settlements, were violently dispersed, with 21 of the protesters arrested by city police.[5] They demanded the immediate release of food aid from the local government (CNN Philippines

2020). Police, on the other hand, claimed residents had violated restrictions on public gatherings by staging a protest without a permit. Six jeepney drivers were likewise jailed on 2 June 2020 in Caloocan (Aspinwall 2020). They rallied for the renewed operation of jeepneys in Metro Manila and the immediate provision of aid by the government. Jeepney drivers lost their wages because of the prolonged suspension of public transportation during the lockdown. Several of them resorted to begging, imploring passers-by and private vehicles for donations (Aspinwall 2020).

Drawing from my own social media network and first-hand knowledge of food provision networks during quarantine in Metro Manila, I observed the development of initiatives like community kitchens (Sitio San Roque's Kusinang Bayan was one such example) and even the private efforts of chefs: Waya Araos-Wijangco of Gourmet Gypsy Art Cafe in Quezon City, for example, transformed her usually bustling kitchen into a food provision hub for frontline workers and drafted guidelines for community kitchens. Other initiatives included those of volunteer groups like Art Relief Mobile Kitchen, which had in the past cooked and provided food for communities affected by disasters. The lockdown gave rise to citizen initiatives propelled by social media, where public calls for contributions, donations, and volunteer work were fielded. They covered a vast array of needs: transportation and lodging for healthcare workers, food relief, direct purchase of produce from farmers, translating health advisories into local languages, and many more.

Artist Nathalie Dagmang reached out to our women partners in March 2020, a day after the lockdown was imposed in Metro Manila. Several of them replied with a sense of panic: the deserted streets meant they would not earn a cent in the coming days, even weeks. Empty streets only meant only one thing: little or to no earnings. Food aid was promised by the national government during the city-wide lockdown. Distribution was left to local barangays (the smallest political administrative units in the Philippines). Our women partners waited for their food packs to arrive, but they had to leave the barangay hall owing to the strict enforcement of curfew during quarantine. Dagmang and I rallied to raise funds for food relief through social media, primarily through a campaign launched by the civil society organisation People for Accountable Governance and Sustainable Action (PAGASA). Food survival packs cost 700 Philippine pesos (US$15 USD or £11) and were meant to tide people over during the first few difficult weeks

Figure 23.4. Plastic chairs in front of a sari-sari store reserved for the arrival of food packs to be distributed by barangay officials, 2020

Source: Photograph by Veejay Villafranca.

of lockdown. Reflecting on her experience distributing the food packs, Dagmang (2020) noted numerous challenges to organising the relief drive, including arbitrary rules concerning checkpoints and curfews and, much later, local officials' requirement that the police or military transport and officially release donations and aid to communities outside Metro Manila.

Supplies of rice, vegetables, and canned goods were delivered to Nathalie at no cost and were brought to Escolta through the efforts of another volunteer. Our women partners helped distribute them. Dagmang (2020) noted that these efforts were carried out 'in the spirit of *bayanihan*', a local expression that refers to a communal spirit and the collective. Environmental historian Greg Bankoff (2020) has cited an even older understanding of *bayanihan* as arising from a 'rootless struggle with an environment where going it alone is dangerous'. How might we rethink the shared need to provide and sustain others during periods of crisis? How can we recuperate the notion of *bayanihan* when it has been deployed by the state in its aid efforts and co-opted in its insidious drive to curtail individual freedoms?

Conclusion: the need for a humane and participatory approach

The authoritarian nature of the Philippine government's policies only worsened the pandemic situation in the Philippines. The state's overtly militaristic approach resulted in arrests, discrimination, and confusion and did not in any way advance the ready provision of aid to those gravely affected by the pandemic. The proliferation of community pantries and community kitchens across the archipelago showed how mobilisations initiated by citizens were more effective in directly providing assistance.

There exists great potential in mobilising women like our research partners from Escolta to restructure food supply chains in cities. It was often the case that our women partners and their children, more than their partners or husbands, provided for their families. This supports the observation that women have always been 'actively involved in

Figure 23.5 and Figure 23.6. Distribution of food packs in Escolta, Manila

Sources: Photos by Richard Quan and Nathalie Dagmang, respectively.
Note: These were delivered through another intermediary.

food systems [yet] their contributions [are often] unrecognised and they face many inequities' (Zseleczky et al. 2020).

Our engagement with our women partners from Escolta helped us realise commonplace understandings of reciprocity and cooperation, specifically those shaped by daily struggles deeply rooted in the structural inequities that pervade life in contemporary cities not only in Southeast Asia but around the globe. Perhaps the vital life lessons we overlook and frequently ignore are those we need to learn again from people whose lives are in perpetual crisis. These lessons include the centrality of social ties in weathering crisis situations and thriving after the crisis has passed. In the Philippines, however, citizen-led initiatives were persecuted and received little support from the state. This was evident in the red-tagging of community organisers and the eventual co-optation of their initiatives and projects by local government units – and even by the military (Robertson 2021; Valenzuela 2021). In the context of pervasive repression, these citizen-led movements should instead take the lead.

Notes

1. Granular lockdowns meant that residents of specific barangays (the smallest political unit in the Philippines) were restricted from leaving their homes, which presented problems for access to food and livelihoods. Some local governments promised the delivery of food packs to affected households, but our experience from 2020 showed that these provisions arrived with great delay. On 19 March 2021, the Philippines recorded the highest count of active COVID-19 cases, at 7,103. 'Circuit-breaker lockdowns' were proposed by local government units instead of the more stringent 'general community quarantine' (GCQ).

2. Summary killings and arrests of activists in Manila and other regions continued. Nine activists were gunned down in the Calabarzon region on 7 March 2020, and many individuals, including lawyers and judges, continued to be 'red-tagged', i.e. accused of being affiliated with the Communist Party of the Philippines.

3. According to Nograles, the National Food Policy was geared towards six result areas: the review and rationalisation of existing policies, rules, and regulations related to zero hunger; ensuring available and affordable food; securing nutrition adequacy; securing food accessibility and safety; ensuring sustainable food systems, food resiliency, and stability; and ensuring information, education, awareness, and participation among the people.

4. The Department of Education endorsed the National Food Policy, as it supplemented the department's existing School-Based Feeding Program (SBFP).

The SBFP provides nutritious meals and milk to learners from kindergarten to Grade 6 whom they describe as 'wasted and severely wasted'. KUMAIN is a consultative platform; it is roughly translated as Practice and Consultation among Citizens on Adequate Food Provision and Nutrition. Pilipinas Kontra Gutom means Philippines Against Hunger.

5. Sitio San Roque used to be home to 17,000 families, many of whom were migrant workers from the provinces. The government entered a joint venture with Ayala Land Corporation to develop the land they lived on. There were numerous demolitions in the area, with the most violent ones happening in 2010 and 2014. As of December 2018, only 6,000 families were left in Sitio San Roque.

Acknowledgements

The author acknowledges colleagues from the Southeast Asia Neighbourhoods Network (SEANNET) research project organised by the International Institute of Asian Studies Leiden; the civil society network PAGASA (People for Accountable Governance and Sustainable Action); Richard Quan Lim; and anonymous donors to the food campaign for our women partners from Escolta, Manila. Photojournalist Veejay Villafranca generously lent his images of the city-wide lockdown in Metro Manila. Ideas for this chapter and other outputs for the Manila SEANNET case study were developed alongside research partners Alma Quinto, Nathalie Dagmang, and our research assistants and workshop volunteers over four years of fieldwork. Foremost, these reflections are shaped by valuable insights of our women partners from Escolta: Brenda Aballa, Arlene Garcia, Gilda Descartin, Cecilia Montemayor, Soledad Peña, Susan Soriano, and numerous others who at some point joined our workshop sessions.

Sections of this chapter were initially presented at the 'Bottom-Up Resilience: Civil Society Responses and Marginalised Publics during COVID-19' webinar organised by APRU Cities and Landscapes Hub and the Pacific Rim Community Design Network in July 2020.

Written consent was granted by participants to the SEANNET project workshops from the latter part of 2017 to early 2020, including those from guardians of children who participated in the nutrition and hygiene workshop at Museo Pambata (Children's Museum) in Manila. Consent includes the use of photos and narratives for purely academic purposes by the researchers.

References

Aspinwall, Nick. (2020). 'Jeepney drivers face charges amid heightened protest crackdown in the Philippines'. *The Diplomat*, 12 June. https://perma.cc /HQ2A-RCTT [Last accessed 25 September 2020].

Aurelio, Julie M. (2020). 'Duterte extends PH state of calamity'. *Philippine Daily Inquirer*, 19 September. https://perma.cc/7RRZ-VBYT [Last accessed 24 September 2020].

Bankoff, Greg. (2020). 'In Search of Bayanihan'. *Philippine Arts in Venice Biennale*. 6 September 2020 https://perma.cc/42ME-MQPP [Last accessed 22 September 2020]. (pg 272).

Bulatlat. (2021). '"Bloody Sunday" spells killings, mass arrests in Southern Tagalog'. *Bulatlat*, 8 March. https://perma.cc/F9WP-7A56 [Last accessed 18 March 2021].

Castañeda, Jason. (2020). 'Why Duterte won't lift world's longest lockdown'. *Asia Times*, 15 May. https://perma.cc/Y2F4-3HB2 [Last accessed 28 September 2020].

CNN Philippines. (2020). '21 protesters demanding food aid arrested in Quezon City', 1 April. https://perma.cc/B9KT-DNWK [Last accessed 25 September 2020].

CNN Philippines. (2021). 'PH daily COVID-19 cases could hit 11,000 by end-March, 20,000 by mid-April – OCTA', 16 March. https://perma.cc/6X NM-7MLD [Last accessed 6 June 2021].

Dagmang, Nathalie D. (2020). 'Responding to Escolta's street vendors: How do we provide relief and security to the economically vulnerable?' *Bulatlat*, 2 May. https://perma.cc/5DDY-WMRU [Last accessed 25 September 2020].

Department of Education. (2020). *Healthy Learners Make Better Citizens, Says Secretary Briones in IATF Zero Hunger Anniversary*, 17 January. https://perma.cc/54PC-6EZC [Last accessed 19 March 2021].

Hinderliter, Beth; Maimon, Vered; Mansoor, Jaleh; and McCormick, Seth (eds) (2009). *Communities of Sense: Rethinking Aesthetics and Politics*. USA: Duke University Press.

IFJ (International Federation of Journalists). (2020). *Independent Journalism and Access to Information Threatened in the Philippines with the Closure of ABS-CBN*, 1 June. https://perma.cc/7J72-JMY2 [Last accessed 24 September 2020].

Luci-Atienza, Charissa. (2020). 'PhilHealth corruption at "pandemic level"; House minority bloc urges "complete overhaul"'. *Manila Bulletin*, 19 August. https://perma.cc/GL7Z-H77E [Last accessed 24 September 2020].

Miraflor, Madelaine B. (2021). 'DA: Food supply enough through 2021'. *Manila Bulletin*, 12 April. https://perma.cc/TY2V-C8QK [Last accessed 4 May 2021].

PSA (Philippine Statistics Authority). (2020). *Updated Full Year 2018 Official Poverty Statistics of the Philippines*, June 2020. https://perma.cc/8ALS -YG4W [Last accessed 18 March 2021].

Rancière, Jacques. (2009). 'Contemporary art and the politics of aesthetics', in Beth Hinderliter, Vered Maimon, Jaleh Mansoor and Seth McCormick (eds) *Communities of Sense: Rethinking Aesthetics and Politics*. USA: Duke University Press, pp. 31–50.

Robertson, Phil. (2021). 'Philippine general should answer for "Red-Tagging"'. *Human Rights Watch*, 10 February. https://perma.cc/LH3Q-6XPG [Last accessed 14 June 2021].

Talabong, Rambo; and Gavilan, Jodesz. (2020). 'Walang wala na: Poor Filipinos fear death from hunger more than coronavirus'. *Rappler*, 2 April. https://perma.cc/RC9D-HYZ9 [Last accessed 28 September 2020].

Trading Economics. (2021). *Philippines Food Inflation*. https://perma.cc /WL3C-ZFKM [Last accessed 18 March 2021].

Zseleczky, Laura; Malapit, Hazel; Meinzen-Dick, Ruth; and Quisumbing, Agnes. (2020). 'Transforming food systems for women's empowerment and equity'. IFPRI Blog, 17 April. https://perma.cc/84CZ-ZZER [Last accessed 18 March 2021].

24. Community responses to gendered issues in Malaysia

Tengku Nur Qistina

The COVID-19 health crisis had a major impact on the world, disrupting the economy, politics, and social life, as well as gender relations. Indeed, COVID-19 exposed long-standing gender tensions and inequalities as the world has struggled to contain its spread.

This chapter examines how women were affected by COVID-19 in Malaysia following the implementation of its first movement control order (MCO), in the first year of Malaysia's version of a quarantine and lockdown. It focuses on the community's role in providing help and assistance to women during an unprecedented health crisis and a unique political shake-up in the country. The political background of the nation yielded a variety of government responses to the few incidents that occurred during the MCO, as voids and holes in the system became apparent following a change of government in early 2020.

This chapter also aims to focus on the community outreach that unfolded both online and offline, as Malaysians and various non-governmental organisations like the Women's Aid Organisation (WAO), which works on domestic violence and advocates for a gendered perspective on social and political matters in Malaysia, rose to the occasion. The MCO also brought new, innovative efforts through online efforts that sought to fill the gaps left by governments and other established institutions as they scrambled to ramp up and pivot their capacities towards dealing with the pandemic. These non-governmental initiatives received a lot of attention and were effective in shaping policy, especially on matters related to domestic violence and women's burden of care.

The pandemic made it clear that community-based organisations and their efforts played a major role in sustaining communities during the MCO. The government was limited in its capacity to engage

How to cite this book chapter:
Qistina, Tengku Nur. 2022. 'Community responses to gendered issues in Malaysia'. In: Shin, Hyun Bang; Mckenzie, Murray; and Oh, Do Young (eds) *COVID-19 in Southeast Asia: Insights for a post-pandemic world*. London: LSE Press, pp. 272–280. DOI: https://doi.org/10.31389/lsepress.cov.x License: CC BY 4.0.

with Malaysian residents. Moving forward, the pandemic proved that community-based efforts in Malaysia need to be further empowered and strengthened to allow them to serve the nation and its residents where the government fails to do so.

First, this chapter looks into the most salient issues Malaysia faced during the pandemic, such as domestic violence and how Malaysia coped with its rise following the implementation of the MCO. Second, it describes the Malaysian political scene that changed drastically overnight at the beginning of the COVID-19 pandemic; this political climate influenced public perceptions of the government and its actions relevant to women and gender. Finally, this chapter explores the different ways in which community responses have filled in the gaps and voids left by the government and its agencies.

Domestic violence

Domestic violence was more prevalent than ever before during the stay-at-home measures introduced as part of the world's fight against COVID-19. The WAO in Malaysia recorded a staggering fourfold increase in the number of calls received compared to before the MCO was imposed (Bernama 2020). The increasing occurrence of domestic violence was observed globally, as UN Secretary-General António Guterres called for a 'domestic violence ceasefire' when the pandemic first hit in 2020 (United Nations 2020). The secretary general also suggested that governments should take more proactive actions in supporting efforts to prevent domestic violence. An example of such support could be supporting civil society efforts and making investments in online services. To help monitor and manage the expected rise in gender-based violence following the pandemic, governments could declare shelters for domestic violence victims and survivors, provide essential services or set up emergency warning systems in pharmacies and grocery stores to increase the accessibility of services for victims (United Nations 2020).

The rise in reported cases of domestic violence was attributed to the stress brought on by lockdown measures. Increased anxiety from financial stress resulting from the concomitant economic crisis set the stage for a worsening domestic violence crisis (Peterman et al. 2020). Malaysia also recorded a rise in unemployment during the first year of the pandemic, defined as March to December 2020. In May 2020, Malaysia's unemployment rate rose to 5.3%, its highest point, with a total of 826,100 Malaysians unemployed (DOSM 2020). Studies in the past have proven a causal link between economic hardships and a rise in domestic violence, especially between intimate partners (Schneider, Harknett, and McLanahan 2016). Rising unemployment numbers brought on by the pandemic thus definitely made domestic violence a cause for concern.

Physical distancing and quarantine measures introduced by government health officials to curb contagion also contributed to the increase in domestic violence (Campbell 2020). They made violence a coping mechanism, as perpetrators felt a loss of control over their lives (Peterman et al. 2020).

Part of this was due to reduced access to support systems, as lockdown and curfews confined victims to their homes, limited contact with persons outside their household, postponed court hearings or counselling services for domestic issues, and allowed perpetrators to more easily restrict victims' access to support hotlines and other services. Additionally, victims struggled to detach themselves and escape abuse due to the uncertainty the pandemic brought. Women might have opted to stay with abusive partners for a host of reasons that were exacerbated by the onset of the pandemic (Peterman et al. 2020).

In providing economic assistance, the Malaysian government first introduced an economic stimulus package called PRIHATIN, which directly translates into English as 'care', at the end of March 2020. Unfortunately, the PRIHATIN package lacked the ability to empower women, who were the most likely victims of domestic abuse: statistics obtained in 2019 showed that 91% victims of domestic abuse in Malaysia were female (Yuen and Chung 2019). The PRIHATIN package provided cash transfers aimed to instantly ease the burden on the community. However, they were given to the heads of households, 80% of whom were men (UNICEF 2020). The situation for women, meanwhile, worsened, as they were often left trapped in their homes and lacked the financial support to escape abuse (WAO 2020).

Fortunately, organisations like the WAO, Sisters in Islam, the Women's Centre for Change, and others included in the Joint Action Group in Gender Equality, a coalition of 13 women's rights organisations in Malaysia, were at the forefront of advocating and protecting women's interests, as they provided gendered perspectives on the pandemic. These organisations were especially active in both highlighting the challenges associated with domestic violence and providing various support services, from raising awareness of shelters for trapped women to advocating for better support and social protections for women (WAO 2020).

The lockdown measures that were introduced to curb the pandemic brought many things to light, including the role NGOs played in intervening in domestic violence in Malaysia. While Malaysia had developed its legal instruments to better protect victims of domestic violence through the Domestic Violence Act (Amendment) 2018, this was not extensive enough to provide victims with protection during the pandemic, as the political will behind such causes changed with the change in the Malaysian government in 2020. Building awareness in communities to collectively protect victims from domestic violence should be the first step in preventing the occurrence of domestic violence during a health crisis like the COVID-19 pandemic.

Politics and policies

At the height of COVID-19's first wave in early 2020, Malaysia went through a political crisis. The Pakatan Harapan (PH) coalition was ousted after 21 months in power. As a result, the nation went through a change of government without holding a general election. The new government from March 2020 was that of the Perikatan Nasional (PN) coalition, which until July 2020 included the United Malays National Organisation (UMNO) – the party that had been in power from the nation's birth in 1963 until its electoral defeat in 2018. The PN government could be considered more right-wing than the previous PH government, which had a more progressive political stance on social issues, especially on those related to gender.

The change in government led to confusion in policies, a lack of coordination, and miscommunication, all of which resulted in backlash from communities. This may be attributed to the fact that Prime Minister Muhyiddin lacked political support in Parliament when the MCO was first implemented in March 2020 (Lee 2020).

The following incidents that occurred during the MCO called into question the PN government's gender sensitivity and awareness in the context of the lockdown.

1. Infographics

The first incident involved the Ministry of Women, Family and Community Development's publication of a set of recommendations and infographics that aimed to advise women on the management of their households to maintain peace and harmony at home. The recommendations, however, which included imitating 'Doraemon voices' and giggling coyly, did not receive a positive response from the community and led the ministry to remove them and issue an apology for their publication (Palansamy 2020). The All Women's Action Society (AWAM), an NGO, called the ministry out for its 'sexist' tips through a series of tweets that condemned the 'recommendations' (Palansamy 2020).

2. Crisis hotline suspension

Another incident was the temporary suspension of the government's crisis hotline, 'Talian Kasih' (*The Star* 2020). When the MCO was first implemented on 18 March 2020, the Ministry of Women, Family and Community Development announced that hotline would be suspended, as non-essential services in the country were suspended for an initial period of two weeks. The criticism this invited led to the suspension being reversed, as politicians from both the government and the opposition cited the dangers that quarantine measures posed for women, which made the availability of the crisis hotline even more important (Chin 2020).

3. Crisis hotline data

Data obtained from calls received through the crisis hotlines provided by the WAO reported a staggering 44% increase in domestic violence throughout the first month of the MCO (Heanglee 2020). Contrastingly, the government's crisis hotline recorded a different trend, as data published on the official government website recorded just a 'slight increase' in the occurrence of domestic violence in the country (Arumugam 2020).

While the data obtained from NGOs does not necessarily coincide with the government's data, this has less to do with the government's capability to provide aid. Instead, it is more reflective of the preference society has for engaging with NGOs rather than government officials, as engaging with NGOs can be less intimidating and confrontational (Sabanayagam 2020).

4. Burden of care

NGOs also shed light on women's burden of care. Women were unequally affected by the increasing burden of care during the MCO (Hisamudin 2020). As families observed quarantine, schools and day care were closed. Women were forced to juggle their responsibilities in taking care of their families, especially children and/or the elderly.

This was on top of the usual housework that women did, such as cooking and cleaning. Normally, domestic helpers that visit homes daily or weekly help lessen the burden of housework, but, with the imposition of quarantine orders, some families no longer had domestic helpers that could come daily, as movement was limited (Hisamudin 2020).

A 2019 report by the Khazanah Research Institute on women's unpaid work in Malaysia highlighted the burden women faced in the country. The report conducted a time use survey that highlighted gender disparities in relation to the burden of care in Malaysian society, as women had to shoulder more responsibilities than men while attending to professional life at the same time, hence the term 'double burden' (KRI 2019). This report highlighted the unequal burden imposed on women given the stereotypical expectations of women in fulfilling housework duties. The unequal burden was further shouldered by women during the pandemic, according to global reports (Thornton 2020).

NGOs highlighted women's problems nationally. Issues akin to women's burden of care had not been previously recognised, with little societal or national awareness. The efforts to highlight this can themselves be said to have resulted in the government's subsequent economic stimulus packages that aimed to address the need for childcare services, including the PENJANA economic stimulus package (Povera, Harun, and Yunus 2020).

The relationship between civil society and the new Malaysian government was responsive. This was seen as subsequent government economic stimulus packages like PENJANA incorporated gendered perspectives that could empower women and families. The PENJANA package was introduced during the country's recovery movement control order (RMCO) that began on 9 June 2020 (Prime Minister's Office of Malaysia 2020). The newly unveiled economic stimulus package paid attention to women's role in driving the economy, with 50 million Malaysian ringgit (roughly US$12 million) allocated for women entrepreneurs in micro-enterprises (Aziz and Zainul 2020). The burden of care faced by women was thus recognised, as childcare support services were provided in the new package. The government also allocated a total of RM200 million (roughly US$50 million) for childcare services to encourage and support parents to return to work (Aziz and Zainul 2020). This was a positive response compared to the government's initial actions, which were shown by civil society to lack a focus on gender issues.

Conclusion

Malaysia's experience of handling the COVID-19 crisis coincided with several other historic political events in the country. The newly formed government's policies left much room for civil society and NGOs to step in and aid policies relating to domestic violence and other gendered issues. The events that unfolded in 2020 with COVID-19 demonstrated and emphasised the lack of gendered perspectives in Malaysian culture and the community at large. This situation signalled larger issues at hand that require the assistance and guidance of civil society and NGOs to ensure the needs of the people are met. To the government's credit, progress was made with subsequent policies like childcare subsidies and flexible work arrangements that were well received by NGOs and the community. The need for faster progress, however, merits exploration, as COVID-19 proved that slow and steady does not win the race when it comes to gender-related policies in Malaysia.

References

Arumugam, Tharanya. (2020). 'All calls to Talian Kasih taken seriously, says ministry'. *New Straits Times*, 4 April. https://perma.cc/995T-YEUL [Last accessed 25 May 2021].

Aziz, Adam; and Zainul, Emir. (2020). 'Malaysia's latest stimulus package PENJANA includes childcare incentives, free internet'. *The Edge Markets*, 5 June. https://perma.cc/W4P8-APQJ [Last accessed 24 May 2021].

Bernama. (2020). 'WAO: Domestic violence calls rise during MCO; more shelters needed'. *New Straits Times*, 5 May. https://perma.cc/TN8T-7Q2Y [Last accessed 1 October 2020].

Campbell, Andrew M. (2020). 'An increasing risk of family violence during the Covid-19 pandemic: Strengthening community collaborations to save lives'. *Forensic Science International*, vol. 2, p. 100089. https://doi.org/10.1016/j.fsir.2020.100089

Chin, Emmanuel Santa Maria. (2020). 'Minister Rina Harun lifts Talian Kasih hotline suspension after bipartisan criticism'. *Malay Mail*, 18 March. https://perma.cc/4W5Q-QXBG [Last accessed 1 October 2020].

DOSM (Department of Statistics Malaysia). (2020). *Key Statistics of Labour Force in Malaysia*, May 2020. Malaysia: Department of Statistics Malaysia. https://perma.cc/5E2T-CXZ8.

Heanglee. (2020). 'Implement emergency response to domestic violence amid COVID-19 crisis'. *Women's Aid Organisation*, 9 April. https://perma.cc/J92G-42S4 [Last accessed 2 October 2020].

Hisamudin, Hakimie Amrie. (2020). 'Women bear a greater burden during MCO, says group'. *Free Malaysia Today*, 21 April. https://perma.cc/2HVQ -8HSJ [Last accessed 1 October 2020].

KRI (Khazanah Research Institute). (2019). *Time to Care: Gender Inequality, Unpaid Care Work and Time Use Survey*. Malaysia: Khazanah Research Institute. https://perma.cc/QSD3-UZS7 [Last accessed 24 May 2021].

Lee, Yen Nee. (2020). 'Malaysia's new prime minister has been sworn in — but some say the political crisis is "far from over"'. CNBC, 2 March. https://perma.cc/5ZVQ-W4FV [Last accessed 14 May 2020].

Palansamy, Yiswaree. (2020). 'Ministry's MCO advice to women: Wear make-up while working at home, speak to spouse in Doraemon voice and giggle coyly'. *Malay Mail*, 31 March. https://perma.cc/9HF4-LJHC [Last accessed 2 October 2020].

Peterman, Amber; Potts, Alina; O'Donnell, Megan; Thompson, Kelly; Shah, Niyati; Oertelt-Prigione, Sabine; and Van Gelder, Nicole. (2020). *Pandemics and Violence against Women and Children*. USA: Center for Global Development Working Paper No. 528. https://perma.cc/KT5Z-ZDJN [Last accessed 23 Aug 2020].

Povera, Adib; Harun, Hana Naz; and Yunus, Arfa. (2020). 'Government announces incentives for working parents'. *New Straits Times*, 5 June. https://perma.cc/6WWZ-B8PL [Last accessed 1 October 2020].

Prime Minister's Office of Malaysia. (2020). Key initiatives of PM Muhyiddin in 100 days. https://perma.cc/TK2E-9DTQ [Last accessed 1 October 2020].

Sabanayagam, Nisha. (2020). 'Was there less domestic violence during the MCO?' BFM, 25 August. https://perma.cc/R3Y3-BNM2 [Last accessed 1 October 2020].

Schneider, Daniel; Harknett, Kristen; and McLanahan, Sara. (2016). 'Intimate partner violence in the Great Recession'. *Demography*, vol. 53, pp. 471–505. https://doi.org/10.1007/s13524-016-0462-1

The Star. (2020). 'Talian Kasih back in service', 19 March. https://perma.cc /4L9A-LQZ9 [Last accessed 2 October 2020].

Thornton, Alex. (2020). 'COVID-19: How women are bearing the burden of unpaid work'. *World Economic Forum*, 18 December. https://perma .cc/2FZB-WV3R [Last accessed 25 May 2021].

UNICEF. (2020). *Families on the Edge: Mixed Methods Longitudinal Research on the Impact of the COVID-19 Crisis on Women and Children in Lower Income Families*. Malaysia: United Nations Children's Fund, Malaysia. https://perma.cc/NP9X-TTFS [Last accessed 1 October 2020].

United Nations. (2020). 'UN chief calls for domestic violence "ceasefire" amid "horrifying global surge"'. *UN News*, 6 April. https://perma.cc/VL6X -AR3C [Last accessed 25 May 2021].

WAO (Women's Aid Organisation). (2020). 'Letter: Prihatin stimulus package does not reach women who are most at-risk'. *Malaysiakini*, 3 April. https:// perma.cc/B5NB-8QHZ [Last accessed 25 May 2021].

Yuen, Meiking; and Chung, Clarissa. (2019). 'Feature: Monster wives'. *The Star*, 18 August. https://perma.cc/G4Z6-G79F [Last accessed 16 November 2020].

25. Building rainbow community resilience among the queer community in Southeast Asia

Cornelius Hanung

When the COVID-19 pandemic hit Southeast Asia, all state leaders in the region imposed measures to tackle the novel coronavirus. By the end of 2020, the measures taken had failed to recognise the intersectionality of the issues that exacerbated the pre-existing vulnerability of marginalised groups (FORUM-ASIA 2020). The queer community, which had been subjected to persistent discrimination and exclusion stemming from the embedded patriarchal, religious, and hetero- and cis-normative values within societies across the region, were among the groups most affected by the pandemic (Hanung 2020).

Queer communities in Southeast Asia faced various challenges and neglect by governments as well as the public on a daily basis owing to negative attitudes towards their sexual orientation, gender identity and expression, and sex characteristics (SOGIESC). The situation was perpetuated because no country in Southeast Asia has anti-discrimination provisions as part of their constitutions or national policies that specifically protect people with diverse SOGIESC (Outright Action International 2017). Furthermore, findings in Indonesia (Saputra 2020), Malaysia (Pillai 2020), and even the relatively more queer-friendly Philippines (Thoreson 2020) in early 2020 revealed a worsening trend of negative sentiments in the region, which blamed the queer community as the source of coronavirus and subjected them to degrading treatment under the pretext of reinforcing COVID-19-related protocols.

In the context of COVID-19, bias and negative attitudes from the governments of Southeast Asian countries resulted in the neglect of the pre-existing issues faced by queer communities, leading to their suffering from mounting physical health, mental health, psychosocial, and socio-economic challenges (Silverio 2020). To survive, queer communities

How to cite this book chapter:
Hanung, Cornelius. 2022. 'Building rainbow community resilience among the queer community in Southeast Asia'. In: Shin, Hyun Bang; Mckenzie, Murray; and Oh, Do Young (eds) *COVID-19 in Southeast Asia: Insights for a post-pandemic world*. London: LSE Press, pp. 281–290. DOI: https://doi.org/10.31389/lsepress.cov.y
License: CC BY 4.0.

in Southeast Asia had to rely on their own capacities to help each other. This chapter seeks to explore various strategies taken by queer communities across Southeast Asia to empower themselves and foster resilience in terms of economy, well-being, and advocacy during the first year of the pandemic.

Community-led initiatives in boosting queer economic resilience

Many queer individuals in Southeast Asia, due to fear of stigma and discrimination in workspace, have relied on jobs in the informal sector as their main source of income. When government measures for COVID-19 subsequently affected that sector, their living conditions worsened, as many of them could not access government assistance. In Thailand, for example, direct assistance provided by the government excluded those who worked in creative industries, nightclubs, and bars, as well as those who were engaged in sex work (Bohwongprasert 2020). In the Philippines, the relief package could only be obtained by people who were married and had families with children (Chong 2020).

As government interventions ignored the specific needs and conditions of queer people, various civil society and community-based organisations helped queer communities to survive by creating initiatives to alleviate the economic distress brought about by the pandemic. One example was the Give.Asia 2020 fundraising by Brave Space and Sayoni in Singapore, both of which were local organisations with specific focuses on empowering marginalised and queer women. The fund provided small grants to queer individuals who were struggling to support themselves and their family due to the loss of their jobs and income.

In Indonesia, communities of transgender women across the country conducted a series of local initiatives such as setting up food banks, distributing food to community members and other people in need, and providing cash assistance to cover rent payments in order to help alleviate the community members' economic burdens. They even enrolled as volunteers in their neighbourhoods to remind people about COVID-19 health protocols in public spaces (Rodriguez 2020).

To meet daily needs, queer and trans women who worked in the nightlife, bars, and sex work sector in Thailand decided to move to online platforms when the government ordered curfews and social distancing as part of its COVID-19 response. For example, they hired remote DJs to perform on Instagram Live and organised drag shows via Zoom. Although the efforts could not cover the full salaries of waiters, bar staff, night taxi drivers, and other secondary jobs that relied on the industry, it at least helped queer-led entertainment businesses stay afloat in the absence of economic assistance during the first six months of the pandemic (Kenyon 2020).

Addressing psychosocial well-being through community-led support

Apart from economic resilience, social and emotional connectedness (both in-person and virtual) helped maintain queer individuals' psychosocial well-being and subsequently strengthened the resilience of queer communities (Anderson and Knee 2020). The isolation imposed by pandemic restrictions compounded existing psychological burdens, and it was further amplified by a heightened risk of discrimination and violence at the hands of their own family members and partners.

The earliest responses by queer community organisations to address the issue of social and emotional connectedness took place through online platforms. In the first three months after the World Health Organization declared COVID-19 a pandemic, various virtual meetings – ranging from webinars and podcasts to community cyber spaces – were convened to discuss the effects of the pandemic on local queer communities in the region. These approaches, however, could not provide sustained and continuous support to facilitate total healing. Therefore, community-led initiatives were focused on providing peer support and counselling that could be accessed anytime by those in need. One of the examples of such a strategy was that implemented by Sayoni in Singapore, which cooperated with AWARE, a local women's organisation, to provide online peer support and a hotline for psychosocial counselling services that could be accessed by queer women in the country.

To support the well-being of caregivers who worked directly with the community, local queer community organisations also cooperated with think tanks, psychosocial institutions, and private donors to establish care programmes for caregivers. For example, the Community Health and Inclusion Association (CHIA), a community-based organisation for HIV-affected populations in Laos, cooperated with various agencies to support their workers by providing them with personal protection equipment, capacity-building for online communication skills, and regular counselling so that they could still conduct outreach to queer communities in need while maintaining their well-being (APCOM 2020).

Realising the paramount importance of providing mental health and psychosocial support for queer communities in pandemic times, community-based organisations and collectives also established online databases of service providers that were available and accessible for queer communities. Such databases were created by Youth Voices Count (YVC Secretariat 2020), an organisation dedicated to queer youth in Asia and the Pacific, and Queer Lapis, a queer community collective in Malaysia.

Although effective in terms of providing immediate support, it should be noted that online platforms had their limitations. As argued by Silverio (2020), there was the possibility that utilising online platforms for building connectedness was exclusionary, as they could only be accessed by communities in urban areas with the privilege of easy access to technology. Finding creative ways to reach the most marginalised of the already-marginalised queer community has yet to be explored.

Addressing stigma and discrimination in pandemic times

In addition to economic, social, and psychosocial supports, the risk of victimisation based on SOGIESC was one of the key determinants for building resilience among queer adults (Shilo, Antebi, and Mor 2014). This challenge was also prominent in the Southeast Asian context, as queer communities in the region remained disproportionately more vulnerable to prejudice or discrimination than their heterosexual or cisgender counterparts.

In commemorating the 2020 International Day Against Homophobia, Transphobia, and Biphobia, United Nations special rapporteurs on human rights warned the public about the imminent threat of queer victimisation and its effects on resilience during the pandemic (OHCHR 2020). The rapporteurs highlighted the increased frequency of hate speech explicitly or implicitly inciting violence against queer persons and blaming the pandemic on their existence. In Southeast Asia, the trend manifested in statements by government officials, political leaders, and religious leaders, as well as in discriminatory treatment and violence carried out by the public.

Many queer community organisations adopted three-step approaches to ensure human rights protections for queer communities. These steps entailed: (1) monitoring and documenting the pattern of violations experienced by the community; (2) providing responsive and restorative interventions to influence law and policy based on the recommendations synthesised from the documentation; and (3) creating an enabling environment through coalition-building (Jaspars, O'Callaghan, and Stites 2008). The community had to take comprehensive steps to ensure the availability of judicial infrastructure and support for victims to obtain justice, even during the pandemic.

A notable example was provided by the Sangsan Anakot Yawachon Development Project, an organisation working to empower queer indigenous and stateless women in northern Thailand. As one of its responses to serve affected community members during the pandemic, it conducted monitoring and documentation on the impact of COVID-19 on women, children, and LGBTIQ youth in indigenous communities. The report was presented at subdistrict and national levels to influence policy interventions. The organisation also submitted the findings to the UN Special Rapporteur on the rights of indigenous peoples, who later issued an official report on the impact of COVID-19 on the rights of indigenous peoples incorporating the voices of the Sangsan community (APWLD 2020).

Conclusion: lessons for moving forward

The examples discussed in this chapter show how queer communities across Southeast Asia, despite various degrees of pre-existing challenges, managed to survive by relying on community-led initiatives as the government's responses failed to address their specific needs. It was not the first time that queer communities had been excluded from discussions related to emergency responses. In 2018, a coalition of civil society organisations in the Asia-Pacific region convened a groundbreaking meeting – 'Pride in the Humanitarian System' – to discuss the continuous exclusion of queer identities from humanitarian and disaster management responses. The organisations called for the inclusion of SOGIESC and the adoption of a feminist lens in recovery, relief, and rehabilitation efforts (UN Women 2018) to avoid further discrimination against the queer community. It was evident that governments in Southeast Asia failed to implement the recommendations in the context of the COVID-19 pandemic.

Queer communities in Southeast Asia demonstrated resilience by performing adaptive actions during the time of extreme adversity (Luthar, Cicchetti, and Becker 2003). The success of such actions stemmed from the essential roles of civil society and community organisations. The cases of queer community-related programmes in Southeast Asia discussed in this chapter show how local actors, who were well-equipped with the knowledge of economic, social, legal, and cultural dynamics, contribute to identifying the needs and developing the strength of queer communities, bolstering agency and self-organisation for queer communities to build resilience. Local actors proved themselves to be able to provide immediate, tailor-made solutions to alleviate burdens and reach out to those in need (Berkes and Ross 2012).

At the time of this chapter's publication, challenges remained. The first was sustainability. Building resilience is a continuous process to enable people to adapt during times of adversity. As there has been no certainty about the end of the pandemic or its re-emergence in the future, fostering resilience should also be accompanied by the availability of sustainable resources. Most of the community initiatives documented here depended on funding from civil society and private donations. There are huge risks associated with putting an additional burden on usually underfunded local organisations (Silverio 2020). This concern led 61 organisations and 142 activists across Southeast Asia to issue a statement calling on donors and funders operating in the region to focus more on building 'rainbow resilience' (ASEAN SOGIE Caucus 2020).

In addition to funding scarcity, civil society and community-based organisations faced a heightened risk of stigma and discrimination. The COVID-19 pandemic, however, pushed them to refocus their efforts on providing direct assistance to queer community members at the cost of reducing resources previously allocated for activities related to the promotion and protection of human rights. Many organisations thus conveyed concerns about juggling the two priorities.

The last challenge was how to plan for recovery. Most of the initiatives discussed above focused on the resilience of the queer community. At the time of publication, however, there was no definite plan for how to assist the queer community to fully recover from the pandemic in a sustainable manner. In October 2020, the governments of Southeast Asia adopted a regional framework of action to help the economic recovery of the region. Reflecting the continuous neglect of the needs of queer communities, the recovery plan did not specifically address the situation of these marginalised communities. With the recovery framework failing to address the specific challenges faced by the queer community, community-led interventions remained the only viable solution to alleviate the burdens on queer individuals and demand a more active role for governments during the recovery period in providing proper remedies for the community.

Figure 25.1. Civil society statement in Southeast Asia calling for donors and funders to focus more on building 'rainbow resilience'

Source: ASEAN SOGIE Caucus.

Acknowledgements

The author would like to convey sincere appreciation for the ASEAN SOGIE Caucus and Sangsan Anakot Yawachon Development Project for their contributions to this chapter and their work towards alleviating the burdens of the queer community in Southeast Asia in the time of COVID-19.

References

Anderson, Austin R.; and Knee, Eric. (2020). 'Queer isolation or queering isolation? Reflecting upon the ramifications of COVID-19 on the future of queer leisure spaces'. *Leisure Science*, vol. 43, no. 1–2, pp. 118–124. https://doi .org/10.1080/01490400.2020.1773992

APCOM. (2020). *How COVID-19 Is Affecting Community-Based Organisation Even with Low COVID-19 Cases: Laos Case Study.* https:// perma.cc/2ZC9-NWBY [Last accessed 23 May 2021].

APWLD (Asia Pacific Forum for Women, Law, and Development). (2020). *Inputs to the Report of the Special Rapporteur on the Rights of Indigenous Peoples to the United Nations General Assembly: Impact of COVID-19 on Indigenous Peoples.* Thailand: Asia Pacific Forum for Women, Law, and Development. with https://perma.cc/8EMF-NZHH [Last accessed 23 May 2021].

ASEAN SOGIE Caucus. (2020). *Call to Donors and Funders Operating in Southeast Asia: Mobilize Rainbow Resilience,* 11 May. https://perma.cc/8FMH -HMH8 [Last accessed 23 May 2021].

Berkes, Fikret; and Ross, Helen. (2012). 'Community resilience: Toward an integrated approach'. *Society and Natural Resources*, vol. 26, no. 1, pp. 5–20. https://doi.org/10.1080/08941920.2012.736605

Bohwongprasert, Yvonne. (2020). 'Hoping for better days'. *Bangkok Post*, 20 July. https://perma.cc/C5A3-5ZA7 [Last accessed 28 September 2020].

Chong, Jean. (2020). 'How Covid-19 affects LGBTIQ people in Asia'. *Asia Times*, 27 May. https://perma.cc/2YXN-EWKY [Last accessed 20 August 2020].

FORUM-ASIA (Asian Forum for Human Rights and Development). (2020). *COVID-19 in ASEAN: The Human Rights Crisis and How to End It.* Thailand: Asian Forum for Human Rights and Development. https://perma .cc/2XRU-R3QU [Last accessed 23 May 2021].

GIVE.asia. (2020). *Relief and Resilience Fund for LGBTQ+ Persons.* https:// perma.cc/953C-HXS8 [Last accessed 18 August 2020].

Hanung, Cornelius. (2020). 'Point of no return: a daunting future of ASEAN LGBTIQ community living in COVID-19 pandemic'. *ASEAN SOGIE Caucus*, 10 June. https://perma.cc/SBL8-PH2V [Last accessed 14 August 2020].

Jaspars, Susanne; O'Callaghan, Sorcha; and Stites, Elizabeth. (2007). *Linking Livelihoods and Protection: A Preliminary Analysis Based on a Review of the Literature and Agency Practice.* UK: Overseas Development Institute Humanitarian Policy Group Working Paper. https://perma.cc/2P8V-SSA5 [Last accessed 23 May 2021].

Kenyon, Barry. (2020). 'Some of Pattaya's gay bars are by no means in intensive care yet'. *Pattaya Mail*, 1 August. https://perma.cc/F7AV-T5GQ [Last accessed 28 September 2020].

Luthar, Suniya S.; Cicchetti, Dante; and Becker, Bronwyn. (2003). 'The construct of resilience: A critical evaluation and guidelines for future work'. *Child Development*, vol. 71, no. 3, pp. 543–562. https://doi.org/10.1111/1467-8624.00164

OHCHR (Office of the United Nations High Commissioner for Human Rights). (2020). *COVID-19: The Suffering and Resilience of LGBT Persons Must Be Visible and Inform the Actions of the States*, 14 May. https://perma.cc/PD4Q-4T6C [Last accessed 23 May 2021].

Outright Action International. (2017). *LGBTIQ Rights in Southeast Asia – Where We Stand and Pathway Forward*, 20 June. https://perma.cc/TH9B-8KM5 [Last accessed 23 May 2021].

Pillai, Vinodh. (2020). 'Blaming LGBT people for Covid-19 is spreading fast'. *Queer Lapis*. https://perma.cc/VL38-L7VW [Last accessed 20 August 2020].

Rodriguez, Diego G.; and Suvianita, Khanis. (2020). 'How Indonesia's LGBT community is making a difference amid COVID-19'. *The Conversation*, 26 June. https://perma.cc/9PSD-JJP3 [Last accessed 15 August 2020].

Saputra, Ramadani. (2020). 'Recent cases of persecution set back LGBT rights advocacy'. *Jakarta Post*, 27 May. https://perma.cc/FF4L-34HR [Last accessed 20 August 2020].

Shilo, Guy; Antebi, Nadav; and Mor, Zohar. (2014). 'Individual and community resilience factors among lesbian, gay, bisexual, queer and questioning youth and adults in Israel'. *American Journal of Community Psychology*, vol. 55, pp. 1–2. https://doi.org/10.1007/s10464-014-9693-8

Silverio, Ryan. (2020). 'Impacts of Covid-19 on LGBTIQ Organisations in the Southeast Asian Region'. *SHAPE-SEA*, 4 May. https://perma.cc/U3RM-KKLW [Last accessed 14 August 2020].

Tan, Nor A. (2020). 'Plight of Rohingyas under COVID-19 spotlights ASEAN's failure'. *The Diplomat*, 16 June. https://perma.cc/3W6H-4T8B [Last accessed 14 August 2020].

Thoreson, Ryan. (2020). 'Philippines uses humiliation as COVID-19 curfew punishment: LGBT people dance and kissed on video'. *Human Rights Watch*, 8 April. https://perma.cc/X3PJ-9PTX [Last accessed 1 October 2020].

UN Women. (2018). *Pride in the Humanitarian System: Consultation Report.* Bangkok: UN Women. https://perma.cc/M7PR-U7MZ [Last accessed 23 May 2021].

YVC Secretariat. (2020). #CopingWithCOVID: Resource list of LGBTIQ organisations and helplines. *Youth Voices Count*, 8 May. https://perma.cc/9RR8-RLQC [Last accessed 23 May 2021].

26. Postscript: in-pandemic academia, scholarly practices, and an ethics of care

Hyun Bang Shin, Yi Jin, Sin Yee Koh, Murray Mckenzie,
Do Young Oh, and Yimin Zhao

As the world struggled to grasp the true scale of the COVID-19 pandemic in early 2020, researchers and academics in higher education across the world suddenly found themselves plunging into an unchartered territory of isolation, online teaching, and a weakened boundary between home and work, if there was any such clear delineation before the pandemic. While the prevailing rhetoric was 'we are all in this together', such experiences were uneven across geographies and along the lines of gender, age, class, race, disabilities, and caring responsibilities.

With the deepening of the pandemic, the authors, located in different parts of the world (China, Malaysia, and the UK) and at diverse career stages, came together to share individual and collective experiences of the pandemic and reflect on some of the emergent literature that aims at contemplating the impact of the pandemic on society and academe. These moments of musing spanned such themes as mobility, knowledge production, ethics of care, and the future of academia.

This volume, *COVID-19 in Southeast Asia: Insights for a Post-pandemic World*, has brought together contributors who have all endured the pandemic-generated stress, angst, and discomfort in the context of an increasingly neo-liberalising academic environment. The contributors are also scholars whose research has been deeply rooted in Southeast Asia, a region that has much to offer to global scholarship in terms of decentring knowledge production in a world where Western scholarship has dominated.

As a way of concluding this volume, we share our own reflections on what it means to conduct academic practices during the pandemic and what the future holds for building a scholarly community that

How to cite this book chapter:
Shin, Hyun Bang; Jin, Yi; Koh, Sin Yee; Mckenzie, Murray; Oh, Do Young; and Zhao, Yimin. 2022. 'Postscript: in-pandemic academia, scholarly practices, and an ethics of care'. In: Shin, Hyun Bang; Mckenzie, Murray; and Oh, Do Young (eds) *COVID-19 in Southeast Asia: Insights for a post-pandemic world*. London: LSE Press, pp. 291–306. DOI: https://doi.org/10.31389/lsepress.cov.z License: CC BY 4.0.

challenges extant power relations and advances an ethics of care as a norm. As scholars who are either based at or were trained in global North institutions, this chapter is also part of our self-reflection on our own positionalities.

Academic (im-)mobility and in-pandemic academia

As the world began to see a rapid increase in the number of COVID-19 cases, lockdowns eventually became the norm for many countries. Numerous media reports and scholarly works were produced to reflect on life under a 'new normal' that was said to have combined imposed physical immobility with the digitalised hypermobility of online activities (see Freudendal-Pedersen and Kesselring 2021). They have also called into question the sustainability of conventional forms of (capitalist) urbanism as a way of life.

While such experiences might have been the norm for many office workers, especially in the global North, many others were excluded from tapping into the new normal because of the inherently mobile nature of their jobs (e.g. delivery drivers, maintenance workers and operators of key infrastructure, and supermarket assistants). Pundits have also highlighted how informal workers in the global South have hardly remained locked down in order to provide services to those who were able to afford working from home. Insomuch as capitalism depends on the flow of goods and capital, it was inevitable that workers were driven to risk their well-being and lives in order to ensure that our physical infrastructure and facilities were attended to and the production of essential goods and food products continued (see Xiang 2020).

As much as the survival of our capitalist economies hinges upon the mobility of goods, capital, and labour, advancing academic careers has also depended increasingly on mobility that revolves around conference attendance, invited talks, field trips, study tours, networking, and workshops, to name only a few. For a long while, we have also been convinced that scholars throughout the world are largely members of an academic 'imagined community' (using Benedict Anderson's term) that prioritised face-to-face communications with their remote peers, facilitated by the rapid development of global transportation, especially the aviation industry. Academic mobility is further influenced by one's performance in relation to research outputs, grant applications, teaching, and service to their host institution (Lipton 2020).

The COVID-19 pandemic significantly disturbed our routinised academic life. The global lockdown distanced most people in the world, including researchers and their peers, their informants, and their co-operators in other places, adding substantial difficulties to continuing ongoing research projects and developing new ones. Moreover, many funding opportunities and academic positions became at risk of disappearing due to budget cuts in the aftermath of the pandemic (*Financial Times* 2021). Academics were unsure at the outset of the pandemic what impact universities' decisions to switch to online distance learning would produce. This seems a cliché as the internet has already penetrated deeply into academic and daily life, but, until recently, reluctance to use webinars or virtual conferences as a mode of their operation prevailed. How will the imagined academic community operate in the (post-)pandemic era, against an increasingly hostile environment and the haunting threat of coronavirus?

The fact that the academic community can be sustained online in such a less expensive and more environmentally friendly way discloses the extant inequity within the academic community. Traditional face-to-face communications, either in lectures or in conferences, and expensive databases and academic books have created many barriers within the imagined academic community. The circulation of knowledge and the interchange of ideas have thus been limited to several centres, even if these ideas and knowledge are of and for people and places afar. In this regard, a by-product of the technology we use is a more open, inclusive, and collective academic community, and perhaps the possibility of avoiding 'embracing the trap of neoliberal scholarship' (Corbera et al. 2020, p.6).

Here, we would like to posit initially that there might still be an upside to the in-pandemic academia. The pandemic unleashed the potential of virtual communications to become one of the major modes of academic interaction at an unprecedented scale. In most cases, with just a link, scholars around the globe, especially those who had not received sufficient financial support to fund long-distance travel, could participate in online lectures and webinars they were interested in and interact with their peers whenever they were available free of charge or at minimal cost. Throughout the COVID-19 pandemic, many scholars became or were pushed to become experts of using virtual communication tools to deliver talks, attend conferences, meet their peers, and even conduct remote interviews or PhD vivas. We have now become adept at picking a nice picture to veil the messy background, as well as promoting our institutions or projects. Indeed, the threshold of engaging with academic activities was dramatically lowered. Digital video conferencing platforms enabled us to virtually meet, exchange ideas, and continue our conversations by thinking and working collaboratively with much fewer concerns for financial pressure and overcoming the immobility and fixity generated by the pandemic.

Compared to physical travelling throughout the world, this is a vivid illustration of an academic version of what 30 years ago David Harvey (1989) called 'space-time compression'. The 'new normal' brought on by COVID-19 has shown the potential for positive developments in the academic community. For example, the Saw Swee Hock Southeast Asia Centre at the London School of Economics and Political Science, with which the authors have been affiliated, hosted all of its research seminars and lectures online in the 2020–2021 academic year. At least a third of the audience came from Southeast Asia, while many speakers also came from the region without the barrier of travel costs. Digital technologies enabled scholars in different parts of the world to connect and support each other. The authors were able to stay in touch and have a series of regular, online face-to-face meetings to reflect on the pandemic and its impact on life and scholarship, which helped them to endure the hardship of the pandemic lockdown. This volume is also the result of such efforts to give more voice to scholars in Southeast Asia.

While the affordances of such online spaces might not have been equally accessed by all, they certainly helped create spaces of solidarity by transcending physical distances and other corporeal travel barriers that would have otherwise limited participation in in-person meetings. Researchers and academics located in the southern hemisphere and the global South usually find themselves unable to participate in events hosted in the northern hemisphere and the global North owing to unaffordable travel costs and sustained travel downtimes. From workshops to writing sessions, seminars to conferences, we were suddenly spoilt for choice as webinars flourished. It seems that scholars from the global South gained access to (more) seats at the table. Their voices started to be heard, and, hopefully, will be included in collective knowledge production moving forward, as has been the case in the production of this volume, which brought together contributors working in/on Southeast Asia.

Digital academe and its limits

While the new digital mode of scholarly exchanges might be a positive development towards a more inclusive and diverse academia, the 'new normal' under the pandemic produced experiences that were unevenly shared depending on one's position and career stage. While experienced senior scholars were likely to continue to benefit from their established reputations, networks, and resources and practised hypermobility, early career researchers found themselves stuck in a myriad of online webinars, pixelated in gallery views on a screen that hardly allowed room for personal interactions that could help build or expand their nascent networks. Movement restrictions and tightened border controls for fear of the spread of the virus extinguished field trips, which would have been key to shaping new research projects, potentially leaving a lasting detrimental impact on those seeking tenure or promotion.

Furthermore, care and intentionality must be consciously considered and interweaved into such virtual meeting projects. In their reflections on pivoting an annual conference online, Goebel et al. (2020) have highlighted the need to consider the diverse needs of participants (e.g. from different career stages, income levels, and time zones) and the appropriateness of technologies in terms of inclusivity, privacy, and security. Most importantly, they have called for a reimagination of academic conferencing, for:

> a new alternative that can address the problems related to geopolitics, continuing colonialism, the soft politics and power hierarchies in academic societies, and the alleged need for extensive and excessive physical mobility. (Goebel et al. 2020, p.813)

In other words, virtual platforms do offer the possibility of transcending some of the existing structures that prevent inclusive participation, but the broadening of participation alone is not enough. Conferences and workshops are key sites for building and growing networks that are crucial for future collaborations, career progression, and collective knowledge production. How might virtual (or new alternatives of) academic conferencing accord more inclusive and productive opportunities for networking that can overcome or reconfigure existing power hierarchies in academia? How might we extend, engage with, and practise care ethics (Lawson 2007) in the creation of new spaces of inclusive possibilities? These are some of the emergent questions that academe needs to address in the coming months and years.

Lastly, it is important to be aware that digital technologies also have a limit. While people in some countries have limited access or no access to video conferencing software, people in conflict zones have limited access to the internet itself. For example, access to the internet has been frequently restricted in Myanmar since the coup in February 2021. How we can collaborate with and support the scholars in such challenging circumstances has become a major challenge for the rest. Furthermore, while many countries introduced technology-driven rapid responses to COVID-19 in order to keep the rate of new infections low and reduce mortality (see Sonn, Kang, and Choi 2020 for the experience of Asian states), the integration of previously disconnected private information altogether and the implementation of various online apps to monitor movements raises concerns for the emergence of digital censorship and surveillance enabled by state-led pandemic responses (see Amnesty International 2020). Several Asian states reportedly took advantage of COVID-19 to justify their controls over online information as well as suppression of dissent (Elemia 2021). More than 100 civil society groups signed a joint statement issued by Amnesty International (2020) to prevent surveillance overreach and safeguard human rights. In fear of the pandemic, people also opted into the digital surveillance led by the state (see, for example, Chok 2020 for the case of Singapore), a phenomenon that is not new to the pandemic world but builds on path-dependency (Chung, Xu, and Zhang 2020). The implication of all these is that the emergent digital opportunities are to be received with caution for heightened possibilities of digital censorship and surveillance that might also affect critical scholarship.

Hyper-productivity versus slow scholarship

The neo-liberal university had pushed us relentlessly, and the pandemic added salt to the wound. During the pandemic, our workloads increased tremendously, our personal spaces of rest and recuperation invaded and taken over by ever-expanding work that has crept into our lives and our homes. Burnout is rampant, affecting academics worldwide across all career stages (De Gruyter 2020; Gewin 2021; McMurtie 2020), and such hardship might have been felt more strongly among those with additional care responsibilities and health vulnerabilities. Where does work end? Does it end? Where and how do we draw boundaries? Can we afford to draw boundaries in the here and now, without unknowingly compromising our futures? Indeed, as Behrisch (2021, p.673) has reminded us, there is 'an opportunity cost to caring [for the self and others], which is not rewarded within neoliberal culture'. As we pondered these questions, in our isolated bubbles that were somewhat out of sync with others who were in differing stages of lockdown, our place within in- and post-pandemic academia came to appear even more uncertain. Where and how do we go next?

Shock and uncertainty were among people's first experiences during the pandemic. They were accordingly shaping our problematics and practices of knowledge production. To do our best to capture the pandemic conditions and their effects, as well as to respond to situations of uncertainty, it would have been very tempting to write and disseminate 'knowledge' as quickly as possible. The dilemma between instant reaction and in-depth reflection is hence brought to the fore and is worth further interrogation. The World Health Organization, for instance, issued its interim guidance on strengthening urban preparedness for COVID-19 in early 2020, when the pandemic was just beginning to unfold (WHO 2020). While it aimed to guide local authorities across the world to take action, the document turned out to be an encompassing void – saying everything and hence nothing. Worse still, we also saw presumptions raised with no solid evidence. For example, it referred to 'the ease of introduction and spread of the virus' in densely populated areas (WHO 2020, p.4), amplifying a long-lasting stigma towards certain urban spaces and residents and testifying, to some extent, what McFarlane (2021, p.6) has termed '[a]n imaginary of *density-as-pathology*' (original emphasis).

The rush to fast production without adequate evidence is not limited to the policy sphere alone. Among the pages of academic journals, similarly, we also saw a quick rise of commentaries and short interventions tackling the conditions of the pandemic. While some of them were relevant and timely in contributing to the collective scholarly response to this pandemic, some others were by and large putting old wine into new bottles, expecting to get more attention or citation with the pandemic as a new buzzword (hashtag) even though little empirical evidence was collected or presented. All of these added fuel to the fire of academe's prevailing culture of hyper-productivity.

The expectation of hyper-productivity might not have been explicitly spelt out but nevertheless was implicitly felt and internalised by many in the neo-liberal university. The metrification of academic work, which continued uninterrupted during the pandemic, 'placed new demands on academics to perform productively and reinvent the self' (Lipton 2020, p.3). Even as some of us succeed in becoming more efficient and more productive, the gauges of 'excellence' are continually being recalibrated upwards. We have no choice but to try to keep up and catch up. The metrified outputs of academics' intellectual work – most notably their publications and grants – cannot be miraculously produced in thin air or through a cookie cutter assembly line. Uninterrupted periods of gestation for deep work and critical reflection are the necessary ingredients for work that can deliver conceptual resonance across empirical contexts. But time and intellectual head space for cognitive processes were increasingly scarce luxuries for many of us during the pandemic. As De Gruyter's (2020, p.18) report on the impact of the pandemic on academics and academic publishing concluded,

> the pandemic has, and continues to be, a time of great stress, insecurity and pressure. These are pressures that will cause career-defining damage that impacts the individual but will also have significant repercussions for scholarship, equality, diversity and research innovation.

The repercussions are either damagingly long working hours to maintain hyper-productivity, erasing time for recuperation and family life, or poorly baked outputs that are equally damaging.

As members of the academic community, we want to call for more ripe reflections and the need to keep a greater distance from such conduct, not least because it is an emerging form of the inflated commodification of knowledge production, inflected by various impact factors and rankings that have long haunted academia. Here, we summon debates on slow scholarship that emerged in the 2010s, well before the pandemic (Martel 2014; Mountz et al. 2015), combined with attention to collective resistance, careful work, and intentional collaboration (e.g. Jones and Whittle 2021; Shahjahan 2014; Wahab, Mehrotra and Myers 2021).

We have certainly been sympathetic to the tendency to respond quickly during the pandemic when so many lives were in danger; however, we see it equally necessary to study this pandemic state of emergency with deep reflection, always focusing on actually existing situations and attending to dialectical relations between instant reaction and in-depth reflection, which might eventually lead us to what David Harvey (2020) would call the 'collective response'. There is no given end to any form of knowledge production in/of the pandemic since the situation is always unsettled. What we should do is respond to ever-changing pandemic conditions collectively, use any convenient way to observe, dialogue, and write, and continue developing those lines of inquiry with colleagues near and far.

There are already plenty of good examples of this kind of knowledge production. Arundhati Roy (2020), for instance, has depicted the 'portal' through which this pandemic was put into play in India. This portal not only revealed the realpolitik at the time of her writing that shaped the Indian government's infamous response to the pandemic a year later, but also explained how and how far this tragedy, though immediate, real, and epic, would not be new at all. 'The tragedy is the wreckage of a train that has been careening down the track for years', says Roy. These sentences were written in April 2020, and they still worked, even more so, in the spring of 2021, when such tragedies became much worse in the same country on the same 'track'. Xiang Biao (2020), on the other hand, has shifted his focus to the social production and reproduction of (hyper-)mobility, endeavouring to explore what happens when global and national economies become hostages of mobility on the one hand, while such mobility is being disturbed by the pandemic on the other. Outside academia, intellectuals and writers of other kinds also worked in their own ways to record the here and now of the pandemic, works that are also worth our attention when documenting the knowledge production in/of the pandemic. The diary of Fang Fang (2020), a novelist living in Wuhan, could be a good case of this kind; both its contents and related controversy in China are artefacts of the pandemic that invite further analysis.

Decolonising scholarship

The imposed restrictions on mobility raise questions about extant practices of knowledge production and academic collaboration, calling for greater attention to new opportunities for decentring academic scholarship in a way that allows room for the growth and independence of local scholarship without subordination to the hegemony of the global North. Conventional international collaborations have been heavily influenced by funding regimes that position scholars in the global North as principal or co-investigators of large grants, while rendering scholars in field sites of the global South local collaborators who carry out data collection based on the prescribed research parameters by grant-holders. The pandemic-generated difficulties in international travel acted as a double-edged sword. On the one hand, they might have aggravated the existing inequity in scholarship by reinforcing the positions of local scholars as data collectors. On the other hand, it might have opened up a new opportunity for local scholars to be able to participate in research projects on a more level playing field based on their superior local knowledge that cannot be stolen by occasionally 'parachuting in' grant-holders. It is the latter that we hope to see blossoming, responding to the emergent calls for decentring knowledge production and decolonising academia.

While the pandemic opened a door to new opportunities that connect scholars across geographies, there is still a challenge for academe to overcome the existing hierarchies that favour the scholarship of the global North. The pandemic environment raised the possibility of immediate hardship to be given priority over a longer-term imperative of building a horizontal network of scholarship to advance the decolonisation agenda in higher education. These issues demonstrate the enduring relevance of Massey's (2004) point, projected through the imperatives of postcolonial thought (e.g. Jazeel and McFarlane 2010; Raghuram, Madge, and Noxolo 2009), that the outward-looking politics of one's connectivity to geographically and professionally distant others is all too easily made secondary to more proximate and immediate concerns.

Amid the myriad personal and professional challenges that the pandemic entailed – challenges that reinforce the fact that being able to write and publish one's thoughts on responsibility already betrays some amount of privilege – the legacies of colonialism have been made readily apparent in the fact that many of the most well-resourced scholars writing on Southeast Asia and other parts of the global South are affiliated with Euro-American research institutions. It is also true, although to a lesser extent than one might expect, of published scholarship. Of the first 856 English-language articles that we collected on COVID-19 in the fields of development, human geography, planning, and urban studies, we found that 71.1% of their first authors are based at institutions in Europe, North America, or Australia and New Zealand. This is an improvement on the percentages of 95.0% and higher that were found in major geography journals by Jazeel (2019, pp.202–203) half a decade earlier.

Such challenges have served as an impetus for geographers' recently mounting efforts to supplement postcolonial and subaltern methodologies by engaging more concertedly with decoloniality and its challenge to the legacies of colonial power preserved in the dominance of the global university and its associated epistemes (see Radcliffe 2017). The epistemological basis for this agenda has been furnished largely by the modernity/(de)coloniality programme, a highlight of which is Mignolo's (2002) argument that coloniality's entanglement with modernity is manifest in the contemporary geopolitics of knowledge that grounds Western epistemology – even when entrained in critical, Marxian, and postcolonial theoretical interventions – in a 'spatial articulation of power' (p.60) that is ineluctably colonial in its disposition.

In this regard, and in light of the pandemic-generated constraints on mobility, we call for the rise of critical scholarship whose line of enquiries by locally embedded scholars starts from the locality where the concrete web of life unfolds and is in need of transformation. Such enquiries are to produce an informed understanding of the locality that is situated in the *interdependence* of all places, to be followed by the reinterpretation and intervention by the enquirers. While we see such practices as part of decentring and decolonising the production of knowledge by adopting 'a pluralistic world view' as a means to challenge the Western hegemony of scholarship, we are also mindful of how such approaches 'may risk falling into the epistemological pitfall of liberal pluralistic thinking, and that a preoccupation with multiplying and pluralising references can potentially neutralise or bypass historical violence and structural hierarchies' (Hae and Song 2019, p.11).

Therefore, it is important to exercise inter-referencing within Asia (and, for this volume, Southeast Asia in particular) in a way that does not entail the erection of another *methodological regionalism*. This entails the recognition of 'linguistic fluidity' (Chen 2010; see also Zhao 2020), which produces a diverse range of translated versions of a concept born out of the experience of the Western modernity. Such fluidity is an indication of how political cultures in (Southeast) Asia can be diverse and differentiated from the West. We ask for more active contributions of locally based scholars who work in and on Southeast Asia, embedded in a horizontal network of scholars across the world, so that pandemic-generated (im-)mobility becomes not a testimony of isolated and individualised regional scholars but an opportunity to rebuild a new network of researchers equipped with decolonising imperatives that contribute to the demolition of existing hierarchies of scholarship. We hope that the co-authorship of this chapter is a small step towards this rebuilding.

Coda: ethics of care

Throughout the pandemic's unpredictable course, surviving and withstanding its threats very much depended on the deepened feelings of care and compassion that COVID-19 motivated. It is this ethics of care to which we turn as we conclude this chapter, for, while a 'resurgence of reciprocity' (Springer 2020, p.112) in the form of mutual aid during COVID-19 provided much that is of interest to the critical social sciences – as is readily apparent in the pages of this book – it also imparted a renewed salience to the question of the social and political responsibilities that are attendant on the production of geographical knowledge (Massey 2004).

For many scholars, the pandemic renewed the challenge of what Massey (2004, pp.8–9) has called 'a hegemonic geography of care and responsibility': a geography that privileges the near over the far and that manifests in distinctly territorial forms. As Massey has acknowledged, there are many reasons for this geography's persistence. Those most apparent for scholars during COVID-19 included the disproportionate burdens of childcare and other domestic responsibilities placed on many academic mothers (Minello, Martucci, and Manzo 2020) and the anxieties of job insecurity and poor working conditions that preoccupied many early career academics (Kinikoğlu and Can 2020). Broadly, as Corbera et al. (2020) have argued, the pandemic highlighted the dearth of care, pluralism, solidarity, and well-being in normal academic practices, for which the pursuit of various standards of professional 'excellence' is often the overriding and unrelenting motive.

The aim of our knowledge production should not be the total number of downloads or citations but instead an ethics of care (Corbera et al. 2020) – the conduct of being collaborative in developing this collective response, we would say, is in itself a form of care and a critical part of the new ethics (see also Shin 2021, pp.67–68). The authors of this chapter have certainly benefited from the regular online meetings we held in 2020, which helped us to form a collective response to a collective dilemma of pandemic constraints without having to feel the urge of rushing into hypermobility and hyper-productivity. Our collective endeavour has also made us realise the importance of maintaining a horizontal network of scholars to overcome an increasingly hostile work environment in higher education and of establishing practices of knowledge production as an exercise that is collaborative, with the pandemic producing new inter-connectivities across great distances, and perhaps even that is therapeutic (in the sense of helping cope with distressing times). Ultimately, we hope an ethics of care becomes the foundation of critical scholarship that is not only confined to the space of the pandemic but a general practice in academia.

References

Amnesty International. (2020). *Joint Civil Society Statement: States Use of Digital Surveillance Technologies to Fight Pandemic Must Respect Human Rights*. https://perma.cc/PZH8-RSQD [Last accessed 19 June 2021].

Behrisch, Tanya J. (2021). 'Cooking a pot of beef stew: Navigating through difficult times through slow philosophy'. *Qualitative Inquiry*, vol. 27, no. 6, pp. 667–676. https://doi.org/10.1177/1077800420941057

Chok, Lazarus. (2020). 'The policy black box in Singapore's digital contact tracing strategy'. *LSE Southeast Asia Blog*, 22 September. https://perma.cc /NC28-325G [Last accessed 19 June 2021].

Chung, Calvin King Lam; Xu, Jiang; and Zhang, Mengmeng. (2020). Geographies of Covid-19: how space and virus shape each other. *Asian Geographer*, vol. 37, no. 2, pp. 99–116. https://doi.org/10.1080/10225706 .2020.1767423

Corbera, Esteve; Anguelovski, Isabelle; Honey-Rosés, Jordi; and Ruiz-Mallén, Isabel. (2020). 'Academia in the time of COVID-19: Towards an ethics of care'. *Planning Theory and Practice*, vol. 21, no. 2, pp. 191–99. https://doi .org/10.1080/14649357.2020.1757891

De Gruyter. (2020). *Locked Down, Burned Out. Publishing in a Pandemic: The Impact of Covid on Academic Authors*. Germany: De Gruyter. https:// perma.cc/YBP9-NW4W [Last accessed 12 June 2021].

Elemia, Camille. (2021). 'At least 10 Asia Pacific gov'ts use COVID-19 for censorship, disinformation'. *Rappler*, 20 April. https://perma.cc/7WKC-8DY2 [Last accessed 19 June 2021].

Fang, Fang. (2020). *Wuhan Diary: Dispatches from a Quarantined City*. UK: HarperCollins.

Financial Times. (2020). 'UK funding cuts are a slap in the face for science', 7 April. https://perma.cc/V5ES-QHE2 [Last accessed 25 June 2021].

Freudendal-Pedersen, Malene; and Kesselring, Sven. (2021). 'What is the urban without physical mobilities? COVID-19-induced immobility in the mobile risk society'. *Mobilities*, vol. 16, no. 1, pp. 81–95. https://doi.org/10.1080 /17450101.2020.1846436

Gewin, Virginia. (2021). 'Pandemic burnout is rampant in academia'. *Nature*, vol. 591, no. 7850, pp. 489–491. https://doi.org/10.1038/d41586-021 -00663-2

Goebel, Janna; Manion, Caroline; Millei, Zsuzsa; Read, Robyn; and Silova, Iveta. (2020). 'Academic conferencing in the age of COVID-19 and climate crisis: The case of the Comparative and International Education Society (CIES)'. *International Review of Education*, vol. 66, no. 5–6, pp. 797–816. https://doi.org/10.1007/s11159-020-09873-8

Hae, Laam; and Song, Jesook. (2019). 'Introduction: Core location, Asia as method, and a relational understanding of places', in Jessok Song and Laam

Hae (eds) *On the Margins of Urban South Korea: Core Location as Method and Praxis*. Canada: University of Toronto Press, pp. 3–20.

Harvey, David. (2020). 'We need a collective response to the collective dilemma of coronavirus'. *Jacobin*, 24 April. https://perma.cc/TP58-FLVS [Last accessed 25 June 2021].

Harvey, David. (1989). *The Condition of Postmodernity: An Enquiry into the Origin of Cultural Change*. UK: Blackwell.

Jazeel, Tariq. (2019). *Postcolonialism*. UK: Routledge.

Jazeel, Tariq; and McFarlane, Colin. (2010). 'The limits of responsibility: a postcolonial politics of academic knowledge production'. *Transactions of the Institute of British Geographers*, vol. 35, no. 1, pp. 109–124. https://doi .org/10.1111/j.1475-5661.2009.00367.x

Jones, Craig Henry; and Whittle, Rebecca. (2021). 'Researcher self-care and caring in the research community'. *Area*, vol. 53, no. 2, pp. 381–388. https:// doi.org/10.1111/area.12703

Kinikoğlu, Canan Neşe; and Can, Aysegul. (2020). 'Negotiating the different degrees of precarity in the UK academia during the Covid-19 pandemic'. *European Societies*, vol. 23, no. 1, pp. S817–30. https://doi.org/10.1080/14 616696.2020.1839670

Lawson, Victoria. (2007). 'Geographies of care and responsibility'. *Annals of the Association of American Geographers*, vol. 97, no. 1, pp. 1–11. https:// doi.org/10.1111/j.1467-8306.2007.00520.x

Lipton, Briony. (2020). *Academic Women in Neoliberal Times*. Switzerland: Springer International Publishing.

Martell, Luke. (2014). 'The slow university: Inequality, power and alternatives'. *Forum Qualitative Sozialforschung/Forum: Qualitative Social Research*, vol. 15, no. 3, pp. 10. https://doi.org/10.17169/fqs-15.3.2223

Massey, Doreen. (2004). 'Geographies of responsibility'. *Geografiska Annaler: Series B, Human Geography*, vol. 86, no. 1, pp. 5–18. https://doi.org /10.1111/j.0435-3684.2004.00150.x

McFarlane, Colin. (2021). 'Repopulating density: COVID-19 and the politics of urban value'. *Urban Studies*. https://doi.org/10.1177/0042098021101481o

McMurtie, Beth. (2020). 'The pandemic is dragging on. Professors are burning out'. *The Chronicle*, 5 November. https://perma.cc/M9F2-XZHM [Last accessed 12 June 2021].

Mignolo, Walter. (2002). 'The geopolitics of knowledge and the colonial difference'. *The South Atlantic Quarterly*, vol. 101, no. 1, pp. 57–96. https://doi .org/10.1215/00382876-101-1-57

Minello, Alessandra; Martucci, Sara; and Manzo, Lidia K.C. (2020). 'The pandemic and the academic mothers: Present hardships and future perspectives'. *European Societies*, vol. 23, no. 1, pp. S82–94. https://doi.org/10.10 80/14616696.2020.1809690

Mountz, Alison; Bonds, Anne; Mansfield, Becky; Loyd, Jenna; Hyndman, Jennifer; Walton-Roberts, Margeret; Basu, Ranu; Whitson, Risa; et al. (2015). 'For slow scholarship: A feminist politics of resistance through collective action in the neoliberal university'. *ACME: An International E-Journal for Critical Geographies*, vol. 14, no. 4, pp. 1235–1259.

Radcliffe, Sarah A. (2017). 'Decolonising geographical knowledges'. *Transactions of the Institute of British Geographers*, vol. 42, no. 3, pp. 329–333. https://doi.org/10.1111/tran.12195

Raghuram, Parvati; Madge, Clare; and Noxolo, Pat. (2009). 'Rethinking responsibility and care for a postcolonial world'. *Geoforum*, vol. 40, no. 1, pp. 5–13. https://doi.org/10.1016/j.geoforum.2008.07.007

Roy, Arundhati. (2020). 'The pandemic is a portal'. *Financial Times*, 4 April. https://perma.cc/76Z8-UXZD [Last accessed 25 June 2021].

Shahjahan, Riyad A. (2014). 'From "no" to "yes": Postcolonial perspectives on resistance to neoliberal higher education'. *Discourse: Studies in the Cultural Politics of Education*, vol. 35, no. 2, pp. 219–232. https://doi.org/10.1080 /01596306.2012.745732

Shin, Hyun Bang. (2021). 'Theorising from where? Reflections on de-centring global (Southern) urbanism', in Colin McFarlane and Michele Lancione (eds) *Global Urbanism: Knowledge, Power and the City*. UK: Routledge, pp. 62–70.

Sonn, Jung Won; Kang, Myounggu; and Choi, Yeol. (2020). Smart city technologies for pandemic control without lockdown. *International Journal of Urban Sciences*, vol. 24, no. 2, pp. 149–151. https://doi.org/10.1080/1226 5934.2020.1764207

Springer, Simon. (2020). 'Caring geographies: The COVID-19 interregnum and a return to mutual aid'. *Dialogues in Human Geography*, vol. 10, no. 2, pp. 112–115. https://doi.org/10.1177/2043820620931277

Wahab, Stéphanie; Mehrotra, Gita R.; and Myers, Kelly E. (2021). 'Slow scholarship for social work: A praxis of resistance and creativity'. *Qualitative Social Work*. https://doi.org/10.1177/1473325021990865

World Health Organization (WHO). (2020). *Strengthening Preparedness for COVID-19 in Cities and Urban Settings: Interim Guidance for Local Authorities*. Switzerland: WHO. https://perma.cc/2TD9-AN88 [Last accessed 25 June 2021].

Xiang, Biao. (2020). 'The gyroscope-like economy: hypermobility, structural imbalance and pandemic governance in China'. *Inter-Asia Cultural Studies*, vol. 21, no. 4, pp. 521–532. https://doi.org/10.1080/14649373.2020.1832305

Zhao, Yimin. (2020). 'Jiehebu or suburb? Towards a translational turn in urban studies'. *Cambridge Journal of Regions, Economy and Society*, vol. 13, no. 3, pp. 527–542. https://doi.org/10.1093/cjres/rsaa032

Index

Page numbers in **bold** indicate Figures or Tables.

Lightning Source UK Ltd.
Milton Keynes UK
UKHW020628180122
397334UK00001B/2